BEYOND 9/11

The BELFER CENTER STUDIES IN INTERNATIONAL SECURITY book series is edited at the Belfer Center for Science and International Affairs at the Harvard Kennedy School and is published by the MIT Press. The series publishes books on contemporary issues in international security policy, as well as their conceptual and historical foundations. Topics of particular interest to the series include the spread of weapons of mass destruction, internal conflict, the international effects of democracy and democratization, and U.S. defense policy.

A complete list of Belfer Center Studies appears at the back of this volume.

BEYOND 9/11

Homeland Security for the Twenty-First Century

edited by
Chappell Lawson, Alan Bersin, and
Juliette Kayyem

Belfer Center Studies in International Security
The MIT Press
Cambridge, Massachusetts
London, England

The MIT Press, One Rogers Street, Cambridge, MA 02142-1209, USA

Typeset in Minion, Source Serif, and Source Sans by Rex Horner.

Printed and bound in the United States of America.

Library of Congress Cataloging-in-Publication Data is available.

ISBN: 978-0-262-04482-0

10 9 8 7 6 5 4 3 2 1

To the women and men who make
America's homeland security enterprise work.
May they keep doing so.

Contents

Preface

This book grew out of two meetings at the Harvard Kennedy School's Belfer Center for Science and International Affairs. The meetings brought together a group of experts, mainly former officials at the Department of Homeland Security (DHS) from the Obama and Bush administrations, to discuss the future of America's homeland security enterprise at a pivotal moment in its evolution.

Seventeen years had passed since the formation of DHS, eighteen since 9/11, and a new president had recently assumed office. Border security and immigration featured prominently on the Trump administration's agenda, and DHS agencies—principally Customs and Border Protection (CBP) and Immigration and Customs Enforcement (ICE)—had drawn extensive media coverage, often negative. All told, the time seemed right for sober reflection on how the government could and should go about securing the homeland.

Political controversies obscure the fact that most of America's homeland security enterprise is largely uncontroversial. Americans might disagree on immigration policy, but few believe that anyone should be able to enter the country whenever he or she wants, regardless of his or her intentions. People might object to lines at airports, but no one disputes the need for aviation security. And Americans generally believe that their government should assist fellow citizens if hurricanes, earthquakes, or other disasters threaten their lives and destroy their homes. When it comes to the nuts and bolts of homeland security, the partisan divisions and political controversies that figure so prominently in media coverage are usually absent or irrelevant.

What is extremely relevant is how good a job the government does at executing these homeland security missions. Can it adjust to circumstances that are very different from those immediately after September 11, 2001, which led to the creation of DHS? Can it identify and respond effectively to new threats—cyberattacks on critical infrastructure by criminals and foreign enemies, devastating natural disasters, and evolving terrorism risks? Can it communicate effectively with the American people about these different threats and build the necessary partnerships to address them? In short, can it do better? Political controversy must not be allowed to distract attention from these pressing questions.

The purpose of this book is to answer them.

In assembling this volume, we received crucial editorial assistance from Karen Motley, Rex Horner, and Sean Lynn-Jones of the Belfer Center. Ben Rohrbaugh and Nate Bruggeman, affiliates of the Belfer Center's Homeland Security Project, provided extensive and extremely valuable feedback on all of the chapters. We owe a special thanks to Tara Tyrrell, Project Coordinator at the Homeland Security Project, for her management and coordination of such a big project; Kate Searle of MIT's political science department for her keen editorial eye; Dan Pomeroy of MIT's Policy Lab for his synthesis of the writers' workshops and subsequent help with policy outreach related to this volume; and Benjamin Porter of Harvard University for his research assistance. We are particularly grateful to the Mexico-based Grupo Seguritech and its president, Ariel Picker, both for his financial support of the project and for his insightful commentary at the first writers' workshop. Finally, we thank Robert Belfer, Renée Belfer, Laurence D. Belfer, Belfer Center Director Ash Carter, Co-Director Eric Rosenbach, and the rest of our colleagues for their support of the homeland security mission.

Chappell Lawson, Alan Bersin, and Juliette Kayyem
Cambridge, Massachusetts, July 2019

CHAPTER 1

Homeland Security Comes of Age

Chappell Lawson and Alan Bersin

FOR MANY AMERICANS, THE TERRORIST ATTACKS OF SEPTEMBER 11, 2001, crystallized the notion of "homeland security." Although the United States had faced the possibility of nuclear attack during the Cold War, it was largely insulated from most foreign threats. The term "civil defense"—perhaps the closest forerunner of homeland security—would have struck people on September 10 as a quaint and nebulous concept.

The threat from Al-Qaeda also clarified the *federal* government's responsibility for homeland security. Although responsibility for public safety in the United States has long resided primarily with state and local authorities, international terrorist attacks on domestic soil clearly involved national policies and agencies. So, too, did related homeland security issues, such as border control, immigrant screening, and disaster recovery.

But what did it mean to secure the homeland in the twenty-first century? Would homeland security resemble old-fashioned civil defense or something entirely different? Where would the line be drawn between classic law enforcement functions within America's borders and "national security" or foreign affairs? In an era of global travel networks, how could America best prevent a small number of potentially dangerous individuals from doing it harm? Was there a tension between unified, top-down action designed to protect Americans at home and a democratic, federal, free-market system, which by design imposed serious constraints on the central government? Finally, as a practical matter, how should the new homeland security architecture be created?

More than seventeen years after these questions were answered—through a more integrated approach to counterterrorism and the establishment of the Department of Homeland Security (DHS)—the time is ripe to evaluate

We thank Juliette Kayyem, Peter Neffenger, Nate Bruggeman, Benjamin Rohrbaugh, Dan Pomeroy, Jason McNamara, Steve Flynn, and Seth Stodder for valuable comments on earlier versions of this chapter.

America's homeland security enterprise. How has the United States gone about "securing the homeland"? What has, and has not, been accomplished? And what is the best route forward?

Overall, efforts to protect Americans from "bad" people, things, and events are far more coordinated and efficient than they were before 9/11. This is particularly true for the functions with which DHS is centrally charged (e.g., border security and disaster response), as well as for domestic counterterrorism (where DHS plays a supporting role to the Federal Bureau of Investigation, or FBI). Terrorists and international criminals, as well as undocumented migrants, have a much harder time entering the country than they did in 2000. The nation is also better prepared to handle many potential disasters (natural or otherwise) if they should occur. But as the homeland security enterprise has matured, the limits of the original reaction to 9/11 have also become clear. Some of the fundamental dilemmas involved in enhancing "security" (including privacy protections) have not been resolved, and the government's ability to respond agilely to emerging threats (such as cyberattacks on critical infrastructure and more destructive natural disasters as a result of climate change) remains uncertain.

This volume tackles the challenges facing America's homeland security enterprise. Each of the chapters that follows focuses on a different mission within this larger enterprise. Their collective goal is to provide background on those missions, illuminate the challenges involved, and identify potential solutions.

In this chapter, we first lay out the broader homeland security enterprise and DHS's role in it. We then review the paradox of DHS's creation, which left it with a potentially misleading name. Next, we describe how DHS has evolved in ways that have increased its coherence and led to crucial improvements within many of its operating agencies (known as Components), but that have not resolved fundamental problems in managing DHS as a whole. The penultimate section discusses some of the generic challenges regarding homeland security, such as the alignment of authorities and missions, challenges of building partnerships, prioritization of threats, and difficulty of measuring success. Finally, we outline the lessons of the book, presenting the conclusions of each chapter and the volume as a whole.

The Homeland Security Enterprise

A wide range of missions falls under the rubric of homeland security: border security and immigration, transportation security, domestic counterterrorism, emergency response and disaster relief, the protection of critical facilities and systems, the protection of dignitaries and high-level officials, prevention of and responses to outbreaks of lethal infectious disease, combating transnational crime, and counterespionage.[1] Ultimately, DHS took over responsibility for only a portion of this larger enterprise; primary responsibility for several homeland security missions would remain with other agencies.

Within a few weeks of 9/11, Senator Arlen Specter introduced legislation to create a new Cabinet Department that would focus on protecting the homeland. Months of deliberation, wrangling between Congress and the executive branch, and bureaucratic battles within the executive branch itself produced the entity now called the Department of Homeland Security. DHS did not constitute a comprehensive federal response to the threat of terrorism on American soil. None of the nation's "three-letter agencies" from the Intelligence Community (IC)—such as the Central Intelligence Agency (CIA) and the National Security Agency (NSA)—nor the Federal Bureau of Investigation (FBI) were incorporated into DHS. The National Counterterrorism Center (NCTC), created to build and manage a terrorist "watchlist", was located in the Office of the Director of National Intelligence (ODNI). Policy related to counterterrorism was made in the White House. As a result, the new Department did not bear close resemblance to a "Home Office" or an "Interior Ministry."

Certain other missions that might be considered part of "homeland security" were likewise conducted elsewhere. Counterespionage, for instance, remained with the FBI and the CIA. Efforts to combat most transnational organized crime continued to be handled by the main federal law enforcement agencies in the Justice Department: the FBI, the Drug Enforcement Administration (DEA), and the Bureau of Alcohol, Tobacco, Firearms and Explosives (ATF). DHS inherited responsibility only for transnational criminal activity related to customs and immigration violations through the Homeland Security Investigations division of Immigration and Customs Enforcement (ICE/HSI), as well as investigations related to counterfeit currency (through the inclusion in DHS of the U.S. Secret Service [USSS]).

Also outside DHS are efforts by the United States to prevent and respond to pandemics of infectious disease. A portion of this mission was at one point passed to the Federal Emergency Management Agency (FEMA), which is part of DHS, but it was later returned to the Department of Health and Human Services (HHS).[2] At present, DHS's role in pandemic preparation and response is focused on helping to screen international travelers and providing support for first responders in emergencies; the main responsible agencies are

HHS's Centers for Disease Control and Prevention (CDC) and Pandemics and Emerging Threats (PET) Office, and the U.S. Army's Medical Research Institute of Infectious Diseases (AMRIID). DHS would have a major role to play if the government ever sought to radically restrict or monitor the movement of people into the United States from the source of an epidemic, as occurred with the 2014 Ebola outbreak, but the infectious disease mission is really "owned" by HHS.

What did end up in DHS was a set of agencies focusing mainly on: (1) border management and security (air, land, and sea); (2) immigration; (3) transportation security, particularly for civil aviation; (4) disaster relief and response; and (5) the protection of critical civilian facilities, systems, and individuals. The border-focused agencies include Customs and Border Protection (CBP), ICE, and the U.S. Coast Guard (USCG).[3] These three agencies, plus Citizenship and Immigration Services (USCIS), also play a prominent role in immigration. Transportation security, and in particular aviation security, became the province of the Transportation Security Administration (TSA), though the USCG retained its role in ensuring the safety of vessels entering U.S. ports. FEMA remains the principal federal agency for disaster management, though the USCG plays a role in the maritime environment, and state and local governments remain in charge of first response to emergencies. Protection of many civilian government buildings and critical infrastructure fell under the National Protection and Programs Directorate (NPPD), now called the Cybersecurity and Infrastructure Security Agency (CISA), and the USSS continued its longstanding role in the protection of dignitaries.[4]

Figure 1.1 conceptually maps different federal agencies to the different missions that collectively form the U.S. homeland security enterprise.[5] Each rectangle represents a homeland security mission that the federal government is expected to perform. These missions involve a large number of tasks and actors, both inside and outside the federal government. For instance, counterterrorism includes everything from drone strikes on suspected terrorists abroad who are plotting an attack on U.S. soil to outreach by local law enforcement to Muslim communities in American cities. Likewise, managing immigration consists of a wide range of activities: interviews by American consular officers from the State Department of foreigners who want to take their children to Disneyworld; processing applications for permanent residency by foreigners married to American citizens (which is the job of USCIS); apprehending undocumented migrants at the U.S. southwest border (handled by the U.S. Border Patrol within CBP); reuniting unaccompanied minors with family members by the Office of Refugee Resettlement (ORR) at HHS; negotiating refugee resettlement through the State Department's Bureau of Population, Refugees, and Migration (PRM); hearing immigration cases through the Department of Justice's Executive Office for Immigration Review (EOIR); and so forth.

Each circle in Figure 1.1 represents an agency, including those agencies outside DHS (grey font) and the major elements within DHS (black font); the size of the circle is roughly proportional to the agency's budget. Overlap between a circle (an agency) and a rectangle (a mission) indicates that a particular agency does things that are relevant for the completion of that mission. In some cases, agencies are devoted entirely to one mission set; for instance, FEMA focuses exclusively on disaster management and emergency response, but that mission also heavily involves state, local, tribal, and territorial governments. In other cases, agencies' activities fall into several different mission sets. For instance, the USCG performs safety inspections of vessels and search-and-rescue operations, as well as patrolling of the littorals and various enforcement activities.[6]

Several things stand out from this diagram. First, as noted above, there is no one "homeland security" mission. Rather, there are a number of separate missions—sometimes adjacent or interrelated, but just as often independent of one another. For instance, counterespionage (and what in wartime might be called "counter-sabotage") is related to domestic counterterrorism and some aspects of immigration, but normally not to controlling deadly infectious disease. As a result, there can be no single "homeland security strategy"; rather, there must be separate strategies for a dozen or so distinct missions. A government can excel at one of these missions while failing badly at another. For instance, Hurricane Katrina in 2005 demonstrated that U.S. efforts to improve disaster response and emergency management had not come nearly as far since 9/11 as had efforts to prevent terrorists from entering the country. (See Chapters 2 and 10.)

Second, a number of homeland security missions remain across different agencies. For instance, efforts to combat transnational crime and domestic counterterrorism involve various government entities that must cooperate and share information to be most effective. More efficient sharing of information about terrorism has been a signal accomplishment of post-9/11 reforms. By contrast, there is far less sharing of information when it comes to law enforcement efforts against transnational crime; different agencies jealously guard "their" sources and cases, and the government lacks anything approaching a unified strategy. (See Chapter 14.)

Figure 1.1. The U.S. Homeland Security Enterprise.

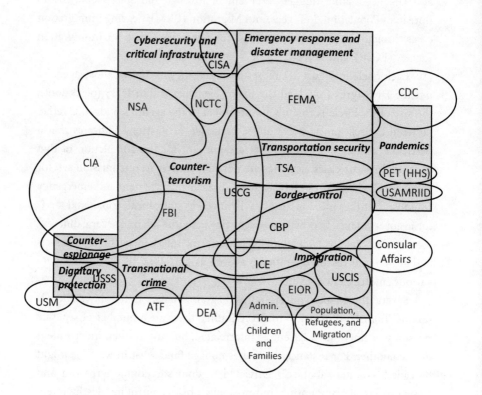

Third, as noted above, DHS itself is focused only on a subset of homeland security missions and plays little role in others. Several of its Components are involved in counterterrorism, but even these agencies have other functions that are typically more central to their roles. For instance, CBP and TSA help keep terrorists off planes, but they rely primarily on adjudications made by the IC when doing so.

Finally, many agencies (including DHS Components) are themselves split among different missions. The operations of CBP, for instance, span classic customs functions such as collecting duties, paramilitary functions such as patrolling the land borders between authorized ports of entry (POEs), law enforcement functions such as preventing the entry or exit of criminals, and counterterrorism functions such as ensuring that terrorists do not enter the country. For its part, the USSS is primarily focused on protecting dignitaries, but it also has an important legacy mission in law enforcement operations against counterfeit currency and a new mission regarding cybercrime.

The Department of Homeland Security

As discussed in further detail in Chapter 3, these separate mission sets create a challenge of organizational coherence for DHS.[7] In some cases, its Components need to work closely together. For instance, the activities of ICE and CBP are intimately related: CBP officers and agents are analogous to the patrolmen or "beat cops" in municipal law enforcement agencies, whereas ICE/HSI houses the "detectives" (that is, those who conduct criminal investigations against smugglers, human traffickers, and employers of illegal immigrants).[8] CBP normally refers its investigative leads to ICE/HSI, and the undocumented migrants who are apprehended and deemed deportable are handed over to ICE's Office of Enforcement and Removal Operations (ICE/ERO). But other Components have far less in common with one another. The USSS, for instance, has no particular need to coordinate with FEMA, and neither of those organizations has much to do with USCIS or TSA.

In this respect, DHS is very different from the Departments of Defense, State, Treasury, Justice, or Transportation. Although several Cabinet Departments include "orphan" agencies or functions that are not directly related to their core mission, DHS's operations are considerably more scattered. Figure 1.2 shows the relative size of DHS's Components. As the graph suggests, none clearly dominates the others. As discussed in Chapter 3, DHS thus looks more like a holding company than an integrated business.

DHS's operating agencies also have very different organizational cultures. Four of the Components (the darker circles in Figure 1.2) are law enforcement agencies: the USCG, the USSS, ICE, and CBP. Their field personnel carry weapons and can make arrests. Three others (the lighter circles in Figure 1.2) are "administrative" agencies: FEMA, USCIS, and TSA.[9] The last, CISA, includes law enforcement agents who manage security at government buildings (recently transferred to another part of DHS), chemical plant inspectors, and other personnel. To use a famous metaphor, each agency has had a different "imprinting."[10] In some cases, this imprinting runs deep: for instance, the Coast Guard and the Border Patrol in their present form are more than a century old.

Given DHS's disparate functions, there is no easy way to summarize what it does. DHS's mission statement reads: "With honor and integrity, we will safeguard the American people, our homeland, and our values." DHS divides that mission into five parts: preventing terrorism, managing borders, administering immigration laws, securing cyberspace, and ensuring

Figure 1.2. Relative Size and Character of DHS Components.

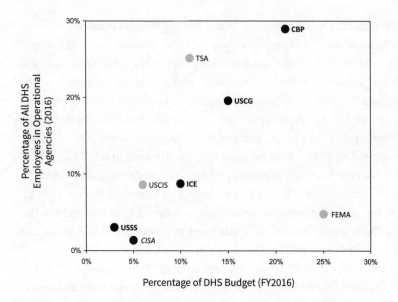

resilience to disasters. Together, these activities do indeed cover the bulk of DHS's operations, but a few caveats are in order. First, although DHS lists counterterrorism as its first priority, most of what DHS does is not directly related to that mission. DHS's main role in counterterrorism is through CBP's National Targeting Center, which determines whether people entering the country fall into suspect categories based mainly on information collected by other agencies.[11] (See Chapter 4.) Second, it is not yet clear whether DHS has a leadership role within the federal government on cybersecurity. It is involved in cyber issues through CISA, but it has never really "owned" civilian cybersecurity. Third, some of the functions that would appear to fall under DHS's mandate do not actually constitute part of DHS's regular operations, even when they are not managed by any other federal agency. For instance, although TSA's mission is "to protect the nation's transportation systems," its primary focus is on aviation; ensuring the safety of trains and urban mass transit remains principally the province of local law enforcement. This division will likely continue until a transit disaster strikes.

Perhaps the closest summary statement of DHS's activities is the one originally offered by Allen Gina, the former Assistant Commissioner for Intelligence, International Affairs, and Trade at CBP, during the second

Quadrennial Homeland Security Review (QHSR): "Protecting the United States from bad people, bad things, and bad events."[12] Even this clever synthesis, however, leaves out many legacy missions in the Components, as well as the crucial importance of resilience in the face of adverse events. The central point is that attempts to describe DHS's core mission are all *ex post*; DHS was not designed in a way that reflected fidelity to any one objective or vision. Placing DHS's disparate activities under a single umbrella definition does not necessarily contribute to an understanding of what DHS does or should do.

In short, DHS remains a bit of a hodge-podge. Its creation lumped together a few core mission sets—borders, immigration, and disaster response—with a number of legacy missions. Meanwhile, several activities that are clearly part of the larger homeland security enterprise (such as counterterrorism, counter-espionage, and handling outbreaks of infectious disease) were left out.

None of this was lost on observers at the time DHS was conceived. Some scholars of public administration argued against the creation of a new Department at all,[13] and others noted that the executive branch had initially favored a very different bureaucratic model.[14] As one skeptic put it:

> If proposals for the creation of a Cabinet-level agency are examined in detail, a disconnect becomes clear. The proposals call for a single official in charge of homeland security, but that official has at his or her disposal, according to the agency design, few assets to actually perform such a role.[15]

Five years later, after DHS had been in place for several years, critics were no less gentle:

> Conceived in haste and crippled by its design, the newest addition to the Cabinet desperately needs an overhaul.... If destiny is largely determined by birth, this is a federal bureaucracy destined to stumble, and perhaps fail.... The Department is a collage of 22 distinct government agencies drawn from different corners of the federal organization chart and glued together into a single, largely dysfunctional unit. Even as they continue doing all the unrelated tasks they brought with them—from screening airline passengers for weapons and explosives to administering the national flood insurance program and rescuing boaters in distress—its Component agencies have been directed to make defending the nation against terrorism their top priority. It is as if a group of widget makers were brought together in a private-sector merger and told they must now start producing software.[16]

Even less ferocious critics acknowledged the same challenge:

> In many ways, DHS's challenges are similar to those of corporate conglomerates that attempt to meld a number of disparate entities and business lines into a single corporation, with the goal of leveraging the strengths of the individual entities to create a stronger, more profitable corporation. Even the merger of similar entities (e.g., two airlines) poses challenges in melding different corporate cultures and such things as personnel and seniority systems, reservation systems, and so forth. In assessing success, corporations usually focus on a single measurable outcome: per-share profits. There is no comparable, easily measured outcome for DHS, nor is it easy to get consensus on what the outcome measures should be and how they might be measured.[17]

Whether the creation of DHS made sense—much less represented the ideal organizational response to 9/11—is debatable. For four reasons, however, the arrangement is not as devoid of logic as critics have implied. First, although DHS Components do not always blend well together, many would not easily blend with any other Department either. For example, the previous location of Customs (which became part of CBP) and the USSS in the Treasury Department were historical anachronisms. Second, the unification of agencies within the same mission set has in practice brought certain unambiguous operational benefits (such as CBP's "One Face at the Border"). Third, seventeen years of operation have made DHS a much more coherent and effective entity than it was in the past. Fourth, and perhaps most important, bureaucratic "lanes" on homeland security within the sprawling federal apparatus are considerably clearer than they were in November 2002.

In general, then, DHS's Components have become significantly more effective and competent over the last seventeen years. For instance, TSA has not prevented all threats to civil aviation, but it has introduced scanning of 100 percent of checked luggage, deployed improved scanning technology for passengers, built crucial partnerships with air freight carriers, worked out kinks in the administration of the terrorism "watchlist" (with CBP and the FBI), created a trusted traveler program, adapted regulations and procedures in response to several attempted terrorist attacks (the 2001 "Shoe Bomber," the 2006 transatlantic aircraft plot, the 2009 "Underwear Bomber," the 2010 cargo planes bomb plot, etc.), and the like. Adversaries would now have a much more difficult time threatening civil aviation than they would have had seventeen years ago. Similar progress in the Components' operational ability is evident throughout DHS, albeit in differing degrees.[18]

By contrast, integration and improvement have been more problematic across the Components and within DHS Headquarters (which has been located in a separate complex from any of the Components).[19] Because many Components have such disparate missions, whether centralized management of DHS actually improves operations is an open question. The alternative of running DHS in the style of a "Cabinet government"—in which the Secretary chairs meetings of the Component heads, who otherwise operate more or less autonomously—is in fact what frequently occurs. The fact that ultimate accountability resides with the Secretary, however, requires her or him to monitor the actions of each of the Components on issues that attract public or media attention. Therefore, there are strong political and bureaucratic incentives to try to centralize management of DHS.[20]

Such efforts have been viewed very differently by different parts of DHS. Headquarters staff are more inclined to believe that centralization of budgeting and planning by "mission set" (rather than by Component) will bring organizational synergies and eliminate redundancies. Field personnel and Component heads, by contrast, are more inclined to view such efforts as operationally pointless, if not active hindrances, and lament the lack of knowledge about Component operations among most Headquarters staff. Secretary Jeh Johnson's attempt to reorganize some DHS operations into regional "theaters," mimicking the military's Combatant Commands, is an excellent example of this controversy.[21] At the same time, there are clearly opportunities for achieving synergy at DHS. Most important, only DHS Headquarters staff—not the individual Components—are in a position to trade off different threats and responses against one another. (For further detail, see Chapter 3; we also return to this issue in some detail in Chapter 15.)

Key Challenges

On Christmas Day 2009, Umar Farouk Abdulmutallab, affiliated with Al-Qaeda in the Arabian Peninsula (AQAP), attempted to detonate an explosive device concealed in his clothing on a commercial flight from Amsterdam to Detroit.[22] The next day, Secretary of Homeland Security Janet Napolitano claimed that "the system worked"—in other words, that the measures in place to protect civil aviation against terrorism had successfully thwarted the plot.[23] Her statement raised eyebrows, given that the attack was actually foiled by a quick-thinking passenger only after Abdulmutallab had lit his trousers on fire.

This episode neatly illustrates several key challenges confronting the homeland security enterprise in general (and DHS in particular). First, as noted above, there remains a fundamental disjuncture between the way most Americans would understand "homeland security" and the statutory authorities vested in DHS. Secretary Napolitano was presented as the public face of the administration following a terrorist attack because her Department was in charge of screening travelers bound for the United States and of domestic aviation security. But in the case of the Underwear Bomber, coordination across the whole government—rather than inside DHS—was the primary source of failure. Indeed, one irony is that the pieces of the system for which DHS was most clearly responsible *had* actually worked: Abdulmutallab had difficulty detonating his device because he was forced to mix several different chemicals together—a result of a DHS-imposed requirement that liquids, powders, and gels be divided into separate small containers. Furthermore, Abdulmutallab had been selected for additional screening at his first point of entry into the United States (Detroit). What broke down so famously was the rest of the system, over which DHS had far less control: security at a foreign airport, the failure of the State Department to rescind Abdulmutallab's visa after his father told American officials that his son had embraced *jihad*, the fact that Abdulmutallab's name was not placed on the "No Fly" list maintained by the FBI-run Terrorist Screening Center (TSC), and so forth. But on Christmas Day 2009, Napolitano was the one called on the carpet.

A second lesson, then, is that "securing the homeland" is not something that any one piece of the government can do alone. DHS clearly lacks the authority to achieve such an ambitious goal. It must rely on partnerships with other federal agencies, state and local governments, foreign governments, private firms (including airlines), and even ordinary citizens to do its job. As noted in Chapter 2, such partnerships are essential even for those homeland security missions that fall squarely within DHS's mandate. Emergency management, cybersecurity, and the protection of critical infrastructure, for instance, require careful coordination with state governments and commercial firms.[24] Building physical barriers along the U.S. southwest border likewise involves negotiating with private-property owners, state and local governments, and the Tohono O'odham Nation (a sovereign Native American tribe whose community spans the Arizona-Sonora frontier). Since its creation, one of DHS's greatest successes has been forming partnerships with state and local law enforcement agencies and with the private sector.[25] Conversely, failures of collaboration and coordination lie behind some of the most glaring failures of the last seventeen years, from disaster assistance during Hurricane Katrina to interior enforcement of immigration laws. And as discussed in several chapters, some of the most creative ways to improve the homeland security enterprise involve establishing new partnerships.[26]

A third challenge concerns the constantly evolving threat scenario faced by America's homeland security enterprise. Abdulmutallab had been identified as a person of interest who would be pulled into secondary screening and questioned further upon landing in Detroit. In other words, CBP's targeting system *had* worked, but it was the wrong system—one geared to preventing terrorists from gaining entrance to the country. Abdulmutallab underscored the fact that terrorists can do damage to the United States if they succeed in boarding a plane in a foreign country, even if they never disembark. Hence there is a need to "push out the border" by obtaining more pre-departure information on passengers from commercial airlines, stationing teams in foreign airports to collaborate with local authorities, and the like. (See Chapter 5.) Threats also evolve dynamically in many other homeland security missions, such as cargo screening for fissile material (given that any nuclear or radiological device could do immense damage before the container carrying it was inspected upon its arrival in a U.S. port); USCG efforts to intercept drug shipments in the Gulf of Mexico (which lead to arrests in international waters for violations of American law); CBP's attempts to prevent undocumented immigration through Mexico from Central America; and FEMA's planning for natural disasters.

A fourth lesson from the Underwear Bomber incident concerns the priority that the government attaches to different threats. Domestic terrorist attacks—however horrible they may be, and however much they disrupt the public sense of safety—are exceedingly rare events. Total deaths from terrorism in the United States over the last two decades, including 2001, constitute a tiny fraction of deaths from drug overdoses,[27] common crime,[28] influenza,[29] and car accidents;[30] even natural disasters have killed more Americans during that period.[31] In a typical year, more people in the United States are killed by lightning strikes than by terrorists.[32] But terrorism receives enormous attention from the media, the public, political leaders, and—as a result—the federal government. The homeland security enterprise is thus obliged to direct disproportionate resources toward this threat.

Despite its rhetorical embrace of an "all-threats" mission in the wake of Hurricane Katrina, the pieces of DHS charged with some role in domestic counterterrorism also tend to direct a disproportionate share of their resources toward that mission. For instance, over 90 percent of the workflow at CBP's National Targeting Center—which vets passenger and container manifests for potentially dangerous individuals and shipments—relates to counter-terrorism. But the National Targeting Center's increasingly sophisticated work has identified only a very small number of suspected terrorists and not a single "bomb in a box" (the dreaded nuclear or radiological device).[33] Considerably less attention at the National Targeting Center is devoted to much more common types of transnational crime (human trafficking, contraband smuggling, and the like).

The point is not that America's homeland security enterprise should ignore terrorism, but rather that resources must be allocated appropriately across different threats. Given the enormous investments that have already been made in counterterrorism across the U.S. government, and the significant success American military forces and intelligence agencies have had disrupting terrorist activities abroad, it may make more sense for agencies like DHS to focus attention on other dangerous or undesirable activities (e.g., cybersecurity). To do so involves not only operational changes but also "fear management"—the conscious attempt by leaders to address public concerns about terrorism in a rational way. (For further discussion, see Chapters 13 and 15.)

A related issue—and this is the fifth lesson—concerns *how* the government must respond. In theory, the government adopts a range of strategies to address threats: protection, prevention, response, recovery, and resilience.[34] In some cases, the sensible operational approach would be to focus not on protection or prevention but rather on recovery and resilience. However, that focus is not always—rightly or wrongly—viewed as politically plausible. Attacks on civil aviation are a classic example. Again, reorientation of government operations will necessarily require better fear management.

Even if a single agency such as DHS were able to alter public discourse about responses to terrorism, as a practical matter, understanding how to manage risk across a disparate set of threats would remain complex.[35] And this brings us to a sixth lesson of the Underwear Bomber incident: how to define "success" in homeland security. (For further discussion of the challenges of measuring success, see Chapter 2.) Does the system work if, every so often, a near-miss occurs? If 99 out of 100 potential attacks are prevented? If disasters occur every now and then, but recovery is far less costly?

Again, threats to civil aviation from terrorists are just one example of the challenges of managing risk; the same challenge of metrics afflicts a host of other activities related to homeland security.[36] When will the U.S. southwest border be "secure"? When will American critical infrastructure—electrical grids, pipelines, dams, etc.—be sufficiently "protected"? When are the ships that enter American ports sufficiently seaworthy? When are high-level officials safe enough? As one example, the United States has made immense improvements in securing the land border with Mexico over the last decade and a half.[37] In Yuma Sector,[38] for instance, the probability of being apprehended while trying to cross the border illegally rose from nearly zero in the late 1990s to over 90 percent in 2010.[39] Unfortunately, such progress has been rewarded by political rhetoric that bemoans the extent of undocumented migration, implies that poor control at the physical border is the main cause of that problem, and incorrectly paints the southwest border region as a locus of massive criminality.[40] Operational effectiveness may be entirely divorced from political perceptions and discourse.

In sum, the homeland security enterprise faces several related challenges. First, missions, authorities, and expectations do not clearly align. Second, as a result, the government must create partnerships with foreign governments, state and local authorities, the private sector, and the public at large in order to succeed in its homeland security missions. Third, threats change, and the government must continuously adapt and redefine its role. Fourth, political considerations encourage the government to focus disproportionately on certain types of risk, as well as (fifth) on the prevention of bad events rather than on recovery from them; senior officials in the homeland security enterprise must find a way to push back against these pressures and allocate resources proportionately. Finally, measurements of effectiveness—and even the very definition of success—are problematic. Leaders thus face the difficult task of articulating when enough security is enough.[41]

Organization of the Book

Eighteen years after the terrorist attacks of 9/11, and seventeen years after the creation of DHS, America's homeland security enterprise continues to wrestle with these challenges. The remainder of this book addresses how best to do so.

Almost all of the chapter authors have held senior positions in DHS, its Components, or other organizations with key roles in the homeland security enterprise. This experience allows them to draw on their firsthand knowledge of how the government actually operates. Their contributions to this volume generally contain extensive descriptive detail on the agencies and policies they discuss, in order to provide context and to serve as stand-alone scholarly references on the topics they address. But the authors deal as much with the strategic "forest" as with the operational "trees." In other words, the chapters that follow represent the best effort by experts who care deeply about homeland security to summarize what has been done and articulate what should be done next.

In Chapter 2, Juliette Kayyem lays out the underlying drivers of the development of America's larger homeland security enterprise and the key questions with which its architects must wrestle. These include coordination within the federal government; the role of the federal government relative to other actors (such as who should pay for homeland security and how disaster response should be managed within a federal system); the proper extent of military involvement, if any, in homeland security; and the perennial challenge of measuring success. One central theme of Kayyem's chapter is that the homeland security enterprise comprises federal, state, local, private, and international players; even at the federal level, homeland security functions are spread across the government. In addition to handling its statutorily-mandated piece of this apparatus, DHS must do a better job of leading the larger enterprise, bringing new issues to the attention of other agencies and ensuring coordination among the disparate players. She closes with several specific suggestions for strengthening the enterprise, including improvements in engagement with nongovernment partners, assignment of responsibilities before a crisis hits, and education of stakeholders, including other federal agencies, about DHS's role and capabilities.

In Chapter 3, Alan Cohn and Christian Marrone take on the challenge of organizing DHS internally. They describe in detail how DHS has cycled through various organizational models in its relatively short life. They conclude that the current arrangement of independent Components reporting separately to the Secretary represents the best (or least bad) option for managing the agency. They emphasize, however, that the Department must find a way to plan and budget coherently across Components, as well as to operate jointly when needed. They close with a number of specific suggestions for improvement, many of which are discussed further in the conclusion.

In Chapter 4, Matthew Olsen and Edoardo Saravalle assess the role that DHS and its Components play in the country's larger domestic counterterrorism enterprise. First they trace the evolution of the terror threat, which increasingly involves self-radicalized individuals and lone-wolf attacks. They then describe how, although DHS's capabilities have matured, it still faces critical impediments in the execution of its role in domestic counterterrorism. These involve not only the architecture of the U.S. counterterrorism effort—which is spread across Departments and agencies—but also public misunder-

standing of what DHS does and how Congress executes its oversight responsibilities.

Chapters 5–9 address the interrelated topics of border control, transportation security, and immigration—missions in which DHS is by far the
dominant bureaucratic player. Seth Stodder (Chapter 5) lays out the central
challenge involved in border management in an era of globalization. Americans
require security, including border security, but they also benefit enormously
from international trade and travel; the challenge is to provide both at the same
time. As Stodder explains, U.S. policymakers accomplished this goal after 9/11
by reimagining the concept of "borders," defining sound border management
not as defending a particular boundary *line* but rather as using broad governmental authorities over entry and exit to secure *flows* across that line. In many
cases, this meant "pushing the borders out"—as with the screening of air
travelers before they left for the United States, rather than upon their arrival in
the country. It required partnerships with the private sector, especially in the
form of advanced information and trusted traveler and shipper programs. It
also meant segmenting flows of goods and people according to the risks they
posed, so that safe shipments and people could move expeditiously through the
system. This transformation represents a major accomplishment for America's
homeland security enterprise and largely resolves the central question of how
to manage borders in an era of globalization.

In Chapter 6, Chappell Lawson picks up where Stodder left off: in the
absence of a universal and comprehensive inspection regime at the border,
how can the U.S. government best divide flows of goods and people into
risky and less risky categories? One strategy involves vetted traveler and
shipper programs, which focus on pulling the least risky entries out of the
system so as not to waste finite law enforcement resources on them. In these
voluntary programs, businesses take steps to secure their own supply lines
and individuals share extensive personal information with the government
in exchange for expedited processing. A second strategy is law enforcement
targeting, which uses data and analytics to identify the highest risk entries.
Lawson concludes by discussing where gaps remain. One particularly challenging policy decision concerns how to secure the vast amount of containerized trade that is regarded as moderately risky—in other words, shipments
that are not part of a trusted shipper program but do not trigger any flags in
the targeting system.

In Chapter 7, Stephen Flynn takes on precisely that issue, including
the specific question of how to prevent a smuggled nuclear or radiological
weapon from entering the United States through the global supply system.

America's current regime involves some inspections abroad, but scanning cargo for radiation normally takes place after the shipments have already reached the United States—too late, in the case of a nuclear weapon. After describing in detail the flaws in the current system, Flynn argues that a pre-arrival inspection regime could be developed in conjunction with the private sector (especially private port operators abroad) and lays out an inventive approach for using existing international law to erect such a regime. Although this system would have costs for consumers, Flynn argues that they are not prohibitive and that better securing the global supply system would have corollary benefits in combating other types of smuggling.

In Chapter 8, Peter Neffenger and Richard Ades tackle the issue of domestic transportation security, where many of the same issues of segmenting risk arise. They first present the evolution of American transportation security, including post-9/11 changes in the USCG and the creation of TSA. They conclude that, unfortunately, existing measures are inadequate to address potential terrorist attacks. The solution that they propose for overall transportation security is akin to the one adopted for securing cross-border flows of people: travelers would provide information about themselves to the government in exchange for rapid movement through the system and reassurances about how that information would be used. By retaining control of their personal data and electing to share it as they thought appropriate (with the understanding that it would not be permanently stored), the system they propose would assuage some privacy concerns. Neffenger and Ades acknowledge, however, that the "new normal" they propose would entail a much greater level of government scrutiny of citizens in some contexts, potentially including more widespread deployment of facial recognition technology and greater access by the government to personal data related to travelers' movements and objectives. Their recommendations thus anticipate the debate over privacy that Stevan Bunnell takes up in Chapter 13, and to which we return in the conclusion.

In Chapter 9, Doris Meissner, Amy Pope, and Andrew Selee address the thorny topic of immigration enforcement and administration. The authors begin by explaining that immigration enforcement has a long history: socio-cultural concerns during the early twentieth century, counterespionage efforts during World War II and the Cold War, and the modern focus on illegal immigration at the southwest border (which began in earnest in the 1990s). Although 9/11 did not mark the beginning of immigration enforcement, it did engender a massive reorganization of the U.S. immigration enforcement structure, with the creation of DHS and its primary immigration-related

Components: CBP, ICE, and USCIS. Meissner, Pope, and Selee argue that bureaucratic and policy changes have closed some gaps in immigration enforcement but left open or created others. Their specific recommendations focus on: improving coordination and connectivity among immigration-related agencies; stricter compliance by international partners with their obligations under the Visa Waiver program; and domestic policies aimed at reducing illegal immigration in general.

Chapters 10–12 shift from border management to the interrelated challenges of emergency response, critical infrastructure protection, and civilian cybersecurity. In Chapter 10, Jason McNamara addresses emergency management, focusing on FEMA. McNamara first documents how FEMA relies crucially on interagency and intergovernmental coordination in order to execute its mission. Following the failures in the government's response to Hurricane Katrina, DHS and FEMA instituted significant reforms, the salutary effects of which were on display during the several subsequent hurricane seasons. But the impact of Hurricane Maria on Puerto Rico revealed that the emergency management community is not yet prepared to address a truly catastrophic disaster. Indeed, it is not fully prepared to address the increasing frequency and magnitude of "normal" disasters. FEMA and its state-level counterparts need to further refine and regularize their response to high-frequency, lower-impact events, while at the same time ramping up for the handful of catastrophes that are most likely to occur. To do so, McNamara argues, they must also better engage the public, treating communities and citizens as partners rather than liabilities.

Chapter 11, by Caitlin Durkovich, addresses the role of federal government in protecting critical infrastructure. The heart of the challenge, Durkovich explains, is that many of the systems and facilities necessary for the func-tioning of modern society are owned and operated by the private sector or (less frequently) by state and local governments. How can the federal government ensure that these systems continue to function, or at least that they recover swiftly after a disaster? This challenge is particularly acute given that failure in one system (such as the electrical grid) can cause other systems to fail. For Durkovich, therefore, critical infrastructure is not a specific set of utilities or pipelines but rather "the increasingly complex and interconnected ecosystem of interacting functions that underpins the flow of people, goods, and services and is essential to a thriving society, robust economy, and national security." Given the scope of the mission, Durkovich argues for more federal regulation to ensure that private firms and subnational governments make the investments necessary to build security into critical systems. This approach includes ensuring that security is built into the design of tomorrow's critical infrastructure sectors (such as driverless vehicles and the commercial uses of outer space).

In Chapter 12, John Carlin and Sophia Brill take on the same challenge with specific reference to civilian cybersecurity, a major vulnerability for America's homeland security enterprise. They first lay out the challenges involved in civilian cybersecurity, the work that has been done to date by the government, and additional steps that could be taken to enhance the response to evolving threats. They begin by breaking down cyber threats into three broad categories, discussing each in detail: threats directed against the federal government; threats against what they describe as "government-adjacent" private actors, defined as entities that could directly affect public safety and government stability; and threats that are caused by rapidly emerging technologies where the safety and regulatory regimes have not kept pace with technological change. Although the government has taken some steps to organize itself better, there are still major coordination problems and ambiguity about where responsibilities lie. In terms of priorities for action, Carlin and Brill recommend enhanced coordination with the private sector, greater regulation of the "internet of things," more robust efforts to protect election infrastructure from cyberattack, and enhanced sanctions against cyber criminals.

Chapters 13 and 14 focus on two crucial issues of law enforcement in the homeland security context: protecting privacy and combating transnational crime. In Chapter 13, Stevan Bunnell discusses how security concerns have led the government to obtain more personal data about individuals and conduct large-scale, highly intrusive searches of individuals. He points out that "privacy" considerations are often misunderstood and misinterpreted. Rather than concern themselves with the simple fact that the government collects personal data to make risk assessments, Americans should focus on what the government actually does with that information. If the data are properly handled, and if using them reduces the need for intrusive physical searches, the result is actually a gain for both security and privacy—or at least for the kind of privacy that most people seem to care about. The future of homeland security, Bunnell argues, should focus on identifying these sorts of win-win solutions based on an enlarged concept of privacy, rather than exclusively on the issue of data collection.

In Chapter 14, we address the issue of combating transnational crime, from smuggling to drug cartels to illegal immigration. We first discuss how traditional criminal justice approaches are unlikely to have much of an effect on transnational crime, in which perpetrators often cannot be brought to justice in American courtrooms and the scope of the problem is too vast to address through criminal prosecution of offenders. We therefore argue for reorienting current efforts to combat transnational crime away from conventional law enforcement efforts (which aim at prosecution of offenders) to "disruption"—that is, preventing or interfering with criminal activity that adversely affects Americans. Because DHS possesses tools that most law enforcement entities lack (including broad search authorities at the border and the ability to deny non-citizens entry into the United States), DHS is uniquely positioned to adopt disruption as its central approach. We close by discussing the specific measures required to move toward a "disruption model."

In Chapter 15, the conclusion to this volume, we return to the central choices confronting the homeland security enterprise going forward. Specifically, we address eight questions:

1. How should America's homeland security enterprise be organized?
2. How should DHS and its Components, in particular, be organized and managed?
3. How should scarce federal resources be reallocated to meet different threats?
4. How far should the United States go in "federalizing" homeland security, and how much of the responsibility for critical infrastructure, cybersecurity, and emergency management can be left to state governments, local governments, or the private sector?
5. How should the United States manage its air, land, and maritime borders in an era of globalization?
6. How should the United States incorporate DHS into federal policymaking on foreign relations?
7. How can the government identify and monitor dangerous individuals while respecting privacy and civil liberties?
8. What should be asked of American citizens and civil society when it comes to homeland security?

In each case, we either articulate the best course of action, when that answer is sufficiently clear, or the tradeoffs involved in pursuing different approaches.

We close by articulating the stakes. The United States has taken remarkable strides toward securing the homeland against an array of threats since 9/11. But it must continue to make progress, against both existing and emerging threats, if America is to be kept safe.

CHAPTER 2

Building a Better Enterprise

Juliette Kayyem

THREE MOMENTS HAVE COME TO DEFINE THE U.S. HOMELAND SECURITY enterprise. First, the terrorist attacks of September 11, 2001, dramatically demonstrated the need for a Department of Homeland Security (DHS). Second, the Homeland Security Act of 2002 legally created it. And third, the epic failures in the federal response to Hurricane Katrina signaled DHS's inadequacy.

It was late in the summer of 2005 when Hurricane Katrina slammed into the Gulf Coast and submerged New Orleans, exposing a Department that had been too focused on nineteen men who had boarded four airplanes and was thus caught with its guard down. The fall of 2005 thus brought a course correction to DHS. Rather than fixating solely on terrorism, DHS was to adopt an all-hazards approach—recognizing a broader scope of threats, assessing each risk, and building resilience-based responses.

All-hazards had, in fact, been a part of homeland security—previously called domestic preparedness—for much of the time leading up to 9/11.[1] But refitting the DHS of 2005 to this broader approach was not easy. Even in its infancy, DHS was large and growing, and that size, along with extreme decentralization, bred dysfunction. A DHS created to stop terrorism realized that to best protect the nation against that risk, it had to find its place in a broader enterprise.

Even if DHS began like the Department of Defense and on a "war" footing, its mission would ultimately require that it learn to behave more like the Department of Education: setting and enforcing standards within a broader apparatus. That pivot—formalized in everything from how money was distributed to states and localities[2] to DHS's new national response plan,[3] which granted DHS broad authority to lead during a crisis—was the beginning of what came to be known as the homeland security enterprise: a broad network of security personnel centered on but reaching far beyond DHS and a strictly "counterterrorism" mission.

The term "enterprise" was itself an acknowledgement that DHS was not alone in the mission to protect the homeland. But fitting DHS into the broader homeland security enterprise raised fundamental questions. How large a role should the federal government play? Should that role be played by civilians or the military? Who would write the rules—the stakeholders or the feds? Who was going to pay? And most fundamentally, how should America judge success? These questions challenged DHS through its establishment, and they are even harder to answer seventeen years later, as the 240,000-person Department continues to struggle to find its place in the broader enterprise.

The next section of this article describes in greater detail what the "homeland security enterprise" is, discussing DHS and the other five primary players—interagency, intergovernmental, media, private sector, and international—that constitute it. Building on the challenges discussed in the preceding chapter, the third section then lays out the questions that have defined the development of the enterprise to date and will continue to define its development in the future. I conclude with reflections and recommendations on how to strengthen and improve the enterprise so it can function more effectively to protect the homeland.

The Homeland Security Enterprise

Although Americans tend to focus on the successes and failures of DHS as a symbol for all of the threats and vulnerabilities the nation faces, the reality is much more complicated.

DHS is big—containing a quarter of a million employees—but it was not built to contain all of the nation's security and law enforcement agencies. Even on matters of homeland security, DHS has to coordinate with a variety of other actors. Who holds the counterterrorism docket, the repository of the government's intelligence on counterterrorism? Not DHS, which is just one among many players feeding intelligence to and receiving intelligence from the National Counterterrorism Center (NCTC).[4] Who investigates counterterrorism cases? Not DHS, which must cede control to the Federal Bureau of Investigation (FBI) in any such investigation.[5] Well, perhaps it can be argued that DHS controls our maritime, land, and air borders? Although DHS does "own" this mission space, it cannot achieve its objectives without engaging with other federal agencies, and state and local authorities. Indeed, given the cross-border nature of border management, DHS must work with an international community to raise the floor of security in any global effort.

Not all of this is intentional. The seeming hodge-podge of Components and agencies drawn together into DHS was based on the unexamined and hasty decisions of a defensive White House in a hurry to head off an assault by Democratic senators clamoring for the Bush administration to bureaucratize the post-9/11 security state.[6] The story of DHS's creation remains illustrative: a gang of five hiding in the White House basement with pieces of paper moving agencies like the U.S. Secret Service (USSS) and the U.S. Coast Guard (USCG) with no vetting by Cabinet secretaries.[7]

The results of this reorganization were imperfect. Notoriously, the founding five did not realize until after moving immigration services to DHS that immigration judges would remain at the Department of Justice.[8] And so DHS's inherently complex coordination problems grew even more difficult. Born out of previously existing agencies with unique interests, cultures, capabilities, and authorities, DHS often has to struggle to keep its stakeholders on the same page. And that is when DHS has all the personnel, capability, and authority that it needs under its roof, an exceedingly uncommon occurrence.

Thus, DHS is often left to organize its counterparts, often without the authority to compel them to act, in order to even address its mission. The homeland security enterprise is the result of this structure, of these diverse players with diffuse authority and often conflicting interest. That is, the enterprise is a collection of interagency, intergovernmental, media, private sector, and international partnerships, with DHS in the middle trying to smooth the edges of jurisdiction.

FEDERAL INTERAGENCY PARTNERS

The threat paradigm facing the United States has shifted, and fixating on terrorism is not enough to keep the nation safe. Today, Americans are threatened by the risks of a deadly pandemic of infectious disease, cyber attacks, transnational crime, and increasingly frequent natural disasters.[9] The challenge for the enterprise is that, as the nature of the threats expands well past terrorism, the subject matter expertise for almost all of America's vulnerabilities resides somewhere outside DHS, and often in other agencies.

Homeland Security Presidential Directive 5 (HSPD-5)—the original (and current) management system for matters of homeland security—designates DHS as the lead authority in crisis and consequence management and establishes a national incident command structure under the Secretary of Homeland Security:

The Secretary shall coordinate the Federal Government's resources utilized in response to or recovery from terrorist attacks, major disasters, or other emergencies if and when any one of the following four conditions applies: (1) a Federal Department or agency acting under its own authority has requested the assistance of the Secretary; (2) the resources of State and local authorities are overwhelmed and Federal assistance has been requested by the appropriate State and local authorities; (3) more than one Federal Department or agency has become substantially involved in responding to the incident; or (4) the Secretary has been directed to assume responsibility for managing the domestic incident by the President.[10]

It turns out that coordinating these resources is quite difficult. There are intense interagency challenges when homeland security absorbs issues as far-ranging as the environment, public health, or military threats. These challenges were not eliminated with the signing of a piece of paper. If anything, HSPD-5's ambiguity accentuated interagency friction, setting the stage for turf battles and coordination nightmares.

Under the HSPD-5 model, DHS is not the sole responding entity in any incident, but it is the lead (or managing) agency for all incidents.[11] This can leave DHS lacking authority in crises it would be positioned to handle unilaterally. Worse, the HSPD-5 model leaves DHS as a middle man when responding to crises where it is relatively lacking in expertise. This sandwiches DHS between the necessary resources and their implementation, creating a management and coordination mess.

Take, for example, a public health incident. The Department of Health and Human Services (HHS) may be the subject matter expert on issues ranging from vaccination manufacturing to isolation protocols, but it is DHS that is supposed to manage the response. That requires, in practice, that other Cabinet secretaries subsume their strong expertise into an incident command structure with which they are probably not familiar and which another Department, DHS, is leading. During public health scares such as H1N1 in 2009 or Ebola in 2015, HHS took the lead in, at the very least, operational health planning and communications.[12] That may be appropriate—seeing medical professionals discuss science is reassuring for the public—but it is a difficult partnership with DHS, which can often find itself "leading" but in actuality on the outside looking in. In times of crisis, it is critical to know who is in charge. But the HSPD-5 model introduces ambiguity whenever DHS works with another agency.

In major incidents, the management of the interagency response is also complicated by the sheer number of participants. In the 2010 Deepwater Horizon oil spill response, for example, over 45,000 responders from 60 agencies and the private sector were involved in the cleanup.[13] This massive response had to be managed by the incident response team led by a DHS operational agency, the USCG. Some agency interests and expertise were obvious and straightforward to incorporate, such as with the Environmental Protection Agency (EPA), which had expertise in the appropriate use and amount of chemical dispersants. Others were not.

The role of the Department of State (DOS) in the oil spill is particularly illustrative of the complexity and intense coordination necessary to compose a comprehensive incident response. At first glance, the DOS might be mostly interested in guiding U.S. relations with Mexico if oil from the spill should make its way to Mexico's shorelines. Mexico and the United States have strong ties and operational agreements that had prepared first responders for plans and positioning should that potential have occurred.[14]

But the DOS's concerns were much broader. The variable that worried the DOS the most was the potential that the loop current would send oil to Cuba, a nation whose relationship with the United States was governed by prohibitions against maritime planning, let alone diplomatic agreements. If oil hit the shore in Cuba, the United States would have had no route to assist. Without a U.S. response and assistance, oil could have ruined the Cuban shoreline, disrupting fishing and commercial capacity, and leading to food shortages, contamination, or other economic emergencies in Cuba. Then, the United States might be facing a mass migration as Cubans tried to immigrate for humanitarian reasons.[15] Under the U.S. government's "wet foot, dry foot" policy and the U.S. law at the time, any Cuban who reached the U.S. shore would have received special immigration status. With that status, the newly arrived Cubans could stay in Florida, a potentially heavy burden that could lead to domestic political consequences. But should fleeing Cubans be picked up in the waters, they would be sent to a naval facility at Guantanamo Bay designed for maritime refugees before being sent back to Cuba.[16] The DOS—then trying to close the terrorist detention centers on Guantanamo Bay—found this possibility particularly alarming, and it was weighed when selecting a response.

This is an example of coordination done right. But had the DOS not been brought into this seemingly unrelated crisis, DHS may have missed the critical Guantanamo Bay consideration. After all, Guantanamo Bay is not closely related to an oil spill response apparatus. Still, coordinating with the DOS brought its own challenges, forcing diplomats unaccustomed to outside supervision to report to relatively less informed DHS personnel through an unclear organizational structure. This is just one example of the extreme importance but also the difficulty of coordinating other agencies through DHS.

INTERGOVERNMENTAL PARTNERS

Although there are many pieces to the homeland security enterprise, none is more crucial to the implementation of policy than the "homeland" itself. Commonly referred to as "intergovernmental" efforts, the interactions between state, local, territorial, and tribal governments and the federal government are deep and often conflict. Dating back to 1803, when a fire tore through a New Hampshire town and prompted Congress to offer emergency relief for the first time, state and federal responders have a long history of cooperation and conflict.[17]

These conflicts between federal and state governments begin with the architecture of the U.S. Constitution. Any power not delegated to the federal government, under the compromise of the Tenth Amendment, is reserved for the states or the people. That includes traditional police matters and public safety. The constitutional structure, which gives special status to Native American interests, also complicates relations with tribal territories. The corollary is that matters of traditional foreign affairs and national security, among others, are the exclusive domain of the federal government.

Homeland security is a source of intense intergovernmental conflict because it does not fit neatly into either level of government's exclusive authority: it is a matter of both public safety and of national security. This means that states have tremendous interests in, and authorities related to, homeland security efforts. This dual sovereign authority is not necessarily bad, but the notion that DHS has some chain-of-command control over the activities of states and localities is belied by the constitutional structure.

This tension and dual authority is most clearly brought to the surface by two important aspects of intergovernmental efforts. First, politics. Politics comes into play in the operational and policy positions of the federal government and the states and localities. President George W. Bush, in his memoir, admitted that he felt his greatest mistake was his failure to unleash the full force of the U.S. military in response to Hurricane Katrina.[18] Bush knew that the people of Louisiana needed help and the federal government had a means of offering it: the Insurrection Act, which is a statute that allows the president to utilize the military on domestic soil in times when states can no longer satisfy the guarantees of government. However, Bush allowed politics to hold him back. He knew that as a Republican president, his use of the Insurrection Act would signal a vote of no confidence in the Democratic, and female, governor of Louisiana, and that this stance would be too difficult to defend.[19]

In 2010, during the Obama administration, five states were impacted by the largest offshore oil spill in American history—Deepwater Horizon.[20] Those states, all of which had Republican governors, were often unhappy with the operational response by the USCG and found themselves in political clashes with a Democratic White House.[21] The 2012 presidential election was part of the narrative of the response's failures and successes: three of those Republican governors would either make overtures to run or actually announce their candidacy against President Barack Obama in 2012. Operations must and should be protected from political considerations during a crisis, but that did not mean that the major political players were silent about their concerns. Politics is a part of American national culture, and it does not ignore homeland security.

The political tension of intergovernmental dual authority is most clearly felt in the immigration and border arenas. Here, DHS has a strong claim. The Constitution vests the federal government with exclusive authority over immigration and borders, and Congress has designated DHS as the responsible federal Department. Moreover, DHS houses the primary immigration and border enforcement agencies: most of DHS's operational Components— the USCG, Immigration and Customs Enforcement (ICE), and Customs and Border Protection (CBP)—are about monitoring and controlling our air, land, and sea ports of entry (POEs). Nonetheless, aggressive interior immigration enforcement by ICE is often met with resistance by urban mayors who claim that aggressive enforcement makes immigrants less cooperative with police, crippling their police forces' ability to interview critical witnesses or even obtain reports of crimes.

This conflict is fundamentally political, and immigration enforcement does not lose its bite when one party leaves the White House. For instance, the Obama administration instituted certain immigration policies against deportation for children who were brought to the United States unlawfully but raised as full-fledged American citizens, as well as the parents of U.S. citizens or lawful permanent residents (the so-called DACA and DAPA programs). A number of Republican governors and their Attorneys General challenged the administration's DAPA program in federal court and won.[22] The Trump administration, in turn, ended the DACA program, but was sued for doing so by various states with Democratic leadership and the University of California system. The Trump administration has, to date, been losing its round of litigation.[23]

After politics, the second intergovernmental tension is the issuance of monetary grants. DHS allocates hundreds of millions of dollars in grants to state, local, territorial, and tribal governments to support their homeland security efforts— $288 million in FY 2017 alone.[24]

In the early years of DHS, when the memory of 9/11 was particularly vivid, grant money flowed with little attempt to organize or institutionalize best practices, priorities, or even assess its effects. In 2005, for example, Newark utilized DHS grant money to buy air-conditioned trash trucks.[25] Since then, the grant process has become more formalized; however, maturation of the grant process renewed tensions between DHS and its local partners.

Rules and guidance were established by DHS to ensure that each state met certain baseline capabilities, but to the states, these requirements constituted a master plan executed by the federal government with little recognition of the unique risks and needs of each locality. For example, in 2007, when DHS released its grant guidance requiring states to spend 25 percent of all their homeland security funding for that year to counter the potential use of impro- vised explosive devices (IEDs), the states publicly balked.[26] State governments pointed out that this requirement was arbitrary and that it did not make much sense to force Oklahoma and New York to invest the same amount in one threat. DHS responded that its obligation was to require a unifying vision for the states. Given our constitutional structure, neither stance is wrong. But adding funding to the picture created a new front to battle over authority.

As the grants process became more exacting, the federal government found a new political and economic tool to compel state and local govern- ments to follow its directives. The rise of the so-called "sanctuary cities" movement, where cities would promise a safe zone for undocumented immi- grants, was met with pushback by the federal government, which threatened to withhold grants from cities that did.

The grant process is further complicated by the congressional process by which funds are appropriated. Because every state has two senators of equal voting power, small states are able to punch above their weight during the funding process. This resulted in the federal government spending four times as much per capita on counterterrorism in Wyoming than in New York.[27] To rectify this disparity, Congress created a separate funding source reserved exclusively for cities in order to buttress more at-risk areas through a grant process known as the Urban Area Security Initiative.[28] These new grants, however, have bred the same political fights as their predecessors.

Thus, DHS finds itself in a paradox. It is often in greatest tension with its state and local partners because of the realities of politics and funding, but in many areas it is most dependent upon those partners to accomplish its mission. The founding five, and ultimately Congress, appear to have given little thought to how this tension would shape DHS and affect the homeland security enterprise.

MEDIA PARTNERS

Even after DHS has fully coordinated with the rest of the government, its work is not done. In American politics, figuring out what is right is only half the battle. Decision-makers then have to sell the result. This is particularly true in a crisis situation, where it is critical to clearly convey information and analysis to the general public.

A lot can be said about the media's role in crises and disaster management—the noise of 24/7 cable, the search for culprits, the unforgiving relentless nature of filling the daily void—but the media also serves as an important amplifier of the government's messages. From the National Weather Service to decisions about sheltering or evacuating, government agencies are dependent on media to inform the public. This is particularly true in the age of social media. Getting accurate information out to the public as quickly as possible can make the difference between a speedy resolution and mass confusion that could worsen a crisis.

The efforts of the media often align well with DHS's goals and are an integral aspect of protecting the homeland. There are times, however, when managing media coverage is critical. False or misleading reports can panic the public or encourage dangerous behavior. Managing coverage is one of the many challenges of coordinating with the pieces of the enterprise that lie beyond government.

Ultimately, effective media coverage begins with smart government. The challenge for government, in particular, is to keep the citizenry informed without terrifying them, urging action without compelling it (such as preparedness or evacuations), and having them "see something, say something" without endorsing vigilantism or racial profiling. This is, again, not new for the enterprise; national education campaigns such as the nuclear-era "Bert the Turtle" were addressed mostly to a white, suburban audience, and failed to provide adequate information to diverse urban populations.[29]

The infamous "color code" system initiated after 9/11 to educate citizens about levels of terror threats ended up being so incoherent and subject to political whims that it was ultimately abandoned, but not before becoming a Saturday Night Live staple.[30] Only by disseminating accurate, timely information through mass media can DHS inform the public and protect the homeland.

PRIVATE SECTOR PARTNERS

Another essential piece of the enterprise is federal partnership with the private sector. There is no single approach to the private sector. The U.S. government enjoys public-private partnerships across many areas, from protecting critical infrastructure to building better detection tools.[31] Some industries are highly regulated, such as nuclear facilities, while others are guided only by advice and best practices from DHS.[32] (For further discussion, see Chapter 11.) Though some at DHS might not like to admit it, the government has found itself dependent on the private sector for everything from prevention to response and recovery. For instance, conditions following Hurricane Katrina famously improved when Walmart was able to deliver necessary goods and commodities to victims of the storm.[33]

More recently, a number of companies have stepped outside their normal operating procedures to assist in disaster management efforts. Tesla helped to provide energy to Puerto Rico after a hurricane devastated its infrastructure; Airbnb provides free home rental services to those evacuating a hurricane; Facebook invokes a disaster tool after a terror attack so that users can notify family members of their whereabouts and wellness.

Although DHS has established a specialized office for private-sector engagement, there are fundamental differences between the incentives and goals of the private sector and the federal government. It is critical for DHS to bridge that divide. Indeed, 80 percent of critical infrastructure facilities in the United States are owned by the private sector.[34] But if critical infrastructure— like an electrical grid—goes down in a storm, the failure to get it back up and running quickly turns into government negligence rather than a private sector failure. Again, DHS often owns responsibility for an issue but not the authority to control it.

In addition, the private sector is often at the forefront of some of the most challenging aspects of protecting the homeland. When it comes to matters of cybersecurity, port security, and oil spills, the private sector is often better equipped than DHS to address security needs.[35] Working closely with private-sector companies can lend DHS access to their tools and expertise, and it gives DHS a leg up in hiring top talent.[36]

Yet, while the benefits of cooperation and synergy are apparent, often the government and the private sector find themselves at loggerheads. For example, the San Bernardino shooting attacks created a conflict between Apple, one of the country's largest companies, and the government, when the FBI tried to obtain access to encrypted information on one of the terrorist's iPhones.[37] For business reasons, Apple was unwilling to provide the help requested by the FBI, forcing the government to find its own way to access the phone. The competing narratives are reflective of the tensions that can arise for Apple; the security of its phones was seen as a critical feature, one which could be lost by helping the government unlock the phone, while the FBI framed Apple's position as costing valuable time and jeopardizing its investigation.

More generally, DHS may struggle to manage critical private-sector partners if it fails to speak their language and address private-sector concerns. The federal government and private companies have different missions—that much is outside DHS's control. But by forming partnerships in advance that are based on mutual interest or beneficial exchange, DHS can ensure that it has the cooperation of its private-sector partners when it matters most. Partnerships help private industry too, promoting innovation through research grants and generally improving private performance.[38] The response to the 9/11 attacks, the Deepwater Horizon oil spill, and hurricanes since Katrina illustrate the power of public-private partnerships to keep Americans safe and deliver resources to those in need.[39] Although the private sector is no substitute for government, it is an effective and necessary component of the homeland security enterprise.

INTERNATIONAL PARTNERS

Even when DHS is successful in coordinating with the full scope of the domestic enterprise—within DHS, interagency partners, intergovernmental organizations, the media, and the private sector—DHS's work is not through. The management of the enterprise extends well past the country's borders, as a core aspect of the U.S. homeland security apparatus is securing the flows of people and goods.

The U.S. strategy has included establishing a minimum standard of security for the global community. Following the attempted airline bombing by the "Underwear Bomber" above Detroit, for example, international airline security changed dramatically as a result of U.S. leadership and pressure to raise global aviation standards and adopt universal protocols.[40]

But creating and enforcing global standards is difficult. Like the private sector, the international community is not a single entity, but rather comprises individual nations and international bodies with their own interests and priorities. Furthermore, DHS does not direct the U.S. government's foreign engagements, which requires DHS to work closely with more outward-facing agencies. In other words, the United States sets standards for itself, but often those standards are only as strong or as lasting as the commitments made by our international partners across maritime, border, and aviation systems. Setting and enforcing standards requires strong leadership internationally and diplomacy—historically the province of the Secretary of State—in areas that are often highly political.

Standard-setting is not, of course, the extent of DHS's international interests. From intelligence sharing to supply chain security to immigration, repatriation, and customs issues, the ability of DHS to meet its objectives is intimately tied to international partners and subject to the complexities of marrying U.S. needs to those of other countries. The "international community" is not a monolith, but America's security is only as strong as the weakest link in an interconnected world.

Questions That Define the Enterprise

As the largest member of the homeland security enterprise, DHS is obligated to play a leading role in shaping the broader apparatus. Shaping the enterprise is about more than safeguarding the homeland. As the enterprise develops, important tensions will have to be resolved about the proper size and function of government and the rights of its citizens. DHS has generally shied away from normative and political debates, but five questions are inevitable: (1) how large of a role the federal government should play; (2) whether the military should be involved; (3) whether federal or state rules should apply during an incident; (4) who should pay for protecting the homeland; and (5) what constitutes success?

HOW LARGE OF A ROLE SHOULD THE FEDERAL GOVERNMENT PLAY?
The scope of the federal government's obligation to the homeland security enterprise falls somewhere along a spectrum. At one extreme is providing all the protection necessary to preserve the homeland, and at the other is never acting directly and instead supporting the capabilities of the private (or state and local government) elements of the enterprise. The alternatives between the extremes are many.

This debate should sound familiar—it has been going on since World War II. It was then that, even a year before Pearl Harbor, President Franklin Roosevelt had to address the possibility that, for the first time since the Civil War, the American homeland was vulnerable to attack. New York City Mayor Fiorello La Guardia, representing the fears of many urban leaders, demanded that the federal government do more than just coordinate. It needed to "initiate and get things going . . . never in our history has the civilian population been exposed to attack."[41] La Guardia wanted a series of protective investments for the American public: bunkers, sirens, and evacuation planning. To La Guardia, the community engagement and radio talks offered by Roosevelt were "sissy stuff" on par with First Lady Eleanor Roosevelt's efforts with community and volunteer engagement.[42]

Even as Roosevelt acceded to some of La Guardia's demands, the president was not convinced that community morale and enterprise engagement should be abandoned.[43] He had, after all, designated his wife as the leader of those efforts. Her goal was to engage the enterprise to support the impending war efforts, one that brought the largest number of women into the labor force in America's history. While the description of "sissy" would not (or, at least, should not) be tolerable in modern times, the tensions between the (hard) La Guardias and the (soft) Roosevelts persists today. The proper role of the federal government in homeland security is far from resolved.

SHOULD THE MILITARY BE INVOLVED IN A CIVILIAN ENTERPRISE?

In the United States, unlike many other countries, public safety always adheres to a civilian command structure; laws, such as the Posse Comitatus Act, prohibit the use of the military in most law enforcement practices.[44] The Constitution, regardless of threat, has no on/off switch to cede control to the military. Even in extreme circumstances, under the Constitution, any domestic military involvement is subject to civilian control—the president— and checks and balances through both Congress and the judiciary, which are independent of the president and the military.

This is not to say that the military is not fully integrated into incident response planning. The National Guard, after all, serves under a governor's command, and every state utilizes National Guard capacity and equipment to assist in disaster management. More troops, through emergency compacts, can be borrowed from other states, but still under the command of the governor. In some circumstances, such as after 9/11, state troops can be utilized for federal purposes, such as protecting nuclear facilities and airports, but again, these troops are still under the command of the governor.

But the tension, indeed fear, is that in exceptional circumstances, there will be an inextricable move to have the "military fix it," summoning troops to defend the homeland in ways that American law and tradition generally do not permit. This is not new; when Roosevelt placed the first "office of homeland security"—called the Office of Civilian Defense (OCD)—in the War Department, public outrage demanded he move it to the White House.[45]

The demand for military involvement domestically became most forceful, in recent history, during Hurricane Katrina. The failed response—at all levels of government—led to one of the greatest military/civilian tensions in U.S. history. Louisiana Governor Kathleen Blanco wanted an increase of troops for hurricane response, but she wanted them under her command: that is, the governor wanted to "borrow" federal troops.[46] That did not sit well with the Pentagon, and her failure to effectively manage the response led to calls for Bush to bypass her and send in troops under his command. Bush declined to do so, but as noted above, he regrets his choice to this day.[47] Had he done so, it would have been an unprecedented use of the military within the homeland. Such an act would have deeply troubled some, but Bush's decision to stay on the sidelines upset many others. This same debate would play out again during the failed response to Hurricane Maria in Puerto Rico in 2017. This is a fundamental challenge in American democracy: the degree of military involvement—a tension between putting what are arguably the best players in the game in order to save lives with creating a sensible method of regulating the military's role.

This challenge was made more vivid when President Donald Trump deployed troops to the U.S. southern border in response to his claims of a "national security" crisis of illegal immigration. The move itself was historic, because the troops were active military rather than the National Guard deployments that are often sent to support state efforts.[48] Initiated just before the midterm elections in 2018 in response to a "caravan" of migrants, Trump's order was viewed as a political stunt, and military members were often utilized for menial tasks or sat bored. Trump pushed the envelope significantly; the question now is whether the genie can be put back in the bottle.

DO FEDERAL OR STATE RULES APPLY DURING AN INCIDENT?

The homeland is diverse, and this is a fundamental challenge for managing the enterprise. Geography, politics, risk assessments, and vulnerabilities all suggest that localities are in the best position to assess what should be the priorities of their security efforts. But the federal government has a responsibility to ensure that there are baseline capabilities across the enterprise—without this floor, weaker links can seriously jeopardize the entire apparatus.

A single standard is not necessarily a bad development. If each jurisdiction and discipline involved with homeland security is allowed to plan and prepare in its own silo, then national efforts would be disjointed, especially in big crises when coordination is most important. This is why coordination efforts during Bush's first term were so essential. Then, finally, the federal government formally adopted the "all hazards" approach to incident command response, creating a unified operational template that serves as a model for any and all disasters.

The ICS (incident command system) model is essentially a plug-and-play structure. It is designed with the flexibility to work for any of the disciplines and geographies that may experience or be involved with an event, and it offers a formalized and uniform process across actors.

The tension between local independence and federal oversight, it should be noted, is closely related to the political tension previously discussed and is not new to DHS. Each president since World War II has struggled with how best to use the levers of federal power—taxes, grants, regulations, zoning laws, criminal liability—to ensure a common operating commitment.

A well-accepted theory of preparedness planning has helped to ameliorate some of these challenges. President Richard Nixon, facing natural disasters as much as the Cold War threat, first authorized domestic preparedness (the precursor to the notion of homeland security) to be employed for "dual use" purposes. This was the first time the federal government understood, as a matter of policy, that funds designated for one threat—in that case nuclear armageddon—could be suited for others. Dual use has animated much of homeland security funding ever since, though in the early years after 9/11, a pure focus on counterterrorism overtook it. Today, dual use is back as "all hazards," after the counterterrorism-only focus was rejected as unworkable as a long-term national policy beginning with the enterprise's failures with Hurricane Katrina.

WHO SHOULD PAY FOR PROTECTING THE HOMELAND?

If homeland security were a traditional war, the answer would be obvious: federal taxes would pay for the effort. But homeland security falls somewhere between war and public safety.

The duties and responsibilities of the federal government for paying have to be balanced by similar duties and responsibilities of other members in the enterprise to pay for their own priorities. For example, federal funds for homeland security are generally prohibited from funding police officers or fire-fighters.[49] The belief is that the federal government should not pay for public safety responsibilities that are primarily local.

Mayors and local officials often feel differently. They counter that homeland security is essentially a federal responsibility, and the federal government should contribute more to the effort.[50] Of course, local officials would like the money to come with as few requirements and restrictions as possible.

Much like protecting local communities, securing critical infrastructure is a good that everyone demands but nobody wants to pay for. Most of the U.S. critical infrastructure is owned by the private sector, which often receives tremendous profits from that infrastructure but with very few security obli-gations.[51] The obligation for a baseline level of protection at, for example, an energy or infrastructure facility may be imposed by the federal government, but more aggressive measures are often challenged on the grounds that they are too expensive for the private enterprise. Funding is a persistent friction point within the enterprise, and one which can be expected to continue if not grow, especially considering the changing and likely increasing threat posed by climate change and natural disasters.

WHAT CONSTITUTES SUCCESS?

Success is a messy concept in homeland security. At the very least, natural disasters are inevitable and the terror threat is persistent. There are no coun-terfactuals to assess responses to crises: a bad thing not happening is hard to quantify, and when bad things do happen, it is hard to separate the inevitable from the preventable. This might sound simple in the abstract, but in the midst of heartbreak, judging success and failure is difficult. If three people die in the Boston Marathon attack, but nearly three hundred people who are rushed to area hospitals survive, what are the successes and failures?

It is easier to tell what success is not than what it is. Success cannot possibly be when nothing bad happens, regardless of how much political discourse treats it as the appropriate metric. And if the goal is to minimize risks and maximize defenses, then there will never be a "finish line," because the flows of people and goods will never stop.

This is the challenge of setting appropriate metrics. There is no perfect answer. On the one hand, safety and security investments are never complete—the risk can always be lower, the defenses always stronger. On the other, these improvements have costs, and when taken too far, they can harm other invest-ments necessary to the growth and development of the country, a modern-day version of President Dwight Eisenhower's "guns and butter" metaphor.[52]

These costs have come into increasing focus at DHS as it has taken its place in the broader enterprise and transitioned away from a singular focus on terrorism.

DHS was born with a simple motto: never again. For some threats, this is an appropriate metric. There are attacks that the United States is unwilling to tolerate: a nuclear attack, a biological weapon of mass destruction, a hijacking of the electrical grid, or another band of terrorists flying airplanes into skyscrapers. For these events, zero tolerance is the only option.

For others, however, "never again" is simply unattainable. DHS cannot stop hurricanes, and it is unrealistic to expect DHS to stop every illegal border crossing or incident of smuggling, absent unprecedented and unpalatable compromises elsewhere. For these—the types of events with which DHS actually deals most often —"never again" is not a workable or desirable metric. Embracing the nuances of DHS's mission allows it to protect the homeland and its values; defining success as "safer" and weighing its benefits against its costs allows DHS to build a safe and sustainable homeland security enterprise.

Building a Better Enterprise

The future of homeland security will always involve the Department built in its name, but DHS will never have complete ownership of the enterprise. In some ways, DHS is left with a lot of responsibility but a lot less authority. For all the debates and chaos around some of DHS's efforts in immigration, border control, cybersecurity, and response capabilities, the absence of a DHS would deprive the public of a single Department remotely capable of integrating these complicated efforts.

Put another way, whether DHS should or should not have been created is past debate; the goal should be to continue to build a better one, one that can better nurture the enterprise. These efforts could include:

- Staffing: DHS leadership should appoint subject matter experts and personnel from state, local, territorial, and private sector stakeholders to leadership roles throughout DHS; clear liaison bodies—such as the Office of Intergovernmental Affairs, the Office of the Private Sector, and the Office of International Affairs—must incorporate professional leaders from the respective fields.
- Training and exercises: Enterprise leaders must be better integrated into federal tabletops and exercises in a meaningful way so that their

roles are understood by DHS and vice versa. When crises strike, it will be an all-hands effort.

- Liaisons to DHS: A better understanding of DHS by the interagency, intergovernmental, private sector, and international players would go far in transparency and understanding. DHS will need to more readily open its own doors to those who might benefit from better understanding through liaison programs.

DHS will be a stronger enterprise the more it can focus outward on its stakeholders. There will always be disagreements, politics, and differing priorities, but they will be better solved with a fully integrated approach to the homeland. Federal protection of the homeland begins with DHS. But it does not end there.

CHAPTER 3

Organizing Homeland Security: The Challenge of Integration at DHS

Alan Cohn and Christian Marrone

THE PRIMARY MANAGEMENT CHALLENGE OF THE DEPARTMENT OF Homeland Security (DHS) has always been integration—how to make the whole of the Department greater than the sum of the parts. At its creation, different communities had very different views of how DHS should operate: some believed that it was nothing more than a holding company for operating agencies (the "Components") that independently conducted their own, often unrelated missions; others believed that DHS's role was ultimately to eliminate these distinctions among Components and create one unified, integrated Department with a single identity and a single operating structure.

Fortunately, neither of those visions has prevailed. Rather, DHS's history over the last seventeen years reveals that it can achieve its highest success by adopting a middle ground—what is known in the corporate world as a "multidivisional organization." In this model, individual operating organizations with deep competencies and rich histories co-exist with integrating structures. These integrating structures apply to both management (how things are budgeted, bought, researched and developed, and so forth) and operations (how mission responsibilities are actually carried out).

No organization, especially the third largest Department of the federal government, can achieve its purpose if it cannot manage itself or effectively conduct operations. Although DHS has converged on the right organizational model, it still must improve on both of these fronts.

In terms of *management*, DHS should pursue further integration based on the principle that decisions should be based on explicit criteria of national interest, rather than compromises among bureaucratic (intra-Departmental or Component-versus-Component) forces. The experience of achieving management and operational integration at the Department of Defense (DOD)—the other major multi-divisional organization in government—is instructive. Since its inception in 1947, when the Departments of War and the Navy were combined, the DOD has wrestled with many of the same challenges that DHS faces, including how to manage budgets. Its experience suggests a roadmap for management integration.

In terms of *operations*, DHS should base its decisions on the concept of applying joint force where it would best achieve specific missions, while enhancing the ability of the Components to conduct their own operations whenever joint force is unnecessary. The idea that "the whole is greater than the sum of the parts" must remain the central tenet of this effort. We believe that this approach, reflected in Jeh Johnson's "Unity of Effort," has enjoyed growing support from key stakeholders in Congress, DHS's workforce, and even some of the Components.

Below, we first discuss the changing homeland security mission, which underscores the crucial importance of organizational effectiveness. We then describe the history of DHS's efforts at internal integration. Third, we sketch out the basics of the multi-divisional design that DHS eventually adopted. Fourth, we discuss the efforts at further managerial and operational integration since then. Finally, we outline the path forward. Our recommendations focus on management integration, where there is greatest consensus about what needs to be done, but we also tackle the more controversial question of operational integration.

We believe that DHS will be in serious jeopardy if it fails to develop its structures and especially its processes. Without continued improvement, it will remain subject to the ever-changing impulses of its political leadership, intensive but capricious attention from Congress and the media, persistent underfunding of key missions, and budgetary uncertainty. Strategy and planning will be largely absent, and DHS will default to tactical reactions to events. Ultimately, without change and growth, DHS will fail to manage existing risks or anticipate new threats, with grave consequences for its standing and for America's broader homeland security enterprise.

The Evolving Homeland Security Mission

Born out of 9/11, DHS always had counterterrorism as a cornerstone mission. The disparate parts of the federal government that were consolidated under DHS tended to share a common theme—how to prevent and respond to a major terrorist attack. That mission included knowing who was in the United States, keeping out those who should not be allowed in, assuring safe travel, and being prepared to respond if disaster struck.

The Homeland Security Act of 2002 was clear as to *which* organizations would compose DHS; however, it was less clear about the rationale for *why* certain organizations and functions would be collected into a new Department or the degree of integration that was supposed to result from this collection. Although counterterrorism was thought to be DHS's primary focus, in reality it had to conduct many different missions.

Over the past decade and half, DHS has dealt with a number of terrorist events: the "Shoe Bomber" Richard Reid, the 2010 Yemen plot using toner cartridges as bombs, the attempted Times Square bombing, the Boston Marathon bombings, and countless other terror-related threats. DHS has also built capabilities to address other types of low-probability, high-risk threats. Preventing or responding to another anthrax-related scare, a stolen nuclear weapon ("loose nuke"), or an attack employing chemical or biological agents ("chem-bio") have long been of concern to DHS. At the same time, it has also dealt with countless major events that had little to do with its counterterrorism mission: Hurricanes Katrina, Rita, and Wilma; Superstorm Sandy; large illegal immigration spikes in 2006, 2014, and 2018; the Ebola crisis of 2015; major cyber incidents like the Sony attack and the Heartbleed vulnerability; and systematic organizational failures in three Components (the Federal Emergency Management Agency [FEMA], the Secret Service [USSS], and the Transportation Security Administration [TSA]). None of these incidents was terrorist-related; each demonstrated the evolving nature of the threats and hazards DHS faces; and each required a wide variety of capabilities to address these challenges. These events often spread DHS's focus too thin and its resources too wide, without a clear mechanism to prioritize across different activities. Furthermore, new challenges have emerged. Most prominently, cyberattacks by nation-states and sophisticated criminal organizations can now wreak havoc with nearly every process upon which Americans rely to carry out their daily lives. (See Chapters 11 and 12 for further discussion.)

As the threats and hazards facing the nation have evolved, DHS's structure and processes have struggled to keep up. Its budget, after dramatic increases in its early years, has been rather flat. Investments have stagnated in many areas, and congressional oversight remains dispersed among a number of committees and subcommittees. A path to effective management and integration continues to elude DHS, its leadership, and its congressional overseers.

All of this speaks to the central question that animates this chapter: Should the Components included in DHS simply be housed within the same federal Cabinet Department, working side by side under the loose supervision of a Secretary and a staff, or is DHS meant to achieve something more? And if it is meant to achieve something more, how exactly should it go about doing so?

Organizing DHS

DHS's first seventeen years saw it cycle through multiple organizational models—not just reorganizations, but wholly different frameworks—without a clear sense of why it should be organized in any particular way. Secretary Michael Chertoff's "Second Stage Review" in 2005 took DHS away from a holding company model and toward a multi-divisional organizational model. The operational experience of Hurricane Katrina taught other important lessons, as did a variety of other operations which DHS led or to which it contributed. Secretary Jeh Johnson's "Unity of Effort" in 2014 focused on greater integration on both the management and operational fronts. Understanding this organizational peregrination is at the core of understanding DHS's well-documented management challenges.

THE ORIGINAL STRUCTURE OF DHS

DHS was created by the Homeland Security Act of 2002, and began operations on March 1, 2003. DHS incorporated all or part of twenty-two legacy agencies and organizations, including whole agencies like FEMA, the USSS, and the Coast Guard (USCG); agencies that would be broken apart and then recombined, such as the U.S. Customs Service and the Immigration and Naturalization Service (INS); and parts of agencies that would remain outside of DHS, such as the Federal Bureau of Investigation's National Infrastructure Protection Center and the executive office of the DOD's National Communications System. The establishment of DHS also involved the creation of its Headquarters (an Office of the Secretary and supporting offices such as the Office of General Counsel, Offices of Public Affairs and Legislative Affairs, and similar organizations). Finally, the Homeland Security Act of 2002 required the construction of new organizations, such as an Information Analysis and Infrastructure Protection Directorate (most of which is now part of either DHS's Office of Intelligence and Analysis or its Cybersecurity and Infrastructure Security Agency) and a Science and Technology Directorate (S&T). DHS was thus a roll-up, a stand-up, and a start-up.

Initially, the Department was organized into five directorates:

1. The Border and Transportation Security (BTS) Directorate, which housed the majority of DHS's law enforcement agencies, including

the newly created Customs and Border Protection (CBP) and Immigration and Customs Enforcement (ICE), the recently-established TSA, the Federal Law Enforcement Training Center (FLETC) from the Treasury Department, DHS's grants office, and the former Office for Domestic Preparedness from the Department of Justice (DOJ);

2. The Informational Analysis and Infrastructure Protection Directorate, which was created to perform DHS's intelligence and critical infrastructure protection functions;

3. The Emergency Preparedness and Response (EPR) Directorate, which essentially housed FEMA;

4. The Science and Technology Directorate, created to oversee Departmental research and development; and

5. The Management Directorate, established to perform management functions for the Department's Headquarters as well as oversee management functions across DHS.

The USCG and the USSS, as well as the new U.S. Citizenship and Immigration Services (USCIS), were not made part of any directorate and instead reported directly to the DHS Secretary.

This organizational structure led to tension between the operating agencies—CBP, ICE, TSA, the USCG, the USSS, USCIS, and FEMA—and the Departmental superstructure of directorates headed by Senate-confirmed Under Secretaries. Leaders of operating agencies were inclined to perceive DHS as a holding company, in which each agency operated semi-autonomously and the Headquarters managed public and legislative affairs, compiling agency budgets into a single volume and providing officials for speaking engagements. Conversely, Headquarters personnel perceived a congressional mandate to merge operating agencies into one unified whole, shedding their individual identities and becoming pieces of a single DHS.

Tensions between these conceptions of DHS integration resulted in barriers to any type of larger integration effort, from joint requirements analysis to joint program construction to integration of regional offices. Almost any initiative meant to harmonize programs or operations across operating agencies was met with suspicion, if not outright hostility. Lack of consensus about how much to integrate led inevitably to an inability to set out a plan for longer-term integration. Compounding matters was the fact that Headquarters staff lacked deep knowledge of the operating agencies they were supposed to oversee and, potentially, merge. Meanwhile, some operating agencies (such as CBP and

ICE), which were composed of pieces of preexisting agencies, were simultaneously wrestling with their own internal integration challenges to bring together "legacy Customs" and "legacy Immigration" operations.

Operationally, DHS largely functioned as if the agencies under its direction were independent entities. The USCG and the USSS continued to conduct their own planning and operations, working together with the military services and others as appropriate. CBP and ICE incorporated their respective operational entities—for example, the Border Patrol, which was moved to CBP from the now-defunct Immigration and Naturalization Service (INS) at the DOJ. They continued to conduct their legacy operations and maintained existing relationships with the Departments of Justice, Health and Human Services, Treasury, Agriculture, and others. The USCG, the USSS, CBP, and ICE all also had their own separate regional structures.

FEMA, in particular, brought with it a distinctive concept of operations and regional structure. FEMA, like many state emergency management agencies, is less a line agency and more a cross-governmental coordinator of activities across the mitigate-prepare-respond-recover cycle. It was organized around ten regions, which were different from the regions that other agencies brought into DHS. DHS's first Secretary, Tom Ridge, proposed conforming all of DHS's agencies and operations to a regional structure based on FEMA's ten regions in 2004, but this initial effort at rationalization failed in the face of almost universal resistance and the reality that the same "regions" did not make equal sense to different agencies.[1] For instance, "the southwest border" might be a conceptually coherent region for CBP, but not for the USCG or FEMA; likewise, "Downtown Washington, D.C." might be an operationally relevant region for the USSS but not for ICE.

THE "SECOND STAGE REVIEW" AND HURRICANE KATRINA
In 2005, Michael Chertoff, the newly appointed second Secretary of Homeland Security, ordered a review of DHS's structure.[2] It was reorganized, with the abandonment of the BTS and EPR directorates, the creation of a new Preparedness Directorate and an Office of Policy, and the establishment of direct reporting lines from the heads of the operating agencies (CBP, ICE, TSA, the USCG, the USSS, USCIS, and FEMA) to the Secretary. In essence, this redesign created three categories of organizations within DHS:

1. The operating agencies, now referred to as the operating Components, which planned, built capabilities, and carried out operations;

2. The Headquarters organizations, sometimes referred to as the support Components, which were tasked with integrating the actions and activities of the operating agencies within specific spheres of responsibility (e.g., policy, management, intelligence, research and development, and operations, as well as specific areas like combating weapons of mass destruction); and

3. The Immediate Office of the Secretary, which had to integrate more than two dozen directly-reporting operating agencies, directorates, offices, and other entities scattered around the national capital region and the country.

Whether intended or not, this reorganization changed the fundamental operating model of DHS. Gone was the holding company structure, as was the concept of a fully integrated Department. In its place was the multi-divisional structure—one pioneered by the legacy U.S. automakers and adapted for government use by then–Secretary of Defense Robert McNamara in the 1960s to create the modern DOD. Left unanswered, however, were questions relating to how DHS should manage itself in this new configuration, and how it should manage its operations.

The first trial for this still-incipient organization came with Hurricanes Katrina, Rita, and Wilma, which lashed Florida and the Gulf Coast in August and September 2005. The damage was the worst in New Orleans and its surrounding areas, where Hurricane Katrina led to a levee failure and a "double disaster" of wind and water—what Coast Guard Admiral Thad Allen would later describe as a weapon of mass destruction without the criminal intent.[3] Although efforts had been made to meld together FEMA's operating concept and structure with DHS's broader mandate as reflected in the new National Response Plan, the institutional and bureaucratic compromises involved had led to unclear lines of authority and incomplete concepts of operation. These deficits were exposed by the overwhelming scale and complexity of this disaster.

All sorts of remedies were proposed for these failures. Some, like the disbanding of the Preparedness Directorate and the reintegration of its functions into FEMA, were mandated by Congress. Others, like better partnership with the private sector, better cross-collaboration among DHS agencies, and a clearer matching of responsibility and authority, would need to wait to be addressed in the context of other disasters, such as Superstorm Sandy, the Deepwater Horizon oil rig disaster, and the Boston Marathon bombings.

The Multi-Divisional Solution

DHS is not the first Cabinet Department—or the first large organization—to wrestle with these questions of management and operational integration. There are principles and models to consider with respect to both management and operational integration, and these principles and models suggest what makes a multi-divisional organization the right model for DHS.

One of the most important considerations when thinking about DHS integration is that DHS is an overwhelmingly operational Department. Although most U.S. government departments make policy, provide government benefits, engage with domestic and international partners, and make grants, DHS is in essence its Components. These agencies field vast numbers of personnel who operate ports of entry (POEs), patrol waterways, conduct investigations, inspect travelers, survey disaster damage and provide assistance, work with private sector cybersecurity operations centers, and the like. As a result, any discussion of DHS integration must focus first on providing higher-order purpose, meaning, and direction to fundamentally operational activities, which are carried out by distinct entities with over-lapping responsibilities and jurisdictions. These entities necessarily compete with one another for resources, attention, and operational primacy—largely to beneficial ends—but the onus is placed on the leadership of DHS to set overall policy and strategic goals, harmonize resource requests and proposed operational approaches, and adjudicate among often equally valid perspectives.

MANAGEMENT

A multi-divisional structure is used when a corporate entity wishes to preserve the distinct identities, competencies, and responsibilities of multiple operating units, but those competencies and responsibilities are not mutually exclusive. Instead, shared business functions such as information technology, research and development, and marketing increase efficiencies, while integrated acquisition and operations enhance effectiveness. In short, a multi-divisional organizational structure is intended to literally make the whole greater than the sum of the parts.

In 1961, McNamara, then the president of the Ford Motor Company, became the Secretary of Defense. The DOD was formed after World War II through the merger of the Department of War and the Department of the Navy, and included four of the five military services within three subordinate Departments (the Marine Corps being part of the Department of the Navy).

In a speech in 1963, McNamara neatly summarized the challenge facing the Secretary of Defense then and indeed the Secretary of Homeland Security today.[4] As he stated:

> The question of how to spend our defense dollars and how much to spend is a good deal more complicated than is often assumed. . . .
>
> You cannot make decisions simply by asking yourself whether something might be nice to have. You have to make a judgment on how much is enough.
>
> I emphasize judgment because you can't even be sure yourself, much less prove to others, that your decision was precisely right to the last dollar—even to the last billion dollars. But the decision has to be made.
>
> There is an important difference between the way we make these tough decisions today, and the way they used to be made. Formerly, an arbitrary budget ceiling was fixed for national defense, and funds were then apportioned among the [military] Services. Today we examine all our military needs, and then decide at what point our military strength is in balance with the requirements of our foreign policy.
>
> There are, of course, sharp differences of opinion on where we should spend our marginal defense dollars. And here is where the responsibility most clearly falls on the Secretary of Defense, because here is where it must fall not only constitutionally but under any rational system. For these decisions can only be made from the point of view of the defense establishment as a whole, not from the point of view of the individual [military] Services.

Managing the DOD in this way was done through a new system for defense resource allocation named the Planning, Programming, and Budgeting System (PPBS). PPBS was based on "six deceptively simple fundamental ideas":

1. Decisions should be based on explicit criteria of national interest, not on compromises among institutional (intra-Departmental or cross-service) forces;
2. Needs and costs should be considered simultaneously;
3. Major decisions should be made by choices among explicit, balanced, feasible alternatives;
4. The Secretary should have an active analytic staff to provide him or her with relevant data and a cross-Departmental, rather than subordinate Department or individual service, perspective;
5. A multi-year force and financial plan should project the consequences of present decisions into the future; and

6.   Open and explicit analysis, available to all parties, should form the
     basis for major decisions.[5]

These same principles apply to DHS; the problem has been putting them into
practice.

DHS OPERATIONS

DHS conducts its missions through its Components, which operate geographically through regions, districts, sectors, and field offices. In 2012, the
Government Accountability Office (GAO) conducted a study for the House and
Senate oversight committees on homeland security concerning DHS's efforts to
realign its field office structure.[6] The GAO set forth four types of operational
realignments:

1.   *Regionalization*, which refers to full-scale realignment of DHS's
     regional/field office structure and includes the establishment of a
     single, commonly-defined set of regions for all Components;
2.   *Co-location*, which refers to the sharing of space, buildings,
     property, or other physical assets by Components;
3.   *Consolidation*, which refers to the merging of organizational
     functions; and
4.   *Integration*, which refers to the coordination of functions across
     Components without consolidation or merger.[7]

The GAO also described four categories of constraints on reorganization:

1.   DHS Components each have a different regional or field office
     structure based on unique mission needs;
2.   Reorganization causes disruption to DHS and Component
     workforce, missions, and operations, as staff are diverted from their
     normal duties;
3.   There are costs associated with relocating facilities and terminating
     leases; and
4.   Statutory provisions may affect DHS's authority to reorganize.[8]

Ultimately, we believe that DHS's operational posture should be determined by mission need. Unlike the DOD, whose forces are meant to be expeditionary, DHS's Components have permanent responsibilities for carrying
out government functions at specific locations (as well as expeditionary or

mobile responsibilities relating to specific campaigns or contingencies). As a result, one single operational posture cannot meet DHS's needs. Instead, individual agency regions, districts, sectors, or field offices may more effectively conduct many of DHS's day-to-day responsibilities (e.g., aviation security screening operations at airports, port safety and security operations in seaports, etc.), while standing "joint" commands may more effectively conduct or direct other activities (e.g., developing an integrated approach to border security or conducting joint investigations), and temporary joint field commands may more appropriately coordinate and direct other activities (e.g., disaster response or search and rescue activities).

To that end, what is more important than the physical layout of DHS's operating regions is DHS's concept of how its operations should be conducted. The proper questions concern (a) the Secretary's planning guidance for the Department; (b) the best way to carry out campaigns pursuant to that guidance; and (c) the best command structures for planning and conducting joint operations.

Steps toward Integration

As noted above, initial efforts to integrate DHS were stymied both by the directorate-focused structure of the Department and disagreement about the imperative to integrate. For example, efforts by a nascent DHS Joint Requirements Council foundered on how to adjudicate legitimate disputes between Components about requirements and whether to force the integration of acquisition programs. Efforts by Secretary Tom Ridge to integrate DHS's regional operations ran into a brick wall of opposition from each of the agencies involved, which questioned why such regional integration was necessary. These disputes led to the Second Stage Review.

After the Second Stage Review's reorganization and the *de facto* adoption of a multi-divisional organizational structure, the path to management integration became clearer, as it could be guided by the DOD's efforts since 1961. However, clarity did not ensure adoption.

MANAGEMENT

Efforts to craft an integrated approach to DHS management began with the formal adoption of a planning, programming, budgeting, and execution (PPBE) process by the Department's management directorate. This process, however, was observed as much in the breach as in the commission. The first Quadrennial Homeland Security Review (QHSR) process included a working group on management integration, but its results were never published.[9] Those efforts did lead, however, to the adoption of a pilot program, the Integrated Investment Life Cycle Management (IILCM) process, during the first term of the Obama administration. The lessons of the IILCM, in turn, led to Secretary Johnson's "Unity of Effort" initiative.

Unity of Effort built on the principles underpinning McNamara's original PPBS process. Johnson's April 22, 2014, memorandum on "Enhancing Departmental Unity of Effort" set out four basic categories of Departmental governance processes for a large-scale, multi-divisional organization such as DHS:

- *Senior leadership decision-making*: Johnson formalized a senior leaders group, integrating the Component heads, the Under Secretaries, and other key Headquarters personnel such as the Chief Financial Officer into a top-level decision-making and oversight body. The Deputy Secretary chaired a similar body at the Deputy level, the Deputies Management Action Group. These bodies formalized previous *ad hoc* arrangements of DHS's senior leaders and placed Component heads on the same level as Under Secretaries for the purpose of Departmental decision-making.
- *Strategy development and strategic analysis capability*: Independent of the groups described above, Unity of Effort gave the Secretary his or her own strategic analysis shop. The objective was to articulate short, direct statements of what specifically the Secretary intended for DHS to achieve; how it would prioritize, deprioritize, or otherwise arrange its activities to achieve these goals; and what resources—budgetary, operational, research and development, etc.—DHS would bring to bear.
- *Linking strategy and policy to investments*: Unity of Effort set out to improve DHS's planning and budgeting, as well as oversight of major acquisitions and investments. The goal was to give the Secretary the ability to ensure that Departmental investments supported national priorities, with budgeting cycles and major acquisitions serving as checkpoints.
- *Linking strategy and policy to operations*: Unity of Effort established field organizations to coordinate the development and implementation of operational plans across Components. This proved to be the most controversial element of the project, because it concerned not only management integration but also operational integration.

These processes were meant to involve leaders across DHS, including both political appointees and senior career officials. By the end of Johnson's tenure, these reforms had been instituted but not fully consolidated.

OPERATIONS

DHS made efforts to examine the consolidation of regional structures, first in 2004 in the Operational Integration Staff's Draft Regional Concept of Operations and later as part of the 2010 Bottom-Up Review. Efforts to select a single regional structure and operating posture for DHS never resulted in concepts that could be implemented, however, and these efforts were ultimately unsuccessful.

The Unity of Effort initiative took a different path, assuming that: (1) most day-to-day activities of DHS could be effectively conducted by the Components with responsibility for those activities managed through their existing geographic structures; (2) responses to disasters were best addressed through the existing concept of operations;[10] and (3) the greatest return on investment for joint operations would come from focusing on DHS's operational responsibilities for border security. This last point meant that joint operations only applied to one of DHS's missions and to only some of its Components. This embrace of three different operating structures for DHS allowed it to focus its operational integration efforts on an area most likely to yield operational benefits.

Ultimately, these efforts came to involve four elements:

- The Secretary's strategic guidance for joint operational planning, which set forth the overall intent for the outcome of those plans;
- Joint commands focused on the U.S. southern border and the Caribbean, together with a joint task force for investigations;
- Standing operations planning and coordination staffs in the joint commands; and
- Joint task-force commanders with the ability to direct the activities of a variety of operational assets provided by multiple DHS Components.

Modeled on the "jointness" initiatives conducted at the DOD pursuant to the 1986 Goldwater-Nichols Act, the new commands were meant to create a coherent approach to joint operational planning and execution for a particular mission.

Unsurprisingly, the joint commands proved more contentious than the first two conclusions from Unity of Effort, which left existing organizational routines in place. Proponents pointed to the poor operations planning capabilities of some Components and the manifest need for a coherent approach to the southwest border. Critics complained that the permanent staffs at the joint commands created an unnecessary layer of bureaucracy and confusion about reporting relationships for Component personnel assigned to them.

The Path Forward

What have we learned from these experiences? Over the past several years DHS has begun to make the changes it needs. But, as in the past, this progress is at serious risk due to bureaucratic inertia, as well as the disruption that typically accompanies a change of presidential administration. To stop efforts toward integration, or to start over with another full-scale attempt to redraw the overall organization of DHS, would cost precious time and generate skepticism both inside and outside the Department. Rather, we believe that DHS should consolidate recent efforts at integration in order to be more effective in addressing future threats. We focus on seven steps.

1. *Decision-making.* DHS leadership must be able to make decisions from a cross-Departmental perspective, and to do this, the Department must create repeatable and sustainable processes to conduct and carry out this decision-making. DHS should reinforce processes such as the Counter-Terrorism Advisory Board, the Joint Requirements process, the matching of policy guidance to budgeting, the investment review process, and campaign planning. These processes need to be routinized during "normal" times, as well as times of high operational tempo.

2. *Breaking down information stovepipes.* DHS's ability to confront and prioritize threats would be greatly enhanced if it had ready access to all of the information needed to make decisions. This is true not just for counterterrorism and cybersecurity, but also for immigration enforcement, border management, and disaster response. On the flip side, DHS should avoid duplication of information collection by Components or Headquarters.

3. *Strategy and planning.* A sharp sense of direction and clear articulation of how to achieve goals are essential to DHS's success. It needs a robust strategic planning and analysis function in the Secretary's

office that can (a) advance secretarial initiatives, (b) gather and present a common fact base for decision-making, and (c) inform the budgeting process. Some individual Components also need to enhance their own capabilities in these areas.

4. *Budgeting.* Budgets should be better focused and aligned around overall missions and priorities, rather than simply around Components. Strategically informed budgeting also applies to investments in capabilities by all Components. The well-publicized "failures" of TSA and the USSS actually began years before they occurred as a result of a failure to invest properly, cannibalizing investment for current operational needs.

5. *Research and development.* DHS research and development should be centralized and aligned with strategy and planning. This includes preparedness and investment for low-probability, high-consequence threats.

6. *Standardization and interoperability.* DHS must continue to create interoperable and standardized policies for how it screens and vets people and shipments, and then build technologies, processes, and operations around those policies. As with information holdings, each Component operates and employs technology differently, creating greater costs and uneven results.

7. *Joint operations.* The joint task force model must serve as an example of how DHS leverages the sum of its operational parts. Its "Southern Border and Approaches" campaign is a good starting point, but the East and West task forces of that campaign must be strengthened. How well these task forces perform—and the extent to which their maturation addresses criticisms—should inform next steps on operational integration.

Achieving DHS's evolving missions requires a coherent organization structure, mature decision-making processes, and ruthless prioritization. It also requires a clear articulation by Congress, the president, and the Secretary that DHS should integrate across Components whenever doing so enhances public safety. The stakes are too high to let bureaucratic resistance or inertia determine what comes next.

CHAPTER 4

DHS and the Counterterrorism Enterprise

Matthew Olsen and Edoardo Saravalle

THE DEPARTMENT OF HOMELAND SECURITY (DHS) WAS ESTABLISHED IN response to the terrorist attacks on September 11, 2001. Despite its limited role in the overall counterterrorism enterprise, domestic counterterrorism has officially remained DHS's top priority. It is likely to remain so, as several DHS functions directly or indirectly support the federal government's domestic counterterrorism efforts against a persistent threat to the homeland. These functions include border security, transportation and aviation security, countering violent extremism, intelligence support to state and local law enforcement, critical infrastructure protection, and initiatives against the illicit acquisition and use of weapons of mass destruction.

Before 9/11, no one agency was responsible for linking these diverse functions under the common rubric of counterterrorism. The creation of DHS was a major element of a massive post-9/11 transformation of the U.S. national security bureaucracy, which was intended to forge the unity of effort and common vision that had previously been absent. In addition to DHS, this change produced several new organizations, including the National Counterterrorism Center (NCTC), the Terrorist Screening Center (TSC), and the Office of the Director of National Intelligence (ODNI), as well as reforms to existing institutions, such as the Central Intelligence Agency (CIA), the Federal Bureau of Investigation (FBI), the Department of Justice (DOJ), and the components of the White House that deal with national security.

As this list makes clear, DHS is only one of many agencies involved in defending the homeland, and it often serves in an enabling role to other agencies with more authority and operational focus on counterterrorism. Several other entities, most notably the FBI and other intelligence agencies, have more direct and substantial responsibility for preventing and investigating terrorism against the United States. Even domestically, primary operational authority for counterterrorism activities in the homeland tends to reside outside of DHS. Indeed, DHS's primary focus on counterterrorism does not accurately reflect its actual authorities or responsibilities, which encompass a wide range of threats to the homeland beyond terrorism and other legacy missions of its principal operating agencies (the "Components").

In addition to the organizational changes mentioned above, the federal government also changed many processes within the government after 9/11, especially regarding information sharing. The objective was to create a whole-of-government effort, rather than perpetuate information stovepipes and disparate activities. As the Obama administration stated in its National Strategy for Counterterrorism, "We are engaged in a broad, sustained, and integrated campaign that harnesses every tool of American power—military, civilian, and the power of our values—together with the concerted efforts of allies, partners, and multilateral institutions."[1]

Finally, after 9/11, the federal government embraced the counter-terrorism role of state and local law enforcement agencies and "first responders." State and local partners are often in the best position to identify suspected terrorists, disrupt plots, and respond to attacks; their sacrifice on 9/11 confirmed their place on the front lines of this national struggle. Security clearances, intelligence sharing, joint "fusion centers," and federal money gave local police forces an unprecedented place in the national security enterprise. These reforms have required DHS to approach its counterterrorism missions in partnership with other entities engaged in homeland security at all levels of government.

This chapter examines the evolving role of DHS and the broader homeland security enterprise in combating terrorism. First, we provide a general overview of the terrorism threat and then proceed more specifically to threats against the U.S. homeland. Next, we discuss DHS's counter-terrorism role. We conclude by identifying the primary challenges facing DHS in the execution of its responsibilities. We highlight the mismatch between perceived and actual responsibilities that encourages duplicative DHS counterterrorism efforts and detracts from a more sustained focus on areas where DHS plays a unique or primary role. One important challenge for DHS going forward is aligning public perceptions and expectations about its capacity to combat terrorism with its actual role within the federal govern-ment's counterterrorism efforts.

The Threat Landscape

Since the attacks on 9/11, the United States has made significant progress in defending the country and its interests overseas against terrorist attacks. In the years before 9/11, Al-Qaeda operated largely without constraint, establishing a safe haven in Afghanistan and moving operatives into Europe and the United States. As the 9/11 Commission documented, a series of operational and strategic failures enabled Al-Qaeda to evade detection and carry out its devastating attacks inside the United States.[2]

Today, through sustained military action overseas, intelligence and investigative efforts around the world, and hardening of defenses in the homeland, the United States has greatly diminished the likelihood of a major terrorist attack inside the country. Military campaigns—including U.S. special forces operations targeting Al-Qaeda leaders—have maintained relentless pressure on terrorist organizations, largely denying Al-Qaeda and related groups the time and space to plan and execute attacks. Revamped and sophisticated intelligence gathering and surveillance activities have provided insights about the capabilities and intentions of terrorist groups at both the tactical and strategic levels. The reform of the Intelligence Community (IC) has streamlined collection and integrated this information across the government. Together, these actions have enabled the United States to map out terrorist networks, target operatives, and disrupt numerous plots.

Law enforcement investigations and prosecutions of suspected terrorists, many captured overseas, have incapacitated hundreds of operatives and facilitators. They have also provided crucial intelligence.[3] Government efforts, in coordination with allies, to map and disrupt the movement of money to terrorist groups have substantially reduced their resources. Finally, the sustained commitment to secure U.S. borders, harden critical infrastructure, and share terrorism information with state and local law enforcement have erected significant barriers against efforts to carry out complex attacks in the homeland.

FROM AL-QAEDA TO ISIS
Despite this progress, however, the threat to the homeland from terrorism remains persistent and potent. To be sure, the "core" Al-Qaeda organization

that carried out the 9/11 attacks has struggled to remain relevant. Most of the group's leadership has been killed or captured and its operational capacity dismantled. Yet, enduring regional conflicts and inadequate governance and security have allowed violent jihadist groups with links to Al-Qaeda to establish footholds in newly ungoverned areas, expand their geographic reach, and adapt their tactics.

In particular, the conflicts and lack of governance in places like Yemen, Syria, Iraq, Somalia, and Libya have provided fertile ground for jihadist ideologies to take root and for terrorist groups to seize and hold territory. Groups such as Al-Qaeda in the Arabian Peninsula (AQAP), al-Shabaab, and the Islamic State (ISIS), have been active over the past several years. In the chaos of civil conflicts and the absence of security forces, these terrorist organizations have subjugated local populations, recruited and trained operatives, raised significant amounts of funding, and planned and executed attacks.

Weak borders have also enabled terrorist groups to move personnel, money, and weapons in support of their efforts with scant resistance. More than 5,000 foreign fighters from the West—including many French, German, British, and Belgian nationals—traveled to Iraq and Syria to join ISIS during the height of its influence. As part of this influx, more than 285 Americans traveled or attempted to travel to Syria or Iraq to participate in *jihad*. These numbers are part of the approximately 30,000 foreign fighters who traveled to Iraq and Syria since 2011. Many have returned to their home countries, battle-hardened and trained in explosives, with access to networks that may be planning attacks in the West.[4]

In areas where state control is particularly weak, territorial sanctuaries have given terrorist groups time and space to incubate complex plots. As Al-Qaeda used its haven in Afghanistan to plot the 9/11 attacks, ISIS, AQAP, and al-Shabaab have used their safe havens to direct, coordinate, and incite attacks outside of their areas of control. In particular, ISIS has demonstrated both the intent and capability to carry out external attacks, even as it has lost control of most of the territory it once occupied. Since its rapid rise in 2014, ISIS has conducted or inspired more than 100 terrorist attacks in at least 29 countries outside of Iraq and Syria.[5] Several of these attacks were conducted directly by ISIS, where the attackers trained with the group in Iraq and Syria. These include the 2015 Paris attack, which killed 130 people, and the 2016 Brussels attack, which killed 32 people. Both attacks demonstrated that ISIS had the capacity to execute sophisticated and deadly attacks in Western Europe and to exploit weaknesses in European intelligence sharing and border security. In Somalia, observers blame al-Shabaab for bombings in Mogadishu in October 2017 that killed more than 500 people.[6]

In other attacks, ISIS played a coordinating role or simply inspired assailants to carry out the acts.[7] Since 2014, ISIS-inspired attacks in Europe and the United States have killed more than 100 people.[8] To foster such a wide network of ideological encouragement, ISIS built a sophisticated media and propaganda machine to radicalize and mobilize followers. ISIS and its sympathizers around the world use social media platforms to disseminate propaganda and encrypted messaging applications to communicate securely with potential operatives globally.

ISIS has varied the scale and sophistication of its attacks. In addition to complex plots, the group directed low-level attacks that have been difficult to detect and stop. These attacks allowed ISIS to maintain its threatening posture even in a time of declining resources. In 2014, an ISIS spokesperson urged sympathizers in the West to launch attacks on their own, calling on them to kill Westerners in any manner available: "Smash his head with a rock, or slaughter him with a knife, or run him over with your car."[9] Attacks in Europe and the United States over the last several years, in which terrorists drove vehicles into crowds, killing bystanders and instilling widespread terror, are consistent with this approach. In October 2017, for example, an ISIS-inspired terrorist drove a rented truck into a New York bike path, killing eight and injuring twelve.[10] Because these simple plots require no advanced skills and minimal planning, they offer little opportunity for security services to detect and disrupt them in advance.

The rise of ISIS is a manifestation of the transformation of the global *jihad* movement over the past several years. The movement diversified and expanded in the aftermath of the upheaval and political chaos in the Arab world since 2010 and the resulting instability and unrest in large parts of the Middle East and North Africa. As a result, the terrorist threat now comes from a decentralized array of organizations and networks.

Even as new threats have emerged, legacy terrorist groups have adapted. Members of Al-Qaeda's remaining leadership, including Ayman al-Zawahiri, remain at large. The group has continued to support attacks in the West and is vying to retain its self-appointed role as leader of the global *jihad*. Al-Qaeda still wields substantial influence over affiliated and allied groups, such as the Yemen-based AQAP. In Syria, veteran Al-Qaeda fighters have traveled from Pakistan to take advantage of the permissive operating environment and access to foreign fighters. They remain focused on plotting against the West.

Al-Shabaab maintains a safe haven in Somalia and threatens U.S. interests in the region, asserting the aim of creating a caliphate across east Africa. In Kenya, al-Shabaab has reportedly increased its recruitment and carried out deadly attacks aimed at destabilizing parts of the country. Finally, Al-Qaeda in the Islamic Maghreb (and its splinter groups) and Boko Haram—now an official branch of ISIS—continue to maintain their bases of operations in North and West Africa and have demonstrated sustained capabilities to carry out deadly attacks against civilian targets.

In the years since 9/11, the United States, along with its allies, has effectively prevented Al-Qaeda from executing another complex, catastrophic attack and, more recently, has substantially diminished ISIS's territorial footprint. Today, the most common terrorist threat comes from self-directed actors. These include lone offenders who are either inspired by jihadi messages online or specifically radicalized and encouraged to carry out attacks by online recruiters.[11] The ability of the terrorist threat to survive U.S. pressure following 9/11 suggests that the danger will adapt and persist. The enduring appeal of the jihadist narrative and the dynamic nature of these terrorist groups will likely continue to pose substantial challenges to the counter-terrorism community.

THE THREAT TO THE U.S. HOMELAND

In the United States, the threat from ISIS and other groups is on a smaller scale than in Europe, but it persists. Government reforms following 9/11 have made large-scale attacks significantly less likely. Yet, new encrypted communication technologies and social media have enabled small-scale planning. For these reasons, lone actors or insular groups—often self-directed or inspired by overseas groups like ISIS—pose the most serious threat to carry out attacks on U.S. territory. Homegrown terrorists are likely to continue to carry out simpler plots that do not require advanced skills or outside training. ISIS-inspired attacks—including attacks in San Bernardino, California, and in Garland, Texas—reflect this trend toward moderate-to-small-scale plots. The online environment and social media platforms—where potential extremists interact with ISIS handlers and recruiters—serve a critical role in radicalizing and mobilizing homegrown extremists toward violence.

The scale of this challenge is alarming. The FBI has opened homegrown terrorist cases in every state, with about a thousand nationwide.[12] Most of these cases are connected to ISIS and point to the potential for an ISIS-directed or inspired attack in the United States. Homegrown, ISIS-inspired terrorists, however, are not the sole homeland threat posed by the group. Americans returning to the United States after fighting in Iraq and Syria also pose a serious potential danger. These returning "foreign" fighters could mimic the complex attacks that foreign terrorists have conducted in Western Europe. Furthermore, ISIS members with European citizenship could potentially pose a homeland threat within the United States by taking advantage of the Visa Waiver Program. (See Chapter 9 for a discussion of the vulnerabilities in that program.)

AQAP also remains determined to strike the U.S. homeland. On three occasions over the past several years, AQAP has sought to bring down an airliner bound for the United States. In 2009, for example, a Nigerian man trained and equipped by AQAP—Umar Farouk Abdulmutallab, the "Underwear Bomber"—nearly blew up a transatlantic airliner as it prepared to land in Detroit. AQAP operatives have developed sophisticated bomb-making capabilities and continue to develop concealed, non-metallic bombs to evade airport security. AQAP leader Anwar al-Awlaki, an American citizen killed in a drone strike in Yemen in 2011, continues to be a source of inspiration to terrorists in the United States and elsewhere through his posthumous online presence.

Finally, in addition to the domestic threat from Islamist terrorism, the United States faces significant threats from radical right-wing terrorism. Although it can be difficult to tally acts of terrorism, some reports indicate that over the past decade there has been a rise in the number of attacks and violent plots originating from individuals and groups who identify with the extreme right wing of U.S. politics.[13] According to the Government Accountability Office (GAO), right-wing extremists have carried out far more attacks in the United States since 9/11 than violent jihadists, although attacks by Islamist terrorists account for slightly more fatalities.[14] Right-wing terrorists carried out the deadliest homegrown terrorist attack in U.S. history, the 1995 bombing of the Alfred P. Murrah Federal Building in Oklahoma City.[15]

Most right-wing extremists fall into one of two broad categories: white supremacists and anti-government extremists, such as militia groups.[16] Like Islamist terrorists, far-right extremist groups have used the internet effectively to spread their ideology and facilitate radicalization. For instance, Keith Luke, who killed two individuals in Brockton, Massachusetts, in 2009, and Dylann Roof, who killed nine in Charleston, South Carolina, in 2015, both appear to have been radicalized online.[17]

In summary, the terrorist threat environment has changed significantly since the 9/11 attacks, from a change in the principal adversary to the rapid rise of the homegrown terror threat. This evolving threat environment has presented a novel challenge to U.S. policymakers and security agencies, including DHS.

DHS's Role in Counterterrorism

DHS's counterterrorism mission has three principal elements: preventing terrorist attacks; preventing and protecting against the acquisition or use of weapons of mass destruction; and reducing the threat to critical infrastructure, personnel, and events. Many DHS counterterrorism functions, however, are not located in terrorism-specific offices. Instead, they fall within DHS Components whose responsibilities are far broader—airline passenger screening at Customs and Border Protection (CBP) and the Transportation Security Administration (TSA), for example.

PREVENTING TERRORIST ATTACKS

DHS's efforts to prevent terrorist attacks fall into four categories: intelligence and information sharing, border security, transportation security, and countering violent extremism. In each of these areas, DHS either has the primary responsibility for the specific function, as in border security, or has attempted to carve out a specific niche within the government.

With regard to intelligence and information sharing, only two DHS Components—specifically, the Office of Intelligence and Analysis (I&A) and Coast Guard Intelligence—are members of the national Intelligence Community (IC), and those entities are limited in size and scope compared to other intelligence agencies. DHS is not positioned to replace the terrorism work of the FBI, the CIA, the National Security Agency (NSA), or other intelligence agencies, which have greater resources, broad authority, and direct access to sensitive sources of intelligence. As a result, the evolution of DHS's intelligence role has reflected a focus on its own operations. This focus—which includes an emphasis on information sharing with state and local law enforcement and first responders—has helped DHS to avoid duplication of effort and to better define its intelligence role within the homeland security enterprise.

The importance of sharing counterterrorism-related information among all levels of government cannot be overstated: Roughly 80 percent of foiled terrorist plots against U.S. interests between 1995 and 2012 were stopped thanks to reports from law enforcement or the general public. By contrast, in five of the seven most deadly or potentially deadly attacks on the United States during this period, at least one entity within federal government either collected initial information related to the threat but did not forward it to all of the relevant agencies, or it passed on the information, but the tip did not result in follow-up investigations.[18]

DHS's intelligence apparatus strives to enable the flow of information between the federal government and local law enforcement. At the front end of the intelligence process, I&A seeks to ensure that DHS's intelligence requirements and interests—i.e., homeland security intelligence requirements—are integrated into and addressed by the IC.[19] DHS facilitates the reporting of relevant homeland security intelligence to state, local, and tribal homeland security and law enforcement agencies through a variety of initiatives.[20] Perhaps the most well-known are DHS-supported state and local fusion centers.

Fusion centers bring together state, local, tribal, and territorial organizations with federal partners including DHS, the FBI, the DOJ, and the ODNI through the program manager for the information sharing environment, as well as with the private sector to support investigations and responses to criminal or terrorist activity.[21] State or local governments oversee each fusion center. The combination of these different levels of government supports the ultimate goal of fusion centers: to act as "focal" vertical and horizontal information-sharing mechanisms.[22] Fusion centers do not replace other information-sharing systems like the FBI's Joint Terrorism Task Forces (JTTFs), because they do not conduct investigations; instead, they complement investigative efforts.[23]

The specific goals of each fusion center vary. Rather than responding to a national unified goal, each center reflects the priorities of the relevant state, local, and federal authorities. Their areas of focus can even be broader than counterterrorism and can cater to local concerns. As one observer has noted, "if you've seen one fusion center, you've seen just one fusion center."[24]

The 2015 San Bernardino attack demonstrates the important role fusion centers can play in "connecting the dots." Immediately afterward, a sheriff's deputy called the Joint Regional Intelligence Center (JRIC), a fusion center covering the Los Angeles region. The deputy reported that a person who matched the description of an individual wanted in connection with providing weapons to the shooters was about to check out of a local hospital.[25] The JRIC, which had taken the lead on developing intelligence on suspects for the attack, shared this information with a task force including the San Bernardino Police Department, the San Bernardino Sheriff's Office, and the FBI. Thanks to this tip, the task force identified the subject and called off a manhunt before it even began.

Although the mission of fusion centers is largely uncontroversial, there are many, including persons in Congress, who have criticized their performance. In 2012, a congressional committee issued a scathing bipartisan report concluding that fusion centers had not produced useful intelligence to support federal counterterrorism efforts and questioning the value of continued federal funding.[26] Some of this criticism seems to stem from the wide variation among fusion centers, with resources sometimes dedicated to state and local criminal threats and natural disasters rather than terrorism. More recent reports from Congress and the GAO have offered a more positive view of the role that fusion centers play and the progress that DHS has made in supporting their work.[27]

DHS further supports terrorism-related information sharing by creating mechanisms to filter information up to federal law enforcement and the IC. The 2004 Intelligence Reform and Terrorism Prevention Act (IRTPA) required the IC to create an "information sharing environment for the sharing of terrorism information in a manner consistent with national security and with applicable legal standards relating to privacy and civil liberties."[28] The 2007 National Strategy for Information Sharing, which created a framework for implementing the IRTPA's requirements, called for a "unified process to support the reporting, tracking, processing, storage, and retrieval of locally generated information [for suspicious activity reports]."[29]

The Nationwide Suspicious Activity Reporting Initiative (NSI) serves as this unified information sharing process.[30] The NSI brings together DHS, the FBI, and state, local, tribal, and territorial law enforcement partners and offers a means of sharing suspicious activity reports (SARs) that are potentially connected to terrorism. From 2010 to 2017, more than 100,000 SARs have led to over 2,300 widely shared SARs that began or improved FBI investigations or were tied to the Terrorist Screening Center's watchlist.[31] Additionally, data from these shared SARs has informed more than 2,000 intelligence products.[32] Notably, an SAR helped the investigation of Faisal Shahzad, the Pakistan-born Connecticut resident who attempted to commit the Times Square Bombing in 2010.[33]

Of course, preventing terrorist incidents requires more than intelligence work; it requires an operational component. Historically, DHS's two primary operational roles in prevention involved border security and transportation security. The scale of these responsibilities is staggering. In the case of border security, for example, between October 2015 and October 2016, CBP inspected more than 390 million travelers at 328 ports of entry (POEs), including more than 119 million people who flew into airports.[34] As of June 2017, Immigration and Customs Enforcement (ICE) forward deployed personnel to 66 offices in 49 countries.[35] And in fiscal year 2017, the U.S. Border Patrol apprehended 310,531 people crossing illegally between the POEs.[36] In addition to CBP and ICE, the U.S. Coast Guard (USCG) plays a pivotal role in the security of maritime approaches to the homeland.

The attention to terrorism in border security, notwithstanding the scale and reach of the current apparatus, is relatively novel. It became a focus of U.S. border security following the 1993 World Trade Center bombing and the interception of the Millennium Bomber in 1999 in Port Angeles, Washington.[37] Following 9/11, the 2002 Homeland Security Act codified "preventing the entry of terrorists and instruments of terror"[38] within the "border and transportation" responsibilities of DHS, a role reiterated by the 9/11 Commission in 2004.[39] As the government's eyes, ears, and enforcement presence at the border, DHS is uniquely placed to detect and repel external threats to the homeland.

One of the notable programs to execute this mission is CBP's effort to target persons and cargo that present a risk. As the 9/11 Commission noted, "Targeting travel is at least as powerful a weapon against terrorists as targeting their money."[40] CBP's National Targeting Center matches traveler data against government watchlists and, for each traveler whose name does not match records, it determines whether the individual is "high-risk" through "rules-based" targeting. The rules-based system compares the subject's information to threat profiles created by intelligence and law enforcement experts.[41] CBP uses a similar intelligence-driven process to screen cargo for possible threats, supporting U.S. defenses against chemical, biological, radiological, and nuclear (CBRN) terrorism.

Part of the counterterrorism border security approach includes helping foreign partners improve their border management and customs capabilities.[42] As then–Secretary of Homeland Security John Kelly noted, "the more we push our borders out, the safer our homeland will be."[43] The 2002 Homeland Security Act authorized DHS to station officers at consular posts which issue visas. Since then, ICE has established units to screen visa applicants before they attempt to enter the United States, and CBP has substantially increased its footprint in partner countries, through pre-clearance and Joint Security Partnerships, for example, to help prevent dangerous persons from reaching the U.S. border in the first place.

DHS's border security efforts work in concert with its transportation security mission. The 9/11 attacks exploited weak security in civilian aviation, an enduring focus of terrorist groups. In response to the systemic failure on 9/11, Congress federalized all airline passenger and baggage screening functions, created TSA, and mandated 100 percent screening of all checked baggage on domestic and international flights to and from the United States. The 9/11 attacks and subsequent legislation also resulted in the transfer of responsibility for matching passenger data against government watchlists from airlines to TSA. TSA now matches 100 percent of passengers on flights in, to, or from, the United States against watchlists as part of the Secure Flight passenger pre-screening process.[44]

Transportation security measures have evolved as failed attacks and intelligence collection have revealed new terrorist techniques. After the attempted attack on Christmas Day of 2009, the U.S. government increased the use of advanced imaging technology for whole-body screening devices, building on recommendations by the 9/11 Commission. Similarly, in response to new intelligence in June 2017, DHS took a further step in enhancing the baseline of security measures for both passengers and electronic devices, as well as additional standards for aircraft and airports in 105 countries.[45] Transportation security has expanded in response to attempted attacks involving liquids, shoes, and non-metallic explosives.

Although significant progress has been made in "hardening" air transportation, security gaps remain in other modes of transportation such as rail systems and buses. The December 2017 attack near a subway platform beneath the New York Port Authority Bus Terminal highlights the potential dangers faced by soft targets. The attacker detonated a pipe bomb in a building that accommodates 220,000 passenger trips per day, injuring three but killing none.[46] The attack came amid increasing attention on securing ground transportation following reports of Al-Qaeda's focus on U.S. rail systems (particularly subways) and similar attacks in Europe.[47]

The threat to surface transportation is reflective of a critical challenge that DHS faces: despite public expectations for DHS, it does not control all aspects of the U.S. counterterrorism mission and there is no consensus that DHS, or even the federal government, should do so. The emerging mission to "counter violent extremism," like transportation security, is emblematic of this challenge.

As discussed above, the most significant threat from terrorism in the United States today comes from homegrown extremists.[48] DHS has sought to undertake what Obama called "the preventative aspects of counterterrorism as well as interventions to undermine the attraction of extremist movements and ideologies that seek to promote violence."[49] Although the focus and the nomenclature of these activities have evolved, within DHS these initiatives all aim to intervene when the threat is too inchoate to be a target of an investigation.

In 2011, the United States began articulating a strategy of "countering violent extremism" (CVE) as part of its terrorism prevention work. The strategy focuses on the world of "open" ideas and engagement rather than "covert" law enforcement actions and intelligence collection.[50] By focusing on preventing terrorism in its embryonic form, this new discipline has brought the fight against terrorism and terrorism recruitment away from the sources (already radicalized individuals) and instead targeted its recipients (susceptible individuals).[51] In 2011, the Obama administration released both Empowering Local Partners to Prevent Violent Extremism in the United States, the first national strategy to prevent violent extremism domestically, and the Strategic Implementation Plan for Empowering Local Partners to Prevent Violent Extremism in the United States (updated in 2016), a planning document with major goals for the initiative as well as primary activities for it.

DHS guides the government-wide CVE effort in partnership with the DOJ through the CVE Task Force. The 2011 Strategic Implementation Plan tasked DHS with 43 of the 62 CVE activities and efforts.[52] In 2016, DHS concentrated the previously scattered CVE components into the since-renamed Office of Community Partnerships. It has also clarified the goals for the program: improving the understanding of the threat of violent extremism and creating ways to counter it; enhancing community awareness through information sharing with community partners; supporting community efforts to counter violent extremism; and better coordination and oversight of DHS CVE activities.[53] DHS's terrorism prevention work includes outreach and engagement with local communities, both to raise awareness of the dangers of radicalization and to eventually detect radicalized individuals and potential terrorist threats. In focusing on the recipients of radicalization efforts, DHS also participates in the marketplace of ideas. Its efforts push back against propaganda through its "counter-recruitment programs."[54]

The Trump administration initiated an end-to-end review of the CVE strategy. Although some officials proposed cutting funds for CVE programs or renaming them to focus on Islamist terrorism, as of this writing, administration officials have suggested that they will maintain the focus on community awareness and education, counter-recruitment, early warning, and stopping terrorist recidivism.[55] These objectives broadly fit into the CVE approach that the Obama administration developed.

Looking ahead, commitment to CVE within DHS, and the government as a whole, is likely to remain controversial. The efficacy of CVE efforts is difficult to measure, and there is a lack of consensus about the role of the government in countering terrorist propaganda. Commentators have also noted that that scope of CVE activity is so broad as not to be descriptive.[56] Still, CVE's focus on education and support to community-based programs in certain cities has proven effective.[57] The government's work on CVE, and the role of DHS in helping to lead this effort, should remain a critical component of the domestic counterterrorism mission.

WEAPONS OF MASS DESTRUCTION

Catastrophic terrorism with weapons of mass destruction (WMD) poses a "low-probability, high-consequence" threat to the homeland. In 2004, the 9/11 Commission recognized this risk when it described attempts by Osama bin Laden to cause his own "Hiroshima," as well as Al-Qaeda efforts to access VX nerve gas in Sudan.[58] The sarin gas attacks carried out in Japan by Aum Shinrikyo in 1995 suggest the feasibility of such an attack, while the anthrax attacks in the United States in 2001 point to the possibility of such risk on U.S. soil.

U.S. policymakers have consistently highlighted this threat. In 2004, the 9/11 Commission stated that "the greatest danger of another catastrophic attack in the United States will materialize if the world's most dangerous terrorists acquire the world's most dangerous weapons."[59] The 2007 National Strategy for Homeland Security noted once again that terrorists had been explicit in their desire to acquire CBRN capabilities. Most recently, the 2017 National Security Strategy noted that CBRN risks are increasing, and made countering them one of the Trump administration's top priorities.[60]

The anti-CBRN effort is dispersed across the government and within DHS. In the federal government, DHS counters this threat alongside the FBI and the Defense, Energy, and State Departments. Inside DHS, the responsibility has traditionally been fragmented, although accountability has increased. In December 2018, DHS consolidated the disparate Components into one entity, the Countering Weapons of Mass Destruction Office. This newly created office will centralize DHS response to terrorist threats, standardize practices across threat categories, and eliminate redundancies within the system.

But consolidating CBRN efforts is just the first step. Within DHS, policymakers must translate the efforts and best practices of the Countering Weapons of Mass Destruction Office (or its successors) across all ranges of CBRN threats. For example, DHS officials have noted that terrorists have used "battlefield environments" to test chemical weapons before considering using them in other conditions. Yet U.S. officials have not applied the lessons learned from efforts like the Global Nuclear Detection Architecture to other WMD threats such as chemical weapons.[61] Eventually, CBRN monitoring and tracking activity should permeate every Component of DHS with roles in border security, transportation security, and intelligence.

Finally, as policymakers unify CBRN responsibilities within agencies, they must unify efforts across them as well. Like DHS, the FBI has a centralized WMD directorate. DHS and the FBI do not have a coordinated plan of action, one which involves other U.S. government entities focused on nonproliferation and countering proliferation finance. Such a plan would be necessary to reduce redundancies, as well as ultimately lowering the overall number of players tasked with protecting the homeland against CBRN dangers.

PROTECTING CRITICAL INFRASTRUCTURE

Not every plot can be stopped in the planning stage. For that reason, DHS also works to reduce vulnerabilities and harden the defenses of potential targets. Some of these efforts yield benefits for threats other than terrorism. For example, improving the security of critical U.S. infrastructure is just as beneficial with respect to attacks from hostile powers, as Iran's cyberattacks on U.S. infrastructure in 2016 illustrated.[62] Consistent with DHS's genesis in the response to the 9/11 attacks, it continues to see a significant part of its counterterrorism role as preventing attacks on "symbolic venues, transportation pathways, mass gatherings, and critical infrastructure."[63]

Experience supports this goal. Infrastructure is a recurring target for terrorists. Between 1970 and 2015, according to one report, a majority of the 2,723 terrorist attacks that were successful, attempted, or foiled in the United States targeted critical infrastructure.[64] The five most targeted sectors for these attacks were commercial facilities, government facilities, healthcare and public health, financial services, and the defense industrial base.[65]

The focus on the terrorist threat to critical infrastructure predates 9/11. In 1998, Clinton issued a Presidential Decision Directive defining critical infrastructure as "those physical and cyber-based systems essential to the minimum operations of the economy and the government."[66] After 9/11, Homeland Security Presidential Directive 7 (HSPD-7) gave the Secretary of Homeland Security the responsibility to "identify, prioritize, and coordinate the protection of critical infrastructure."[67] In 2013, the Obama administration's Presidential Policy Directive 21 (PPD-21) identified sixteen critical infrastructure sectors—

with associated sector-specific agencies tasked with overseeing them—and outlined Departmental roles in the protection of critical infrastructure.[68] (For further detail on critical infrastructure protection, see Chapter 11.)

Within DHS, the Office of Infrastructure Protection within the National Protection and Programs Directorate (NPPD, now called CISA) leads the work to manage risks to critical infrastructure. Various DHS initiatives target terrorist threats to critical infrastructure specifically. As Caitlin Durkovich describes in Chapter 11, for example, the Chemical Facility Anti-Terrorism Standards program ensures that high-risk chemical facilities have risk-reduction policies in place. Globally, DHS supports multilateral programs like the World Customs Organization's Program Global Shield to track the movement of precursor chemicals for explosive devices and improve security standards.[69] In line with the limited and incomplete scope of DHS's counter-terrorism efforts, while it coordinates the overall effort to protect critical infrastructure, PPD-21 delegates the primary counterterrorism role to the DOJ.

Conclusion: Three Challenges for DHS

Since DHS's founding, its leaders have faced a challenging task: managing an unwieldy organization with an all-encompassing mission and expectations that are nearly impossible to fulfill. Leading a Department formed from twenty-two agencies, DHS leadership has had to play a significant role in the fight against terrorism, even though many of the tools at the Department's disposal appear to be suited for other missions. The fragmented and often dysfunctional system of congressional oversight has routinely exacerbated these challenges. DHS leadership has also had to navigate the complex politics of counterterrorism, enduring the swings in political and public support for counterterrorism measures and shouldering the expectation of complete prevention of terrorist attacks. In concluding, we focus on three challenges that DHS must manage to succeed in its counterterrorism mission: managing expectations, streamlining congressional oversight, and addressing the politics of counterterrorism.

First, an overriding challenge for DHS is the gap between its capacity to prevent terrorism in the homeland and the expectations about its responsibilities in the counterterrorism effort. There are several dimensions to this challenge. The most obvious is DHS's limited authority. As described above, DHS's counterterrorism authorities are limited by the responsibilities of the agencies it controls: border security, immigration, and transportation security.

72

In contrast, the FBI has primary authority for counterterrorism investigations, and the IC handles most intelligence collection and analysis regarding terrorism. Meanwhile, DHS's Components must execute a range of missions beyond counterterrorism: countering transnational crime, preventing illegal immigration, marine search and rescue, aviation security, etc. Furthermore, DHS has limited resources to dedicate to counterterrorism. Consistent with its diverse responsibilities, DHS must devote personnel and other resources to several missions that are relevant to, but broader than, counterterrorism. Finally, as a result of its limited authority and resources, DHS depends on partners at the federal, state, and local levels to execute many of its responsibilities within the counterterrorism mission.

Nevertheless, DHS is often viewed as playing a leading role in the counterterrorism effort in the homeland. This perception comes in part from the genesis of DHS in the aftermath of 9/11. It also stems from DHS's own rhetoric and mission statement, identifying the prevention of terrorism as its number one priority. A challenge for DHS going forward, then, is to align public expectations about its capacity to combat terrorism with its actual role within the nation's counterterrorism efforts. To address this challenge, DHS leadership should emphasize the enabling role the Department plays in the homeland counterterrorism mission. DHS should clearly articulate the important functions, such as border and aviation security as well as intelligence sharing with state and local law enforcement, that do indeed provide critical support to the security of the homeland. Furthermore, DHS should highlight and continue to build on the close counterterrorism partnerships it has forged with other agencies at all levels of government. Finally, DHS should ensure that public statements and strategy documents reflect its specific role, and that those communications do not overstate DHS's authorities or capabilities.

A second enduring challenge for DHS is the fragmented and redundant regime of congressional oversight. The 9/11 Commission recommended that Congress create "a single, principal point of oversight and review for homeland security."[70] The commission recognized that this was both an important recommendation and one that was difficult to implement, but that in the absence of congressional reform, "the American people will not get the security they want and need."[71] As many commentators have pointed out, this recommendation has remained unaddressed.[72] In fact, by some measures, the problem of disjointed congressional oversight has gotten worse. When the 9/11 Commission issued its report, DHS leaders appeared before 88 congressional committees and subcommittees. Ten years later, more than 100 committees and subcommittees asserted jurisdiction over DHS.[73] This is in comparison to the 36 committees and subcommittees that oversee the Department of Defense (DOD), whose budget is an order of magnitude larger than that of DHS.

The failure of Congress to reform and streamline its oversight of DHS adversely impacts the Department's counterterrorism efforts, along with its other core mission areas. For one, the fragmented nature of congressional oversight impairs Congress's ability to provide programmatic and comprehensive guidance to DHS. DHS's counterterrorism activities cut across several DHS Components, each subject to the oversight of myriad congressional panels. As a result, no single committee has the ability to look across DHS's counterterrorism mission—to oversee this mission as a cohesive whole and to aid DHS in reconciling competing priorities. As former members of the 9/11 Commission observed, "Emblematic of this inability is the fact that Congress has not, since the Department's creation, enacted a final comprehensive DHS authorization bill setting policy and spending priorities."[74]

The overlapping jurisdiction of congressional committees also drains limited DHS resources. In the 112th Congress, DHS personnel took part in 289 hearings before the House and Senate (which involved 28 committees, caucuses, and commissions requiring the testimony of over 400 witnesses from DHS) and participated in over 4,300 congressional briefings and non-hearing engagements.[75] These substantial demands from the hodge-podge of congressional panels with some degree of oversight for DHS's counter-terrorism efforts divert DHS officials from their operational responsibilities. As the 9/11 Commission recommended years ago, Congress should substantially reduce the number of committees with jurisdiction over DHS and consolidate primary jurisdiction of its counterterrorism mission under one committee in the House and one in the Senate. Ideally, the oversight structure for DHS would be comparable to the oversight of the DOJ and the DOD.

Third, a root cause of many of the challenges facing DHS is the "cyclical politics of counterterrorism."[76] Because of the nature of many counter-terrorism activities, the threats that an entity like DHS analyzes or prevents are not apparent to the public on a routine basis. For this reason, the public may consistently underestimate the terrorism threat. Yet, after the occurrence of a domestic act of terror, public opinion focuses on the threat and demands swift responses. In such galvanizing moments, policymakers are often able to overcome many of the same procedural obstacles that had proven insurmountable in times of lower perceived threats. Over time, however, as these new tools work and once again diminish the public's perceived threat of terrorism, support for such counterterrorism measures declines once again.

DHS owes its role and mission to the expansive policymaking that immediately followed such a galvanizing event. From the beginning, preventing terrorism has been one of its primary objectives. At the same time, its leaders and its founding documents have recognized the difficulty of achieving such a goal. This reality has put DHS in a bind. On the one hand, it is tasked with preventing terrorism. Therefore, it must take active steps to stop attacks on the United States. On the other hand, even DHS's guiding documents acknowledge that it is difficult to stop every attack.[77] Furthermore, ensuring both the security of the homeland and the dependable international flow of goods and people—which immediately following 9/11 came to a halt—requires an approach that balances the two priorities. DHS has therefore wisely adopted a "risk-based" approach. (For further discussion of risk segmentation, see Chapter 6.) Under this method, DHS focuses most of its attention and resources on the biggest threats and saves time and money on analyzing low-risk targets. This "shrinking the haystack" approach has led to pre-screening programs like TSA's Pre✓ initiative, which allows expedited inspections for low-risk travelers.[78] DHS has also worked on resilience initiatives and on lowering U.S. vulnerability in the case of a successful attack.

The competition between total prevention (on the one hand) and a risk-based policy combined with resilience (on the other hand) may undercut DHS's counterterrorism mission. To be sure, the goal of prevention offers the best way to ensure that parties will share information across levels of government. An excessive focus on prevention, however, undermines the planning for future threats and the development of a long-term homeland security strategy. Because of the prevention-centered approach, any successful attack on the homeland does not simply register as a possible inevitable result of growing threats. Instead, it comes to represent a failure of intelligence, coordination, or interdiction.

Therefore, a prevention-focused approach ensures that the immediate outcome of a successful attack will be fault-finding and backward-looking criticism. This approach will lead to a reactive homeland security policy and will forestall proactive planning for better future prevention and resilience.[79] A better-defined articulation of the duties of DHS would clarify expectations for the Department. Looking ahead, DHS should focus its counterterrorism efforts on its core areas of expertise and authority—including, for example, its mission to collect and disseminate travel and immigration data across the intelligence and law enforcement communities. This approach will position DHS to continue to play a vital role in preventing and disrupting future threats in the evolving terrorism landscape.

Rethinking Borders: Securing the Flows of Travel and Commerce in the Twenty-First Century

Seth M. M. Stodder

THIS CHAPTER FOCUSES ON THE ROLE AND FUNCTIONING OF INTER-national borders in the twenty-first century's ever more borderless, "globalized" world. It addresses how, in response to the terror attacks on September 11, 2001, the United States and its international and private-sector partners worked together to manage risks and reinvent how borders function. The result made America and its partners safer and more prosperous—making it much harder for Al-Qaeda or ISIS to send terrorist operatives or weapons across international borders, while speeding through the lawful commercial activity and travel so essential to a thriving economy.

In the eighteen years since the 9/11 attacks, there have only been approximately one hundred deaths in the United States caused by Islamist terrorism directed or inspired by Al-Qaeda or ISIS. Of those tragic killings, most were committed by native-born American citizens radicalized in the United States. Since 9/11, the United States has strengthened its borders so much that Al-Qaeda and ISIS have been forced to resort to their "Plan B"—either radicalizing and "inspiring" Americans to commit terrorist attacks, or attacking elsewhere.

Meanwhile, and despite this strengthened security, cross-border commerce and travel are at all-time highs. The security measures taken in the wake of 9/11 have not obstructed legitimate travel and trade. On the contrary, both are booming. What happened? How could this be?

The modern approach to borders began dramatically—in the aftermath of the 9/11 attacks. Immediately after the terrorists struck, the two U.S. government agencies then responsible for securing the land borders—the U.S. Customs Service and the Immigration and Naturalization Service (INS), which have since been recombined into Customs and Border Protection

(CBP), Immigration and Customs Enforcement (ICE), and U.S. Citizenship and Immigration Services (USCIS) as part of the creation of the Department of Homeland Security (DHS)—went to "Level One Alert," the maximum level of security at the borders short of outright closure.

Although the Level One Alert did not literally shut the borders, the way the order was implemented had the effect of grinding North American commerce to a halt. Security checks of nearly every privately-operated vehicle and commercial truck resulted in massive traffic jams—twelve- to fourteen-hour waits for trucks to enter the United States across the Ambassador Bridge from Windsor, Canada, and similar delays at other ports of entry (POEs) on both the U.S.–Canada and U.S.–Mexico borders. Far from just being irritating to truck drivers, these delays were in fact catastrophic for modern supply chains, which have reduced reliance on expensive stationary warehouses in favor of shipping goods "just in time" within intermodal containers across borders to their intended destinations. (For further discussion of the global supply system, see Chapter 7.)

As a result of the lengthy delays at the U.S.–Canada border, automotive assembly plants in Michigan were beginning to shut down, with potentially cascading economic impacts across the entire North American economy. This was a crisis—one as threatening, if not more so, to the U.S. economy and way of life than the 9/11 attacks themselves. In short, misguided policies and instinctive—but, in retrospect, wrong—reactions to the terrorist attacks presented their own distinct and potentially catastrophic threat.

It also revealed a crisis in thinking about borders—specifically, that the security and enforcement responses that might have been sensible in the context of the twentieth century's less globally-integrated economy were downright dangerous to the twenty-first century's globalized economy— with so many products now manufactured and assembled in various places, and parts sourced from all over the world, delivered just in time for use in putting together the finished product. The twentieth century "playbook" for responding to a security event at the borders—ramping up security inspections or shutting down the border—ended up being a catastrophic "cure," far worse than the terrorist threat's "disease."

And this intellectual crisis was not limited to land borders or to the security of cargo. It also permeated how the government addressed the flow of millions of people transiting through airports and other POEs—especially as the United States, in the days after 9/11, once again began the flow of aviation into the country and the granting of visas to international travelers. In the new, post-9/11 world, how could one spot the terrorist needles in the vast haystack presented by the millions of international air, land, and sea travelers crossing U.S. borders? Or among the vast numbers of people applying for visas? How could the government manage those risks without squelching the flow of international travel so vital to the U.S. economy and the world's? U.S. policymakers—and the American people as a whole—needed a wholesale paradigm shift. America's borders, and those of its international partners, required dramatic reinvention to address the challenges and opportunities of the twenty-first century world.

This chapter tells the history of this post-9/11 reinvention and lays out the new strategy that was ultimately developed by the Bush and Obama administrations to secure and facilitate the flows of lawful commerce and travel into and out of the United States. The chapter is broken into several sections.

First, the chapter discusses the basics of border management and security. These include the legal authorities at and between the POEs, the mechanics of visa issuance, and the post-9/11 institutional reforms, specifically the creation of a single border agency—CBP—presenting a single face at the border. Understanding the legal and institutional basics is key to understanding how the post-9/11 paradigm shift was implemented.

Second, the chapter discusses the immediate actions taken by the Bush administration to ease the crisis at the borders shortly after 9/11, and then walks thematically through the key doctrines, laws, institutions, and initiatives created in the wake of 9/11 that defined the Bush and Obama administrations' innovations in border strategy. The "alphabet soup" of acronyms that burst out of this era—C-TPAT (Customs-Trade Partnership Against Terrorism), CSI (Container Security Initiative), NTC (National Targeting Center), API/PNR (Advance Passenger Information/Passenger Name Record data), among many others—still guide America's approach to borders, and how CBP works to secure the flows of travel and commerce so essential to the global economy and American prosperity. This chapter will discuss some of those key programs.

This section also discusses how the post-9/11 strategy has become globalized into a consensus *international* approach to borders—as the United States worked with its international partners both bilaterally and multilaterally, as well as the global private sector, to secure and facilitate the lawful flows of commerce and travel *throughout* the global economy. The aftermath of the 9/11 attacks taught us that unilateral "America first" or "Germany first" or "Mexico first" solutions to inherently transnational threats were invariably the wrong answer. More important, it was vital that the nations of the world and key private sector players get on the same page strategically and share information in order to work collectively to spot and interdict threats as early as possible, ideally before they even entered the global transportation system. The *United States* wants to know if an ISIS fighter is traveling from the Middle East to Europe, because it matters not only for European security, but also for *American* security, not only given the possibility of travel to the United States, but also because of the integrated nature of the global economy and, therefore, America's global economic and security interests. Moreover, the government requirements, data collection standards, and inspection protocols also need to be harmonized to the greatest extent possible, so as not to bedevil global businesses or travelers with having to comply with dramatically conflicting security rules.

So these principles had to be globalized—and, in part due to the leadership of the Bush and Obama administrations, they have been, both bilaterally with key partners like Singapore and the European Union, and multilaterally through key instruments like the World Customs Organization's SAFE Framework of Standards to Secure and Facilitate Trade and the United Nations Security Council Resolution 2178 (adopting a global approach to interdicting the travel of foreign terrorist fighters), among other efforts. While these global partnerships have fallen short in implementation thus far, and there is still insufficient regulatory uniformity throughout the world, these multilateral agreements establish a set of standards that all nations seeking full access to the global economic and transportation system must work toward.

Third, the chapter briefly addresses the specific context of North America—where, in the years since the 9/11 attacks, the United States, Canada, and Mexico (as well as other key hemispheric partners) have worked to secure its continental perimeter, reduce barriers to travel and commerce, and realize the economic promise of the North American Free Trade Agreement (NAFTA), now the United States–Mexico–Canada Agreement (USMCA). The North American project is perhaps the most important outcome of the post-9/11 era, in that it broadly succeeded in securing the North American perimeter against international terrorism. At the same time, it established an integrated North American manufacturing platform that is the most competitive in the world. The ever-closer North American partnership since 9/11 is truly one of the great legacies of the Bush and Obama years. With luck, it will survive the Trump years and not be undermined by the needless construction of walls between the North American partners (both literally and figuratively).

In sum, this chapter tells the story of the reinvention of international borders in the wake of the 9/11 attacks and, subsequently, the rise of ISIS. It addresses the challenge of how to manage risks by sifting through the vast amounts of travel and commerce moving through global systems of transportation through official POEs into and out of the United States and other nations. It does not purport to address the totality of border security or border management, of course; there are myriad other issues, such as controlling regular and irregular migration flows, addressing asylum seekers seeking humanitarian protection, combating transnational crime, enforcing trade law, securing land borders between official POEs, and securing maritime borders, among others. This chapter is focused on the reinvention of borders in the wake of the 9/11 attacks; other border-related topics are addressed elsewhere in this volume (especially Chapters 6, 7, 8, 9, and 14).

Basics: The Border, Border Authorities, and Border Institutions

To start with the basics, what do we mean by the "border"? As noted by former CBP Commissioner Alan Bersin, "the purpose and function of borders in world history has been and remains to delineate and demarcate—that is, to differentiate—one sovereignty from another."[1] Often established by military developments and resulting treaties, such as the Treaty of Guadalupe Hidalgo after the Mexican-American War or the French reannexation of Alsace-Lorraine after World War I, borders "define a homeland" and help identify the "us" who get full rights in a national community, and the "them" outside the border lines who do not.[2]

Although it is certainly true that the twenty-first-century global economy is becoming ever more "borderless" functionally—defined as it is by the trans-national flows of travel, trade, money, and data that crisscross the world across national frontiers—Americans emphatically do *not* live in a post-Westphalian world where, as Bono sings in the U2 song, "Invisible," "there is no them, only us" and borders no longer exist.[3] Most people very much believe that there is an "us" and a "them," and see strong national borders as necessary for clearly drawing a line between the two—no matter how integrated the global economy may be.

Legally, it is helpful to divide the concept of borders in two: first, official POEs, such as Los Angeles International Airport, the San Ysidro border crossing between Tijuana and San Diego, the UPS Worldport international express mail facility in Kentucky, and the Port of Charleston, South Carolina; and second, the vast lands and maritime areas between the POEs, such as stretches along the Rio Grande, the hinterlands along the Montana-Saskatchewan border, or the coastlines of the Great Lakes. In most countries, America being no exception, it is generally illegal for a person to simply enter between the POEs. There are some exceptions to this principle required by international law, such as the rules governing asylum seekers, but for the most part, people (even U.S. citizens) cannot simply stroll into the United States from Mexico or Canada between the POEs, or land a boat somewhere on the shoreline and walk in. Under U.S. law, they are required to present themselves at an official POE to an immigration and customs officer (usually a CBP officer), and establish admissibility into the country—generally by showing a passport, a visa, or some other valid travel or entry document. A CBP officer will then determine if they—or shipped goods, or other items—are allowed into the country, and if they owe any customs duties. There are also controls going the other way, as CBP also enforces laws governing controls on exports and tracks aliens who leave the country.

These checks at the POEs are performed by CBP's Office of Field Operations. Between the POEs, the border is policed by the U.S. Border Patrol, another branch of CBP. Here, the job is straightforward. Anyone the Border Patrol encounters coming across or, to some extent, even near the border is subject to questioning, apprehension, potential removal, or even prosecution (as happened to many when the Trump administration implemented its "family separation" policy in 2018). This is because, as noted, it is generally illegal to enter the country between the POEs.

At the POEs, the job is more complex—as officers must identify and sift the inadmissible travelers and unlawful contraband out of the huge haystack of legitimate travel and commerce seeking entry or exit through the official POEs. In doing this, traditionally it has often been a zero-sum game—as inspections increase, delays for legitimate travel and commerce also increase, thereby disrupting lives, invading civil liberties, and squelching the economy. The Level One Alert after 9/11 was an extreme example, but getting the balance right is a daily challenge.

To assist CBP in doing its job, it is afforded the broadest authorities of any law enforcement agency. As noted by the Supreme Court in *United States v. Flores-Montano*, "the Government's interest in preventing the entry of unwanted persons and effects is at its zenith at the international border."[4] Accordingly, the Supreme Court has repeatedly held that "searches made at the border, pursuant to the longstanding right of the sovereign to protect itself by stopping and examining persons and property crossing into this country, are reasonable simply by virtue of the fact that they occur at the border."[5]

Thus CBP's "customs border search authority"—together with authorities granted by the Immigration and Nationality Act governing admissibility—allows its officers to open any container, inspect any shipment, or ask any question of anyone seeking entry into the United States, without any level of suspicion whatsoever (neither "reasonable suspicion" nor "probable cause"), and without any judicial warrant.

There are some twists to this, as the Supreme Court has required reasonable suspicion for "non-routine" searches—such as the invasive personal body search and detention at issue in *United States v. Montoya de Hernandez*.[6] This issue has also come up recently in the context of CBP's searches of electronic devices, including smartphones, iPads, and laptops. On occasion, CBP seeks to inspect an electronic device—as some data may itself be inadmissible contraband (such as digital child pornography) or may be evidence showing inadmissibility (such as communications indicating that an alien seeking entry might be a terrorist or a criminal). The problem, of course, is that inspecting all the data on a device takes time, is invasive of peoples' personal lives (as so much personal information is kept on smartphones), and the devices and data are often encrypted. Therefore, CBP is sometimes required to seize the device and hold it for an extended period—often days or weeks—until the encryption is broken and the data is reviewed. Some travelers or criminal defendants have claimed that this is an overly-invasive "non-routine" search requiring a warrant under the Fourth Amendment or, at a minimum, reasonable suspicion or probable cause. Cases addressing this question have been moving up through the courts, but the Supreme Court has not yet resolved it.

This issue aside, CBP (as well as ICE and the Coast Guard [USCG]) has extraordinarily broad legal authority. And this broad authority has been critical to America's ability to reinvent how its borders work in the wake of the 9/11 attacks, because CBP has been able to leverage this authority—plus others granted by Congress—to extract cooperation from shippers, airlines, international partners, and others, to "extend the border" out to secure the flows of travel and commerce well before they reach American shores.

In discussing the basics of the border, we must also consider the State Department's Bureau of Consular Affairs—the entity that oversees all the consular officers stationed at embassies and consulates around the world, and who grant immigrant and non-immigrant visas for travel to the United States. Consular officers are vital parts of how the United States secures its borders—as most aliens require visas to immigrate or travel to the United States[7]—and, much like CBP's authority to refuse admission to an alien deemed inadmissible at the time he or she arrives at the border, consular officers must also refuse to grant a visa to an inadmissible person.[8] Thus, in many respects, CBP officers and consular officers perform a similar border function—and, as with CBP officers' admissibility decisions, consular officers possess broad authority in making visa determinations that, with certain narrow exceptions, are unreviewable by the courts.[9] And, in much the same way that the Level One Alert at the borders threatened the North American economy, so did post-9/11 policies tightening visa issuance threaten to seriously disrupt legitimate travel by foreign persons who wanted to visit, study, or work in the United States.

In the wake of the 9/11 attacks, the United States revamped its border institutions. As part of the creation of DHS in 2003, the United States broke up and recombined the Customs Service and the INS to create three brand new agencies—CBP, ICE, and USCIS. CBP is the frontline border agency at the POEs and along the land borders, while the USCG patrols the maritime borders. The creation of CBP unified all the border inspectors that had previously been in the Customs Service, the INS, and the U.S. Department of Agriculture, and established "one face at the border"—a unified inspection force at all POEs. In addition, CBP includes the Border Patrol, which guards the borders between the POEs. ICE includes all the special agent investigators from the former Customs and INS, as well as all the officers involved in detaining and removing inadmissible foreigners. USCIS performs all the non-enforcement "service" functions of the old INS, including citizenship and immigrant and non-immigrant petitions, as well as asylum and refugee processing.

This reorganization, while controversial and having some issues, has been effective in strengthening and rationalizing America's border management capabilities.[10] It also has been influential to some degree, as several other countries, such as Australia and Canada, have similarly combined their frontline inspection and patrol functions into a single entity like CBP. This reform has been key to the ability to reinvent borders in a holistic way— addressing the movement of both people and goods through global transportation systems and across international borders. Previously, those functions had been broken up into an immigration agency like the old INS and a customs agency like U.S. Customs, both placed in different Departments of government often at bureaucratic odds with one another (with INS in the Department of Justice and Customs in the Treasury). As a result, there was no overarching strategy for how to manage global transnational flows of travel and commerce. The creation of CBP and similar agencies around the world enabled such a unified, holistic strategy to emerge.

Risk Management: Securing and Facilitating the Flows of Lawful Travel and Commerce

The post-9/11 approach to international borders arose not out of the World Trade Center ruins, but instead out of the gridlocked line of trucks stuck on the Ambassador Bridge, awaiting clearance as Customs used its broad legal authorities to perform Level One Alert security checks following the terrorist attacks. It also arose out of the extraordinary delays in visa processing caused by post-9/11 security measures, and in the frustration of Muslim visitors singled out and forced to "register" as part of the National Security Entry-Exit Registration System (NSEERS). It also arose out of the fear that, even with the Level One Alert, the United States had still failed to address other serious security vulnerabilities, such as the threat presented by the millions of sea containers and air cargo parcels moving through completely opaque global supply chains, headed to American seaports and airports, and containing who knows what—but hopefully not a smuggled weapon of mass destruction. Or the possibility that terrorists might first travel to Canada or Mexico, and then slip through the untamed forests of the northern border or hide within the flows of undocumented migrants coming from the south. So, in the days and weeks after 9/11, the United States had the worst of all worlds—blocked trade and travel, discriminatory policies, *and* serious security vulnerabilities still left unaddressed. America needed a new approach.

The country first needed to solve the immediate problem caused by the Level One Alert—the fourteen-hour traffic jams at key POEs on the U.S.–Canada and U.S.–Mexico borders that were threatening to shut down the North American economy. The U.S. government had caused the problem, but it could not go back to the pre-9/11 security posture; the terrorist threat was too pressing and real. In the immortal words of Abraham Lincoln, which I had pasted to my wall in my office at Customs during those early days, "as our case is new, so we must think anew, and act anew."[11] Government officials (specifically policymakers at CBP) needed to figure out a way to better secure the border while also facilitating the movement of commerce so vital to America's prosperity. Easy to say, but quite a challenge. And the government could not do it alone. It could throw bodies at the situation—making inspectors work overtime to keep all the lanes open and get more trucks through. But this would not be enough to meet the challenge, especially over the long haul. The government needed help.

The first step was reaching out to the private sector. Kevin Weeks, the Customs Field Director in Detroit—acting under the direction of incoming

Customs Commissioner Robert Bonner—immediately met with the automotive industry, and worked with them on a plan.[12] Initially, these discussions focused on efforts to ameliorate the traffic jam—rerouting to other POEs and posting wait times on the Customs website, among other measures. Weeks also met with bridge owners, shipping companies, and other key stakeholders in the Detroit area with an interest in addressing the border crisis. These were small steps at the start, but they set the stage for the larger dialogue to come between Customs (and then its successor agency, CBP) and the global private sector, focusing on how to meet the "twin goals" at the border—security and the facilitation of legitimate commerce.

Over the succeeding months, these discussions ultimately led to some of the most important public-private partnerships to emerge in the wake of 9/11, including C-TPAT—a partnership between CBP, importers, and other key players in the global supply chain to establish agreed-upon supply chain security standards and supply chain visibility all the way back to a foreign supplier's loading dock, in exchange for expedited clearance by CBP at the borders. Of course, the government had leverage—as it could use its broad legal authorities to stop and inspect any shipment it wanted. And it used this leverage to convince the private sector that there was a better way, enlisting importers and others to secure their own supply chains, which would provide some assurance to CBP that shipments moving through those C-TPAT-certified supply chains were lower risk and thus not worth spending much time on.

C-TPAT still exists today, and it is a cornerstone of America's supply chain security strategy, now with more than 11,000 certified C-TPAT partners, including importers, highway carriers, rail and sea carriers, customs brokers, non-operating common carriers, and freight consolidators, among other participants in the global supply chain. These certified C-TPAT partners are essentially "trusted" shippers that CBP can expedite across the border, with only occasional verification checks, so its officers can focus on those shipments warranting greater scrutiny.

The problem with the Level One Alert was not the increase in security; that was necessary. It was its indiscriminate nature—all vehicles and shipments were suspect, therefore all required time-intensive scrutiny, leading to the massive delays at the border. C-TPAT adopted a different model: Partnership with the private sector, in order to assess risk and segment it. The vast majority of shipments present zero risk, so why should the government spend any time on them, as opposed to focusing on the known risks or the unknowns? C-TPAT partnership enlisted the private sector—the owners of their own supply chains, and with a keen interest in not having them infiltrated by terrorists or criminals—to identify those low- or no-risk shipments that could be cleared quickly, thereby allowing CBP officers to focus on the real threats.

Other public-private partnerships also arose out of these early discussions. On the land borders, CBP also created a companion program—called Free and Secure Trade (FAST)—aimed even more expressly at reducing wait times for lawful commerce. Under FAST, if an eligible truck driver moving goods within a C-TPAT certified supply chain enrolls with CBP and completes a background check, that truck driver can drive his or her truck through dedicated FAST lanes at POEs on both the U.S.–Canada and U.S.–Mexico borders. As with C-TPAT, the FAST program allowed America to achieve both "twin goals" at the border—expediting lawful shipments driven by FAST-certified drivers, while allowing CBP to focus its scrutiny on non-FAST, non-C-TPAT shipments requiring a closer look.

Together, C-TPAT and FAST provided a template for how the United States could work in partnership with the global private sector to achieve greater security, while also expediting clearance of the lawful commerce so essential to the economy. They demonstrated that, far from being in tension, security and trade facilitation were actually two sides of the same coin—one couldn't be done without the other. The United States could *only* improve security of global supply chains if it worked with the trade community to identify and then expedite low-risk lawful commerce—reducing the "haystack," so that CBP officers could review a smaller, more "needle-rich" haystack.

Another key partnership was the one with the air cargo industry—called the Air Cargo Advance Screening (ACAS) program—that was established after the 2010 attempted attack by Al-Qaeda in the Arabian Peninsula (AQAP) on a UPS flight using an explosive hidden in a printer cartridge. As with C-TPAT, the ACAS program is a true partnership—UPS, FedEx, DHL, and other express carriers voluntarily provide data on shipments to CBP and TSA at the earliest practical point, which enables CBP and TSA to analyze that data to assess risk and spot potential threats like the printer-cartridge bomb, ideally before they are put on planes. I will come back to the importance of data analytics below, but ACAS is yet another example of the U.S. government working in partnership with the private sector to both secure their supply chains *and* expedite commerce across borders.

So, the first step out of the post-9/11 crisis was the United States working in partnership with the private sector. The second step was reaching out to international partners. Indeed, they beat U.S. policymakers to the punch.

Within an hour of the 9/11 attacks, Customs received a telephone call from Denis Lefebvre, the Assistant Commissioner for Operations for the Canadian Customs and Revenue Agency, offering whatever help Canada could provide.[13] Similar discussions were also held with Mexican counterparts, and then ultimately with partner nations around the world. Ultimately, policymakers in the United States, Canada, and Mexico came to the same insight—a nation operating alone could not address the transnational threats moving within traditional flows of travel and commerce, short of building a wall or a moat and, like North Korea, cutting itself off from the world. The only way to do it was to embrace global interdependence and tackle the problem together. Only by working in *partnership* could the nations of the world successfully secure and facilitate the transnational flows of travel and commerce so essential to every nation's prosperity.

This was especially true in North America, where the United States, Canada, and Mexico had to act quickly and in concert to escape the Level One Alert quagmire. Over the succeeding eighteen years, this paved the way toward a deep North American security and economic partnership—perhaps the most important positive legacy of the 9/11 attacks. One key example is the partnerships that were forged in the context of maritime shipping. The eleven million or so containers that entered U.S. seaports every year presented a scary problem in the days after 9/11. What was in those containers? On a good day, CBP inspected 1–2 percent of them. What was in the others? What if Al-Qaeda got its hands on a nuclear weapon? Could it smuggle it in one of those eleven million boxes, and then detonate it on arrival at the Port of Los Angeles? At seaports, inspections occur *after* the containers arrive, often after they sit on the docks for days. But isn't that too late if a terrorist wants to attack the seaport itself—especially a seaport, like Seattle or Los Angeles, in a heavily populated urban area?

This was a scary problem: the "sum of all fears," as Tom Clancy put it in his novel of the same name. And the only way to solve it was to figure out a way to inspect high-risk containers before they were put on ships bound for the United States. But given that the seaports of Hong Kong, Rotterdam, and Yokohama were not on U.S. territory, how could CBP put officers in those seaports? Well, the first step was to ask. This was the start of what became the Container Security Initiative, or CSI. It began in partnership with Canada in early 2002, with the United States stationing inspectors in the ports of Halifax, Montreal, and Vancouver—and, in turn, the Canadians stationing inspectors in Newark and Seattle. From there, CSI expanded to seaports throughout the world—first to Rotterdam in the Netherlands and Le Havre in France, then to Singapore and Hong Kong, and then, over a period of several years, to nearly sixty major seaports around the globe—with CBP inspectors working overseas in partnership with host nations to inspect high-risk sea containers *before* they headed to the United States, and certain nations also stationing officers in U.S. seaports.

CSI's unprecedented set of operational bilateral partnerships brought greater security to over 85 percent of all U.S.-bound maritime cargo—and, in concert with C-TPAT partnerships with the private sector, transformed how the United States secures its borders. Instead of thinking solely in terms of security *at* America's physical borders, the goal was to "push the borders out," working with the private sector and international partners to secure the transnational flows of commerce at the most important points in the system. Through C-TPAT and FAST, CBP worked with the private sector to secure supply chains from end to end, as importers compelled their suppliers and carriers to adopt security protocols aimed at preventing terrorists from infiltrating supply chains. Though CSI, CBP worked with partner countries to inspect high-risk containers *before* they departed for U.S. seaports. And conversely, C-TPAT and CSI allowed CBP to identify low-risk supply chains and container shipments, and expedite them through the border—achieving the "twin goals" of security and trade facilitation.

In addition, for cargo, a key piece of the twin goals strategy was the deployment of scanning and radiation detection technology—both at CSI ports and U.S. seaports and land POEs. This scanning equipment allowed for quick inspections of high-risk containers using radiographic imaging systems that allow CBP officers to spot potential anomalies—or variations from the container's manifest. Only when a problem is revealed by the scanning equipment will CBP then take the next step—a time-consuming full physical inspection of the shipment.

CBP also developed similar strategies for securing the flow of travel through global transportation systems. For example, under CBP's Pre-clearance initiative, the Immigration Advisory Program (IAP), and the Joint Security Program (JSP), CBP has stationed inspectors in airports around the world—either fully pre-clearing air passengers before they head to the United States (in various airports in Canada, Ireland, the United Arab Emirates, and several locations in the Caribbean) or, through the IAP, working with the airlines and host governments to identify high-risk passengers and pull them aside for questioning before they board their flights. As with the "sum of all fears" problem that CSI was designed to address, the IAP and pre-clearance programs aimed to prevent the next Richard Reid—the "Shoe Bomber," who, after boarding his December 2001 flight from Paris to Miami, attempted to bring down the plane by igniting explosives hidden in his shoes. Of course, CBP and its partners needed to improve scanning technology at airports in order to better detect smuggled weapons (yes, this is why you take off your shoes at airports), but in addition, high-risk passengers like Reid needed to be identified and questioned before they boarded their planes. And, because CBP officers are stationed in foreign airports under the pre-clearance, IAP, and JSP programs, this often happens—and it could only be done in close partnership with international partners and the airlines.

The first two steps in the reinvention of international borders after 9/11 focused on partnerships—with both the private sector and international partners. Only through embracing interdependence could the United States truly address the transnational threats all countries face at the earliest point, while at the same time expediting the flows of low-risk commerce and travel across shared borders.

So far, so good. But this begs the obvious question—how can the government determine who or what is high- or low-risk? The third step provided the answer to this question. Certainly, trained officers have a sort of "spidey sense" and can sometimes spot individuals or shipments that are a little off—and require more scrutiny. An example of this is Customs Inspector Diana Dean, who stopped Millennium Bomber Ahmed Ressam at Port Angeles on the U.S.–Canada border in 1999, thereby preventing him from carrying out his plan to attack Los Angeles International Airport. Ressam was not on a watchlist, and Inspector Dean had not received any alert from Head-quarters—but her training and instincts allowed her to detect something unusual in Ressam's agitated, "hinky" demeanor, as she later said. And she was right. After being selected for secondary screening, Ressam tried to flee and was then arrested; on inspection, his car trunk was found to have more explosives than were in the truck used in the attack on the Alfred P. Murrah Federal Building in Oklahoma City in 1995.

This is an extraordinary story, and one should never discount the impor-tance of trained officers. But in the context of the modern global economy, with millions of individuals and shipments crossing international borders every year, the United States cannot depend entirely on those instincts. The government does not have nearly enough inspectors to do that. And in any event, relying on them—and on manual watchlist checks of every individual and shipment upon arrival—could substantially slow down travel and commerce, as we saw in the Level One Alert days and weeks after the 9/11 attacks. The country needed a new approach—one that could replicate Inspector Dean's instincts as much as possible on a larger scale, and also leverage the vast amounts of data and intelligence that border agencies receive on a daily basis.

Luckily, an alternative was close at hand. In fact, the private sector had already come up with the basic idea. In the days before 9/11, the airlines had grown tired of long delays at airports, caused by Customs and INS officers checking traveler information against watchlists while those travelers waited at primary inspection booths. During high volume periods, this often meant that planes would sit on the tarmac for hours, because the lines were so long getting through the primary inspection, and the space to wait in the airport was full. So, the airlines worked with Customs and INS on a different idea—what if information on passengers could be provided *in advance of arrival*, so the border agencies could perform their watchlist checks in advance? This would allow Customs and the INS to speed low-risk passengers who were not on any watchlist through the primary inspection, and conversely allow officers to focus their resources on known risks. This idea had an immediate impact. Under this voluntary initiative, the airlines began transmitting Advance Passenger Information (API) to Customs and the INS in advance of passengers' arrival, as well as giving these agencies access to reservation information, called Passenger Name Record (PNR) data. These border agencies could then analyze the API/PNR, identifying those individuals who warranted secondary inspection and those who could be sped through on primary inspection. This had the dual benefit of reducing delays at airports *and* improving security—a victory for the twin goals of security and facilitation.

After 9/11, Congress made the pre-arrival transmission of API and access to PNR mandatory for all international air travel to the United States. This allowed Customs and INS, and subsequently CBP, to run watchlist checks on *all* travelers to the United States well in advance of arrival. In addition, given the richness of API and, especially, PNR data (which includes ticketing details, credit card information, seating assignments, and routing, among many other things), this allowed CBP to begin performing ever-more sophisticated analysis of the data—essentially bringing CBP into the twenty-first century's data analytics revolution. CBP began using its Automated Targeting System or ATS platform, frequently upgrading its algorithms and rules based on intelligence, to spot linkages between passengers and known intelligence, or to spot potential terrorist or criminal travel patterns. Indeed, it was through the analysis of PNR data that Customs was able to identify all nineteen of the 9/11 hijackers—within an hour or two of the attacks.

Over the eighteen years since 9/11, CBP has only become more and more sophisticated in utilizing API/PNR and other data to assess the risks presented by international air passengers, working in concert with the National Counterterrorism Center (NCTC) and other agencies. And, as the terrorist threat evolved, CBP began to see the need to obtain this data and analyze it *before* planes depart for the United States. This was clear after the Shoe Bomber incident, and became ever clearer after the 2006 "liquid explosives" threat, where Al-Qaeda had plotted to attack planes traveling across the Atlantic using liquid explosives. In the wake of these incidents, CBP promulgated regulations mandating that airlines provide access to API/PNR data in advance of departure so that CBP could run analytics on air passengers before wheels-up. In addition, given the risks presented by Visa Waiver Program (VWP) passengers (such as the liquid explosives plotters, who are UK citizens)—who do not submit visa applications and are not interviewed by consular officers—CBP also obtains data on them through the Electronic System for Travel Authorization (ESTA), as all VWP travelers must receive ESTA clearance before traveling to the United States.

In addition, many travelers—both air passengers and those seeking to cross U.S. borders by land—voluntarily provide additional information so that CBP can perform more extensive background checks and then, if these checks are clear, allow them expedited clearance through POEs. These "trusted traveler" programs, such as Global Entry, NEXUS, SENTRI, and TSA's similar Pre✓ program, are essential parts of the information-based risk assessment strategy. They give CBP and TSA the information they need to, ideally, assess these trusted travelers as low-risk, and speed them through inspection—thereby allowing CBP officers and TSA screeners to focus their energy on the known and unknown risks.

CBP's strategy of receiving and analyzing data before departure, as well as further reducing the haystack of risk through the trusted traveler programs, was not limited to air passengers. Indeed, it actually started with cargo. As I mentioned above, in 2002, CBP had launched the Container Security Initiative, and deployed officers in seaports around the world in order to inspect high-risk cargo containers before they were shipped to U.S. seaports. But there was no way that CSI could work unless Customs—and later, CBP—had information on shipments before they departed. Before 9/11, carriers provided information on shipments in advance of *arrival*, and importers upon entry—often after the shipments were already in the country. To implement CSI's "beyond the borders" strategy, this obviously needed to change. Therefore, Customs promulgated the "24 Hour Rule," which mandates that ocean carriers provide information on shipments 24 hours before they are loaded on a vessel headed to a U.S. seaport. This allowed Customs inspectors to analyze the shipment data and identify the high-risk shipments that CSI teams, working in concert with local officials at the foreign seaports, would inspect before departure.

CBP also needed better data. Before 9/11, shippers commonly listed shipments as containing "freight all kinds," or other vague terms. If CBP was to be able to identify what shipments presented higher risks, it needed more than that. The 24 Hour Rule also required far more specificity in what was reported. And in 2008, empowered by the Trade Act of 2002 and the SAFE Port Act, CBP ultimately went even further, with the so-called "10+2" Importer Security Filing rule, which required both carriers *and* now importers to provide much more detailed information on shipments (such as the manufacturer name/address, seller name/address, importer of record, and country of origin, among other elements), 24 hours in advance of loading, and before a ship departed for a U.S. seaport. Armed with this information, CBP was now in a position to truly assess the risk presented by any maritime container shipment, and to identify those higher-risk shipments requiring greater scrutiny at CSI ports.

To summarize, in the years after 9/11, Customs—and then CBP— completely revamped its risk assessment capabilities, otherwise known as "targeting." Following the same strategy across the board, CBP pushed for and often mandated the collection of advance information on international travelers, maritime container shipments, and air cargo shipments, as well as truck and rail shipments, to the greatest extent possible. In addition, with regard to international travelers who are not U.S. citizens, DHS also required the collection of biometrics—fingerprints—at the POEs. With regard to most foreigners seeking to travel to the United States by air, CBP now has a rich array of data—biographical data from visa applications, ESTA (if the indi- vidual is traveling under the Visa Waiver Program), API/PNR, and other sources, as well as biometric data. For some, the government also has global entry information. CBP is then able to marry that biographical and biometric data with intelligence and other law enforcement information, run it against watchlists, and also analyze it for linkages and patterns using the ATS. CBP assesses the risk presented by any individual passenger, and then this infor- mation is communicated to the IAP inspectors stationed in foreign airports or to the frontline inspectors here in the United States, who are in turn equipped to determine whether to admit the individual into the United States, or send him or her to secondary inspection for further examination.

A similar process is performed to assess the risk of cargo shipments, and all of this analytical capability is housed at CBP's National Targeting Center (NTC). Established shortly after 9/11 in a tiny room at CBP Headquarters, the NTC has since grown into a massive nerve center housed in an enormous building in Virginia. If anything symbolizes the complete transformation of international borders since 9/11, it is the NTC—CBP's state-of-the-art data analytics facility that is at the heart of CBP's risk management strategy. With its analytical capabilities, the NTC—now working in concert with the Trump administration's new National Vetting Center (NVC)—*assesses* and then *segments* risk, identifying the low-risk travelers and shipments that CBP allows to speed through the global transportation system and across U.S. borders and targeting the higher-risk or unknown travelers and shipments requiring additional scrutiny from CBP officers in the field.

This was the strategy developed by both the Bush and Obama administrations in the wake of the 9/11 attacks. Far from building walls or digging moats around America, the Bush and Obama administrations responded to 9/11 by embracing *interdependence*—partnerships with both the global private sector and international partners to facilitate the transnational flows of lawful travel and commerce, and to secure those flows against the transnational scourges of terrorism and crime. These officials recognized that America could not wait until those threats were at its shores. It had to work with its partners to address these threats well beyond U.S. borders, securing the key entry points and transit nodes in the global transportation system, and working with the private sector to secure supply chains from end to end.

In addition, the Bush and Obama administrations embraced *technology* and the *data analytics* revolution as vital pieces of the border risk management strategy. From the deployment of cargo scanning equipment to the development of biometrics capturing devices to the installation of the bandwidth required to transmit data and scanning images around the world, the U.S. border strategy depended on the most advanced technology. The United States also revamped its data collection and analysis capabilities—creating the National Targeting Center, continually upgrading the Automated Targeting System, and developing the Automated Commercial Environment (ACE), among many other capabilities, and enacting laws and regulations mandating the collection of vital information on international travelers and shipments. These steps allowed CBP and other agencies to analyze vast amounts of data in order to spot the high-risk travelers and shipments and speed the lower risks on their way.

This strategy has been extraordinarily successful—and it was bipartisan. It is amazing to think that, for all of the tension and threats of the years since 9/11, only 102 people have been killed in the United States by Islamist terrorism, and, of those, most—76—were killed by U.S. citizens who were born and radicalized *here*. With the exception of Tashfeen Malik (the wife of San Bernardino killer and U.S. citizen Syed Rizwan Farook) and of the other 26 perpetrators who were killed by their own acts of Islamist terrorism since 9/11—in Boston, Chattanooga, New York, and elsewhere—most (such as the Tsarnaev brothers and Chattanooga terrorist Muhammad Youssef Abdulazeez) had come to the United States as children and, in Abdulazeez's case, were eventually naturalized as U.S. citizens. These were all tragedies, but *none* of these incidents involved Al-Qaeda or ISIS operatives who successfully entered the United States by crossing its borders. This is quite a statement about the effectiveness of U.S. border strategy.

The world has seen this success and has embraced the strategy for the most part, although global implementation has lagged. In the cargo and supply chain security arena, the United States and several other nations led the development and worldwide adoption in 2005 of the World Customs Organization's SAFE Framework of Standards to Secure and Facilitate Trade. This agreement committed the nations of the world to a strategy very much like that developed in the United States, which hinged on partnerships with the global private sector (embracing Authorized Economic Operator [AEO] programs such as C-TPAT), partnerships with international partners to screen high-risk containers before *departure,* not on arrival as with CSI, use of scanning technology, and data analytics engines to assess risk.

Similarly, in the wake of the rise of ISIS—and the threat presented by the flow of foreign terrorist fighters— in 2014, President Barack Obama led the United Nations Security Council to pass Resolution 2178. This resolution similarly embraces interdependence and partnerships in order to address threats, calling for robust international sharing of intelligence and information on travelers, and also calling upon all nations to collect and analyze API/PNR in order to spot high-risk travelers moving through the global transportation system as early as possible. There have also been other multinational agreements through groups such as the International Civil Aviation Organization (ICAO).

In short, in the years since 9/11, the nations of the world and the United Nations have adopted strategies very similar to the successful one developed since 9/11 by administrations of both political parties in the United States. While much remains to be done in terms of implementation, the strategy itself is sound. The key threat now is nationalist politicians stirring fear and seeking to erect walls instead of deepening the international collaboration that has been so vital to the post-9/11 strategy's success.

Securing the North American Perimeter

In addition to implementing the global strategy outlined above, the Bush and Obama administrations also worked close to home, building strong partnerships with North American neighbors Mexico and Canada, and then branching out to other key hemispheric partners, such as various Caribbean nations, Panama, Chile, Brazil, and others.

This was an immediate priority, of course, given that the Level One Alert had the greatest impact on the U.S. land borders with Mexico and Canada. American policymakers needed to work with those countries immediately to figure out a way to strengthen security against terrorism without shutting down the North American economy. This, in turn, led to longer-term U.S. discussions with both countries and the signing of various "Smart Border," "Shared Border," and other similar accords, all essentially aiming at two key points.

First, North American countries wanted to remove unnecessary barriers to lawful travel and commerce within the continent. But this was tricky, because so long as the United States lacked confidence in the willingness or ability of Mexico and Canada to prevent potential terrorists from entering *their* countries, it would be hard for the United States to lessen defenses at its borders. Indeed, the Ressam case demonstrated this very threat—that a terrorist could get into Canada or Mexico, and then seek to enter the United States. This led to the *second* key priority in discussions with Canada and Mexico—namely, how the United States could work with each country to secure the entire North American perimeter from the entry of terrorists such as Ressam.

And, over the last eighteen years, the United States has done just that. Indeed, for all of the recent rhetoric about the purported need for a "wall" across the U.S.–Mexico border, the reality is that in the years since 9/11, Mexico has become one of America's most important security partners. Mexico is represented at the National Targeting Center, and the United States and Mexico work together to analyze the API/PNR data on all travelers flying *into* Mexico. Therefore, it does not help a terrorist to fly to Mexico in order to get into the United States—U.S. personnel and their Mexican colleagues will greet that terrorist at the Mexico City or Cancún airport. A similarly close relationship has also developed with Canada, though it differs given certain legal issues that have precluded implementing the kind of joint targeting that the United States coordinates with Mexico. But Canada and the United States share watchlist information; Canada is represented at the NTC; and the two countries work together to harmonize how they analyze API/PNR data and identify targets for secondary screening. The United States also uses the Secure Real Time Platform (SRTP) and other systems to vet all visa applicants and refugees seeking entry into Canada, running its biographical and biometric data against U.S. watchlists and informing Canada if it spots a problem. The United States also works closely with Mexican and Canadian partners on securing the flow of trade to North America. Indeed, the Container Security Initiative was first deployed with Canada, and the United States and Canada jointly presented the CSI concept to the World Customs Organization.

The Bush and Obama administrations—along with the Fox, Calderón, and Peña-Nieto administrations in Mexico, and the Chrétien, Martin, Harper, and Trudeau administrations in Canada—all recognized the essential interdependence of the North American countries. Interdependence involves not only perimeter security, but also interdependent economies, linked by transnational infrastructure—cross-border bridges, pipelines, rail lines, and binational urban areas, among other things—and family relationships. Indeed, since the ratification of the North American Free Trade Agreement (NAFTA) in 1994, trade within North America has roughly quadrupled, and now well surpasses $1 trillion. CBP simply could not allow the terrorist threat to get in the way of this continental economic juggernaut—and because of the wise policies implemented by all three countries since 9/11, aimed at securing the perimeter and reducing unnecessary barriers to lawful travel and commerce, it did not. In fact, the opposite happened. The integrated North American market of 550 million people is now the most dynamic, competitive economy in the world.

This deepening North American partnership has also allowed the three countries to work more closely together on other key issues, such as fighting transnational crime and controlling the flow of irregular migration. Indeed, there is no way the U.S. government could be dealing with the recent Central American migration crisis without such a close partnership with Mexico—for it has been Mexico that has brought some order to the situation, better securing its borders with Guatemala and Belize, controlling transit points up to the U.S. border, and implementing humanitarian screening (to determine if certain migrants require asylum protection). More recently, Mexico's northern cities such as Tijuana have had to operate as "way stations" for asylum seekers trying to enter the United States, as CBP has allowed only limited numbers of individuals to apply for asylum each day. This has been an imperfect process, but without the partnership with Mexico, the Central American migration challenge would be much more difficult to address—and more Central American migrants and asylum seekers would be losing their lives.

The deepening security, economic, and law enforcement partnerships of the United States, Canada, and Mexico is one of the truly great developments since the 9/11 attacks, and it is a cornerstone of the post-9/11 reinvention of thinking about international borders. Without that partnership, U.S. land borders would be far less secure from terrorism, and North American countries would be far worse off economically. With that partnership, the opposite is true.

Conclusion

The paradigm shift in how we think about international borders is one of the great yet lesser-known stories of the years since 9/11. For all of the recent political rhetoric about terrorism and border security, the actual reality is that U.S. borders are more secure now than at any point in history. The small number of deaths caused by foreign terrorist operatives in the United States since 9/11 is a testament to that fact.

This did not happen by accident. It happened because the United States and its international and private sector partners led the world in developing a new strategy for managing risks at U.S. borders—one that recognized that only through embracing global interdependence could countries address the inherently transnational threats they all faced without unnecessarily interfering with the flows of lawful travel and commerce that are so vital to the global economy. Policymakers recognized that securing national borders themselves was not enough and, in fact, could lead to bottlenecks that could harm economic growth. Instead, countries needed to secure and facilitate the global flows of transnational travel and commerce—and do this at the most logical points, and ideally far away from physical borders. Walls and moats could not protect anyone from the terrorist needles flowing through the giant haystacks of global travel and trade. Countries needed to secure the flows themselves, and this could only be done in partnership with other countries, with international organizations, and with the global private sector.

The United States also embraced technology, and especially the data analytics revolution—building the National Targeting Center and using its capabilities to analyze the vast amounts of traveler and trade data available to the border agencies in order to assess risk, spot potential threats, and speed everyone else through the global transportation system. In this way, CBP could simultaneously increase security and expedite lawful flows, because it could focus its attention on known or unknown risks. CBP also invited shippers, through "trusted shipper" programs like C-TPAT, and individuals, through "trusted traveler" programs like Global Entry, to help—working in partnership with the government to provide information that CBP could analyze. If they presented little risk, they could move along. Through all of these efforts, the government reduced the bottleneck, and focused its gaze at smaller, more "needle-rich" haystacks of potentially higher risk travelers and shipments.

And finally, the United States paid particular attention to its North American neighbors—building a security perimeter around the continent while, at the same time, building an integrated continental economy that is the envy of the world, and working to address the continental problems of transnational crime and irregular migration *together*.

The success of this strategy speaks for itself. Because of the interdependence adopted after 9/11, Americans are far safer and far more prosperous than they were before. The only threat to this regime is Americans themselves—specifically, whether fear and demagoguery will bring back the unwise, "America-first" pre-9/11 strategies such as the Level One Alert, isolate America from its natural partners, and blindly undermine the global interdependence that the Bush and Obama administrations so successfully embraced in the years after 9/11.

CHAPTER 6

The Trusted and the Targeted: Segmenting Flows by Risk

Chappell Lawson

Preventing "bad people" and "bad things" from entering the United States is a core element of homeland security. But as Seth Stodder describes in Chapter 5, finding dangerous or undesirable entries amid the vast flows of legitimate travel and commerce is like looking for a needle in a haystack. In fact, the haystack in question is extremely large, and the needle is likely to be straw-colored.

This chapter discusses the strategies for and mechanics of sifting through oversized haystacks. It focuses on how the government might best execute that task in the context of international flows through authorized ports of entry (POEs), which is the province of Customs and Border Protection (CBP)—the largest operating agency of the Department of Homeland Security (DHS). The same lessons, however, generally apply to domestic aviation, which is handled by the Transportation Security Administration (TSA), also an operating agency of DHS.

In the first section of this chapter, I present the magnitude of the challenge that DHS faces: that is, the volume of legitimate, beneficial flows relative to potentially dangerous or illegal flows. In the second section, I discuss the pros and cons of universal inspection regimes, in which—to continue the metaphor—every single piece of straw would be scrutinized. The third section assesses alternatives to universal inspection: non-inspection, which essentially accepts a baseline level of undesirable or dangerous entries; random inspection, which aims to establish a baseline deterrent against undesirable activity and thus reduce many undesirable flows; and selective

I thank Steve Flynn, Seth Stodder, Benjamin Rohrbaugh, Nate Bruggeman, Juliette Kayyem, and Alan Bersin for useful comments on earlier drafts of this chapter.

inspection, which directs law enforcement resources toward the most suspicious shipments and individuals. The fourth section discusses the two main elements of any selective or "risk-based" inspection regime worth its salt: blowing some of the hay off the stack by not inspecting entries presumed to be safe (through vetted shipper and traveler programs) and getting better at finding the needle (through law enforcement "targeting" and watchlisting).

In the fifth section, I suggest some opportunities for improvement in the way DHS performs its mission to secure and expedite flows of goods and people through the United States—in particular, increasing inspections of potentially risky shipments and improving targeting. I close with a discussion of the crucial unresolved challenge of how to secure the large amount of trade that falls into the "low-to-medium risk" category, especially transoceanic shipments. (Chapter 7 takes up this issue in greater detail.)

The Scope of the Challenge

DHS's mission entails securing the flows of goods and people into the United States in order to facilitate legitimate commerce and travel in an era of globalization. Each day, on average, CBP's Office of Field Operations (OFO) processes close to one hundred thousand shipments and more than one million travelers entering the United States through the POEs.[1] Within these flows lurk a comparatively tiny number of dangerous, unlawful, or otherwise problematic entries.

Consider the POEs along the U.S.–Mexico border, supposedly the vector for massive contraband smuggling and undocumented immigration.[2] There is indeed a problem of illegality at the POEs in the form of thousands of unlawful crossings each year (by migrants concealed in vehicles or using fraudulent documents) and billions of dollars of smuggling. But these flows are minuscule compared to legal commerce and transit. Illegal drugs, for instance, constitute perhaps one five-thousandth of 1 percent of trade at the POEs (measured by weight).[3] With respect to persons, there were over 185 million legal crossings into the United States from Mexico through the land POEs in 2016; illegal crossings at the POEs thus constitute far less than 1 percent of total entries.[4]

Data from random secondary inspections at the POEs reveal that in 98–99 percent of the cases, the vehicles and individuals who cross the southwest border at the POEs are entirely compliant with all federal laws and regulations.[5] Equally important, the bulk of the violations that are discovered in these inspections are trivial—as when a daily commuter between Tijuana (Baja California) and Chula Vista (California) neglects to declare an orange in the glove compartment of her car. Drug mules, travelers using fraudulent documents, illegal immigrants hiding inside truck trailers, and other undesirables constitute a truly tiny fraction of the people who attempt to enter the United States each day from Mexico through the POEs.

The needle-in-a-haystack metaphor applies with even greater force to other border environments: the U.S.–Canada land border, airline passengers flying into the United States from abroad, passengers on ships, international air freight, maritime commerce, and all outbound travel or shipments.[6] For instance, consider the U.S. northern border. Most of Canada's population lives within one hundred miles of the frontier, and the two economies are tightly interwoven—from tourism (e.g., Niagara Falls) to automobile manufacturing supply chains to natural gas pipelines. Some smuggling does exist (e.g., shotguns, cigarettes, and prescription pharmaceuticals); as with the southwest border, a portion of that smuggling takes place through the POEs. Contraband, however, remains an infinitesimal fraction of the legal flow. Travel across the border by suspected criminals or terrorists is likewise minimal at best. For the *domestic* travelers and shipments (including air passengers and air freight) with which TSA must contend, the ratio of illegal to legal activity is even smaller.

Throughout the homeland security enterprise, then, the story is one of scarce, minuscule illegal "needles" within much larger, entirely legitimate "haystacks." The rarer the pernicious activity—for instance, spies or terrorists attempting to sneak into the United States—the smaller the needle and the harder it is to find.

The immense size of the haystack at the POEs, of course, reflects the globalization of travel and trade. That process has continued steadily as transportation costs have diminished, tariffs have largely disappeared, and the logic of economic complementarities around the world has played out. Despite appropriate policy debates over certain aspects of globalization—e.g., the details of "free trade" agreements with developing countries—there is no doubt that Americans derive immense benefits from traveling internationally, admitting tourists from foreign countries (who spend money in the United States), purchasing foreign-made products that would otherwise be unavailable or hopelessly expensive (from bananas to apparel to petroleum), and exporting American-made products. Even if certain aspects of economic globalization (e.g., imports of manufactured goods from China) were significantly restricted, however, the challenge of border management would remain daunting; the volume of international trade and travel will always be vast relative to the "dark side" of commerce and transit. A central question for the homeland security enterprise, then, is how to find the handful of harmful things and people amid the much larger flow of legitimate cargo and people.

Universal Inspection

One natural, intuitive response to this challenge would be a *universal* and *comprehensive* inspection regime. Every person, every conveyance, every parcel, every pallet, and every shipping container passing into or through the United States would be searched (hence "universal"). Furthermore, each of these inspections would be thorough enough to detect anything illegal or dangerous (hence "comprehensive").[7] Because inspections take time and can impose considerable costs, this approach inherently gives less weight to facilitating free flows of legitimate travel and commerce and assigns more weight to catching "bad things" or "bad people."

Such searches would, of course, present a host of practical challenges. As discussed in Chapter 5, the attempt to impose such an inspection regime in the immediate aftermath of the 9/11 attacks proved enormously counterproductive. That fact has led many people in and out of government to dismiss the notion of universal inspection out of hand, even if it only focuses on certain threats (and thus is not "comprehensive"). Nevertheless, governments do maintain large-scale, universal inspection regimes of one sort or another for certain types of contraband in certain environments. For this reason, it is worth examining more carefully the value and limitations of universal inspection.

One well-known example of a near-universal inspection regime is the scrutiny of air passengers (including domestic air passengers). This regime is not truly universal (i.e., it does not apply to every person), because flight crews are not subjected to the same scrutiny as ordinary travelers and, since the launch of TSA's Pre✓ in 2011, some passengers receive less scrutiny. It is also not truly comprehensive (i.e., it is not designed to detect all threats): metal detectors, body scanners, and baggage x-rays are intended to protect civil aviation, rather than identify run-of-the-mill contraband. But passenger inspections for aviation security do indicate the scope of inspections that are possible, even in an era of globalized travel networks.

There are also foreign precedents for regimes that approximate universal inspection at POEs (e.g., Israel). Even in the United States, most travelers entering the country have historically been subject to light "primary inspection"—that is, they have been forced to interact with a customs or immigration officer in some way, even if they are not physically searched.

The downside, of course, is that a universal inspection regime imposes significant costs in an era of global supply chains and travel networks. For travelers, searches would mean longer wait times, effectively restricting freedom of movement. Inconvenience would be particularly pronounced for business travelers and those with relatives abroad, especially residents of twin communities along America's northern and southern land borders (e.g., Nogales in Arizona/Sonora and Sault Ste. Marie in Michigan/Ontario). A universal inspection regime for shipments (the main vector for contraband) would likewise disrupt manufacturing systems and retailers that depend on just-in-time delivery of parts and supplies, making goods more expensive for American consumers and rendering U.S. manufacturers less competitive internationally. The more comprehensive such inspections were—that is, the greater the variety of undesirable activity they were designed to address—the more burdensome and economically destructive they would be.

A less obvious problem is that universal inspection regimes generally cost the government a great deal of money in personnel, technology, etc. Where the vast bulk of the flows is safe, the expense involved in searching for a particular type of bad thing could be wildly disproportionate to any benefits gained. The opportunity cost of applying universal inspection to one species of threat in one particular modality (e.g., inspection of maritime cargo for explosives) looms particularly large in a context of fixed resources and multiple potential threats—precisely the environment in which DHS operates.

Yet another limitation is that universal inspection regimes do little to reduce flows of undesirable things or people whenever the POEs constitute just one smuggling vector. For instance, consider a universal inspection regime designed to detect methamphetamine, in which every person and every container entering the United States by air, land, or sea was searched for crystal meth. Even if such a regime could be devised and was not prohibitively expensive, it would do relatively little good. Smugglers would adapt rather easily, redirecting that particular type of contraband through tunnels under the southwest border or into the wide expanses between the POEs (including the littorals), thereby foiling the inspection regime. Universal inspection can look even less attractive from the broader perspective of protecting public safety (rather than the narrower perspective of intercepting things at the border). For instance, crystal meth is something that can be made inside the United States at a cost not much greater than the cost of smuggling it in from Mexico. To the extent that stepped-up border enforcement was intended to reduce the availability of crystal meth in the United States, the ultimate effect on public health would be modest and evanescent.[8] Universal inspection thus makes the most sense for modalities where the displacement effect of inspections is small and the reduction effect potentially large.

One example that highlights the challenges of universal inspection concerns the radiation portal monitors (RPMs) installed at POEs.[9] Every truck or train coming into the United States, as well as every container leaving an American seaport for somewhere else in the country, must pass through such a device. Unfortunately, these monitors activate whenever the containers passing through them hold trace amounts of radioactive material; kitty litter, ceramics, certain medical devices, and other innocuous cargo often trigger alarms. At some POEs, as many as one out of every 150 or so trucks originally had to be pulled over for secondary inspection.[10] Worse still, the monitors are not always directionally sensitive enough to determine which lane an offending vehicle occupies; as a result, CBP officers must sometimes pull over more than one vehicle each time the alarm sounds. Not for nothing did one customs officer on the southwest border describe the RPMs to me as "the bane of our existence." Needless to say, not one of the hundreds of thousands of such alarms has been triggered by someone attempting to smuggle a dreaded "bomb in a box" into the United States.[11]

Furthermore, as with our putative methamphetamine smugglers, the efficacy of this universal inspection system is uncertain. To skeptics, the deployment of RPMs is premised on the notion that terrorists who are sophisticated enough to obtain fissile material, assemble a device, and smuggle it into the United States would not also be sophisticated enough to mask its signal.[12] Finally, from the larger perspective of public safety, malefactors could do massive damage to the United States when they arrived in a major port city before they passed through the RPM. Even if a universal inspection system were put in place for all maritime shipments bound for the United States *before* they entered the country, a nuclear weapon could still cause massive devastation if it were detonated just over the border from a major U.S. city (such as San Diego or Detroit), without ever having been brought into the country. For this reason, analysts familiar with non-proliferation efforts agree that investing in the sequestration of fissile material at its sources and securing specific "choke points" in the international transportation system would be far more efficient and effective than universal screening of cargo bound for the United States.[13] Of course, the current regime may be helpful as part of a layered defense system, and it could be combined with other scanning technologies or screening techniques to improve detection of smuggled devices as discussed in Chapter 7.

When, then, is a universal inspection regime worth the price? The answer, of course, depends on the costs (both to the government and to the economy as a whole) and the benefits of threat reduction. On the threats side of the equation, protecting against some sorts of illegal activity—such as smuggling pirated DVDs or knock-off designer bags—would presumably not justify significant government expenditures or severe economic dislocations. By contrast, the widespread deployment of scanning technologies that detected smuggled people or certain particularly dangerous items might be worth the investment. It might also make sense to invest in the *capability* to conduct universal inspections should the need arise, even if the regime were not continuously employed. For instance, use of the RPMs that are already in place would make sense if fissile material were already known to have fallen into the hands of those who sought to smuggle it into the United States. Likewise, screening systems for febrile illness at certain airports might be justifiable if their operation slowed the speed of transmission of a deadly infectious disease during the beginning stages of an epidemic, even if the system were not used most of the time.[14]

The cost side of the equation depends heavily on the difficulty of detection. Inspection is costly in terms of both manpower and delays. And inspection is vastly more time-consuming if the "bad thing" in question cannot be identified through non-intrusive scanning: it is much harder to pull over a truck and search inside its trailer than to drive the truck through a high-energy x-ray machine. Not surprisingly, the availability of safe, cheap, reliable, and accurate scanning technologies emerges as the pivotal factor in cost-benefit modeling exercises on universal inspection.[15]

Non-intrusive inspection technologies range from cheap and accessible (low-energy x-rays that can detect things such as weapons in carry-on luggage) to costly (large-scale backscatter that can detect contraband inside trucks) to currently non-existent (scanners that can identify smuggled gemstones) to impossible even in theory (inspection technology that can differentiate between emeralds from countries subject to international sanctions and emeralds from countries not subject to sanctions). The more comprehensive an inspection regime attempts to be, the more likely it is that scanning technologies will not exist for at least some of the targeted species of contraband. Therefore, a universal inspection approach would only make sense for contraband that was highly dangerous and reasonably easy to find.

Alternatives to Universal Inspection

At the other end of the spectrum from universal inspection is the absence of any inspection regime at all. Again, there are both domestic and foreign examples of such regimes. Many countries have no customs inspections for travelers from "safe" places; for instance, air passengers arriving in Italy from the United States are simply not inspected upon their arrival.

There are certainly points of origin for which inspection upon arrival in the United States would be of dubious value. For instance, cargo flowing through Japanese seaports is more secure than cargo flowing through American seaports, and there is probably little point in searching American tourists returning from a trip to Iceland. Indeed, there is a strong rationale for eliminating primary inspections of individuals at air POEs, which have typically been quite cursory. To abandon entirely the goal of identifying bad things and bad people *en route* to the United States, however, would be an abdication of quintessential government functions.

One alternative is a random inspection regime. CBP conducts random secondary inspections at most POEs (as does TSA at domestic airports). Some other countries rely almost entirely on such regimes.

The central purpose of random inspection is to establish a minimum deterrent against doing illegal things: travelers are directed to secondary inspection frequently enough to remind them that they could be caught if they engage in smuggling. This same premise underlies random inspection regimes in many spheres of policy: income tax audits, workplace drug-testing programs, etc.

The deterrent effect of random inspection is much more potent when the guilty party is at hand to be apprehended. For this reason, random inspection makes more sense for passengers (and their luggage) than for cargo shipments. Random inspection can still deter smuggling in a cargo environment if a compromised shipment can be clearly linked to an individual who might subsequently be arrested (as with air parcels delivered to a specific individual at a specific domicile), but in many cases, apprehension of the smuggler and his confederates is difficult. Random inspection is thus a rather ineffective deterrent in the cargo environment.

The deterrent effect of random inspection can also break down for other reasons. First, random inspection may not constitute an adequate disincentive to illegal activity when the perceived payoff is very high. For instance, there remains a ready supply of drug mules from developing countries despite the non-trivial risks of getting caught.[16] Likewise, it is not clear whether a 10-percent-greater chance of getting caught would deter prospective suicide bombers.[17] Second, random inspection is ineffective in discouraging naïve couriers. This applies both to travelers and to legitimate shippers whose supply lines have been corrupted without their knowledge. Third, random inspection is of limited value when even a small number of successful evasions would compromise the entire system (as with smuggled nuclear weapons or the entry of contagious individuals during the initial outbreak of a deadly infectious disease).

A final consideration is that, although random inspection is far cheaper than universal inspection, it can still be extremely expensive relative to the value it provides. The inefficiency of the regime is particularly striking where the background rate of illegal activity is extremely low (resulting in a very large proportion of false positives) and where the inspection itself will not always detect the illegal activity (in other words, a large number of false negatives). As an extreme example, consider a hypothetical random inspection regime designed to detect foreign agents infiltrating into the United States at POEs by randomly interviewing one out of every thousand travelers. Such an inspection regime would cost the government tens of millions of dollars per year, not to mention the burden it would impose on selected travelers who were asked a battery of questions about their kindergarten teacher and which television programs they favored as adolescents. It would probably never select a single spy for interrogation, however, because such individuals constitute far fewer than one-tenth of one percent of travelers. Furthermore, an actual spy would likely have a sufficiently convincing legend to pass such an interrogation even if randomly selected (i.e., to be a false negative).

A fourth inspection regime, then, is *selective*—or, in homeland security parlance, "risk-based." Risk-based regimes focus enforcement efforts on people or shipments that seem suspicious.[18] For some types of people or shipments (for instance, individuals on a "watchlist" or travelers returning from the epicenter of an outbreak of hemorrhagic fever), a risk-based approach would function like universal inspection. For travelers or shipments at the other end of the spectrum, it would typically function as either a no-inspection regime or a random inspection regime (with the goal of "keeping the honest honest").[19] For those in-between, the probability of inspection and the level of scrutiny would be a function of potential risk.

Ultimately, the goal of a targeted approach should be to segment risk along the entire continuum, as depicted in Figure 6.1. Some flows (the darkest

Figure 6.1. Segmented Risk Flows.

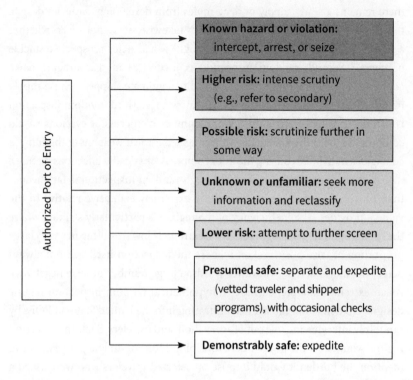

shading) are presumed to be dangerous or illegal and need to be intercepted. In the passenger context, this might include individuals with outstanding arrest warrants (inbound or outbound), those on TSA's "No Fly List," those on the Centers for Disease Control and Prevention (CDC)'s "Do Not Board" list, etc.: for instance, "Chappell Lawson is the subject of an Interpol Red Notice." In the context of cargo (inbound or outbound), such entries might include shipments about which a reliable source had provided specific information: for instance, "A ship named the *Alba Varden*, sailing for Cape Town from Los Angeles, is carrying two large wooden crates filled with undeclared bulk cash on the aft deck."

Also toward the darker end of the spectrum are entries about which law enforcement has some derogatory information, even if that information is not conclusive. For instance, an individual with a series of past convictions for customs-related offenses might merit greater scrutiny at a POE, even though he may not be carrying anything illegal this time around. An international parcel from Palermo addressed to a company suspected of being a front for the Sicilian Mafia, even if it otherwise seemed innocuous, would fall in the same category. Tips from the public and judgments by officers about whether an individual is behaving suspiciously (based on what Seth Stodder calls officers' "spidey sense" in Chapter 5) also signal high-risk shipments or passengers.[20]

Less obviously problematic but still worthy of scrutiny are travelers and shipments whose characteristics suggest a greater threat than average, even in the absence of specific derogatory information—for instance, middle-aged Nigerian women who fly once per month from Lagos to New York City, staying only forty-eight hours or less before returning, and whose ticket was often purchased in cash. (It was precisely for such suspected heroin "swallowers" that certain types of imaging machines were first installed in airports.) On the cargo side, there might be shipments that, from the information available about them, simply do not "make sense." For instance, a large shipment of a certain chemical that could be used in processing drugs to a fast food restaurant in Anacostia might raise eyebrows. Most law enforcement "targeting" (discussed further below) is based on such rule-sets.

The middle of Figure 6.1 indicates entries about which law enforcement simply knows nothing. In the case of a shipment, it could be from a previously unknown exporter to a previously unknown importer that otherwise raises no particular flags—a crate from an unfamiliar shop in Napoli supposedly containing mozzarella cheese destined for a deli in Hoboken, an air freight box of machine tools from a company in Slovenia to a newly incorporated manufacturing firm in Chicago, a package of silk fabric from China to a dressmaker in San Francisco who has not previously imported anything, etc. In the case of a person, it could be an individual whom DHS has not encountered before: for instance, a Korean exchange student beginning his study in the United States, a seventy-eight-year-old American veteran traveling back from Vietnam on his first commercial trip abroad, a Brazilian couple with two small children on their way to Orlando, etc. The background probability of any of these entries being problematic remains low, but because they are unfamiliar, CBP cannot be sure they are not "cleanskins."

The less concerning, or "bluer," end of the risk spectrum (shaded lighter in Figure 6.1) comprises those individuals about whom the government already has some exculpatory information—for instance, short-term travelers from locations that are not hotspots for transnational crime (e.g., Stuttgart) and have never been found in violation of any regulation when they were randomly selected for random inspection in the past. The same logic applies to shipments—for instance, furniture from an established carpentry workshop in Kitchener, Ontario, to Restoration Hardware in Boston.

Even further along the spectrum are those entries that are familiar and almost certainly unproblematic. For instance, the manifest of a truck crossing into the United States from Windsor, Canada, may indicate that it contains auto parts from a subsidiary of an American auto company in Canada to a different subsidiary of the same firm in Michigan—the thirty-seventh identical shipment between that sender and that recipient in thirty-seven months. The truck's trailer *could* contain ivory from poached African elephants or pharmaceuticals that are subject to countervailing duties or hidden Hezbollah operatives, but the possibility is remote—especially if the firm's facilities themselves are known to be secure. Likewise, an American executive returning from her annual meeting of senior Microsoft managers in Hong Kong *could* be smuggling opium resin in her Gucci clutch, but the probability is so low as to be laughable.

Finally, there are some individuals or shipments whose inspection is—and should be regarded as—entirely pointless. (In homeland security circles, this is known as the "Should-Colin-Powell-really-have-to-take-off-his-shoes-at-the-airport?" problem.) For instance, there is not much point in searching an airplane pilot for hazardous material; he knows the risks of carrying lithium ion batteries better than anyone, and if he wants to destroy the airplane, he can find another way.

For those passengers and shipments on the less worrisome end of the spectrum, a risk-based system should be much cheaper than universal inspection; it would involve only occasional, random checks. For entries at the most dangerous end of the scale, a risk-based approach should be far more effective at preventing smuggling than a random inspection regime (or no inspection at all). The degree to which it combines the best of both worlds, however, depends on how good a job it actually does of segmenting risk, especially in the large middle categories. This task in turn depends on the quality of the information available to authorities about how suspicious each individual or shipment is.

The Trusted and the Targeted

As the foregoing discussion implies, there are two basic strategies for applying risk segmentation to the "needle in a haystack" problem. The first involves identifying dangerous people or things in the vast flow of legal goods and travelers (i.e., getting better at finding the needle). This can be done directly by law enforcement agents based on observation of apparently suspicious activity ("spidey sense") or based on more systematic information; the latter, which is the focus here, is known as *targeting*. The second approach involves pulling out of the system those individuals or shipments that pose no risk (i.e., blowing some of the hay off the haystack, in order to see the needles more easily). In the homeland security context, this takes the form of *trusted traveler and shipper programs*.

Ideally, targeting would involve mustering all the information available to the government about an entry and fusing it together rapidly enough to be able to make an operational decision. (This decision usually takes the form of a green, yellow, or red light: allow in, inspect further, or deny entry/apprehend.) In theory, DHS has a great deal of information upon which to draw when making determinations about travelers. With regard to air passengers, for instance, the government collects advanced information about passengers—their name, gender, nationality, identity documents, and (for foreign nationals) address while in the United States, among other things. DHS can also exploit data from customs declaration forms and (for some foreigners) visa applications. All of this information can then be combined with past travel records, previous encounters with law enforcement, and the like. Finally, DHS's data can be combined with separate information from other sources that might be linked to one of the elements in the advanced passenger information, visa application, or customs declaration form. For instance, DHS can determine whether the address listed on a form is also listed by a known or suspected malefactor, or whether the credit card used to purchase a plane ticket was also used to purchase the ticket of a different individual found to be a "bad guy."

In the customs context, targeting rule-sets and algorithms are designed to divide the middle categories in Figure 6.1 more effectively. The more reliably and precisely they do so, the sounder the risk-based approach will be. The most precise rule-sets reflect specific tips and are sometimes limited to particular POEs: for instance, "Be on the lookout for recently washed, white vans with Sinaloa license plates crossing at Eagle Pass before noon." Less precise are rule-sets based on analysis of trends or other intelligence (e.g., "illegal prescription drugs are being smuggled into Washington state from British Columbia on afternoon ferries"). By contrast, rule-sets based on general information about travelers are notoriously imprecise. For instance, the lowest false positive rate for algorithms that rely on travel history and demographic variables alone is around 97 percent. (In other words, only three out of every hundred individuals who meet the designated criteria actually merit the additional scrutiny they receive.) The problem is mechanical: with only a small number of categories in the advanced passenger data that CBP receives and so many travelers, most "cells" in the data matrix will inevitably contain a large number of people. Rule-sets in the passenger environment outperform random inspection, but not always by much.

This problem is even more acute for shipments, for two reasons. First, customs manifests contain information about the cargo itself, shipper, importer, ultimate consignee, customs broker, etc. These data are not particularly rich or predictively valuable compared to the travel history data of passengers.[21] Second, the manifests may not accurately reflect what is inside the container: unlike with passengers, where biometric identifiers can be used to ensure that the "wrapper" is actually associated with the data that DHS has on a particular individual, there is no obvious way to do so in a cargo context without actually scanning or opening a shipment. Screening of shipments is thus more akin to guessing whether an otherwise typical traveler is smuggling contraband on her person than it is to the less daunting challenge of assessing whether an individual is likely to be a "bad guy." Unsurprisingly, CBP's Automated Targeting System (ATS) did not originally outperform a random inspection regime in identifying contraband,[22] and it is not clear whether meaningful improvement has been made since then. Devising the optimal screening-and-scanning model for container security thus remains a major technical challenge.[23]

Hence the other half of a risk-based strategy: reducing the number of entries on which law enforcement must focus its attention. With regard to cargo, the central program is CBP's Customs-Trade Partnership against Terrorism (C-TPAT). Participating companies voluntarily agree to secure their own supply chains, meet basic security standards for access control, and seal containers and truck trailers at points of origin. Their facilities are subject to inspections and their security practices are reviewed. In theory, firms are also expected to work collaboratively with CBP to develop a proper threat assessment and mitigate risks. In exchange, participants receive expedited processing at POEs (for instance, their shipments are not normally inspected at the border) and other potential benefits (for instance, priority in business resumption after a crisis).

On the passenger side, CBP runs four "white lists" that operate in more or less the same way: NEXUS, for crossing between the United States and Canada; Secure Electronic Network for Travelers Rapid Inspection (SENTRI), for crossing between the United States and Mexico; Global Entry, for international air passengers; and FAST (Free and Secure Trade for Commercial Vehicles) for commercial truck drivers.[24] In each case, participants voluntarily submit to a background check, surrendering information not normally required of travelers, and are interviewed by a CBP officer.

In exchange, they are subject only to occasional random inspections when returning to the United States.

Trusted trade and trusted traveler programs intersect when it comes to vehicle operators. In North America, C-TPAT members whose truck drivers are participants in FAST can use dedicated lanes at the POEs. In this situation, the driver of the truck is the last piece of the supply chain, and he receives the benefits of a SENTRI/NEXUS traveler for his vehicle when hauling his load across the border.

The whole point of vetted traveler and shipper programs is to extract from the system large numbers of "blue" entries. Consequently, the value of trusted trader and traveler programs is greatest if a relatively small number of reliable individuals or shippers constitute the bulk of the entries. When it comes to cargo, C-TPAT largely accomplishes this objective: its 11,400 participants (including 4,000 or so shippers) comprise more than half of all containerized trade.[25] In other words, they blow a great deal of hay off the stack.

For travelers, by contrast, efficiency varies considerably across programs. SENTRI comes closest to the desired model: the relatively small number of SENTRI passholders accounts for about 15 percent of all entries along the southwest border.[26] The percentage of entries for NEXUS on the northern border is similar.[27] By contrast, the four million Global Entry[28] members account for a little less than 1 percent of international air passenger entries.[29] Global Entry still pulls out of the system more than a million entries per year that presumably should not be the focus of DHS's attention; however, the haystack remains almost the same size as before.

All told, the main instrument of risk segmentation on the cargo side is vetted shipper programs, which eliminate from inspection up to half of all shipments; targeting contributes much less to solving the "needle in a haystack" problem. On the traveler side, the two strategies contribute more evenly. In the international air passenger environment, watchlisting and targeting do the bulk of the work, while whitelisting does much less.

Another feature of the current regime is that targeting efforts focus much more heavily on counterterrorism than on other threats (e.g., transnational crime). For contraband, there is nothing remotely approaching the elaborate watchlisting process or link analysis done by the Intelligence Community (IC) to identify potential terrorists. Likewise, in the cargo environment, there is nothing remotely approaching universal radiation scanning for "ordinary" contraband, and much more effort is expended at CBP's National Targeting Center on counterterrorism than on other smuggling.

Targeting algorithms for shipments are likewise underdeveloped when it comes to contraband, both because of CBP's priorities and because of the paucity of useful data.

Improving the System

Wherever the government pursues a risk-based strategy, improvements must focus either on better targeting or on enhancements in vetted traveler/ shipper programs. In both cases, the opportunity for improvement is greater when it comes to contraband than counterterrorism. And within the range of contraband materials, there is greater potential for progress in some areas than in others.

With regard to cargo, DHS could no doubt take certain steps to strengthen compliance by C-TPAT partners with the rules of the program, given that C-TPAT itself may now include companies that have invested less in security than the original members.[30] For instance, inspections of facilities could be accomplished more efficiently by using new technologies (e.g., drones); joining forces with Canadian and Mexican agencies would expand the number of inspection facilities; more systematically assessing the appropriate number of random inspections conducted on C-TPAT partners would enhance compliance; and the like.

But the biggest weakness on the cargo side concerns the riskier half of shipments that remain in the system. Only a tiny percentage (less than 2 percent) of such shipments are inspected, and the false negative rate for the inspections that are actually carried out, usually non-intrusively, is not zero. This remains a significant hole in the current risk-based approach. The very large category of "medium- to low-risk" shipments—those that do not activate targeting rules and do not fall under a trusted shipper program— simply goes uninspected.

The easiest route to improvement within this system would be to develop better targeting algorithms for cargo. Although some progress could be made by overlaying more advanced analytics on the data that CBP currently has, progress really depends on bringing new data to bear. The first step would be to integrate the data that the government already has on people with the data it already has on shipments. The operating principle here is that "bad things" are rarely shipped between "good" people; it is much more likely that they will be shipped from one malefactor to another. The second step would be to bring in more data that can readily be cross-referenced with information on manifests—such as lists of valid addresses and names of suspected front companies.

Unfortunately, it is not clear how effective a targeting regime in cargo can ever be, given that manifests do not necessarily reflect what a shipment actually contains and that random inspection is an ineffective deterrent to smuggling. A more ambitious approach, therefore, would be to scale up the rate of inspections to a much higher percentage of non-C-TPAT shipments.[31] This approach would presumably focus first on maritime trade through certain ports and, to a lesser extent, truck and train shipments across the southwest border. Specific tactics might include collaboration with private port operators to expand pre-departure inspections,[32] the use of drones equipped with sensors that could scan containers for certain types of dangerous materials while in transit,[33] the installation of sensors inside shipping containers for similar scans in transit, and increased inspections at POEs.

One corollary benefit of scaling up inspections at POEs is the salutary effect it would have on C-TPAT. As the background rate of inspections increased, the benefits of being a trusted shipper would grow significantly. More shippers would join the program, and CBP could demand that program participants invest even more in securing their own supply chains.

Because the desirability of a more intensive inspection regime depends so heavily on its costs, which in turn depends on the existence of non-intrusive scanning technologies, one important preliminary step would be to better evaluate the likely long-run costs and efficacy of scanning. This calculation is not straightforward, because a government-mandated inspection regime that covered a larger portion of shipments and searched for a larger range of contraband would create a new market for scanning technologies, leading in turn to new inventions.[34] Therefore, more sophisticated modeling of the costs is needed to provide the basis for better decision-making.

The net benefit of a stricter regime thus remains unclear. Very high rates of inspection of non-trusted shipments would almost assuredly prove ineffective or prohibitively expensive when it comes to certain types of contraband (such as gemstones or intellectual property violations), where non-intrusive inspection is generally impossible. In the case of the highest value forms of contraband, such as drugs, tougher inspection might not significantly enhance public safety because of the existence of other smuggling and production modes. On the other hand, the value of stricter inspection is likely to be higher when it comes to the smuggling of both humans and nuclear material.

Turning from cargo to people, enormous progress has already been made on vetted traveler programs and the use of targeting to identify potential terrorists. Again, some improvements are possible at the margin for trusted traveler programs: Global Entry can continue to enroll more people; partnerships with other countries that allow members of their own trusted traveler programs to qualify for Global Entry can be expanded; re-vetting of participants in SENTRI and FAST can be improved; information on criminal offenses recorded by the subnational governments of foreign countries can be incorporated into the vetting; each element of the interview process required for participation in the program could be systematically tested for efficacy; and the like.

The most promising opportunities for improvement in risk segmentation, though, will come from better targeting of people, especially for transnational crime. CBP's targeting efforts have improved dramatically since 9/11, especially with the deployment of a new, more user-friendly system that has incorporated modest automated link analysis in the last five years. Targeting, however, could still be enhanced in three general ways. First, the system needs more and better data. An ideal targeting regime would incorporate all information available to federal governments—including from state, local, tribal, territorial, and foreign partners—and bring that information to bear every time that any individual attempted to enter the country. For example, as discussed in Chapter 14 of this volume, one important missing element when targeting for criminal activity concerns certain types of financial information. Second, more advanced analytics can be run on the existing data. At present, link analysis at DHS is an artisanal activity: investigators or analysts craft charts that plot specific links between individuals who are usually already known to be involved in criminal activity. A better system would allow computers to run automated link analyses on the available data, and then have analysts rate these products, gradually "training the computer" to find connections that could be used to identify suspect individuals or shipments. Third, an optimal targeting system should learn from each encounter with an individual, in preparation for future encounters. Whenever a traveler is searched or interviewed, law enforcement officials know more than they knew before. Much of that information is currently lost in the process of "processing" travelers and shipments.

Conclusion

DHS currently operates a range of different screening systems for different sorts of risks. When it comes to the safety of civil aviation, something approaching universal inspection (for people and baggage) is the norm. The same is true (upon arrival at U.S. POEs) for cargo that might contain fissile material. For other threats, the regime is much closer to a risk-based model, albeit with varying levels of intensity, sophistication, and efficacy depending on the type of illegal activity and the threat vector.

An inspection regime that is both universal (i.e., applies to every entry) and comprehensive (i.e., seeks to detect every possible threat) is infeasible and prohibitively expensive; in this sense, DHS is appropriately wedded to a risk-based approach. The current system, however, remains imperfect—particularly when it comes to maritime shipments not assumed to be low-risk.

Some improvements are certainly possible through better targeting methods that bring new data and methods to bear on an age-old problem. That is clearly the first step. A more aggressive approach would be to move toward broader non-intrusive inspection of cargo, especially certain classes of shipment containers entering the country from selected foreign ports.

How far and how fast the United States should go beyond that is unclear. Although there is a strong argument for expanding the number of inspections of shipments that are not part of C-TPAT, the case for a universal inspection regime—at least for anything other than radioactive material—remains weak. That approach, of course, leaves a vast amount of cargo uninspected, and no simple route forward to securing the portion of the global supply chain that runs through the United States.

CHAPTER 7

The Challenge of Securing the Global Supply System

Stephen E. Flynn

ON FEBRUARY 20, 2017, I STOOD AT THE ENTRANCE GATE OF ONE OF THE world's busiest marine terminals. I was there to observe the security procedures for processing inbound trucks carrying cargo destined for foreign ports. As each vehicle arrived, it waited to be checked in by a security officer who would walk to the back of the truck to examine the seal on the cargo container's door latch. The seal, which is actually a colorful metal bolt with a number etched on it, is the primary physical safeguard for assuring the integrity of global containerized cargo. If the number on the door seal matches its corresponding cargo manifest, the assumption is that there has been no tampering with the container's contents. After the officer records the seal number, the truck is cleared for entry into the terminal. Once in the container yard, the box is hoisted from the truck's chassis and placed into a stack until it is ready to be loaded aboard a ship for its overseas journey.

The process I observed in Hong Kong is replicated around the globe for more than one hundred million containers that circulate through the world's ports each year. The intermodal transportation system is the "overlooked-in-plain-sight" conveyor belt upon which global supply chains and much of the global economy depends. Twenty-foot and forty-foot containers akin to massive Lego blocks are moved interchangeably from truck to train to ship without unloading and reloading the cargo they hold. For virtually all of them, as long as there is a seal on the door and they originate from a "known" or

---

This chapter was adapted from a final report for a project supported by the John D. and Catherine T. MacArthur Foundation and undertaken with the assistance of John Holmes, Sean Burke, and Connor Goddard, to whom the author is indebted for their contributions to the research and the development of the chapter's recommendations.

"trusted" shipper, the common practice is to allow them to flow unimpeded across national borders.

During my visit to the marine terminal in Hong Kong, I witnessed something out of the ordinary. When one of the entering trucks came to a stop at the gate, the driver jumped out of the cab, scurried to the back of the rig, and quickly attached the seal to the door of the container. I was taken aback: the seal is supposed to be attached once the container is loaded at a factory or cargo consolidation center as a safeguard against the contents being tampered with during the transit to the port. I asked the security manager who was escorting me why he supposed this protocol had not been followed. He replied that some drivers did this as a way to reduce the risk of cargo theft on the way to the port: would-be cargo thieves are on the lookout for containers with potentially valuable cargo. The absence of a seal would lead the thieves to believe that the container was empty and not worth trying to hijack.

My port visit in February 2017 reinforced what I have been observing for more than a quarter of a century about the state of cargo security. Criminals and other nefarious actors target containers to steal from them or to smuggle contraband. Narcotics, weapons, cash, hazardous waste, and counterfeit goods routinely move through the global supply system; cargo theft and trade fraud remain ongoing challenges. This is true despite the myriad security initiatives since September 11, 2001, the avowed aim of which has been to bolster port and cargo security.

The problem is not just that contraband continues to find its way into containerized cargo carried by trucks, trains, and ships. It is also that these giant colorful boxes are workhorses of the international trade system. Should the flow of these boxes be disrupted for more than a few days, it would sever the worldwide supply chains that connect suppliers to consumers. The result would be immediate shortages of pharmaceuticals, auto and machine parts, health-care supplies, and virtually everything that can be found in Walmart and Target. Assembly lines would grind to a halt, and stores would run out of stock to put on their shelves.

What could lead to the disruption of this system? Natural disasters and transportation labor issues have wreaked havoc locally and regionally in the past, but the system has been able to devise workarounds. The biggest risk would be a major security incident that leads public officials to order stepped-up inspections for all inbound containers, causing almost immediate system-wide congestion as ships were delayed from offloading their cargo. Port terminals would run out of space to hold the outbound boxes arriving by trucks and trains, and the intermodal transportation system would end up in gridlock. It would take weeks to clear the backlogs.

Such a scenario remains all too real because existing arrangements all fall considerably short of meeting three imperatives required to safeguard the global supply system. First, security measures should deter criminals and terrorists from trying to exploit or target the system. Second, should deterrence fail, security measures should boost the odds that contraband (including a smuggled weapon of mass destruction, or WMD) could be successfully detected and intercepted. Third, even in the worst case, such as a terrorist organization that successfully pulls off an attack by using a container as a "poor man's missile," there should be the means in place to quickly conduct the forensics to isolate where and how the security breach occurred. In short, there must be sufficient confidence in the safeguards in place so that any incident does not trigger the kind of response witnessed on 9/11.

This chapter assesses the current state of security for the global supply system. Although the aviation sector and the southwest U.S. land border have commanded tremendous attention and resources, efforts to safeguard the global flows of containerized cargo remain largely fragmented and woefully under-resourced given the potential stakes. But this situation can be turned around. The key will be to move beyond a primary reliance on government efforts to detect and intercept dangerous contraband within supply chains to one that fully engages with industry. The maritime and surface transportation industry, particularly major port operators, should be made active partners in investing in new cargo security technologies, gathering and sharing data, facilitating inspections, and working collaboratively with the public sector on response and recovery from incidents when they occur. Forging a close partnership between the public and private sectors is essential to ensuring that the global supply chain is secure and resilient in the face of ongoing criminal and security threats.

The Neglect of Global Supply System Security

Any effort to bolster the security and resilience of the global supply system requires an understanding of how the system works. Remarkably, this critical foundation of the modern global economy has come into being largely through an *ad hoc* process. There never has been a modern master plan for constructing the interconnected surface and maritime transportation systems and the logistical networks that manage the movement of the overwhelming majority of the world's goods. Nor has there ever been an overarching authority for managing the risks associated with these systems and networks.

Instead, decades of largely localized decisions at the individual business and government levels have cumulatively contributed to the system's evolution. It is a bit like the story of the internet, except that the internet can at least trace its origins to the government-sponsored ARPANET; there is no similar public-sector parentage for the global supply system.

The cargo container dates back to 1956, when the owner of a trucking company, Malcolm McClean, upended the longstanding process for shipping cargo by loading fifty-eight containers on a converted tanker to sail from Newark, New Jersey, to Houston, Texas. Up to that point, longshoremen would remove cargo from an arriving truck and manually load and tie it down to make it secure within the hold of a ship. When the ship arrived at its destination, the process was reversed. The cargo was removed by stevedores from the hold of the ship, typically to be moved to a dockside warehouse, and then loaded into the back of a truck for final transport to the consignee. The process was labor-intensive, occasionally dangerous, and time-consuming.

McClean saw a way to streamline this process: placing the cargo into a container and then moving the container from truck to ship to truck. His approach was brilliant, but putting it into effect on a global scale ended up taking more than two decades. The main obstacle was the lack of common standards for the construction of containers and agreed-upon conventions for the chassis of trucks and trains needed to convey them. Trucks for moving cargo came in a variety of sizes. Ship owners did not want to reconfigure their vessels to carry containers if there were no gantry cranes at their ports-of-call to unload them. Ports did not want to invest in cranes to offload the containers as long as there were not enough ships carrying containers to make that investment worthwhile. It would take until the 1970s until these issues were sorted out enough to support regular transatlantic and transpacific containerized cargo service.[1]

Containerized cargo took off in the 1990s, as countries liberalized their economies and global trade grew. This growth created an enormous demand for new maritime transportation and logistical infrastructure to support these cross-border trade flows, with Asia leading the way. Larger vessels were constructed to meet this demand, growing from a small number of container ships carrying 1,500 twenty-foot-equivalent units (TEUs) in the mid-1970s to the modern fleet of over 5,000 container ships making transoceanic voyages today, with the latest ships carrying more than 20,000 TEU from "mega-ports" such as Singapore, Rotterdam, Dubai, Hong Kong, and Shanghai.

As container vessels grew bigger, they required upgraded port infra-structure to accommodate them. Given the large capital investments required, governments increasingly turned to the private sector to self-finance and build that infrastructure. Large companies such as Hutchison Ports (Hong Kong), PSA (Singapore), and Maersk (Denmark) constructed the piers and container yards, dredged the slips to accommodate deep draft vessels, and procured the large gantry cranes used for loading and unloading containers from ships. Governments provided these companies with decades-long leases to privately operate these terminals as a means for industry to recoup its investment.

Ships earn no money when they are tied up at a pier or resting in an anchorage; any port delay merely adds to their costs. The goal, therefore, is to load and offload cargo as rapidly as possible so ships can be on their way. The larger the vessel, the more pressure there is turn it around quickly. With four gantry cranes assigned to a container ship, a marine terminal is able to move as many as 120 containers on or off a vessel in a single hour. As the volume of containers grew, the trucks that move them in and out of the terminals needed to be tightly scheduled and nimbly processed at the arrival and departure gates to prevent congestion within the container yards. The primary focus of port operations has been to achieve assembly-line levels of speed and efficiency.

All of these investments translated into explosive growth in the volume of containerized cargo handled by the world's ports. The number of containers handled by port terminals in 1993 doubled by 1998 and quintupled by 2008; the global recession that year slowed things down only temporarily. This rapid expansion in containerized cargo was both a response and a contributor to the success of major retailers such as Walmart and Target, which revolutionized logistics as a means of driving down the cost of the merchandise they sold to consumers. Increasingly, companies realized that they could avoid the expense of maintaining large inventories in warehouses or in the backrooms of department stores. Instead they relied on "just-in-time shipping," where the transportation system effectively served as a mobile warehouse. As these companies grew, so did their global transportation needs. And as the number of overseas containers they needed to ship increased, they acquired the leverage to squeeze shipping lines into offering lower rates. The consequent thinning of profit margins generated yet more pressure for the transportation industry to lower costs by achieving greater economies of scale and efficiency in operations.

In short, the modern network that underpins the global flows of containerized cargo has resulted from commercial drivers seeking economic efficiency. In this objective, the global supply system has succeeded. In 2016, a U.S. retailer could order nearly thirty tons of cargo in Shanghai, have it loaded into a container, and ship it to Los Angeles for as little as $1,200 in trans-oceanic shipping costs. This makes the average postage stamp for mailing a letter seem expensive by comparison. But one unintended consequence of the market-driven evolution of this system is that it created a longstanding bias against investing in security. For many years, incidents of smuggling and cargo theft were quietly accepted as "the cost of doing business." The market drivers to improve efficiency and drive down costs generated enormous economic benefits which largely trumped periodic expressions of concern that the system was vulnerable to criminal elements, as well as potentially more serious security breaches.

With the benefit of hindsight, the public interest would have been well-served if the global supply system was not just low-cost but also had adequate safeguards against contraband smuggling, cargo theft, and terrorist exploitation or targeting. Specifically, as this system evolved, governments should have pressed for sufficient visibility and accountability in order to accomplish three goals:

1. Monitor the integrity of authorized shipments to ensure that they have not been compromised as they move through the system.
2. Support the timely and surgical interception of a shipment when intelligence is available that it might pose a potential threat.
3. Facilitate forensics efforts immediately after a security breach to assess and quickly isolate where and how a shipment was compromised.

These three objectives could be accomplished if tracking and monitoring technologies were embedded within transportation and logistical networks to support routinely locating, identifying, and assessing the transit and condition of containerized shipments from their origins to their final destinations. To date, however, there have not been sufficient market drivers for creating an end-to-end system for the near real-time tracking of containerized shipments that would provide general oversight of cargo integrity. Containers typically are handed off to multiple transportation providers as they move along their journey. The common method by which carriers manage the transfer of cargo is with a "waybill" that shows the names of the consignor and consignee, where the shipment originated from, its destination, and its route. Waybills also provide a general description of the goods, but the carrier has no binding obligation to confirm that these descriptions are accurate. As a general rule, transportation providers have no reason to be interested in the specific contents of the containers that they are carrying. Unless a shipment poses a potential risk to the safety of the conveyance or the operators, carriers are primarily interested only in where a container is heading and the time by which it needs to be delivered.

An additional factor complicates the tracking of the integrity of a shipment once it is in transit— the fact that so many containers hold multiple shipments from multiple consignors. Most individuals and companies that want to ship goods do not require a full forty-foot box for what they are sending. Middlemen known as freight forwarders, or more technically, non-vessel operating common carriers (NVOCC), organize these consolidated shipments. NVOCCs will load containers and then contract with a transportation provider or multiple carriers to move the goods to their final destinations. Most of the goods that freight forwarders receive are already packaged, much like a UPS parcel picked up at a home or an office. Carriers will likely weigh the item, but they generally take the word of their customers about what is being sent. There is no system in place for routinely subjecting shipments to non-intrusive inspections (i.e., scanning). As a result, when assessing risk, customs authorities depend almost completely on what individuals and companies declare that they are sending. It is essentially an honor system.

Although supply chains have become increasingly complex in modern times, as a rule, manufacturers and retailers only become interested in trying to determine the location of their shipments when confronted with the relatively rare instances when they go missing or are delayed. The reliability of the modern supply system translates into goods almost always arriving when they are supposed to. As a result, supply chain managers are not inclined to invest in capabilities that would allow them to track the real-time location of their shipments while in transit.

To summarize, transportation providers know the locations of their conveyances and the containers they are carrying, but rarely know the contents of those containers. Supply chain managers or the beneficiary cargo owners know what is being shipped and when their goods are supposed to arrive, but not the location of those goods at any given time. The system has evolved in such a way that there was no imperative for developing the means to match a specific shipment with a specific location once goods are in transit. Nor is it possible to confirm that what a consignor declares it is shipping is the same as what is being actually shipped until it reaches the consignee. The operative assumption of the system is that its users are honest and legitimate.

Flaws in the Post–9/11 Effort

Since World War I, the federal agency with the lead role for securing ports is the U.S. Coast Guard (USCG). During the early years of the Cold War, there was considerable anxiety over the possibility that the Soviet Union might use a merchant ship as a way to target U.S. port cities with nuclear weapons. But with the advent of intercontinental nuclear missiles, such concerns faded away. By 2001, port security was relegated to a part-time function managed by the U.S. Coast Guard Reserves, whose focus was not even domestic. Instead, these reserve Port Security Units were trained to deploy overseas to provide security in support of the U.S. Navy operating out of ports near warzones.[2]

Cargo security also suffered longstanding neglect at the turn of the millennium. U.S. authorities essentially operated blind when it came to assessing the risk of containerized cargo. This is because importers were not required to provide cargo manifests to customs authorities until the container neared the end of its journey. For imports that were destined for an inland port of entry (POE), such as Chicago or St. Louis, the standard practice was for port officials to automatically allow overseas cargo arriving in Seattle or Los Angeles to travel by truck or train for the many days or even weeks it might take to reach a bonded facility in America's heartland. The importer would then provide a paper manifest and pay any required customs duties; at that point, the customs inspectors would authorize its release into the economy. Furthermore, when it came to describing the container's contents, importers were often notoriously vague. The most frequently used descriptions on cargo manifests were "FAK" and "GM," which were abbreviations for "Freight All Kinds" and "General Merchandise," respectively. As a practical matter, this translated into making it impossible for inspectors to assess risk prior to a container's arrival in the United States, and in many instances, even well afterward.

A security initiative in the fall of 2001 illustrates how little attention was being paid to the cross-border flows of containerized cargo shipments, even in the immediate aftermath of 9/11. With funding from the Defense Advanced Research Projects Agency (DARPA), an interagency group of officials in New England and a group of engineers at the Volpe National Transportation Systems Center collaborated on a project dubbed "Operation Safe Commerce."[3] The project's objective was to monitor the location and integrity of a container from the time it was loaded with automotive parts in Slovakia until it arrived at an assembly facility in New Hampshire. The container traveled by truck across the Czech and German borders, was loaded and sailed by ship from Hamburg to Montreal, and was then transferred to a truck that crossed the U.S.–Canada border at Highgate, Vermont, for the final three-hour journey to the facility in Hillsborough, New Hampshire.

The technology used in this initiative was relatively primitive. To track the location of the container, the engineers mounted a GPS antenna on the rear of the container. The antenna was attached to a wire that was fed through the narrow gap of the closed container door to a power source (an automotive battery) that was mounted on the interior floor. They also placed a light sensor inside the container to detect any possible intrusion. When the project team briefed the interagency group on their prototype, a senior U.S. customs official expressed some apprehension. He pointed out that the antenna, wiring, and battery would look suspicious to an inspector who might mistakenly conclude that the container had been armed with an explosive device, or perhaps even something worse. He asked the project team if they had briefed the customs agencies in the jurisdictions through which the container would be passing about the pilot project. The engineers replied that they had not. After a debate about what to do, it was decided that there was not time enough to alert the many customs entities involved without delaying the shipment. Nonetheless, the group decided to go ahead with the trial. Embarrassingly, it turned out that the concerns of the U.S. customs official were unwarranted. No one at the Czech border, the German border, the port of Hamburg, the port of Montreal, or the U.S.–Canada border reported noticing the unusual antenna with the wire passed into the interior of the container. Because the box had come from a "trusted shipper," apparently no border inspector even took the time to check if it had a seal on its doors.

Given this sorry state of security, there were stepped-up efforts by multiple agencies to bolster port security and container security beginning in the fall of 2001. But no one agency was put in charge of intermodal transportation security. As a result, the overall approach ended up being uncoordinated and fragmented.

In the fall of 2001, the USCG led an initiative to set common international security standards for port facilities and ships. It worked through the International Maritime Organization (IMO), a specialized agency of the United Nations headquartered in London, to establish the International Ship and Port Facility Security (ISPS) Code. The code, which went into effect on July 1, 2004, established minimum security requirements for vessels, shipboard personnel, and port facilities to "detect security threats and take preventative measures against security incidents affecting ships or port facilities used in international trade."[4] The sanction for ports that were determined to be non-compliant was that all vessels visiting that port would potentially be subjected to a comprehensive security inspection by the authorities in any of the next ten ports they visited. Because such inspections typically result in significant delays, shipping lines would find it cost-prohibitive to load or offload cargo in a non-compliant port and would forgo servicing these ports. Given the potential risk of being cut off from global shipping, countries have a compelling incentive for ensuring that that they remain in compliance with the ISPS Code.

The U.S. Customs Service, which subsequently became part of Customs and Border Protection (CBP), also created a stricter regime. Customs officers now have the authority to perform an exam of all inbound cargo, detain shipments, and, where appropriate, seize or re-export that cargo. As Seth Stodder discusses in Chapter 5 of this volume, CBP drew on their authority in November 2001, with the launch of the Customs-Trade Partnership Against Terrorism (C-TPAT),[5] followed in 2002 with the Container Security Initiative (CSI).[6] C-TPAT identified supply chain security "best practices" that companies involved with importing goods into the United States were asked to adopt voluntarily. Companies that signed on to C-TPAT were told that they would be considered low risk, which would translate into "facilitated" entry into the United States. The unambiguous message that the agency conveyed was that non-C-TPAT companies would be far more likely to be targeted for inspection, with all the associated delays involved.

In the other major program, CSI, foreign government counterparts agreed to play host to U.S. customs inspectors and collaborate on inspecting U.S.-bound containers that had been identified as high risk at the ports of loading. An additional requirement of becoming a CSI partner was that foreign customs agencies had to procure and maintain non-intrusive inspection (NII) and radiation detection technology to support cargo inspections.

Finally, in 2003, in order to improve its ability to assess risk prior to cargo arriving in the United States, CBP imposed new requirements on importers with respect to the timing and details of cargo manifests. Cargo manifest information could no longer be submitted after the container arrived at the U.S. POE, but had to be provided twenty-four hours prior to a container being loaded onto a U.S.-bound vessel in a foreign port. Six years later, CBP implemented the Importer Security Filing "10+2," which required the electronic submission of more detailed cargo information as a part of the twenty-four-hour rule.[7]

While the USCG and CBP were busy launching their separate efforts to strengthen port security and cargo security, the U.S. Department of Energy (DOE) focused on the challenge of detecting and intercepting nuclear materials hidden within cargo shipments that were being transported across foreign borders. The National Nuclear Security Administration (NNSA) was established within the DOE in 2000, and was tasked with developing and deploying detection technologies that would support U.S. nuclear counter-terrorism and counterproliferation objectives. Specifically, the NNSA oversaw the Second Line of Defense Program, which involved bilateral arrangements whereby the NNSA provided direct assistance for strengthening the techno-logical capabilities of partner countries to combat smuggling of chemical, biological, radiological, nuclear, and explosive (CBRNe) materials.[8] In 2003, the NNSA launched the Megaports Initiative, through which it provided foreign customs, port authorities, and port terminal operations with radiation detection equipment, along with the training and technical support to operate and maintain that equipment.[9] While the NNSA dealt with the nuclear trafficking risk overseas, the Domestic Nuclear Detection Office was created within DHS in 2005, and was assigned the responsibility of managing the risk of WMD terrorism at U.S. border crossings and U.S. POEs.

The U.S. Department of Defense (DOD) also decided to take on the nuclear counterterrorism mission with the creation of the Proliferation Security Initiative (PSI) in 2003. Working with the U.S. Department of State (DOS), this program focused on obtaining agreements from individual countries that would allow specialized teams to board and interdict suspected WMD shipments at sea.[10] Nations with large numbers of commercial vessels within their ship registries were of particular interest. They were pressured to agree to an expedited process for approving boarding requests on their flag vessels.

After 9/11, the DOS undertook a major diplomatic effort to have the United Nations adopt a requirement for all member states to adopt legal and regulatory measures on preventing WMD proliferation. UN Security Council Resolution 1540 was adopted in 2004, along with the creation of a committee to oversee its implementation. The resolution did not provide the 1540 Committee with enforcement powers; instead, member-states were left to determine the degree to which they devised and invested in implemen-tation plans.[11]

On its face, when all these initiatives are outlined together, it seems that the U.S. government has been pursuing a comprehensive approach to reducing the opportunity to exploit or target the global supply system by terrorists or by those involved in circumventing nonproliferation protocols. But if a U.S. ambassador were asked to provide a briefing on the overall approach to the foreign country to whom he or she is accredited, it would be difficult to convey much in the way of coherence. Some requirements are voluntary, while others are mandatory. Some are reached through international agreements overseen by international organizations, while others are essentially dictated by U.S. agencies and imposed on major trade partners. Some require foreign governments to invest their own resources in new inspection technologies, while others are supported by direct U.S. assistance. Finally, some are largely market-oriented, expressing a sense of trust that companies will find it in their best interests to bolster cargo security, while others rely on regulations that impose new requirements on importers with penalties for non-compliance. In sum, the briefing would outline the following regime:

- The U.S. government supports a multilateral approach for establishing universal security standards for ships and port facilities. The USCG will conduct periodic audits to check that individual countries are abiding by the ISPS Code developed by the International Maritime Organization. The consequences of not being in compliance would likely be a drop-off in global shipping to their ports to transport imports and exports.
- For cargo security, the U.S. government wants individual foreign governments to agree to participate in CSI. A condition of entering into CSI agreements is that the foreign governments purchase and deploy their own NII equipment to scan cargo containers identified by U.S. inspectors as posing a high risk prior to loading them onto U.S.-bound ships. CSI participants are also expected to support the permanent hosting of a team of U.S. customs agents and facilitate their work with local counterparts.
- The U.S. government also wants individual governments to participate in the Megaports Initiative. But unlike CSI, where participants are required to procure NII equipment, the DOE will provide radiation portal detection equipment to them at no cost, as well as training for operating and maintaining that equipment.
- Foreign governments are encouraged to join the PSI, which will allow special teams to be unilaterally deployed by the DOD to intercept illicit nuclear materials that are identified to be within their ports or onboard their flag vessels.
- The U.S. government wants companies involved with imports to adopt the cargo security best practices outlined within the C-TPAT program, for which they will be rewarded with fewer inspections,

but they must also abide by new regulations that mandate the presentation of more detailed advance cargo information.

- Finally, the U.S. government encourages foreign governments to fully abide by the multilateral UN Security Council Resolution 1540 and develop and enforce appropriate legal and regulatory measures to prevent the spread of nuclear weapons and materials to non-state actors. But how they choose to implement the resolution is up to each government to determine.

The lack of strategic coherence in the post-9/11 approach to advancing global supply system security is largely the inevitable outcome of the *ad hoc* nature with which the many new security initiatives were developed and deployed. The authorities that are involved with ports, ships, cargo, counterterrorism, and counterproliferation are spread across an array of U.S. Departments and agencies, with both domestic and foreign policy implications. Given the sense of urgency to redress the many longstanding lapses in trade and transportation security, each agency felt compelled to take actions that drew on the capabilities they thought they could bring to bear. In theory, the National Security Council staff within the White House should have been on the lookout for gaps and redundancies and forged coordination through the interagency process. But during the Bush administration, container security was viewed primarily as a homeland security issue rather than a national security matter, and was assigned a relatively low priority.

Obama identified nuclear proliferation as a top national security priority. During his two terms in office, he hosted four nuclear summits animated by publicly stated concerns over loose nuclear material, nuclear terrorism, and Iranian and North Korean nuclear programs. Nonetheless, his administration did not make any significant changes to the port and cargo security measures inherited from his predecessor. In fact, the interagency review that he called for to assess global trade security programs took more than two years to complete and resulted in the 2012 release of what may be the thinnest strategy document ever issued by the White House. The National Strategy for Global Supply Chain Security is just over five pages, including a one-page executive summary. The strategy outlines as its two goals: promoting efficient and secure movement of goods and fostering a resilient supply chain. The approach is informed by two guiding principles: galvanizing action and managing supply chain risk. The document tasked DHS to lead "a six-month engagement period with the international community and industry stakeholders."[12] This document is a case study on how agencies can successfully create top cover for preserving the status quo by providing vacuous strategic guidance and calling for further engagement.

If the array of U.S. port and cargo security initiatives put in place after September 11, 2001, were individually and collectively effective, then the scattershot way in which they were developed and deployed would be of little consequence. The reality, however, is that each of these programs has serious flaws; combined, they do not pose a significant barrier to an adversary intent on targeting the global supply system. Furthermore, there is a substantial risk that a major security incident will place each program under a glaring spotlight. They will likely be found wanting, and public confidence in the entire security regime will be undermined.

The International Ship and Port Facility Security (ISPS) Code should be applauded on its face for its ambition in establishing worldwide standards that addressed the nearly wholesale neglect of security within the global maritime transportation system. Because any given port basically serves as an on-ramp and off-ramp for cargo moving to other ports, the objective of getting maritime nations to agree collectively on the approach to enhancing port and ship security and then codify it as a resolution within an international convention is an admirable one. Additionally, the code goes beyond requiring that an inbound ship must certify that it is ISPS-compliant. A ship must also be able to confirm that the maritime terminals that it has been in contact with for its last ten port calls are also in compliance with the code. This provides a significant market-based incentive for ships to avoid contact with port facilities that are non-ISPS compliant, as well as pressure on marine terminals and the countries that rely on them to trade with the world to make sure they are assessed as abiding by the code.

The ISPS Code, however, has some serious shortcomings. Its Achilles' heel is that the code overtly sidesteps the issue of cargo security even though the most serious risk connected with the maritime transportation system is derived from the cargo that ships carry. The ISPS provisions relating to port facilities focus solely on the ship and port interface and punt on cargo containers—what the code identifies as "closed cargo transport units" or "closed CTUs." Instead, the International Maritime Organization adopted a resolution on December 12, 2002, that "invites the WCO (World Customs Organization) to consider, urgently, measures to enhance security throughout international movements of closed CTUs."[13]

Security has been improving at many port facilities in no small part because USCG personnel are sent to foreign ports to verify compliance with the ISPS Code. Ports that are found wanting are placed on a kind of probation, which triggers additional security precautions, including requiring a vessel sailing from a non-compliant port to wait in an anchorage until it is boarded by the USCG and provided permission to enter.[14]

C-TPAT and CSI also have serious weaknesses. The carrot of facilitation along with the stick of potential delays associated with stepped-up inspections for non–C-TPAT members led to a rush by members of the trade community to enroll in the program. By 2017, CBP reported that there were 11,400 certified C-TPAT partners that account for over 50 percent of cargo, by value, imported into the United States.[15] The numbers are impressive, but they also underscore the challenge of monitoring so many partners. CBP does not have adequate manpower to provide periodic audits of partners that are certified by C-TPAT. As such, CBP has no way to distinguish between those companies that are making good-faith efforts to implement supply chain security best practices and those that are simply going through the motions. Nor does CBP have adequate resources to step up inspections of companies that opt out of C-TPAT without creating backlogs. As a result, most companies notice no meaningful difference in the number of inspections to which they are subjected, whether they belong to the program or not.

With regard to CSI, one significant limitation is the quality of the risk assessments or "targeting" that informs which shipments CBP selects for inspection. CBP's Automated Targeting System processes cargo and conveyance information that shippers forward electronically twenty-four hours before a container is loaded aboard a vessel bound for a U.S. port and then uses algorithms to assess risk (focusing almost exclusively on terrorism). CBP officers working at the National Targeting Center also check the information against intelligence and law enforcement databases. Potentially dangerous shipments are then examined. If the shipments are hazardous enough to pose a risk to the vessel or the arriving port, they should be examined before leaving the foreign port. If the shipment is suspected of containing contraband, it may be better to intercept it once it arrives in the United States, where the federal authorities have full legal jurisdiction.

This targeting approach is straightforward and seems perfectly logical, but it is not designed to foil a terrorist plot. Criminal organizations strive to find weaknesses in the global trade systems that they can exploit on an ongoing basis, as opposed to the kind of one-off operation that a terrorist group would engage in. Since legitimate companies have safeguards in place for detecting, investigating, and sanctioning employees who violate security protocols, these companies are difficult for criminals to penetrate and any success in doing so is likely to be short-lived. But terrorists need to succeed only once. For this reason, they are likely to find it attractive to compromise a shipment of a legitimate company with a well-known brand name. In other words, they can game the risk-based system.

Another serious limitation of CSI is that not all ports participate in the program. For those that do, foreign customs authorities are responsible for conducting the inspections, and occasionally they resist CBP's recommendations. All told, only a very small number of containers are actually being examined at the 58 CSI ports in the thirty countries where CSI is operating. Based on the last publicly available figures from 2013, there is an average of five examinations per CSI port per day (approximately 290 per day worldwide) for the more than 50,000 TEU that arrive in U.S. ports each day.[16] The overwhelming majority of these— about 80 percent—are examined once they have already arrived at U.S. ports.[17] Should one of those "high risk" shipments end up having a weapon that is set to trigger upon arrival, these inspections will come too late.

With respect to cargo that poses potential threats of nuclear terrorism and proliferation, the post-9/11 programs launched by the DOD, the DOE, and the DOS are also problematic. The DOE's Second Line of Defense program has two serious limitations. First, its focus has been primarily on deploying radiation detection technologies within major seaports and at border crossings, where these radiation detectors are only able to send alarms on unshielded radiological materials.[18] It is difficult to imagine that criminals or terrorists who have gone to significant lengths to obtain nuclear materials or a nuclear weapon would not take the precaution to shield it with a material as commonly available as lead in order to avoid detection. Second, it turns out that what this equipment is quite good at detecting is radioactive waste from medical and industrial devices. Properly disposing of radioactive materials such as cobalt-60, cesium-137, and strontium-90 is quite costly. This makes it tempting to forgo the strict handling and disposal protocols and instead slip these materials into cargo flows where they can be dumped in unsuspecting jurisdictions. Discovering this "nuclear junk" ends up posing a significant challenge for the public or private entities that operate the detection equipment, because they then becomes responsible for safely handling and disposing of these materials. Not surprisingly, this ends up becoming a disincentive to routinely operate these portals and respond to alarms, given the hassle and expense of dealing with these orphaned nuclear materials.

For the PSI (by the DOS and the DOD), the central challenge is that, as a practical matter, it is operationally impossible to gain access to containerized cargo shipments at sea. When containers are stowed, there are only eighteen to twenty-four inches of space between them, within stacks that are ten or more containers deep below decks and as much as twenty containers deep across. Accordingly, having foreign nations agree to allow the DOD to deploy specialized teams while ships are in transit is unworkable, because there is no easy way to open a container's door. Instead, the ship must come into a port in order for a gantry crane to remove the containers stacked on top of and around the suspected container, at which point it would make sense simply to unload it onto the pier for inspection. This reality notwithstanding, the DOD and the DOS have negotiated agreements with more than one hundred countries to participate in the PSI.[19]

To encourage greater international effort in managing the risk of nuclear terrorism, the DOS succeeded in getting the United Nations Security Council to pass Resolution 1540 in 2004. This resolution calls on all UN member-states to "refrain from providing any form of support to non-State actors that attempt to develop, acquire, manufacture, possess, transport, transfer or use nuclear, chemical or biological weapons and their means of delivery, in particular for terrorist purpose."[20] Specifically, member-states are required to adopt and enforce appropriate laws and put in place "other effective measures to prevent the proliferation of these weapons and their means of delivery to non-State actors."[21]

The primary shortcoming of this initiative is that the 1540 Committee is not authorized to confirm compliance by member-states. It can call on member-states to prepare national implementation action plans, but these are done on a voluntary basis. The committee has no dedicated program for guiding member-states on what they should be doing to mitigate the risk of non-state actors transporting WMD through ports within their jurisdictions and across their national borders. In 2011, however, the UN Security Council extended the mandate of the 1540 Committee through 2021.[22]

One might argue that despite the flaws outlined above, which are associated with each of the major post-9/11 trade and transportation security initiatives, these programs can still be judged as an overall success in light of the fact that there has not yet been a WMD incident involving containerized cargo. It may indeed be true that repeated public assurances by officials about the security benefits of these efforts have been accepted at face value by terrorist organizations and have dissuaded them from using a container as a modern-day Trojan horse. But there also have been dramatic breaches that have highlighted the degree to which these controls continued to be circumvented. Three such incidents underscore this reality, given that they involve the most closely regulated segment of the maritime transportation system: the handling of hazardous materials.

First, the M/V Hyundai Fortune was destroyed after a shipboard explosion off the coast of Yemen on March 21, 2006. The source of the explosion was presumed to be a containerized shipment of hazardous materials that was not revealed in the cargo manifest provided to the maritime carrier. The container ended up being inadvertently stowed below deck, where the combination of heat and inadequate ventilation led to the ignition of the hazardous cargo, setting off a chain reaction that destroyed the 5,500-TEU container vessel.

The second event involved a cargo container that arrived in Genoa, Italy, on July 13, 2010, emitting cobalt-60. The source was likely a medical device or a machine used to sterilize food. Since disposing of this kind of industrial -use radioactive material is very expensive, it was likely placed into the container simply to get rid of it without incurring those costs. There was no established protocol for what the terminal operator should do with this highly radioactive waste. The container sat in the port for over a year as Italian authorities pondered what to do with it. After a media report brought attention to this orphaned container, it was finally disposed of with the assistance of the DOE on July 29, 2011.[23]

The third case involved a series of explosions that killed 173 people and injured nearly 800 others on August 12, 2015, in the port of Tianjin, China. The explosions occurred at a container storage station operated by Ruihai Logistics, an approved operator for handling these hazardous materials in the port. The source was likely the improper storage of an overheated container of dry nitrocellulose, which is a highly flammable compound.[24]

These three incidents highlight both the uncomfortable reality that highly dangerous materials continue to evade safeguards within the maritime transportation system and that the consequences can be highly disruptive and destructive. More important, should a terrorist organization decide to put the current security measures to the test by intercepting a container from a "trusted shipper" and inserting a shielded "dirty bomb," the result would likely undermine public confidence in the entire port and container security regime. If such a container held cargo that was likely shipped by a firm that was a C-TPAT participant and if it transited through multiple ISPS-compliant, CSI ports, it would also likely have passed through multiple radiation detectors at border crossings and within seaports without setting off alarms. In the aftermath of such a scenario, the PSI would be exposed as impotent because it could not gain access to suspicious containerized shipments at sea. The multilateral efforts to address this risk at nuclear proliferation summits and through UN Security Council Resolutions would be judged as toothless.

Significantly, the many years of public officials' overstating the efficacy and downplaying the shortcomings of the post-9/11 port and cargo security measures would add fuel to post-incident public anxiety about the dangers posed by uninspected cargo containers. This would be compounded by the fact that Congress passed legislation that Bush signed into law on August 3, 2007, mandating that by 2012, 100 percent of U.S.-bound cargo containers be subjected to non-intrusive imaging and radiation detection equipment prior to their being loaded overseas. The Implementing Recommendations of the 9/11 Commission provided the Secretary of Homeland Security with the authority to delay implementation of the law in two-year increments, which Janet Napolitano did in 2012 and Jeh Johnson did again in 2014 and 2016.[25] Following an incident involving an undetected WMD entering a U.S. port, however, the decade-plus delay in implementing this law would likely generate a serious political backlash. There would be enormous public pressure to implement 100-percent overseas container scanning as a condition for resuming foreign trade, which would be impractical to accomplish in the near term.

The Path Forward

The homeland security enterprise needs a more integrated and comprehensive approach to cargo security. The good news is that there is a path forward that can leverage many of the positive elements of the current array of security initiatives. However, it will require committed leadership, lacking to date, that is capable of forging common ground among the complex array of public and private players who have a stake in global supply system security and resilience.

The first step involves enlisting as full partners the infrastructure owners and operators who directly handle virtually all of the world's maritime containers. Governments do not have routine contact with much of the world's cargo, but there are six major companies that do. APM Terminals (Netherlands), DP World (Dubai), Hutchison Port Holdings (Hong Kong), Port of Rotterdam (Netherlands), Shanghai International Port Group (China), and PSA International (Singapore) combined manage container movements in all of the world's megaports. These companies also operate terminals in many of the smaller regional ports that send containers on to the megaports. This places them in a unique position for helping to devise and implement tools and applications for enhancing the visibility and accountability of the cargo that passes through their facilities and transforming such a regime into the industry-wide standard.

The world's largest port terminal operators have a direct commercial interest in the reliable functioning of the global supply system, because a major security breach would generate massive disruption to intermodal logistics. Additionally, should this nightmare scenario come to pass, it is very much in their interest to be widely seen as a force for good that has been actively working to manage the threat, as opposed to being on the receiving end of public recriminations and draconian new security requirements when the post-mortem reveals longstanding security lapses.

If the major global port operators are so well-positioned to play a meaningful role in bolstering the security of the global supply system, why have they largely remained on the sidelines? First, they have not been asked. U.S. officials have been more comfortable collaborating with their public-sector counterparts than reaching out to the industry leaders who run companies headquartered outside of the United States. Second, because the supply system is global, the approach must be global as well so that it can be consistently applied across the entire maritime transportation industry. Third, there is a collective action challenge. As private entities, port operators are not in a position to invest independently in additional security measures without a universal mandate for doing so. This is because a company ends up placing itself at a competitive disadvantage if it tries to absorb or pass along added security costs when its commercial counterparts can elect not to make such investments.

These issues can be resolved by centering port and cargo security measures around the universal counterproliferation requirement set forth in UN Security Council Resolution 1540. Under this mandate, nation-states are supposed to be developing and maintaining "appropriate effective border controls and law enforcement efforts to detect, deter, prevent and combat ... the illicit trafficking" in nuclear, chemical, or biological weapons and their means of delivery.[26] Putting these controls in place would also enhance the ability of states to deal with other threats such as contraband smuggling, cargo theft, and customs fraud, because living up to security obligations would require the routine NII of containerized shipments being transported from their jurisdictions—inspection that could be used to identify ordinary smuggling.

The 1540 Committee is tasked with engaging with relevant international organizations and forging effective partnerships with the private sector and industry so as "to support national and international efforts to meet the objectives of the resolution."[27] Accordingly, the 1540 Committee would be well within its mandate to work with the International Maritime Organization on incorporating the counterproliferation requirement into the ISPS Code.

Specifically, the guidance contained in Part B of the ISPS Code should include recommended practices for ensuring that the containerized cargo entering port facilities does not pose a WMD risk to the ships and crews transporting that cargo. This would have the constructive effect of making the maritime industry a partner in cargo security while simultaneously establishing common standards for the entire global maritime transportation system. Because the ISPS Code applies to all ports engaged in foreign trade, major port operators would have an incentive to devise uniform approaches that they can embed into their worldwide operations. They would also have the means for recovering the costs associated with stepped-up security measures, because the ISPS Code authorizes port terminals to levy a Terminal Security Charge to offset the expense of deploying and maintaining the measures necessary to comply with its code. This charge is incorporated into the price of moving freight.[28]

The principal tenet of the new Part B guidance should be that port operators must verify that the cargo that is passing through its seaports is safe. One crucial step would be for port operators to routinely scan all containers entering their facilities in order to confirm that the contents do not pose a security risk to the terminal, the ship, and the crew. The logic of making this fundamental shift—from a default of no inspection to a default of inspection—derives from the fact that it is easier to prove a negative than a positive. That is, in order for a container to pose a risk of nuclear terrorism, it would have to contain both radioactive material and shielding to prevent detection of that material. A radiation portal monitor can determine the presence of radiation, but the contents of the container would need to be scanned in order to identify heavy metals with sufficient density that can provide shielding to defeat radiation detectors. These metals would need to be made of lead or another chemical element with a high atomic number, generally referred to as "high-Z" materials. Accordingly, the use of NII could be largely automated. If a container driven through a radiation detection and scanning portal had neither radioactivity nor high-Z materials—and the overwhelming majority of containers do not—it could be automatically cleared to be stored in the container yard or transferred directly for loading aboard another vessel.

If inspections to support the interception of more traditional contraband such as drugs, currency, or counterfeit goods are done at the port of arrival instead of the port of loading, it should be possible to routinely subject containers to NII before they are shipped without creating any meaningful delays to cargo handling. Such contraband is unlikely to pose a direct threat to the safety of terminals or container ships, so it does not need to be interdicted before loading. Furthermore, the laws defining contraband are not universal; this means that goods are potentially legal in the exporting jurisdiction even though they are illegal in the importing jurisdiction. Accordingly, it makes sense to house the locus of enforcement at the port of arrival, where customs officials can use the risk management tools normally available to them, augmented by the additional data provided by the non-intrusive image captured at the port of loading.

Of course, the contents of some containers would set off the radioactive or high-Z alarm, and port operators would have to have protocols in place for handling those situations. The approach should be to immediately direct a container that triggers an alarm to be transferred to a secondary inspection area for further scanning of its contents by more sensitive NII equipment. In most instances, this more detailed examination would resolve the concern in minutes and the container could then be cleared to be transferred back into the yard in time to make its scheduled onward voyage. This additional scanning data could also be forwarded to customs inspectors in destination ports to supplement their information.

The NII technology continues to improve. Particularly promising are new passive system technologies first invented at Los Alamos National Laboratory. The current version allows for automated alerts on radioactive material, material discrimination based on density and automated material identification alerts, and a machine-learning library that can support the continued refinement of algorithms to interpret imaging accurately.[29]

In the rare instances where alarms cannot be resolved by the secondary inspection scanning, the protocol would be for officials in both the loading and destination ports to be alerted and to move the container to a secure holding area where its contents could be inspected by local officials or in collaboration with CSI teams that the United States has deployed overseas. Breaking the containers' seals to gain physical assess to the containers' contents would only be done by authorized inspectors.

When it comes to integrating NII equipment into port operations, industry managers are best positioned to address the operations management and system engineering issues. Embedding drive-through portals into the terminal gate structure is relatively straightforward. Placing the equipment in the container yard or quayside to support the scanning of transshipment containers is a more complicated traffic management challenge, but not an insurmountable one because the images can typically be collected in less than a minute.

Beyond deploying equipment to routinely collect images of a container's content, port operators should also implement the secure data management processes that can support the automatic transfer of NII data to officials who may be interested in reviewing it. The objective should be for this data to be shared as soon as it is collected. Rapid sharing ensures that government agents can exercise oversight of the port operators or (more likely) the bonded third-party entities that operators contract with to manage the on-the-ground container-screening process. Having direct access to this data would also allow government inspectors to examine images of cargo that they have determined might pose a high risk before it is loaded. In this way, they could resolve their concerns without needing to alert the port operator or even the local government. In the case of contraband, they may also decide to allow the container to move through the supply system unmolested to gather intelligence and secure evidence of trafficking without alerting the criminal conspirators.

It is the capacity that automatic scanning of all containers provides to "pull bits" instead of "pulling boxes" that can make it cost-effective. In the first comprehensive analytical and technical assessment of the operational impact of container inspections in international ports, a 2010 study collected detailed data on the movement of more than 900,000 individual containers at two of the world's largest international container terminals. The project used these records as the basis for a simulation analysis that estimated the effect of a number of inspection protocols on terminal operations. Containers typically arrive two to three days before their voyage, so by the time they are identified for inspection by U.S. customs officials, they are almost always already sitting in a stack in the container yard, waiting to be loaded onto a container ship. Containers are typically stacked up to six high in most major ports. This translates into the need to lift and move the containers on top of a targeted container out of the way in order to transport it. The container must then be placed on drayage to be carried to the customs inspection facility, await scanning, and then be transported back to the stack. The 2010 study calculated that the cost of these inspections would average $110 each and could create significant backlogs at inspection facilities if overseas officials were directed to inspect as little as 5 percent of U.S.-bound cargo at any given time using CSI protocol. The study also determined that automatically scanning all containers upon arrival would be more operationally efficient, with the inspection cost being covered by a $15 per container Terminal Security Charge.[30]

In some instances, the NII detection equipment may identify nuclear waste that is being illegally dumped. Currently, there is no established protocol for disposing of these extremely hazardous materials, which also pose the risk of finding their way into the hands of terrorist organizations who are looking to fabricate a nuclear dispersal devise or "dirty bomb." Working with the International Atomic Energy Agency (IAEA), the updated guidelines for Part B of the ISPS Code could establish appropriate handling and disposal procedures that could be undertaken by a specialized hazardous material team. The cost of deploying these teams could also be incorporated into the Terminal Security Charge.

An additional benefit of the approach outlined above is that it would allow the U.S. Secretary of Homeland Security to certify overseas ports to be compliant with the 100 percent NII scanning mandate embedded in the 2007 Implementing the 9/11 Commission Recommendations Act. It would also require U.S. ports to similarly monitor outbound container traffic, defusing a longstanding complaint by foreign governments about the lack of reciprocity when the United States often imposes security requirements on its trade partners.

To summarize, global supply system security and resilience can be advanced by undertaking the following five actions:

1. Linking the currently disconnected global counterproliferation mandate established by UN Security Council Resolution 1540 and global port security requirements embedded in the ISPS Code so that nations abide by uniform standards.

2. Inviting the world's major port operators to actively partner with governments, the International Maritime Organization, the IAEA, and the World Customs Organization in providing recommended guidance to be placed within Part B of the ISPS Code for uniform, performance-based standards for NII equipment to be used in maritime terminals.

3. Creating the means for the world's major port operators to provide the data collected by NII equipment to government officials at both the port of loading and the port of arrival as requested. This includes securely sharing and storing all NII data for an agreed-upon time period.

4. Authorizing bonded third parties to partner with governments to address and resolve alarms generated by NII equipment when they occur.

5. Allowing port operators to levy an estimated $15 to $20 per container as part of the authorized Terminal Security Charge to support the cost of security upgrades.

Conclusion

Given the longstanding vulnerabilities of the global supply system, it is surprising that it has not been targeted or exploited by terrorist organizations in the way that passenger aviation, air cargo, mass transit, and, more recently, trucks have been. But the absence of attacks to date should not be cause for complacency. The stakes associated with safeguarding the intermodal transportation system are enormous given that the overwhelming majority of the world's manufactured goods move through that system. In an age of "just-in-time" inventories, the weeks-long disruption to supply chains that a major security breach is likely to generate would have devastating economic consequences as well as real human costs, given that life-sustaining medical supplies also rely on this system.

The relative lack of progress on this critical issue can be attributed to three important shortcomings associated with the post-9/11 measures to bolster cargo and port security. First is the uncoordinated way in which U.S. agencies and Departments pursued their respective security initiatives. Second, no meaningful effort was made to enlist global port operators as active partners in developing and sustaining the protocols for managing the security risk associated with containerized cargo. Third, there is a pervasive lack of understanding by policymakers of the economic and operational realities that animate the global supply system.

Despite these constraints, the building blocks are largely in place for assembling a comprehensive and sustainable approach to improving cargo and port security. The latest generation of NII technology, big data, and decision-support tools can reinforce the routine confirmation that low-risk containerized cargo is indeed low risk. UN Security Council Resolution 1540 and the ISPS Code provide an international mandate and a framework for pursuing a comprehensive system-wide approach. Finally, programs such as C-TPAT, CSI, and the PSI have fostered private-public and multinational collaboration that can be leveraged in taking global supply system security to a new level.

The primary missing ingredient in moving from where we are to where we need to be is leadership. A comprehensive approach will also require close collaboration and coordination among major trading nations who share an interest in global supply system resilience. Also key to the effort is a willingness on the part of the CEOs of the world's largest port operators to commit to playing an active partnership role. All of this is achievable if there is a shared willingness to acknowledge that more can and must be done to safeguard one of the world's most critical infrastructures.

CHAPTER 8

Rethinking Transportation Security

Peter Neffenger and Richard Ades

With my signature, this act of Congress will create a new Department of Homeland Security, ensuring that our efforts to defend this country are comprehensive and united . . . the new Department will bring together the agencies responsible for border, coastline, and transportation security. There will be a coordinated effort to safeguard our transportation systems and to secure the border so that we're better able to protect our citizens and welcome our friends.[1]

THE GLOBAL TRANSPORTATION NETWORK UNDERPINS AMERICA'S economy. Each day in the United States alone more than two million travelers on average pass through checkpoints at some 450 U.S. commercial service airports. All told, "personal, business, and government purchases of transportation goods and services accounted for 8.9 percent of U.S. gross domestic product in 2014."[2] An efficient and integrated transportation network gives firms access to materials and markets, thereby making economies of scale in production commercially valuable, and gives people the opportunity to travel for business or pleasure. However, people's ability to move about freely and in some cases anonymously, and to ship goods everywhere—in other words, the very efficiency and openness of the transportation system—creates critical vulnerabilities.

Collective approaches to transportation security across the United States are a direct outgrowth of the events of September 11, 2001. Transportation provided the weapon of 9/11 and was central to the success of Al-Qaeda's strategy that day. Transportation offered the means (*aircraft*) and the instrument (*aircraft as weapons*) for Al-Qaeda and its operatives to strike at America.[3] Transportation also provided the mechanism for the nineteen hijackers to travel and coordinate their plot.

If the 9/11 attacks were the catalyst for the subsequent and ongoing national dialogue about the protection of the U.S. homeland, then concern about transportation security was arguably the imperative for the creation of the Department of Homeland Security (DHS). Concerns about transportation security continue to strongly influence DHS policy and decision-making, particularly in light of the role of transportation systems in border control and immigration.

In this chapter we provide an overview of federal efforts at transportation security as those efforts have developed in the years since 9/11, primarily under DHS auspices. We argue that transportation security as currently defined and deployed in the United States is no longer sufficient to address the terrorist threat as it has evolved, in part because current security regimes have been largely bolted on to existing transportation systems and have not advanced to become fully integrated into the transportation environment. Moreover, current approaches to transportation security have been heavily weighted toward aviation, with particular emphasis on protecting aircraft, whereas the threats have become ever more diffuse and distributed across the various transportation modes.

We then outline some of the key challenges facing security professionals and suggest a strategic framework for rethinking transportation security in order to design more integrated, holistic, and continuously evolving security systems. In so doing, we highlight the various authorities that have given rise to current strategic and operational thinking and discuss the evolving nature and challenge of the terrorist threat. We point to a few of the promising new technologies and approaches to security that illustrate the innovative thinking that is challenging the current system architecture and could lead to a wholesale transformation of security across the nation's transportation systems. Finally, we emphasize that all security systems must anticipate and prepare for the potential for terrorists to succeed on occasion; therefore, response, recovery, and resilience must be integral to the design of security systems.

Changes in Transportation Security after 9/11

Transportation as a target of terror is not new. During the three decades preceding September 11, 2001, there were 1,343 terrorist attacks worldwide on airports, airlines, maritime, or other transportation targets; sixty-eight of these attacks occurred in the United States.[4] But there was something new, sinister, and more alarming about the 9/11 attacks. That "something new" was the recognition that transportation could serve not only as a facilitator and target of terrorism, but also as a weapon.

This recognition invalidated an entire set of assumptions that had previously informed transportation security in the United States—a set of assumptions that had largely viewed transportation security as the responsibility of the private sector, public operating agencies, and local authorities. Transportation security in the United States had been disaggregated, piecemeal, and distributed among multiple jurisdictions and entities. Enforcement was inconsistent; information generally not shared; federal oversight limited; and national strategic planning absent with respect to the security of aviation, maritime, or surface transportation. Aviation security, in particular, had been viewed primarily as protection of aircraft from hijackers and was considered the responsibility of airline companies, with passenger screening carried out primarily by independent contractors to individual airlines (as compared with aviation *safety*, which had long been carefully and directly regulated by the federal government).

Two initial steps after 9/11 were the establishment of the Transportation Security Administration (TSA) within the Department of Transportation in November 2001 and a rapid reorientation of the U.S. Coast Guard (USCG) toward maritime security as a primary mission, with reduced emphasis on traditional missions of drug interdiction, search and rescue, regulation of commercial shipping, and protection of the marine environment. By the time the USCG was transferred from the Department of Transportation to the newly formed DHS in March 2003, it was laser-focused on maritime security and counterterrorism—mission areas not emphasized since World War II. The cultural change within the USCG was profound and was vividly reflected in the service's bumper sticker change from "The Lifesavers" to "The Guardians."

AVIATION SECURITY

Whereas the USCG asserted its responsibility for direct oversight of maritime security, overall responsibility for transportation security in the United States was specifically given to TSA, an agency that was also transferred to DHS in March 2003. Congress had established TSA within the Department of Transportation in the immediate aftermath of the 9/11 attacks expressly to create a federal agency with the authority to direct and oversee collective approaches to the security of the transportation systems of the United States. Of paramount concern was the aviation system (including the operation of airport passenger and baggage screening), over which TSA was given direct responsibility, in addition to indirect oversight of maritime and surface transportation. TSA was also given responsibility for the Federal Air Marshal

Service (FAMS), a federal law enforcement agency specifically tasked with protecting commercial aircraft in flight.

The National Strategy for Aviation Security defines the aviation system as "a broad spectrum of private and public-sector elements, including: aircraft and airport operators; over 19,800 private and public use airports; the aviation sector; and a dynamic system of facilities, equipment, services, and airspace."[5] This expansive definition encompasses all possible entities and activities in and around aviation. The federal government's role in aviation security is specifically delineated by the Aviation and Transportation Security Act (Public Law 107–71, November 19, 2001), the act that established TSA as the federal agency with direct responsibility for the security of the aviation system, especially commercial passenger and cargo-carrying aircraft.

MARITIME SECURITY

As with aviation, the National Strategy for Maritime Security defines the maritime domain as "all areas and things of, on, under, relating to, adjacent to, or bordering on a sea, ocean, or other navigable waterway, including all maritime-related activities, infrastructure, people, cargo, and vessels and other conveyances."[6] Maritime security had long been a narrowly defined responsibility of the USCG, primarily focused on protection of critical maritime ports, facilities, and operations during times of conflict. The 9/11 attacks brought renewed concern about the potential for maritime transportation to be used not only to facilitate the movement of terrorists and their weapons, but also for the possibility that water-borne vessels could be used as weapons in a manner similar to the way in which aircraft had been used to attack the United States.

This concern about maritime security ultimately led to the passage of the Maritime Transportation Security Act of 2002 (Public Law 107–295, November 25, 2002). This act significantly expanded the USCG's authority with respect to the security of the commercial maritime industry and that industry's activities within the jurisdiction of the United States. Among its many provisions, the act required vessel owners and operators to develop USCG-approved security plans for their ships, establish security credentialing and training standards for people employed in maritime industries, install fences and access controls for port areas and terminals (including locked gates and barriers, positive ID checks for employees in the form of the Transportation Worker Identification Credential,[7] and continuous escorts of visitors within seaport facilities), create a national security exercise program, deploy more extensive and comprehensive cargo and personnel reporting requirements for vessels en route to U.S. ports, and develop a national system for signaling the relative level of security threat to any given port area.[8] It further extended specific security requirements to foreign ports interacting with vessels bound for U.S. waters. The USCG also led the development and implementation of the International Ship and Port Facility Security (ISPS) Code under the auspices of the International Maritime Organization (IMO). The ISPS Code, which entered into force on July 1, 2004, built upon longstanding protocols and agreements regarding maritime safety and established a corresponding international framework for global maritime security.[9]

Customs and Border Protection (CBP) also plays a role in maritime security—specifically with respect to tracking, targeting, and inspecting maritime cargo and vetting foreign crews against terrorist databases. Two programs in particular focus on preventing terrorists from exploiting the maritime supply chain: the Container Security Initiative (CSI) and the Customs-Trade Partnership Against Terrorism (C-TPAT). Much of the information gathered and operations generated by these programs are coordinated through CBP's National Targeting Center (NTC) in Sterling, Virginia, which performs the daily work of targeting, tracking, and identifying cargo and individuals of interest or concern.[10] CBP is also responsible for implementation of the World Customs Organization's SAFE Framework of standards to secure global trade in the United States.[11]

One of the overarching concerns of DHS has been the potential for terrorists to use the maritime supply chain to facilitate the movement and use of weapons of mass destruction (WMD) by terrorists. DHS's Countering Weapons of Mass Destruction Office, established in December 2018, coordinates and supports the efforts of the USCG and CBP to identify and track WMD as a key element of national maritime security.[12] In total, the authorities, programs, operations, and efforts noted above have resulted in a maritime security regime that is among the most comprehensive and consistent globally in both application and implementation across all transportation modes.[13]

SURFACE TRANSPORTATION SECURITY

Land transportation is the most diverse of the three primary modes, consisting of heavy rail (freight and passenger), mass transit systems (trolleys, subways, streetcars, city buses, etc.), motor coaches (Greyhound, Trailways, and the like), hazardous materials conveyances (primarily tractor-trailer trucks and rail cars), and interstate pipelines. According to the U.S. Bureau of Transportation Statistics (BTS), there are nearly 4,000 rail stations, approximately two million miles of pipelines, and more than 600,000 bridges in the United States.

There has been increased federal engagement and involvement since 9/11 by TSA through its Surface Transportation Program,[14] through which the agency develops and distributes security training courses and materials, helps to administer DHS security grants programs to state and local transportation systems, and oversees a national security exercise and evaluation program. That said, nearly all of the direct responsibility for the security of the various means of surface transport still remains in the hands of other federal, state, and local agencies; local law enforcement entities; and the private sector. Indeed, there is, as of this writing, no national security strategy for surface transportation and its many diverse components.

In 2007, Congress passed and the president signed into law the Implementing Recommendations of the 9/11 Commission Act of 2007 (Public Law 110-53, August 3, 2007), in part to address the perceived lack of national focus on surface transportation security. Among its many provisions, it called for specific additional federal security oversight, as well as identification and coordination by TSA of security training for the various surface modes of transportation. TSA has yet to publish regulations to implement many of the requirements called for by this act. There are two primary reasons. First, unlike in the aviation system, TSA was not given direct responsibility for ensuring security for the various surface modes. Security, as noted, is distributed among various other federal, state, and local entities. This distributed responsibility results in a multitude of approaches to security, complicates oversight, and slows the development of federal regulations required to implement the law in that many more voices must be considered in the course of developing new regulations and requirements. The multiplicity of voices further dilutes the sense of urgency in considering any specific approach. Second, the relative level of risk of terrorist attacks across the various forms of surface transportation is still relatively low compared with aviation, especially in the United States.[15] Hence, there is less urgency within DHS to seek modifications to a system that generally looks satisfactory and well-managed in its current form.

ASSESSMENT OF TRANSPORTATION SECURITY

Of the three modes of transportation, TSA's day-to-day efforts remain overwhelmingly focused on threats to the aviation system. Aviation still holds the greatest potential for catastrophic impact—both psychological and economic. Terrorists still consider airlines and airports to be high-value targets, and the global aviation system (especially commercial passenger aircraft) remains a primary target of every global terrorist network. That has not changed since 9/11.[16]

It follows, then, that the most restrictive and intensive security procedures are in place in and around commercial airports and aircraft. The procedures and equipment in the aviation security system focus on infrastructure, cargo, and people. They consist of:

- physical perimeter barriers, such as hardened bollards and Jersey barriers (K rail) along roadways, fences, and locked access doors;
- surveillance cameras on access roads, throughout airport terminals, at secure access points, and in the checkpoint environment;
- access controls in the form of TSA checks of passenger IDs and boarding passes, in addition to employee secure-access badges and controlled-access privileges;
- physical and virtual passenger screening through vetting of passenger names against terrorist databases;[17]
- the detection of prohibited items through the use of metal detectors, on-person imaging technology to detect metallic and non-metallic devices, explosive trace detection, bottled liquid scanners, x-ray and computed tomography scanners for carry-on and checked baggage, and extensive use of bomb-sniffing dogs (also used to screen cargo intended for air shipment);
- periodic FBI and law enforcement background investigations of airline and airport employees;
- local airport security plans; and
- shared threat intelligence among federal, state, and local law enforcement and national intelligence agencies.

In addition, there are aviation security training and exercise requirements, along with periodic TSA oversight inspections and testing to ensure required security processes and procedures are in place and operating as intended.

The Federal Air Marshal Service (FAMS) has also grown and expanded. Originally comprising eighteen or so volunteers from within the Federal Aviation Administration (FAA), FAMS traces its origin to March 1962 and President John F. Kennedy's order to protect certain high-risk commercial flights. Responsibility for populating and operating the Air Marshal program expanded at times from the FAA to the former U.S. Customs Service and the U.S. Department of the Treasury. Following 9/11, FAMS was specifically designated a federal law enforcement agency and placed as a semi-autonomous entity within TSA. The number of federal air marshals has grown considerably from the handful in existence prior to 9/11, and today consists of several thousands of agents whose primary mission is still to protect commercial passenger aircraft from terrorists.[18] Beginning in 2004, however, federal air marshal responsibilities expanded to include the operation of teams of air marshals and TSA officers known as Visible Intermodal Prevention and Response (VIPR, pronounced "viper") teams. VIPR teams, authorized by the Implementing Recommendations of The 9/11 Commission Act of 2007 (Public Law 110-53, Title XIII, Section 1303), focus on providing an overt and highly visible federal law enforcement presence, primarily in surface transportation venues and particularly during high visibility events. Given the critical national importance of transportation systems, having a sworn federal law enforcement capability exclusively focused on transportation security allows for direct liaison with other law enforcement agencies, rapid response to transportation incidents, and the ability to detain and arrest those who plot against or harm travelers and transportation systems.[19]

Much of this current aviation security system evolved from the many disparate and inconsistent approaches in place prior to 9/11 and was mostly added onto existing infrastructure. New, larger, and more equipment-centered passenger screening checkpoints were shoehorned into airport terminals that had not been designed with security in mind. Equipment-intensive checked baggage screening systems were retrofitted into existing baggage transport systems, often straining the ability of the infrastructure to accommodate the new equipment. Once the new systems (passenger screening checkpoints, checked-baggage screening devices, and the like) were in place, they became the defining system for the future. Modifications to airports had to accommodate the systems already in place.

Perhaps most interesting, the aviation security system is still designed primarily to protect the aircraft itself from harm. It is a system that has performed well in defending aircraft against attacks by terrorists, organized or otherwise. But it is a system that is fundamentally reactive in nature—one that generally responds to the latest threat by instituting methods to counter that threat. For example, metal detectors were installed to stop guns and knives from being carried onto airplanes, and terrorists countered with non-metallic devices for which metal detectors were of little value. Systems were then developed and deployed to detect non-metallic items, following which terrorists devised liquid explosives that could be disguised in everyday items such as bottled drinks, shampoos, and other everyday liquids. This resulted in the deployment of bottled liquid scanner technology coupled with regulations banning liquids in containers exceeding 3.4 liquid ounces (100 milliliters) from being carried onto aircraft. This cycle continues, and it puts enormous responsibility and pressure on security personnel and first responders to identify and react to threats in real time.

In contrast to aviation, security systems and responsibilities in maritime and surface transportation are distributed among many stakeholders. In its oversight role, TSA establishes guidelines and relies upon many private- and public-sector agencies and entities throughout the nation to ensure security.[20] Although many of the same systems are in use—perimeter barriers, access controls, surveillance systems, and the like—they are far less intrusive or extensive than those used in commercial aviation. Maritime and surface transportation systems are, by definition, more open and accessible, and imposing aviation-style security in its current form would likely cripple the efficiency and capacity of these systems as they are currently designed and operated.

Perhaps understandably, aviation security generates the most concern among citizens and attracts the most intense oversight from the federal government. Aviation security in the form of TSA is the retail face of government—where the federal government most directly and consistently interacts with the daily lives of the traveling public. While acknowledging that each transportation mode has its own unique challenges, aviation provides for a visible real-time laboratory for techniques and systems that may be generally applicable and transferable to the surface and maritime modes, in addition to informing approaches to the larger challenge of protecting the open venues and public spaces which have increasingly been targets of opportunity for terrorists to attack. Changes to the aviation security system can be immediately noticed. Moreover, many of the concepts, technologies, and systems in place or in development today will likely form the underpinnings of the holistic approach to transportation security described later in this chapter.

The Evolving Threat

More than a decade ago, the National Strategy for Aviation Security observed that the terrorist threat was continuously evolving, "changing in form and intensity as terrorists' intentions and capabilities change and counter-measures are instituted." Noting terrorists' adaptability, flexibility, and complexity, the report concluded that "the type, location and frequency of terrorist attacks cannot be reliably extrapolated from historical patterns, and therefore current threats must be regularly reassessed."[21] Notably, that was in 2007. It was an assessment issued well before the widespread use of social media, which has perhaps illustrated terrorist evolution and adaptability the most vividly. Indeed, Twitter was in its infancy, Facebook was new, and Instagram was still on the drawing board; these are now three of the social media platforms that have become important tools for terrorists to use to communicate, motivate, and activate.[22]

Today's threat environment is in many ways more dynamic, profound, and complex than ever before, and certainly more so than the one faced when DHS came into being. Transportation systems are still high on terrorist target lists, and the threat picture today presents a multitude of configurations and pathways, with domestic radicalization increasing. Today, the global threat to transportation is from a diffuse and dispersed enemy that manipulates communications and media, not only to direct attacks but also to inspire, enable, coordinate, and claim credit. Terrorists are entrepreneurial, exceptionally adaptable, and creative by nature—the very embodiment of asymmetry. To defeat them, everyone involved in transportation security must be even more entrepreneurial, adaptive, and creative.

This is all the more important as the timeframe from idea to action has been compressing, which leaves less time, and hence fewer opportunities, for attacks to be thwarted. Perhaps the most frightening and difficult to predict are the increasing number of seemingly sudden attacks by terrorists driving vehicles into random crowds of pedestrians. In 2016 and 2017, such attacks occurred in London, New York City, Barcelona, Stockholm, Berlin, Jerusalem, and Columbus, Ohio.[23] Attacks on transportation and public gatherings create great spectacle, sow fear and panic among the populace, generate dramatic headlines and video, destroy lives, and cause significant economic loss and disruption.

Arguably, a turning point in TSA's thinking about transportation security occurred on March 22, 2016, the day of the terrorist attacks on the Brussels airport and metro systems.[24] While over the years airports around the world have effectively created perimeters and secure areas within airports and around airplanes and airport operations areas, the attacks in Brussels demonstrated that perimeter barriers and checkpoints are not sufficient to stop or deter terrorists. The Brussels airport bombers never attempted to pass through the passenger checkpoint. Perimeters and barriers are good at protecting things such as aircraft and secure areas within terminals that are beyond the checkpoint. But the aircraft and secure areas are not the only parts of the system that need protection, or that are vulnerable to attack. Open, public, non-secure areas can also be exploited by terrorists, and the Brussels attacks were a tragic illustration of this lesson.[25]

Toward a New Security Architecture

In the years since the National Strategy for Aviation Security assessment cited above, much has been done to address terrorist threats to the United States. Massive resources from federal, state, local, and tribal governments and the private sector have been marshaled toward a broad national approach to the challenges of terrorism. Intelligence capabilities at the federal, state, and local levels have been more fully integrated across the nation, and new security technologies have been introduced. These technologies include more advanced uses of biometrics for identification, more comprehensive camera surveillance throughout security-sensitive venues, greatly improved screening and imaging equipment throughout the aviation system, improved means of identifying and targeting of maritime cargo of concern, and the use of large-scale imaging equipment to screen maritime containers. The vastly improved national interagency intelligence network has become nimbler at both sharing and acting upon intelligence—determining threats and instituting processes to better address and neutralize those threats.[26] Indeed, intelligence and information sharing has become fundamental to understanding how to better predict the types and locations of terrorist attacks—learning who and where the groups and individuals of interest are; determining their targets and their plans for attack; and defining and prioritizing critical infrastructure in order to understand and mitigate the vulnerabilities of that infrastructure.

However, much of the current design of transportation security systems, particularly at airports, remains focused on preventing "things"—guns, improvised explosive devices, knives, liquids, and the like—from being brought into secure areas or aboard commercial aircraft. Indeed, aviation security still relies heavily upon checkpoints and barriers to deter, detect, and disrupt terrorists by finding prohibited items and preventing them from being carried through. Security systems are, of course, always interested in identifying the people who might try to get something past security. Agencies within DHS (CBP, TSA, the USCG), along with other government agencies (the National Counterterrorism Center and the Terrorist Screening Center) examine passenger manifests, scrutinize flight crews, and track known or suspected terrorists, in addition to encouraging travelers to sign up for DHS trusted traveler programs such as CBP's Global Entry or TSA's Pre✓. These voluntary programs help in identifying low-risk travelers by collecting identity information and conducting background checks against criminal and terrorist databases—ideally, separating travelers who need less attention from those who may warrant more. Although these programs are still limited in enrollment, they provide the seeds for a more holistic, integrated approach, as discussed further below.

Transportation security can, and must, evolve from a system focused primarily on cordoning off and protecting certain areas and objects to one in which security is integrated into the very architecture of the ecosystem. The current approach puts considerable pressure on checkpoints and barriers, especially in aviation.[27] For example, airport checkpoints screen every traveler (even those in the existing trusted traveler programs), despite the fact that the overwhelming majority of people moving through the system pose minimal security risk. Of course, there will likely always be a need for checkpoints and security barriers to conduct physical checks, including pat-downs when necessary, in addition to serving as visible deterrents. Indeed, TSA remains hard at work fielding new technologies that improve detection at the checkpoints and increase efficiency to meet the needs of a burgeoning air travel population.

But successful security systems also incorporate a disaggregated and distributed approach to their design. What if the bulk of low-risk travelers could be identified as low-risk in a more comprehensive and effective manner, and well before the checkpoint, thus relieving pressure by reducing the extent to which known travelers need to be screened? This could enable the checkpoint to focus on the few people about whom less is known, or about whom concerns have been identified.

Consider the manner in which safety is woven into the fabric of daily life. One seldom thinks about the design of highway systems, for example. Yet the size, location, and design of highway signage, the width and marking of highway lanes, the length of exit lanes—all are designed to more effectively engage drivers, lessen distraction, and dramatically reduce the risk of accidents without hindering traffic flow. The evolution of aviation safety is also instructive on this point. One seldom considers, or even understands, how fully the systems and culture of safety are integrated into every aspect of the aviation system—except perhaps during the inflight safety briefing. Similarly, transportation security systems need to evolve such that security culture is as fully integrated and as often unseen as that of safety.

Today security professionals are developing systems that seamlessly and discreetly collect and integrate information about users of the transportation system (travelers, employees, shippers, and so forth) from "reservation to destination," providing visibility and identities of travelers and other system users throughout their journeys. Such systems would be able to assign risk categories based upon how much was known about any individual or thing (such as cargo) moving through the system. This risk-based approach would seek to "subtract" known or trusted travelers and cargo from categories of concern in order to focus on those about whom less is known. The vast majority of people and goods would be expected to move through with minimal inconvenience.

One of the most significant challenges in building such a system is ensuring the privacy and protection of personal information. It is no small matter to ask people to voluntarily share personal information about themselves and their travels, to ask them to trust the owners and operators of the system to protect that information from compromise or misuse, and to further trust that their information will be used responsibly and only for the purpose of ensuring transportation security—and only for the duration of their travels.

There is an understandable concern over how personal data is used and controlled by both the government and the private sector.[28] People supply vital, personal financial information to the government when filing taxes; they are required to do so. People willingly, if at times grudgingly, provide sensitive personal information to a myriad of private-sector entities, from shopkeepers to large corporations to financial institutions, in order to transact business. People also freely share detailed personal information across social media platforms, often resigned to the fact that they have little awareness or influence about the ways in which the information provided will be used or protected. The increase in the unauthorized use and security breaches of personal information are major issues with which both the government and the private sector are grappling. Future transportation security systems must address these concerns in order to develop a system rooted in the trust that is at the heart of a free and open society, and one that is safeguarded by a transparent system of checks and balances.

Rethinking Transportation Security

Governments and security experts have become adept at looking in the rearview mirror to analyze what happened and reconstruct the actions leading up to an attack. Security professionals subsequently do a good job of designing new processes and procedures to prevent similar kinds of attacks from happening again. Countermeasures to terrorist tactics are, of course, necessary. Security is additive, as terrorists have not been known to remove a tool from their kit. A security system that changes based primarily on reaction to the most recent attack, however, is a security system that will eventually fail. As events have demonstrated, adversaries are constantly adapting and evolving—devising new means of attack and developing new tactics, techniques, and procedures for using those new means. Success against these evolving tactics demands systems that anticipate and predict—systems that think differently about how to approach the security of the movement of people and things, the overwhelming majority of which pose little or no risk.

To answer the need that current and future challenges present, a holistic approach would evolve transportation venues from a reliance on providing points of security to developing a continuous flow of security—both seen and unseen—to create a security ecosystem. It entails expanding the focus from primarily protecting the conveyances of transportation systems to one that seeks to understand and secure the movements and flows of people and goods. As previously noted, the U.S. government already has a formidable intelligence network that coordinates efforts nationally and with global partners to detect and disrupt attacks. The key to the future of transportation security is to use information and intelligence to implement systems that can include the ability to identify anomalies within and among the people and goods moving through the system, with the potential to detect malicious intent before adversaries can act.

There are three core elements that form the foundation of an effective transportation security system:

- Visibility: seeing the people and things of concern or interest that are moving through the system;
- Identity: knowing who and what those people and things are as they move through the system; and
- Purpose: knowing why those people and things are there.

Knowing where someone is, who they are, and why they are there allows for a determination of relative risk through verification against databases of people known to have a reason for being present (they are scheduled on a flight, they work at the airport, and the like). Identity can be compared with databases that tell more about whether a specific individual is someone known or suspected to be a threat. Purpose provides a sense of intent. Are the individuals' actions consistent with their stated or implied reason for being in the system? For example, airport employees may have access to secure areas and certain locations. If one of those employees accesses a secure area at an odd, off-duty time, or through a door not normally used by that employee, it can and should prompt further investigation.

Moreover:

- Visibility provides scope, location, and scale. How many people and things are in the system? Where in the system are they? How are they distributed throughout the system? Visibility highlights, for example, where large crowds may be congregating or where there are bottlenecks that can impact security or hamper movement through the facility.
- Identity answers "what" or "who"—such as traveler, employee, or cargo. Identity also helps to quantify risk. Is this a regular customer, a frequent traveler, a twenty-year employee, or cargo from a known and trusted shipper? TSA Pre✓ and CBP's Global Entry, the voluntary programs mentioned above, provide information about identity. Through voluntary participation, registered passengers are assigned to a lower category of risk in order to allow TSA and CBP to pay more attention to those about whom less is known.
- Purpose implies, and often clarifies, intent. What is the purpose of that person or thing—an employee going to work, expected cargo going to a routine and expected destination, a passenger with a flight that day?

In 2004, the U.S. Congress passed the Intelligence Reform and Terrorism Prevention Act (Public Law 108-458), which, among other provisions, required DHS to develop a biometric entry and exit system for the United States. In 2013, CBP was tasked with developing and implementing the system in order to positively account for the entry and exit of all non-citizens visiting the United States, in addition to positively identifying individuals boarding planes for international destinations. CBP had used fingerprints since 2004, but in 2016, it began piloting the use of facial recognition for what it refers to as Biometric Air Exit.[29]

CBP's pilot projects using facial recognition to identify people entering and exiting the United States could inform the design of a new system architecture that would enable visibility, identity, and purpose. CBP tests how biometric technology can be used to confirm identity. The program matches existing photographic records (from passports, visas, and other travel documents) with a photograph of the traveler taken just before departure.

CBP discards the photos of U.S. citizens within twelve hours after their identities have been verified and deletes the photos of non–U.S citizens from CBP systems within fourteen days.[30] As of this writing, CBP was operating twenty-eight facial recognition pilot programs in partnership with a number of airports and airlines and one cruise ship terminal, with the airline partners concurrently piloting facial recognition as a potential replacement for traditional boarding passes.

In 2017, CBP approached TSA and additional airlines about the potential to benefit from the use of this facial recognition technology throughout the airport environment. The envisioned system would use common facial recognition systems at airline check-in, at TSA checkpoints as a replacement for the current document check, upon exit from the United States if traveling internationally, and at boarding in lieu of a boarding pass. CBP has suggested that such common use of facial recognition would create efficiencies, make for a better and more seamless travel experience, and create a more secure airport environment. Additionally, commonality could further reduce cost and error rates, would help to address the desire for continuous visibility and identity of travelers moving through airports, and would improve coordination among airport entities tasked with ensuring security.[31] TSA, for its part, has independently begun to explore and test the use of facial and fingerprint recognition technologies.[32] In September 2018, TSA released its roadmap for expanding biometric technology.[33] And in October 2018, Congress passed the first-ever TSA reauthorization act, which specifically empowered TSA to expand field testing of advanced screening technologies.[34]

It is important to note that there have been serious questions raised about CBP and TSA facial recognition programs. These include concern over the cost relative to the actual security benefits, the potential for recognition errors, and the overarching privacy implications of government collection and use of this data, not to mention a fundamental question about whether the federal government even has the authority to collect such large-scale biometric data on travelers and visitors.[35] These concerns highlight the significant challenge in designing and implementing a more holistic security system while ensuring that individual privacy is protected.

Evolving a Holistic Approach

How, then, does the nation move to a more secure system—one in which visibility, identity, and purpose are established—without violating individual privacy rights and exposing personal data to potential misuse as a by-product of a large-scale government and private-sector program? The answer may lie in finding a way for travelers to control their personal information and then voluntarily permit it to be used to generate a risk "score" that would be assigned for the duration of the journey, ensuring that control of personal data would at all times be retained by the individual. Travelers could permit access to the data that they carry (and generate) in a manner that permitted the various entities with whom the traveler interacts during a journey to transact for purposes of identification and clearance, while at all times ensuring the traveler's continued independence, privacy, and personal ownership of the data. The traveler could "choose" to remain continuously visible and identified.

Blockchain technology, which at the time of this writing is finding its way into mainstream applications and uses, provides an intriguing potential new method for how individuals could maintain ownership of their personal data, yet still share it in a way that leads to greater system security. Though popularized as the technology behind digital currencies, blockchain has been called a "foundational technology" in that it holds great potential to provide new means of affording privacy protections while allowing for the use of data for other purposes.[36]

How might this look in practice? Consider the air traveler. From the moment a traveler makes a reservation at her destination, she has exchanged data with a number of databases and information repositories: the airline of choice; a frequent flyer program; the Secure Flight program; taxi, ride hailing, ride-sharing, and car rental or parking reservation services; government agencies; and perhaps even airport concessionaires, to name but a few. The traveler has provided information, often willingly, to various public and private entities that can collectively identify this traveler. For the most part, this information is held independently and in disconnected databases. But what if the traveler could control her information using blockchain and then voluntarily permit it to be accessed across the system to keep her visible and identified in order to generate a personal risk "score" that would be assigned for the duration of her journey? The traveler would "choose" to share her data to ensure her security (and reduce inconvenience) during her journey. Moreover, as the number of travelers voluntarily participating increased, then the "system" would gain a greater measure of awareness and predictability in order to better identify anomalies.

By integrating the three core elements of visibility, identity, and purpose, transportation system managers and operators could have at their disposal a continuum of security throughout the transportation network. The operational doctrine to implement this strategy could enable engagement across all transportation touch-points—from routine services such as taxis and ride-sharing services, baggage handling, and ticketing to law enforcement and security matters. Such a doctrine could form the foundation for a new comprehensive transportation security system built on secure, coordinated and time-limited (duration of travel) data collection and sharing, supported by integrated operations networks and rapid engagement and response capabilities extended across all transportation modes.

The Role of DHS

The central mission of DHS is, quite simply, "to ensure a homeland that is safe, secure, and resilient against terrorism and other hazards." DHS's mission statement further observes that

> hundreds of thousands of people from across the federal government, state, local, tribal, and territorial governments, the private sector, and other nongovernmental organizations are responsible for executing these missions. These are the people who regularly interact with the public, who are responsible for public safety and security, who own and operate our nation's critical infrastructures and services, who perform research and develop technology, and who keep watch, prepare for, and respond to emerging threats and disasters.[37]

DHS is uniquely positioned to lead the transition of the transportation security enterprise into a more holistic and integrated system. Difficult challenges are not new to this nation, and there are many examples of disruptive, entrepreneurial, and imaginative undertakings. The United States has seen great success in areas where the public and private sectors jointly engage on a grand scale—from conquering diseases to space exploration to the marvels of the information age. The sheer unwieldy nature of protecting the nation's many and diverse transportation systems demands that the government lead on this front. DHS holds authorities, as embodied in its various agencies and entities, along with the ability to convene and coordinate among many stakeholders to exercise those authorities in a collective and focused manner. Moreover, DHS plays a key role in the broader national security enterprise, which has learned much more about the identities, intentions, and capabilities of the nation's enemies. The federal government is perhaps the only entity with the comprehensive ability to convene, facilitate, and empower the many agencies, state and local governments, private companies, passengers, cargo operators, and other transportation stakeholders needed to succeed at such a venture.

However, envisioning, developing, and implementing a new approach to transportation security is not a task that could be easily handed to DHS or its agencies. DHS is, first and foremost, a collection of operating agencies with demanding daily missions. These daily missions make it challenging to implement fundamental change. Operating agencies that have an imperative to get something done every single day (passenger screening, clearing inbound cargo, inspecting ships, patrolling the border, responding to disasters, and so forth) understandably tend to get locked into particular ways of doing things. There is little incentive to develop a dramatically new approach because the status quo works well enough, and there is an entire system of policies, procedures, and training in place to support the current ways of doing business. Change is hard, disruptive, and, if not done carefully, hazardous.

Even the entities within DHS whose job it is to innovate, such as the Science and Technology Directorate or TSA's Innovation Task Force, are generally tasked with driving innovation and implementation of new technologies within an existing system architecture.[38] TSA established its Innovation Task Force in 2016 as a permanent entity to reimagine the current approach to aviation security and become a driver for innovative, entrepreneurial thought. Since then, the task force has been hard at work testing and implementing new passenger screening checkpoint enhancements such as automated screening lanes, computed tomography carry-on baggage scanners, and advanced uses of biometrics. But even innovative efforts such as these are naturally focused more on modernizing and adapting existing systems and less on developing entirely new ones. This is due to the daily operational demands that require optimal performance of the current system.

A coordinating entity could be established within DHS and specifically tasked with overseeing the development of a fully integrated and holistic approach to security across the Department. Such an entity would be less constrained by existing system design and daily operational demands, and as such could focus its energy on driving a much more comprehensive and strategic transformation. Moreover, a DHS-directed approach could unify the current, often disparate and disconnected efforts of the various agencies within the Department with respect to transportation security. Such an approach would be less beholden to existing system architecture and afford the freedom to think and act expansively and imaginatively and convene the many stakeholders—public and private—in such an effort.

Resilience

The focus of this chapter has been on the protection of transportation systems and the prevention of attacks through a comprehensive system of identity, trust, and clearance. But effective transportation security must always balance security measures and protocols with the need for the free movement of people and goods. This, by definition, accepts risk—since the only risk-free transportation is that which does not move. There is no perfect security system, and terrorists and other attackers sometimes succeed.

Security systems, therefore, must acknowledge and prepare for this potential. While transportation facilities must be designed and operated in ways that reduce the impact of attacks, they must also incorporate a comprehensive approach to responding and recovering rapidly and effectively. A speedy, effective response has the further potential to reduce the psychological effects of terror by rapidly returning to normal operations, ultimately helping to reduce the perceived value of the system itself as a target. As President Barack Obama put it in a September 2016 interview:

> From Boston to San Bernardino to Orlando, we've seen how important it is for communities and first responders to be ready if and when tragedy strikes. That's a critical part of preventing attacks from causing even greater loss of life. It's a key part of our resilience. It's one of the ways we can show terrorists that they will not succeed—that Americans get back up and we carry on, no matter what.[39]

Hence, security systems must include comprehensive response and recovery protocols. The various stakeholders from the private sector, government, and even the traveling public need to be educated and trained (together where possible) and kept up to date, not only in the systems and elements for which they are directly responsible, but in interacting, coordinating, and integrating with the many other players and elements within the system. The ability to work across institutional boundaries—to work as an integrated team to respond quickly and effectively to a security event—is critical to saving lives, mitigating further damage and destruction, recovering effectively, and helping to reduce the motivation for future attacks.

Conclusion

Some might argue that current security systems are good enough, and that the significant commitment and cost needed to transform transportation security as discussed in this chapter would greatly outweigh the benefit, given the overall low probability of attacks. This argument suggests that society would benefit more by focusing efforts on more urgent and compelling national problems, such as reducing the number and frequency of highway traffic accidents.[40] Periodic terrorist attacks have occurred for decades, if not throughout human history, with most being relatively small in scale and overall impact. The probability of dying or being injured in a car accident is far, far greater than the probability of being killed or injured in a terror attack.[41]

The flaw in this argument, however, is that the nature and consequences of terror argue against rational thought and empirical data. As physicist Lawrence M. Krauss has said, "it is terrifying to know that there are individuals living among us with the express intent of killing randomly, for effect."[42] The psychological and economic impacts of a terror attack, the opportunity to inspire other terrorists to act, and the inevitable cascade of disruptions beyond any given attack are all strong justification for continuing to invest in transforming and evolving security systems in order to ensure the ongoing ability to deter, detect, and disrupt terrorists and their plans, as well as building resilience into the system.

The fundamental premise of this chapter is that the transportation security of today cannot be the transportation security of tomorrow. The United States may never return to the levels of openness enjoyed prior to the tragedy of 9/11. But we can envision a future in which security is more seamless—more transparent even—reducing the attractiveness and vulnerability of the transportation system to terrorists and other attackers while eliminating some of the procedures and encumbrances that create friction for all who depend upon America's vast transportation networks.

CHAPTER 9

Fragmentation in Unity: Immigration and Border Policy within DHS

Doris Meissner, Amy Pope, and Andrew Selee

ONE OF THE PRINCIPAL FACTORS MOTIVATING THE CREATION OF THE Department of Homeland Security (DHS) in 2003 was to reorganize the agencies responsible for border security and immigration and put them under the same roof. The 9/11 attacks had revealed vulnerabilities in the way the U.S. government managed borders and immigration policy, and this reorganization was designed to ensure both greater clarity of mission in each new agency and greater coordination among them.

Two of the principal agencies that had been responsible for border and immigration issues—the Customs Service in the Treasury Department and the Immigration and Naturalization Service (INS) in the Justice Department— were divided up into three agencies and placed within the newly established DHS. The three new agencies that emerged from this reorganization—Customs and Border Protection (CBP), Immigration and Customs Enforcement (ICE), and Citizenship and Immigration Services (USCIS)—were designed to have more targeted responsibilities than their legacy agencies. Their inclusion within the new Department was designed to ensure operational coordination and common policy formulation.

Overall, the agencies have been fairly successful in managing expanding immigration, tourism, and trade while addressing ever more complex security threats. At a time when many people feared a wave of foreign terrorist attacks on the United States or growing paralysis in immigration and trade, the three agencies have largely succeeded in keeping U.S. borders open to legal crossings while implementing measures to keep the country safe from outside threats. They have done so by embracing new technology platforms that allow for information sharing among agencies, employing risk management techniques, pushing their functions increasingly away from the border itself, and coordinating actively with foreign governments. These improvements came with new resources. The U.S. government now spends 25 percent more on immigration and border enforcement, most of it through these three agencies, than it does on all other federal criminal law enforcement functions combined.[1]

However, the three agencies have had uneven degrees of success in developing their particular mandates. Legacy systems and overlapping missions with other agencies elsewhere in the government have undermined some of the clarity of mission and action that was supposed to have emerged from the reorganization. And politicians have added additional mandates along the way that have often redirected attention away from central priorities.

More important, the reorganization did little to create overarching mechanisms for setting policy or even ensuring cooperation among the three agencies. As a result, policymaking and coordination on immigration and border issues remain fragmented within DHS and across the U.S. government more generally. In particular, weak policy coordination has made it difficult for the three agencies to anticipate and readily respond to quickly changing conditions on the ground and to conduct political debates with coherent strategies and ideas for better managing borders and the immigration system.

This chapter begins with a historical review of the U.S. approach to national security and immigration, including the decade that preceded the 9/11 attacks. We then examine briefly the deficiencies in the U.S. immigration enterprise that contributed to 9/11 before discussing the changes to the enterprise following the attacks. Having explained how the government reorganized its immigration functions, we next review key immigration policy issues in order to illuminate how the government has focused on pushing its borders out and the importance of information sharing and fusion. We conclude with recommendations to further reform and strengthen U.S. immigration agencies, policies, and processes.

The History of National Security and Immigration

There were few immigration restrictions (and no federal agency charged with restricting admissions to the United States)[2] until the 1880s, when Congress began to pass immigration legislation as the number of immigrants rose and concern about their impact on the economy increased.[3] The original focus was on keeping out "idiots, lunatics, convicts, and persons likely to become a public charge"; it was expanded to cover polygamists, those convicted of crimes of moral turpitude, and those suffering loathsome or contagious disease.[4]

The situation changed in the twentieth century as the primary U.S. national security concern became the influence and intent of other nation-states such as the Central Powers, the Axis, or the Soviet Union. The threat was that individuals posing as legitimate migrants, refugees, or travelers would work on behalf of one of these nations to undermine or destabilize the United States. As a result, immigration and national security policy evolved to give the government the power to interrogate and remove or deny entry to nationals of these countries.[5] During World War I, the Immigration Service was given responsibility for interning "enemy aliens," although its primary responsibility remained regulating admissions based on criteria such as health, resources, and literacy.[6] The Immigration Act of 1918 also prohibited any membership in anarchist groups, as well as any group that advocated the violent overthrow of the U.S. government.[7] National security concerns began to play a larger and more dominant role in U.S. foreign policy, particularly with the decrease in immigration during the Great Depression. The newly created INS focused increasingly on removing criminal and subversive aliens, and on working more closely with the Federal Bureau of Investigation (FBI) to counter such threats.[8]

In 1940, the INS was moved from the Department of Labor[9] to the Department of Justice to provide more effective control over foreign nationals in the public interest.[10] During World War II, the national security responsibilities of the INS became more explicit and included fingerprinting every alien in the country, operating the internment camps for enemy aliens, and conducting record checks for immigrant workers in the defense sector.[11]

Following World War II, the United States shifted its attention to admitting war refugees persecuted under the Italian or German governments and managing the increasing numbers of unauthorized migrants crossing the southwest border. Individuals admitted under the Displaced Persons Act of 1948 were subject to "a thorough investigation and written report made and prepared" by the government regarding each individual's history, character, and eligibility for the program.[12] Still, concerns lingered, particularly in Congress, that the refugee admissions program could be a shield for Communists to be admitted to the United States and engage in subversive activity.[13] The resulting screening process—in which applicants were interviewed multiple times, including by security officials—forms the basis of today's refugee screening program.[14] It was not until the late twentieth century, however, that terrorists acting independently of a nation-state became a much more significant threat to U.S. interests.[15] The 1983 Beirut barracks bombing and the 1993 bombing of the World Trade Center in New York highlighted this concern.

In the 1990s, the focus of policymaking on immigration and borders shifted noticeably to preventing unauthorized immigration across the southwest border. Congress authorized a major expansion of the Border Patrol, then within the INS; the first fencing for urban areas near the border; and, in 1996, a reform of immigration policy that limited legal immigrants' access to certain benefits and enhanced penalties for illegal entry.

Despite this shift in focus, federal officials recognized the need for a comprehensive counterterrorism approach to combat misuse of immigration tools, particularly after the 1993 bombing of the World Trade Center. The Anti-Terrorism and Effective Death Penalty Act of 1996 (AEDPA) prohibited providing material support or resources to designated foreign terrorist organizations, and made it a basis for excluding or removing foreign nationals.[16] There were also nascent efforts to build out the INS's counterterrorism capability. The INS set up a National Security Unit in 1997 to track potential terrorist cases for possible immigration enforcement action; automated a terrorist watchlist; increased work with other law enforcement agencies and the Department of State (DOS) to identify suspected terrorists; and granted immigration officers access to classified information.[17]

Nonetheless, fundamental policy questions—such as whether the Central Intelligence Agency (CIA) could complete background checks prior to naturalization—were not resolved. Furthermore, inspectors at ports of entry (POEs) often relied on paper watchlists and did not realize that they were checking for terrorists when comparing the names of incoming passengers to the automated watchlist. Programs to track foreign student visa compliance and tracking travelers' entry to and exit from the United States were initiated but not completed.[18]

By March 10, 2000, the National Security Council Principals' Committee recognized the need to strengthen immigration law enforcement, recommending increases to the number of INS agents assigned to the FBI's Joint Terrorism Task Force (JTTF) and activating a special court to enable the use of classified evidence in immigration-related INS cases.[19] Yet the funding available for the counterterrorism mission was limited, and the efforts remained incomplete and in competition with more politically charged demands such as stemming unauthorized crossing at the southwest border. Eighteen months later, Al-Qaeda successfully carried out its spectacular attacks on U.S. soil, fueling a rapid review and reorganization of U.S. immigration capabilities. The events of 9/11 dramatically demonstrated that a sophisticated, patient, well-financed terrorist group that sufficiently understood the U.S. visa and immigration system could place its operatives in the United States. Countering this threat was the primary reason for updating America's immigration regime.

The Impact of 9/11 on Immigration and Border Policy

Prior to 9/11, there were two federal agencies responsible for administering the immigration system. First, the INS managed immigration functions at the POEs. It also was the parent agency of the Border Patrol, which was responsible for security between the POEs. Finally, the INS also was responsible for citizenship and immigration benefits functions, including refugee admissions and the detention and deportation of individuals in violation of U.S. immigration law. Second, the Bureau of Consular Affairs within the DOS screened applicants for visas. The Customs Service managed POEs along with the INS, but was not an immigration enforcement agency. The Coast Guard was involved with maritime border control but, aside from interdicting or rescuing migrants at sea, had no role in the immigration system.

As outlined above, national security responsibilities had long been part of the core mission of immigration agencies; however, the resources and political will devoted to them were often drowned out by other priorities and concerns, and terrorism had not been, historically, a core concern. The 9/11 Commission Report identified a host of operational failures and opportunities indicting immigration screening processes, among other failings by relevant agencies. These include:

- Failures to include individuals on the terrorist watchlists and No Fly lists;
- Failure to inform the FBI about one hijacker's visa or travel to the United States;
- Failure to discover false statements on visa applications;
- Failure to recognize false passports; and
- Failure to properly screen and search airline passengers.

At the heart of the problem was the failure to connect the dots between those who had the relevant intelligence about terrorist plots and those who could act on that intelligence to protect U.S. borders. Consideration was given to increasing the intelligence capabilities within the border and immigration screening agencies to improve the connectivity with the Intelligence Community (IC). Ultimately, however, the solution became institutional changes and better tools to identify potential bad actors.

INSTITUTIONAL CHANGES AFTER 9/11

The overarching organizational response to 9/11 was the creation of DHS. The Homeland Security Act of 2002 made counterterrorism the central mission for agencies tasked with border and transportation security, and recognized the importance of connecting the mission and functions of the agencies that manage the border.[20] Prior to the Homeland Security Act, no single government entity was charged with border management and transportation security.[21]

Within DHS, the act created a Directorate of Border and Transportation Security, pulling together under one organizational roof the Customs Service and the Federal Law Enforcement Training Center from the Department of the Treasury, the INS from the Department of Justice, the Federal Protective Service from the General Services Administration, the newly created Transportation Security Administration (TSA) from the Department of Transportation, and part of the Animal and Plant Health Inspection Service from the Department of Agriculture. Together, this new entity was responsible for:

- Preventing the entry of terrorists and the instruments of terrorism into the United States;
- Securing the borders, territorial waters, ports, terminals, waterways, and air, land, and sea transportation systems of the United States, including managing and coordinating those functions transferred to DHS at POEs;
- Carrying out the immigration enforcement functions vested by statute in, or performed by, the Commissioner of Immigration and Naturalization;
- Establishing and administering rules governing the granting of visas or other forms of permission, including parole, to enter the United States to individuals who are not citizens or aliens lawfully admitted for permanent residence in the United States; and
- Establishing national immigration enforcement policies and priorities.[22]

Soon after, DHS reorganized to create two bureaus: CBP and ICE.[23] The responsibility for immigration and border management within DHS thus breaks down as follows:

- CBP is the U.S. government's unified border management agency, which is responsible for managing and securing the flows of goods and people into the United States. The Border Patrol, a CBP component, remains responsible for security between the POEs.
- ICE is responsible for interior immigration enforcement through its office of Enforcement and Removal Operations (ERO). ICE also has an investigative arm, Homeland Security Investigations (HSI), which has broad jurisdiction to investigate crimes with a border nexus.
- USCIS is responsible for overseeing lawful immigration to the United States. It administers the adjudication of immigration benefits, including eligibility for admission to the United States for a range of non-immigrant visa programs, such as foreign student stays; adjustment of status to permanent residence ("green card" eligibility); naturalization; and admission of refugees and asylum applicants.

As significant as the creation and organization of DHS was, it was not an all-encompassing, comprehensive fix. Other key agencies that bear a significant responsibility for homeland security and immigration—including the DOS's Bureau of Consular Affairs, the Department of Justice's Executive Office for Immigration Review (EOIR), the FBI, and the intelligence agencies, including the National Counterterrorism Center (NCTC)—remained outside DHS, leaving many longstanding turf battles unresolved and information silos in place. Likewise, the move did not automatically create the infrastructure, policy, and incentives to link together disparate agencies. It divided the INS into three separate agencies—CBP, ICE, and USCIS—which meant that they were no longer sharing information, technology, acquisitions, or even offices.

The result has been a fracturing of mission that may have exacerbated some of the gaps identified by the 9/11 Commission. Thus, most agencies still cannot search across federal information and identity databases. Agencies rely on data dumps from one database to another or send requests to each other. In many cases, agencies search individual databases separately, rather than one aggregated set of information. While individual databases and agency experts are becoming increasingly sophisticated and are finding ways to bridge the gaps in their information, they still largely function as "silos of excellence."

Two examples illustrate the problem. Consider first the "life cycle" of a foreigner's journey to the United States. ICE/HSI may be following the movements of a criminal suspect across Latin America, but when that person attempts to cross the border, the responsibility shifts to CBP. After CBP apprehends the individual, it transfers him to ICE's other division, Enforcement and Removal Operations, or ICE/ERO, for deportation. Once the person goes into immigration proceedings in the Department of Justice's EOIR files, ICE/ERO no longer regularly receives information about that individual, even if he has been ordered removed, particularly if he is not in immigration detention.

USCIS experiences similar problems in its vetting work. Because applicants may hide their true intent or background in applying for immigration benefits, USCIS carries out internal and external security checks in deciding upon applications. USCIS has two components—the Fraud Detection and National Security (FDNS) and the Service Center Operations Directorate (SCOPS) Background Check Unit (BCU)—that oversee applicant vetting. These components verify fingerprints through the FBI, but do not have automatic access to the FBI's Integrated Automated Fingerprint Identification System (IAFIS). Instead, USCIS must solicit (and pay for) checks on individual applicants. When there is a match, the FBI uploads any record of arrests and prosecutions into USCIS's biometric system. Separately, USCIS must run a fingerprint check through DHS's US-VISIT system for any applicant who is applying for a benefit which, if granted, would permit the applicant to remain in the United States for more than a year.[24] If an applicant applies to adjust her status (for example, to change from a student visa to an immigrant visa), USCIS will petition the FBI for a name check, a more in-depth search which queries FBI databases for any records in which she was the primary person of interest or was referenced. Likewise, the adjudicating officer will run an applicant's name through Treasury Enforcement Communications System name check, a database that incorporates law enforcement–related information from twenty-six federal agencies.[25] Any time these searches reveal a match to a name in the database, a USCIS officer must investigate and resolve the issue before granting any immigration benefits.[26]

Although the checks are comprehensive, the primary weakness is that USCIS is tapping outside agencies for information integral to its decisions. USCIS does not have connectivity with the FBI, ICE, or the intelligence agencies. Like ICE and CBP, it suffers from the same disconnect over the life cycle of an individual case. Information available to one agency is not available to all.

In practice, in cases involving the most serious national security threats, agencies are likely to remain in close contact, but there is no automatic connection between the multiple agencies to ensure a seamless transition of information over the life of an individual's immigration case. It also means that an individual who is not detained—either in ICE/ERO or Bureau of Prisons custody—can be far more difficult to locate once he has been ordered removed or if national security concerns surface later. The agencies try to coordinate respective priorities. And there are places such as the El Paso Intelligence Center where the agencies meet regularly, identify shared targets, and share information to overcome institutional barriers.[27] DHS Secretary Jeh Johnson's creation of regional task forces was in part a response to these challenges.[28]

The fact that such a plan was required demonstrates that the realignment of agencies within DHS did not, by itself, significantly improve national security in the way that was anticipated. In some cases, because of inadequate information connectivity between agencies and within DHS, agencies may be worse at sharing information today than they were before 2001. Information and capabilities that were at one time housed within the INS are now split between ICE and CBP, and ICE has not been equipped to play a stand-alone role in many cases.

When it comes to adjudicating immigration cases, the system is also slow. USCIS still adjudicates many of its cases using paper files, despite decades-long attempts to establish a centralized, account-based electronic environment. In its most recent effort, both the Government Accountability Office (GAO) and DHS Office of the Inspector General (OIG) reported that the new system was slowing adjudication instead of improving it.[29] Additionally, as of July 2015, only 2,215 out of 19,000 employees and contractors had access to the system.[30] In March 2016, the OIG reported that USCIS had potentially sent hundreds of permanent resident cards to incorrect addresses because the online system would not let employees update applicants' addresses.[31] By November 2016, USCIS had received roughly 200,000 reports from applicants whose applications were approved but who never received their cards. In addition, USCIS issued 19,000 cards with either incorrect information or as duplicates.[32] The errors associated with the online naturalization adjudication process were compounded as the system either did not complete background security checks or provided inaccurate information regarding the results of those checks. Given the cascading errors, in January 2017, the OIG recommended against reinstating the electronic system;[33] USCIS planned to automate all its benefits and services by 2019, at a cost of up to $3.1 billion.

Because of the repeated errors and failures to connect the dots within its own agency, USCIS's actions have exacerbated national security vulnerabilities. And although it has become a stand-alone, benefits-granting agency, its responsibilities entail ensuring essential security and other protections that have not been able to be successfully reconciled with the goal of a customer-service orientation and culture. In this sense, USCIS has not resolved the problem of reconciling security with facilitation of legitimate travel and immigration.

POST 9/11 PROCESS CHANGES

Although many of the post-9/11 changes were bureaucratic—creating new agencies or reorganizing old ones—significant changes were also made to the way those agencies did business. The ethos of the most successful initiatives has been the concept of driving the borders outward. (For further discussion, see Chapter 5.) The more clearly a determination about a person's identity and intention can be made before they reach American borders (air, land, or sea), the easier it is to protect the United States from harm. Part and parcel of these initiatives has been managing and improving access to information to enable advanced risk assessment and identification of threats.

The central challenge is how to best isolate threats while facilitating the mobility and travel that is essential to U.S. global competitiveness and the domestic economy. Programs such as the Visa Waiver Program (VWP), the refugee screening program, land border controls, and the so-called ENTRY-EXIT all illustrate the difficulties of maintaining that balance.

THE VISA WAIVER PROGRAM. Well before boarding a flight to the United States, travelers must be screened by U.S. officials. This happens through the visa adjudication process or the VWP. The VWP permits visa-free travel for up to 90 days for citizens of 38 partner countries, and accounts for over 20 million visits to the United States per year.

Every two years, VWP travelers must submit a short online application (ESTA) providing key identifying information before they can board their flights. The information is checked against an array of U.S. government databases. In some cases, a traveler is directed to a U.S. consulate for a visa. In others, a traveler may be denied entry. Once the traveler is bound for the United States, CBP's National Targeting Center uses the traveler's information to identify persons who should be further inspected or denied entry.[34]

VWP travelers do not have to be interviewed by a consular officer. The VWP thus facilitates the legitimate travel of millions of visitors to the United

States. From a national security point of view, the risk of not inspecting and interviewing each individual traveler is mitigated by information-sharing agreements with the participating countries. By statute, participating countries must report lost and stolen passports to Interpol, share information on known or suspected terrorists, and update shared information from their own encounters with known or suspected terrorists.

In theory, the information-sharing agreements give the United States access to sophisticated data about nationals of the participating countries. The VWP also frees U.S. officials to focus on more questionable travelers. In practice, it is a more complex story, and the program has evolved as the threat landscape has shifted.

Based on the 9/11 Commission Report, Congress passed legislation that altered the eligibility requirements for countries joining the program. Previous guidelines required that countries have a visa refusal rate of no more that 3 percent. The new law permitted DHS to waive this requirement for countries that had visa refusal rates between 3 and 10 percent.[35] In exchange, countries agreed to cooperate with the United States on counterterrorism information sharing and initiatives and have sufficient security measures in place to assure that involvement in the VWP would not pose a risk to U.S. immigration and criminal law enforcement or national security interests.[36] The law increased the responsibilities of the admitted countries in other important ways.

Yet lawmakers continued to express concerns that foreign fighters would be able to enter the United States using VWP country passports. Congressional committee members were further concerned that VWP countries were not consistently sharing vital terrorism data until after high-profile terrorist attacks occurred in other countries.[37] In August 2015, DHS Secretary Jeh Johnson announced that new security measures would be added to the VWP, requiring that all participating countries use electronic or e-passports for all VWP travelers coming to the United States. The new measures required that VWP travelers be screened through Interpol's Lost and Stolen Passport Database (LSPD) when traveling. Finally, countries had to consent to the expanded use of U.S. federal air marshals on flights to the United States from VWP participant countries.[38]

After the November 2015 terrorist attacks in Paris, DHS again announced new and expanded changes to the VWP. Legislation in 2015 formalized many of the policy changes and also excluded from the program any VWP national who had previously travelled to Iraq, Syria, or a country designated by the Secretary of State as supporting terrorism. Travelers who are dual citizens of a VWP country and one of the countries of concern were also ineligible for the program. The legislation also increased the demands on participating countries—for example, shortening the time in which a VWP participant could report a lost or stolen passport.

In practice, the VWP relies heavily on the sophistication, skill, and political will of the participating governments. For years, many European governments were prohibited by their privacy laws from collecting or sharing certain information on their nationals with the United States, particularly absent a criminal conviction. Compliance with the requirement to report lost and stolen passport data to Interpol was strikingly low.

Likewise, many European governments did not have comprehensive screening mechanisms in place, particularly when travelers crossed at land or sea ports. For partner countries like Greece and Italy, hit hardest by the waves of migration from North Africa and the Middle East, improving their own border controls is dependent on systematic identification of those entering their countries. For countries like Germany, France, and Belgium, which have comparatively high numbers of nationals who have left to become foreign fighters, sharing information on the travel patterns of these individuals, as well as encounters with them, is key. Even with the threat of termination, the economic and diplomatic repercussions of such a decision have meant that the U.S. government has been unwilling to pull the trigger, relying instead on carrots versus sticks to encourage compliance.

Given the evolving threat and the low compliance rate of participant countries, the United States is increasingly focused on strengthening information sharing between U.S. agencies and their partners—for example, establishing direct data-sharing relationships with every European country in the VWP, and continuing to build these relationships through multiple different channels and agencies. In the past two years, the U.S. government has offered technical exchanges with both the FBI and CBP to help European partners maximize their use of U.S. terrorism information, as well as securing real-time access to U.S. biometric data sets to support refugee and immigration processing, terrorist and foreign fighter screening, and border security. Likewise, the DOD is working with European partners to expand their screening and vetting capabilities through various security sector assistance programs and initiatives and working with NATO to establish common data-sharing capabilities and architectures that can be used to support both military operations and other national security screening activities through cross-domain data sharing frameworks.

Additionally, the U.S. government is working with Interpol and Europol to share more criminal and terrorism information, as well as lost and stolen passport information and other threat stream data. In recent years, following the passage of UN Security Council Resolution 2178 in 2014, more European partners have passed counterterrorism legislation that provides the legal authority to more robustly share data with the international community to help identify and interdict criminals, foreign fighters, and terrorists attempting to cross international borders.

Ultimately, the VWP enables a sophisticated information-sharing system between governments that allows for accurate and sophisticated identification of bad actors. The value of this exchange outweighs the information that can be obtained in any one visa interview. But the ultimate success of the program directly correlates to the participating governments' ability to collect, update, and share this information and the U.S. government's ability to compel compliance with the statutory mandates.

REFUGEE SCREENING. The refugee admissions program has been the target of intense scrutiny in recent years. In his first immigration executive order, President Donald Trump severely curtailed refugee admissions on national security grounds.[39] Refugees, by definition, are often fleeing war-torn locations where the threat of terrorism is significant and their ability to document their identity may be limited. At the same time, the world is now facing the biggest crisis related to displaced persons and refugees since the United Nations began keeping statistics on refugee movement.[40] So the question is how well refugee vetting protects the United States from national security threats.

Refugees are people outside of their country who are unable or unwilling to return home because they fear serious harm. The definition of the harm for asylum and refugee status is essentially the same, but the key difference is the location of the applicant. People making an asylum claim are already at or across the U.S. border; the government has no direct control over who shows up—particularly at land borders—to claim asylum. A refugee remains outside of U.S. borders until admitted. For refugees, the process for admission is strictly controlled, time-consuming, and unpredictable, involving multiple agencies. In the United States, the process for admission—once a person has been identified as eligible for resettlement—can often take more than a year.

The review process for refugee resettlement is the most thorough for any immigrant or non-immigrant population.[41] Refugee security screening has been significantly enhanced over recent years, particularly for individuals coming from places such as Syria. Under current procedures, applicants undergo biometric (fingerprint) and biographical checks and a lengthy interview by specially trained USCIS officials who scrutinize the applicant's explanation of individual circumstances.[42] Significantly, in recent years, many of these agencies are co-located so that they can share information in real time, and their electronic sharing of information has been improved. Additionally, the United States prioritizes the admission of those determined to be the most vulnerable and therefore posing a decreased security risk—for example, female-headed households, children, survivors of torture, and individuals with severe medical conditions.[43] Refugee applicants undergo recurrent vetting throughout their application process, so if there is any doubt about whether refugees poses security concerns, they are not permitted to enter the United States.

From a security perspective, the slow, cumbersome process for admission of refugees for resettlement in the United States leaves the primary pressure on partner countries; this can significantly strain their resources and capacity. From a U.S. homeland security perspective, refugee resettlement does not pose the security risks some suggest. In fact, a bad actor who intends to do harm in the United States would likely fare better seeking admission through *any* other process. Not only is the security screening exhaustive and recurrent, but the United States is at best admitting about 0.1 percent of the 65 million displaced people in the world. The likelihood of being admitted if one is male, single, and of military age is significantly lower.

SOUTHWEST BORDER ENFORCEMENT AND "THE WALL." At the land borders, there are significant pressures that do not exist at airports. Government officials do not benefit from the advance notice available with air travel to assess the threat posed by individual travelers. It is easier for a person or illicit commodity to enter the United States undetected at the land borders than via air.

Although it may appear that the best opportunities for evading detection would occur between the POEs, criminals and other bad actors are more often exploiting the opportunities created by the sheer number of people and goods transported at these ports. CBP statistics show that 81 percent of the 265,500 pounds of hard drugs caught at the U.S.–Mexico border from fiscal year 2012 to fiscal year 2016 was stopped by CBP officers at POEs, rather than by Border Patrol agents working in the deserts and wilderness between authorized crossing points.[44]

In fact, the most significant gains in enforcement have been in curtailing criminal activity between POEs. Border patrol staffing, technology, and infrastructure improvements (including extensive fencing) have reached historic highs, while the number of unauthorized migrants apprehended crossing the southwest border dropped to a forty-year low by 2017.[45] Although a wall would provide one more layer of defense against an unsophisticated bad actor seeking to cross the land border without detection, in reality, additional physical infrastructure would not mitigate national security threats.

DHS efforts have also focused on building in as much advance notice as possible of national security threats, so that the first encounter with a threatening individual is not at the border. This model is best highlighted by DHS's strategy in responding to Special Interest Aliens (SIAs)—migrants who are traveling from thirty-five countries in Asia, the Middle East, or Africa where there is known terrorist activity—who may be crossing the land borders.[46] The plan is to develop the capacity of other countries in the Western Hemisphere to screen, investigate, detain, and remove SIAs, including by collecting and sharing biometric and biographical information of SIAs encountered by foreign-country border officials.[47]

In particular, DHS has prioritized the development of cross-agency and cross-border relationships with partners in the Western Hemisphere. For example, DHS partners with the DOD's U.S. Northern Command, as well as the DOS's Bureau of International Narcotics and Law Enforcement Affairs, to initiate the sharing of biometric information with the National Institute of Migration in Mexico. DHS also uses the Biometric Identification Transnational Migration Alert Program to help partner countries develop the ability to collect biographical and biometric data. The countries enrolled in the program provide information to law enforcement and intelligence agencies on any SIA encountered by law enforcement or border officials, as well as any gang member, and on any national security concerns encountered.[48]

Finally, the U.S. government has increasingly recognized that until the underlying drivers of migration are fixed, no wall—no matter how tall or wide—will keep out the most desperate people or the most sophisticated criminals.[49] Transnational criminal organizations, which reap significant profits operating across the border, adapt to enhanced border enforcement measures.[50] For this reason, coordinated engagement, including the provision of foreign assistance, is critical. Traditional migration is best dealt with by focusing on improving the ability of foreign partners to address the crime, violence, and lack of opportunity. Improved border security results when partner countries can play a meaningful role in providing the intelligence, deterrence, and border security along their own borders to identify strategic threats—both to their own interests and to the United States.

In short, the answer to managing U.S. border security is addressing migration well before it reaches the United States. Doing so depends crucially on relations with Mexico. For example, in 2014, the most important factor in slowing the wave of Central Americans coming to the southwest border was Mexico's willingness to secure its own southern border. Once Mexico enhanced its own border security—often with the instruction of U.S. Border Patrol and immigration agents paid for by the DOS—the total number of migrants dropped by more than 14,000 in just one month in the Rio Grande Valley alone.[51]

Panama, Costa Rica, and other countries in the region have also become valuable partners in managing today's migration and identifying national security risks along the way to the southwest border. The ability of the countries in the Western Hemisphere to manage their aviation security—to identify who is traveling into their countries and whether they have a past record suggesting terrorist activity—is one of the most significant ways to mitigate the threat to the United States through its land borders. As a matter of national security, it is much more effective for a country like Ecuador to identify an SIA on the U.S. terrorist screening database and stop that person at their national airport than for a CBP official to stop that person at the vast U.S. land and sea borders.

At the land borders, CBP cannot receive the same benefits from the powerful analysis and resources that its National Targeting Center provides at airports. For that reason, the answer is to build an early warning and information-sharing system with bordering countries. To do so requires building partnerships with foreign governments in the Western Hemisphere and continued investment in the region.

As Congress has done with other foreign assistance, U.S. investment should be paired with meaningful and measurable outcomes to demonstrate that foreign partners have the ability to use the information and enhanced security to the benefit of the hemisphere. Such cooperation should enhance information sharing, including name and fingerprint queries; making improvements at the border; and denying terrorists and transnational criminal actors the ability to use any country as a transit point. Given the ability of bad actors to breach a wall, investments in partnerships in the Western Hemisphere and in their technical capacity will have a more long-term and meaningful impact and are a much better value for the money. Smart and targeted investments in these partnerships are an investment in U.S. border security.

ENTRY-EXIT CONTROLS. A final issue that has bedeviled U.S. Congressional and executive branch officials for years has been creating an exit system at U.S. land and air ports. The 1996 Illegal Immigration Reform and Immigrant Responsibility Act (IRRIRA) required creation of an entry and exit control system that would record each entry and exit in an online database. The system could not excessively increase the time taken to complete the inspection process.[52] Although the INS tested a variety of programs, every option increased the amount of time needed to cross the border.[53]

In 2000, Congress again instructed the INS to develop an entry and exit data collection system at all POEs. After the attacks on September 11, 2001, Congress issued the INS yet another mandate to expedite the development of an entry and exit data system and to establish an interoperable database with other existing systems.[54]

In 2003, the newly created DHS launched an automated entry and exit system called United States Visitor and Immigrant Status Indicator Technology (US-VISIT). Commercial carriers flying foreign nationals to or from the United States were required to submit manifest information electronically to DHS prior to arrival or departure that contained the biographical information of each traveler, as well as any information regarding his travel documents.[55] These requirements were subsequently expanded to include passport information, biometric identifiers (including fingerprints), and digital photographs.

Passenger manifest data significantly helped DHS identify suspicious travelers before they entered the United States. Collecting exit data, however, still proved to be elusive.[56] Despite congressional demands, US-VISIT continued to struggle to implement biometric exit, even at airports.[57] Travelers did not comply in pilot testing of solutions, such as the use of self-service kiosks, and enforcement was difficult.[58] DHS tried multiple solutions, but each one proved to be unsatisfactory.

In 2013, DHS reassigned responsibility for complying with entry and exit requirements from US-VISIT to CBP, effectively killing US-VISIT.[59] CBP continues to develop biometric exit capability. It increasingly relies on other mechanisms to document departure, however, including using information from and cooperation with ICE, the FBI, and an enhancement between DHS's Arrival and Departure Information System (ADIS) and TSA's Alien Flight School Program Data Exchange.[60]

To plug the gap at the land borders, the United States negotiated an agreement with Canada to exchange border-crossing information, so that an entry into Canada could be used as a record of exit from the United States. As of 2018, the match rate was just over 98 percent. Although the United States does not have a similar agreement with Mexico for the southwest border, a significant portion of Mexican border departures are reconciled due to the frequency of crossings. Once a foreign national reenters the United States, as cross-border commuters frequently do, the previous arrival is closed.[61] CBP continues to test programs to confirm exits through tools such as social media analysis, publicly available information, and facial recognition.[62] The pilot program matching passenger manifest photos to travelers has resulted in a matching rate of 96–98 percent in the three pilot airports, and is currently being tested in six airports with the expectation of future widespread implementation.[63] CBP is also testing facial recognition technology at two land ports.[64]

Thus, although DHS has failed to meet the congressional requirement of establishing a comprehensive biometric entry and exit procedure at all POEs, it is able to match 97 percent of departing aliens to their arrivals.[65] This high match rate does not account for some unknown number of people who enter and never depart. But given the effort that has gone into developing a solution over the years, the question is whether other improvements in sharing information now outweigh the value of a record of exit. Furthermore, given the difficulty in tracking down individuals who have not departed the United States and the sheer number of the visa overstayers already in the United States, as well as ICE's limited resources to track down any one individual, the benefit may no longer be worth the cost.

Once DHS knows that an individual has not exited the United States on time, the next question is "so what"? The government does not have sufficient resources to take enforcement action against every overstay, so the value of recording exits is diminished. Even if information surfaces about a particular individual to suggest that he is a suspected terrorist, the lack of information about that individual's exit is of minimal value. U.S. officials are far more likely to identify the presence of any one individual in the United States through a host of traditional law enforcement techniques. The money and attention would be better spent improving connectivity between agencies in the first instance.

Conclusions and Recommendations

Immigration and border management have been controversial and difficult for much of U.S. history. One result is that the federal government and the public can easily yield to decisions (including investments of resources) that do not actually make Americans safer. The 9/11 Commission Report unflinchingly detailed the risks of failing to remedy known gaps in American security.

There has been tremendous progress over the past eighteen years in closing those gaps. At the same time, more needs to be done in the ways that government agencies carry out their national security missions. The government cannot control the thinking and actions of those who intend to harm the United States, particularly through increased asymmetric threats and radicalized lone wolves who commit terrible, low-cost acts of violence. Policymakers can, however, continuously learn from past mistakes.

There is also an opportunity in the future to consciously rebalance the need for national security with the U.S. national interest in economic development. As it turns out, many of the things that make Americans safer—enhanced policy and operational coordination among agencies, pushing the border out, and separating high- and low-risk flows—also facilitate the commercial and individual border crossings that make the United States competitive in an era of globalization. Most of the time, national security and competitiveness do not require choosing trade-offs, but actually benefit from the same policies that enhance efficiency and coordination.

We believe that the following recommendations would help improve the work of the agencies charged with managing immigration and borders within the U.S. government and create greater coherence for policymaking around these issues:

Strengthen policy coordination among agencies within DHS that are tasked with border and immigration management. CBP, ICE, and USCIS have deeply interconnected mandates, yet no overarching policymaking structure exists below the level of the Secretary or Deputy Secretary. In some cases, DHS Office of Policy has been able to impose a degree of policy coherence. But this only works when the Secretary empowers this office to have those responsibilities, and it depends enormously on the personalities involved. (For further discussion about the role of DHS Office of Policy, see Chapter 15.) Another option would focus on regular meetings among the heads of the relevant agencies, overseen by the Deputy Secretary. Still a third option would be to create an Under Secretary for Immigration and Border Policy with oversight over CBP, ICE, and USCIS, in order to ensure greater coordination in day-to-day decision-making as well as policymaking. Whichever option is pursued, greater coordination is clearly needed. Given the salience of border and immigration issues in Congress and across the U.S. government, it is essential for DHS to have a united voice in formulating and advancing policies that respond to ongoing political debates.

Enhance connectivity among agencies within DHS—particularly with respect to technology and acquisitions. The creation of DHS did not go far enough in achieving connectivity among its Components and may have disrupted existing connectivity in counterproductive ways. Each DHS Component tends to act independently of other agencies and self-maximize its mission within the Department, despite—in the case of the immigration agencies—being responsible for different aspects of a single immigration system. Acquisitions, including IT, are made independently by each agency. Operations are planned and executed and information is collected and stored independently. Systems do not "talk" to each other. Although DHS agencies collect a tremendous amount of information, it is not effectively shared among Components. Success in integration will require political will from the Secretary (or Deputy Secretary) of DHS.

Increase coherence in oversight. Also problematic is the fact that Congress, when creating DHS, did not consolidate congressional oversight of its Components. Therefore, the Components report to different congressional committees, and their budgets are decided within different appropriations subcommittees. Until congressional committees of jurisdiction are better aligned, DHS will have even greater difficulty in developing a unified strategy and securing funding for it.

Enhance connectivity between federal agencies with responsibility for immigration and national security. While purporting to consolidate all agencies responsible for homeland security into one Department, glaring exclusions have hampered DHS's success. The most obvious is having left the FBI in the Department of Justice. By all accounts, this decision resulted from an inability to force the FBI into a bureaucratic restructuring, rather than a conclusion that the FBI's mandate was incompatible with DHS.

Likewise, retaining the responsibilities of Consular Affairs within the DOS has required constant engagement and coordination. The DOS has made significant efforts to build bridges to the relevant DHS agencies, but many see divergent and sometimes incompatible goals. As a result, the burden often falls to the president and the National Security Council staff to ensure compatibility between agencies. Improved cross-agency sharing of data is essential. Until the federal government can trace the life cycle of an immigration case—

from the time the foreign national is identified as a person of interest even before entering the United States, through the border crossing, immigration detention, case adjudication, etc.—it is at a disadvantage imposed by its own fragmentation.

Ensure that Visa Waiver Program partners meet their statutory obligations. Increasing numbers of VWP participant nationals have been radicalized to violence or are known foreign fighters. The perpetrators of various attacks across Europe were largely nationals of their Western European countries, not refugees, asylees, or new migrants. It is critical that participants in the VWP take seriously their obligations to share information and report encounters with known or suspected terrorists, report lost or stolen passports to Interpol, and meaningfully screen travelers crossing their borders. Countries that do not or cannot meet their obligations should be reevaluated for participation.

Focus resources and attention at the southwest border on building capacity at land POEs and partnerships with Western Hemisphere governments. A border-wide wall is an outdated, inefficient, and expensive border security solution. As with all border security, the best solutions are those that push out U.S. borders and segment flows into those with higher and lower risks. Given the shifting demographics of migration and the likelihood that suspicious aliens are most likely to fly into airports in the Western Hemisphere, efforts should be focused on improving personnel and resources at U.S. land POEs and building partnerships throughout the hemisphere.

Mexico plays an increasingly important role as a buffer between the United States and migration from other parts of the world. The United States should embrace Mexico as an essential partner. Improved security throughout the hemisphere is more difficult due to limited buy-in by foreign partners and differences in state capacity. Still, the United States should continue to invest in information sharing and capacity building as fully as possible.

Pause the expensive, low-yield border enforcement goal of biometric exit in favor of deepened database connectivity and cross-agency coordination. The value of biometric exit as a national security tool is questionable, especially in light of the significant advancements in information sharing and collection across the federal government enterprise. The goal should be to better identify threats to the United States, including where individuals may be located. To that end, it would be better to invest in information-sharing technologies, including a cross-DHS platform that allows access to agencies regardless of provenance.

Even more effective would be improvement of information sharing across the federal intelligence and law enforcement agencies. Negotiating individual memoranda every time agencies want to share information generates delays, duplication, and hoarding of information.

Invest resources in addressing the threats of tomorrow. A key lesson from 9/11 was that public officials knew they needed to do more to address the evolving threat of terrorism, but did not take action soon enough. We know that cyber threats, emerging infectious diseases, and transnational criminal organizations will be more prevalent and menacing as the world becomes increasingly mobile.

The U.S. government should not limit improvements in information sharing and coordination to terrorism. Instead, it should invest in combating the threats on the horizon—conducting meaningful analysis of the cost to U.S. lives and resources of these threats and making proportionate investments to address them. Every event improves the response. For example, the 2015 Ebola outbreak demonstrated that terrorist targeting tools could be used to identify travelers at a higher risk of infection and led to a supplemental appropriation. The significant governmental cyber breaches—from the Office of Personnel Management breach to the infiltration of the U.S. electoral system—led to greater clarity of agency roles and responsibilities.

None of these threats has received the same level of sustained governmental attention and resources as U.S. domestic counterterrorism efforts. The Intelligence Community, the FBI, CBP, ICE, the DOS, and other organizations all have pieces of the solution, but like the days before 9/11, there has not been sufficient priority given to next-generation needs. Government officials must change that dynamic, and Congress should provide the resources to do so.

CHAPTER 10

Emergency Management
and DHS

Jason McNamara

SUCCESSFUL, NATIONWIDE EMERGENCY MANAGEMENT IS A CRUCIAL element of the homeland security enterprise. When disasters—whether they are natural or man-made—strike, citizens must be able to turn to the government for assistance. And in a country as large as the United States, disasters frequently do strike. In a ten-year period from 2004 to 2014, the United States experienced more disasters than any other country except China, at a cost of $443 billion in damages.[1]

Coordinating the country's response to these disasters falls to the Federal Emergency Management Agency (FEMA), which is part of the Department of Homeland Security (DHS). In America's federal system, however, emergency management functions differently from most of DHS's other operating agencies ("Components"): it is built upon a foundation of state, local, tribal, territorial, and federal cooperation. FEMA can be successful only when intergovernmental cooperation works well. In short, FEMA's success is dependent upon its ability to consistently and continuously coordinate the actions and resources of the entire federal interagency and intergovernmental community.

FEMA was much criticized in the wake of Hurricane Katrina in 2005, which shone a spotlight on leadership and program deficiencies both at FEMA and within DHS as a whole. Afterward, FEMA implemented significant improvements; until Hurricane Maria made landfall in Puerto Rico on September 20, 2017, and caused widespread destruction, FEMA enjoyed generally positive reviews from critics both inside and outside of the government. But the 2017 hurricane season—and in particular the effects of Maria—portends a future in which disasters and emergencies regularly overwhelm the U.S. government's capacity to effectively respond and recover.

Indeed, a continued increase in the impacts and costs of disasters can be expected, for three reasons. First, the variability and intensity of hazards are increasing. Second, exposure to natural hazards is also on the rise. And third, vulnerability to disasters—both social and structural—has continued to grow. The United States needs to address these challenges now to reduce the risk of catastrophe, some examples of which are already looming.

To provide context on FEMA, this chapter first discusses the challenges that the agency faces regarding its role within the homeland security enterprise and specifically within DHS. It then discusses the history of federal emergency management, which underscores the reactive nature of policy-making. It concludes with an assessment of where FEMA is now and provides recommendations for strengthening FEMA's (and the broader emergency management community's) capabilities in the future.

FEMA and DHS: Challenges of Culture and Mission

Emergency management—and specifically, FEMA—occupies a somewhat awkward position within DHS and the larger homeland security enterprise. Unlike most of the other Components of DHS, such as Customs and Border Protection (CBP), FEMA has no responsibility for federal law enforcement. Although DHS's primary statutory mission is to "prevent terrorist attacks within the United States,"[2] FEMA's mission is focused on supporting "our citizens and first responders to ensure that as a nation we work together to build, sustain and improve our capability to prepare for, protect against, respond to, recover from and mitigate all hazards."[3] Most of these hazards do not involve terrorism; they are far more likely to be the product of extreme weather, earthquakes, or other natural disasters.

FEMA's mission and its cultural differences from many parts of DHS generally are significant, so much so that there was extensive debate regarding the appropriateness of FEMA's inclusion in DHS at all. Although this organizational debate has been settled, the mission and cultural differences remain.[4] In practice, these differences often result in FEMA's resistance to DHS efforts at unification of administrative functions such as acquisitions, human resources, and information technology, because such centralization of functions does not result in direct benefits to the FEMA mission. For example, FEMA has no equities or interest in DHS efforts to achieve economies of scale by making large-scale purchases of ammunition. Furthermore, although FEMA's Administrator reports to the Secretary of Homeland Security, Congress also designated the Administrator as "the principal advisor to the President, the Homeland Security Council, and the Secretary for all matters relating to emergency management in the United States"—a different position than other Component heads enjoy.[5] Differences in mission focus, coupled with statutory language passed in the aftermath of specific incidents, create an ongoing tension between FEMA and DHS as a whole.

Another crucial distinction between emergency management and the remainder of DHS's missions and functions concerns the concept of prevention. Although governments can take measures to reduce the impacts of disasters and emergency events, floods, hurricanes, earthquakes, and other natural events cannot be "prevented." FEMA operates on the principle that bad things—no matter the cause—will eventually happen, and that the nation must be prepared to respond to and recover from such incidents.

A second difference, noted above, concerns FEMA's relationship to subnational authorities. FEMA maintains the strongest and most regularized programmatic, policy, and financial ties to state, local, tribal, and territorial governments. FEMA's success, particularly in the response and recovery phases of disasters, is dependent upon full coordination and cooperation with them. Indeed, except in very limited circumstances, FEMA cannot take action without the consent of and close partnership with the affected governments.[6]

FEMA is also the only DHS Component—and perhaps one of the few executive branch agencies—that is governed by laws, regulations, policies, and processes that are purposely built upon the foundation of federal interagency coordination and cooperation. Many DHS Components must collaborate with other agencies to fulfill their mission, but FEMA's success is particularly dependent upon its ability to consistently and continuously coordinate the actions and resources of the entire federal interagency community.

A final organizational challenge with which FEMA must wrestle is the high visibility and intense media interest that individual disaster incidents generate. All DHS Components must, of course, face public scrutiny when things go awry, but natural disasters are more common than major terrorist attacks, and responsibility for managing them is more specifically directed at one organization. Success or failure in disaster response has long-term consequences for both individual political appointees and their associated organizations. Effective action and government competence following a disaster or emergency are necessary to ensure that elected and appointed officials—such as the impacted governor, the FEMA Administrator, the Secretary of Homeland Security, and even the president of the United States—maintain the confidence and the support of their constituents, and in some cases, their jobs. In the wake of a disaster, government officials are not afforded second chances, the space to consider all options before making a decision, or the opportunity to revisit policies and processes at a later date. Under the most intense levels of scrutiny by both the media and the public, numerous self-appointed "experts" are pleased to second-guess government decision-making. Unclear lines of authority or failure to demonstrate leadership in disaster response are readily apparent to the media and the public: there is no hiding bureaucratic incompetence. In these complex environments, successful leadership requires a somewhat different skill set than is generally needed in the traditional federal appointee or executive. (Conversely, the relative frequency of federally-declared disasters provides DHS with the opportunity to regularly demonstrate its competence in responding to major incidents, as well as reinforcing the intergovernmental cooperation required to protect the nation from emergency incidents of all types.)

It is important to note that the challenges FEMA faces within DHS are organizational and cultural; they do not mean that emergency management is alien to the homeland security enterprise. The successful nationwide practice of emergency management has always been a critical resource for DHS and for the homeland security enterprise as a whole. By performing coordination functions for a range of incidents (regardless of which federal agency is designated to lead by statute), FEMA and the emergency management community supports DHS leadership in fulfilling the Department's role as the leader for domestic incident management, as well as supporting other federal agencies that lack the resources to maintain the full complement of coordination mechanisms (e.g., 24/7 emergency operations centers and interagency funding mechanisms).[7]

The Evolution of Emergency Management

Throughout the history of disaster response and recovery in the United States, major incidents have always served as the driver for significant, lasting policy change in the emergency management community. Specifically with respect to FEMA—which was established in 1979 for reasons that are strikingly similar to those stated for creating DHS (e.g., consolidating functions to cut duplicative administrative costs and strengthening the nation's ability to deal effectively with emergencies)—major incidents, and the perceived failures of government action in response to these incidents, have driven large-scale changes within the organization.[8]

In 1989, widespread problems in the federal response to the Loma Prieta Earthquake in California and Hurricane Hugo in South Carolina focused major national attention on FEMA. The Bush administration and FEMA attempted to address the agency's shortcomings by developing and publishing the Federal Response Plan (FRP) in April 1992. Approved and signed by the leadership of twenty-seven federal Departments and agencies and the American Red Cross, the FRP provided "the mechanism for coordinated delivery of Federal assistance and resources to augment efforts of State and local governments overwhelmed by a major disaster or emergency."[9] Despite this important advance in federal coordination efforts, FEMA's response to Hurricane Andrew in August of 1992 brought significant additional criticism, as well as calls for reform from Congress; "some members of Congress even threatened to abolish the agency."[10]

In 1993, the Clinton administration and FEMA initiated a number of major reforms. FEMA Director James Lee Witt "streamlined disaster relief and recovery operations, emphasized preparedness and mitigation, and focused on customer service. At the same time, the reduction in geopolitical tensions occasioned by the end of the Cold War enabled the agency to redirect [numerous human and physical] resources from civil defense to disaster relief, recovery, and mitigation programs."[11]

The Great Midwest Floods of 1993 and the Northridge (California) Earthquake of 1994 clearly demonstrated the potential value of increasing the use of hazard mitigation techniques and grant funding to reduce the financial and human impact of future disasters. Specific steps included acquiring high-risk properties within flood zones, encouraging communities to adopt better building practices and codes, and focusing federal mitigation grant funds on critical facilities in earthquake zones, such as hospitals. Continued focus on the importance of mitigation by the Clinton administration following these two disasters resulted in the passage of the Disaster Mitigation Act of 2000, which provided FEMA with the legal basis to mandate mitigation planning requirements for state, local, tribal, and territorial governments as a condition of mitigation grant assistance.[12]

At the same time, FEMA and the emergency management profession as a whole worked to become more professionalized through the development of training and certification programs. In 1993, the International Association of Emergency Managers (IAEM) began accepting the first applications for its Certified Emergency Manager (CEM®) designation, and issued 211 CEM certifications later that year.[13]

In 1995, the bombing of the Alfred P. Murrah Federal Building in Oklahoma City increased the federal government's emphasis on terrorism preparedness and response. This change in emphasis forced greater coordination and cooperation at all levels of government between the law enforcement and emergency management communities. Incident management concepts that had traditionally been utilized by the fire service, such as the Incident Command System (ICS) and the Multi-Agency Coordination System (MACS), began to be adopted by multiple response disciplines. These concepts were widely tested in 1999 as the nation prepared for the Y2K conversion and its anticipated adverse impacts. On December 31, 1999, the emergency management, law enforcement, information technology, critical infrastructure protection, and national security communities worked in close coordination at both the federal level and on a state-by-state basis to monitor the transition and respond to any incidents as they arose.

Despite the magnitude of these disasters, and the enormous loss of life associated with them, FEMA's post-disaster assistance programs were generally able to address the impacted population's needs within FEMA's statutory and funding authority.

In the immediate aftermath of the attacks of September 11, 2001, FEMA and the emergency management community continued to demonstrate the ability to effectively coordinate resources within and across all levels of government. However, 9/11 did significantly change the landscape of federal emergency management policy. Terrorism preparedness and enhancing the response to terrorist incidents became a principal driver for changing the focus, practice, and priorities of the emergency management community. This emphasis on preparedness for terrorism overshadowed the historical emphasis on preparedness for natural disasters and other types of emergencies. Enormous financial resources were devoted to the creation of new federal grant programs that were intended to enhance preparedness for terrorism nationwide. These enhancements, however, often came at the expense of other preparedness activities that may have been better suited to the more likely threats and vulnerabilities in specific states. Further complicating this competition for resources, many states created the stand-alone position of homeland security adviser or coordinator, often with a direct reporting relationship to the governor. These appointments created a competition for resources between the emergency management and homeland security directors.

In March of 2003, FEMA joined twenty-two other federal agencies, programs, and offices in forming DHS. Two years later, under Secretary Michael Chertoff (who had succeeded the first Secretary, Tom Ridge), DHS reorganization "moved virtually all of the remaining preparedness capabilities in FEMA to a new Office of Preparedness, leaving FEMA to focus exclusively on response and recovery. This situation was similar to what existed [prior] to FEMA's 1979 creation when Federal emergency management and disaster assistance capabilities were scattered across the Federal government and in the White House."[14]

Balancing and Solutions

In August 2005, Hurricane Katrina starkly demonstrated the failure of splitting the preparedness and response-and-recovery functions (and more broadly, separating homeland security and emergency management). This devastating event showed that natural disasters could be as bad as—if not worse than—terrorist attacks on the homeland. At least 1,100 Louisianans died as a result of Katrina, revealing the enormous shortcomings of a federal response organization that should have addressed the readily apparent needs of the impacted populations.[15] (There were also, of course, significant failures at the state and local levels.)

Numerous reports, congressional investigations, and other criticism following Katrina resulted in the passage of the Post-Katrina Emergency Management and Reform Act (PKEMRA), which for the first time defined the role of FEMA and federal emergency management in the context of DHS.[16] The PKEMRA clarified both the special advisory role of FEMA's Administrator and FEMA's relationship with state, local, tribal, and territorial governments. It further professionalized the practice of emergency management at the federal level by statutorily defining the qualifications required of presidential appointees to the agency. From 2007 until the 2017 hurricane season, FEMA was generally able to successfully navigate multiple record-breaking disaster years by managing the federal government's response to multiple large-scale natural disasters, including devastating tornadoes in the Midwest as well as Hurricanes Irene, Matthew, and Sandy. Although the response to and recovery from each of these disasters created novel problems and received their share of criticism from the impacted populations, the level of concern with FEMA's overall competence did not approach the calls for abolishment of the agency that occurred after Hurricanes Hugo, Andrew, and Katrina, as noted above.

Still Unprepared

The United States faces the very real threat of a major catastrophe, the likes of which the nation has never experienced before. In fact, despite recent disasters such as Katrina, Sandy, and the 2017 hurricanes, the nation has never truly experienced a catastrophic disaster, in the sense of an incident where the resources that can be brought to bear to protect the population, save lives, and safeguard property have been completely overwhelmed. The current emergency management system is still far from prepared to fully address the needs that would be created by a disaster of this scale. A large magnitude earthquake in Southern California, along the New Madrid fault in the central United States, or in the Cascadia subduction zone would result in thousands of casualties, millions of displaced residents, and tens of billions of dollars in damages.[17] Although FEMA and other federal agencies have invested millions of dollars in studying and planning for catastrophic incidents, real progress in developing capabilities to address all consequences of such incidents has been limited.

Although the initial response to Hurricanes Harvey and Irma in 2017 indicated a high level of resilience and adequate intergovernmental coordination, that same season demonstrated that there is a point after which—often driven by novel circumstances—the federal government's response becomes ineffective. In the case of Hurricane Maria in Puerto Rico, the island's distance from the mainland and the failure of FEMA both to provide enough logistical resources prior to landfall and to anticipate the difficulties in transporting and distributing mass care supplies on the island resulted in an inadequate federal response in the early days of the disaster that has been widely, and justifiably, criticized.

The principal factor preventing progress in preparing for catastrophe is that DHS, FEMA, and the federal government still plan for what the government is capable of doing, rather than planning for what could actually happen. Currently, the emergency management system is much more comfortable planning and budgeting for the normal annual occurrence of disasters; this planning approach is predictable, budgets are defensible, and it fits in well with the normal appropriations process. Any of the aforementioned catastrophic events, however, would quickly break down current systems and structures. The government would not have enough resources to address the impacts of such disasters, it would not be able to save lives, and recovery programs would take years if not decades to implement. In order to be successful, the future of emergency management requires a shift in the current thinking about what could happen, and what the government can or cannot do about it.

The increasing number and scale of disasters suggests further cause for concern. Superstorm Sandy in 2012 and Hurricanes Harvey, Irma, and Maria in 2017 provide additional evidence that the number, magnitude, and cost of natural disasters will continue to increase (see Figure 10.1). According to the Government Accountability Office (GAO), from fiscal years 2005 to 2014,

Figure 10.1. Federal Emergency and Disaster Declarations, 1950–2015.

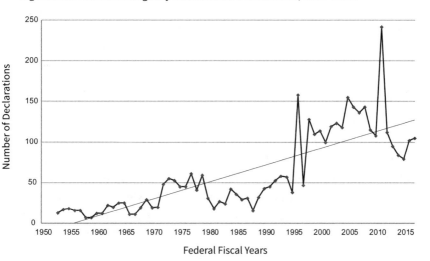

federal Departments and agencies required at least $277.6 billion in disaster assistance, an average of $27.76 billion per year.[18] The 2017 hurricane season was officially the most expensive ever, racking up $202.6 billion in total damages (including physical damages, clean-up expenses, and lost business activity), and for the first time in official records, three Category 4 storms hit U.S. shores, with Hurricane Harvey becoming the first major hurricane to slam into the United States since 2005.[19]

Emergency managers typically assess hazard risk based on the historical record, but prior experience is no longer a sufficient predictor of future conditions. Climate change is challenging the traditional, history-based approach to risk assessments, forcing emergency managers to find new ways to accommodate greater uncertainty in decision-making processes.[20]

More than half of the U.S. population lives in coastal areas. As Superstorm Sandy clearly demonstrated, large-scale disasters in densely populated coastal cities present a new set of complex challenges. The insured value of property along the Atlantic and Gulf coasts has also risen, from $7.2 trillion to $10.6 trillion during 2004–2012.[21] This is a recipe for disasters that cost more money and threaten more lives.

Diminishing federal budget resources, reductions in annual grant funding, and competing budgetary pressures at the federal, state, and local government levels have negatively impacted the disaster preparedness and response capabilities and capacities in many jurisdictions. At the federal level, and particularly from members of Congress, there have been consistent proposals to reduce federal expenditures associated with disasters.[22] At the same time, there has been enormous resistance from state and local governments against proposals to shift the financial burden for disasters down to state and municipal governments. In an era of decreased government resources, the emergency management community cannot hope to see significant increases in their budgets and resources in the coming years.

Based on the trends described above, the future holds more catastrophic incidents in store for the nation. In addition, a variety of other factors will serve to increase the complexity of managing emergencies, including the proliferation of social media and real-time media coverage of events; increased operational interdependencies within and across critical infrastructure sectors, including power, water, and transportation; and the existence of novel threats that have unclear consequences or untested response strategies, such as attacks on the cyber infrastructure or chemical, biological, radiological, and nuclear (CBRN) terrorism. In summary, the future promises more, not fewer, challenges for the homeland security and emergency management communities.

What Should We Do?

Emergency management agencies at all levels of government must undertake a number of initiatives to enhance the nation's ability to prepare for, respond to, recover from, and mitigate against future vulnerabilities. I offer three straightforward but critical recommendations to build the nation's preparedness posture and to assure continued improvement in the nation's emergency management system.

BUILD UPON LESSONS LEARNED AND PRIOR SUCCESSES

FEMA and state governments need to maintain their current readiness posture and continue refining their approaches to "regularized" disasters—those incidents that we understand will happen with relative frequency on an annual basis. Increasing the efficiency and effectiveness of processes to manage such disasters is critical for controlling costs, building public confidence in DHS, FEMA, and the emergency management profession, and preserving as many resources as possible for large-scale catastrophic events. In the future, the response to a three-county flood event along the Mississippi River should be quick, efficient, cost-effective, and minimally disruptive. Although such an incident may be devastating to many individuals and families, the government's response should be so scripted and routinized that the chance of failure is almost nonexistent.

HOPE FOR THE BAD (I.E., "NORMAL" DISASTERS), PLAN FOR THE WORST

The emergency management community needs to adopt a planning and budgeting posture that focuses resources on the most likely catastrophic events. Federal leadership is absolutely necessary to drive preparedness priorities. FEMA must define the limits of federal government capabilities to address the most catastrophic incidents; develop an in-depth understanding of where capability gaps exist across the nation; and fill these gaps with government, private sector, or voluntary and nonprofit resources. The simple fact is that the government, as whole, does not have enough capacity to respond effectively to the most catastrophic disasters. Government-centric solutions to catastrophic disaster response will not survive first contact. One possible approach is to significantly enhance the partnerships and co-ordination with the private sector, particularly on enhancing the resilience of the supply chains and other critical infrastructure. This approach would require close coordination with other Components of DHS such as the Cybersecurity and Infrastructure Security Agency (CISA), and may have the effect of increasing cooperation within the Department itself. (For further discussion of CISA, formerly known as the National Protection and Programs Directorate [NPPD], see Chapter 11 in this volume.)

VIEW THE PUBLIC AS A RESOURCE, NOT AS A LIABILITY

Although it was encouraging to see the resilience of communities in Texas and Florida following the 2017 hurricanes, the population as a whole remains unprepared to deal with the consequences of disasters. In 2014, FEMA found that the percentage of surveyed individuals taking recommended preparedness actions had remained largely unchanged since 2007.[23]

In order to reposition the public as a force multiplier—as opposed to a drain on scarce resources—the federal government should research and implement the most effective alert and warning systems and methodologies. Efforts should focus on providing clear and concise messages that allow the public to take definitive action to protect themselves and their communities and how to best deliver those messages. FEMA must maintain a real-time understanding of the advances in communication technologies and methodologies in order to understand how to reach the most people in the shortest time. At the same time, through the use of social media and other emerging technologies, FEMA and the emergency management community need to adopt policies and procedures that make the best use of and take advantage of information provided by the public through social media. This information can be used to increase situational awareness, identify and direct needed resources, and determine the location of the most highly impacted or vulnerable populations. As noted above, however, such strategies will only work when the public is viewed and activated as a full partner in preparedness and response.

Despite the challenges that FEMA has faced throughout its integration with DHS, it is clear that FEMA brings a critical intergovernmental perspective and cooperative approach to the practice of homeland security. FEMA can continue to enhance DHS's relationship with state and local governments by building more partnerships, providing technical and financial resources, and maintaining close contact with DHS's most critical partners—the state governors and elected leaders of municipalities throughout the nation.

CHAPTER 11

Protecting Critical Infrastructure

Caitlin Durkovich

My former colleague in government, Jason McNamara, notes in Chapter 10 the awkward position that emergency management occupies within the homeland security enterprise. The mission of protecting critical infrastructure also sits uneasily alongside border control and counter-terrorism, because most infrastructure is owned by the private sector.

Because its uninterrupted operation is essential to the owners and operators themselves, privately owned infrastructure has not always been regarded as something that the federal government needed to protect. At the same time, certain types of infrastructure (such as the electrical grid, communications networks, and water systems) are basic services that underpin American society and are increasingly essential to the operation of other systems. If something so fundamental fails, so do large swaths of the economy. American society thus depends on this "system of systems," and the American people depend on its protection in carrying out their everyday lives.

Various regulatory regimes have established standards intended to encourage the private sector to take into account the reliability and security of infrastructure. In some cases (as with cyber threats to some parts of the financial sector), long-established, sector-specific regulatory agencies have been able to ensure that necessary changes to private sector operations were made. In other cases, as with chemical plants, new legislation and policy changes have forced compliance with measures that the federal government deemed necessary for public safety. For the most part, however, the United States has depended mainly on partnerships between the federal government on the one hand and a wide array of private firms and state or local authorities on the other. "Security," where it exists, is primarily the product of voluntary cooperation.

These partnerships have been reasonably successful because many critical systems (e.g., local water utilities) were contained and bound; the disruption of one system did not necessarily destabilize others. In general, the likelihood and costs of disruption have largely fallen in the bottom-left quadrant of a typical risk matrix (low-probability, low-consequence events). Unfortunately, the increasing interconnectedness of systems to each other and to the internet means that what were once low-cost, isolated events are increasingly high-cost and cascading. Meanwhile, changes in the threat environment—especially low-grade cyber warfare and aging infrastructure under stress from increasingly severe natural disasters—make once low-probability events more likely and more consequential. In this context, existing arrangements are no longer adequate to protect the complex ecosystem that underpins the American way of life.

This fact raises crucial questions for the homeland security enterprise—and specifically, for the relevant operating agency at the Department of Homeland Security (DHS), which is now known as the Cybersecurity and Infrastructure Security Agency (CISA). What responsibility does the federal government have to protect critical infrastructure? What new authorities or capabilities does it need in order to do so? Can the private sector still act as a first line of defense against certain types of threats? Who should pay for required security improvements?

In this chapter, I first describe critical infrastructure. I then discuss the federal government's role in its provision and protection, including the creation of the voluntary partnership regime and the salient steps in its evolution after September 11, 2001. In the conclusion, I offer a set of specific recommendations for improvement.

All told, I argue that the voluntary partnership model continues to make sense for many sectors, including infrastructure designated by the federal government as "critical." On the other hand, certain "lifeline" sectors whose uninterrupted operation has major implications for the economy and society—such as energy, communications, and water—remain concerningly vulnerable. Owners and operators do not have sufficient capability to ensure the security of the system of systems in this complex risk environment. In particular, sophisticated cyber attacks and increasingly extreme weather have revealed the inadequacy of existing incentives for security-conscious behavior, especially for smaller, less sophisticated companies that are often the weak link. Modest government action now to ensure better private-sector behavior and adherence to security and resilience best practices would help to prevent serious incidents (as well as potential regulatory overreaction in their wake).

The federal government must also be proactive in setting up appropriate regulatory regimes for those emerging sectors that will become tomorrow's critical infrastructure—"smart grids," smart cities, autonomous vehicles, electronic voting technologies, and the commercial use of outer space. In many of these sectors, security has simply not been a consideration in system design. It needs to be.

Finally—and perhaps most controversially—I argue that the federal government faces a significant challenge in dealing with sectors at the outer edge of what is considered "critical." More frequent cyber and terrorist attacks on soft targets make it likely that the federal government will feel compelled to play a role in the security of facilities and systems (e.g., schools), which are not necessarily vital to the operation of other systems but which are nevertheless part of the fabric of American life. A federal commitment to protect such critical infrastructure would require a thorough revision of the current system.

What Is "Critical Infrastructure"?

A modern and functioning infrastructure is an important part of what differentiates the developed world from the developing world. Most Americans take safe, functioning infrastructure for granted and organize their lives around the notion that it will operate smoothly. In this sense, they implicitly assume that the government will ensure its continued operation.

Most of the infrastructure on which Americans depend, however, is not owned by the U.S. government; the majority is owned and operated by the private sector. Private water and wastewater service providers, for example, support the needs of nearly seventy-three million people in the United States.[1] Some of the private firms that provide basic services are national or even international companies; others, like many of the investor-owned electric utilities, are regional.

Infrastructure that is not owned by the private sector is generally owned by state and local governments. States and municipalities, for instance, frequently fund and operate transportation networks, electric and water utilities, and dams. As infrastructure modernization and maintenance have become costlier, however, financially strapped state and local governments have increasingly outsourced such operations to the private sector. Many "public services" are thus privately provided.

The owners and operators involved in providing these services have different incentives from government, most notably profit. Their incentive to invest in security is usually weak. At best, they will take steps to protect their own facilities and build basic business resumption capacity. But of course they do not have an incentive to take into account what economists call "externalities"—the fact that a disruption in their business may trigger a cascade of failures in other businesses or systems. In the absence of regulation or incentives, therefore, they will underinvest in both protection and resilience.

When most people think of "infrastructure," they tend to think of a set of roads or pipes. Though factually accurate, this imagery is misleading because it does not capture the increasingly complex and interconnected nature of infrastructure. In a modern economy, infrastructure is actually a "system of systems," in which the operation of one part can have a profound effect on the others. The failure of the electrical grid is one obvious example: it affects not only whether people have lighting in their homes but also whether traffic lights work and subways run (the transportation system), whether water pump stations operate (the water system), and whether people can charge their cellphones or access the internet (the communication system). Counterintuitively, the connectivity of these systems to each other by way of the internet has exacerbated this problem; the disruption of one system can cause broad problems for society. One feature that makes a particular system "critical," then, is the degree to which failure in it will spill over to other systems.

The federal government views certain infrastructure functions as "critical" not because of their interconnectedness but because they are essential in their own right; their demise creates profound disruptions in society even if other systems are not particularly affected. These include:

> systems and assets, whether physical or virtual, so vital to the United States that the incapacity or destruction of such systems and assets would have a debilitating impact on security, national economic security, national public health or safety, or any combination of those matters.[2]

Nuclear power plants, dams, water systems, energy infrastructure, communications networks, financial services, and government facilities are among the sectors considered "critical" for this reason.

Sometimes it is not until the moment of failure and its impact on the "American way of life" that a particular type of infrastructure is revealed to be "critical." For instance, electoral systems in a given county may not seem worthy of national focus until that county becomes pivotal in a presidential election. At that point, it becomes obvious that each of the tens of thousands of independent decisions about electoral registries and voting technologies made by states and counties across the nation affect the fundamental legitimacy of the nation's political system.

Current government policy (under Presidential Decision Directive 21, or PDD-21) defines sixteen sectors of "critical" infrastructure, several of which have many "subsectors" or "segments." These include:

- Chemical plants and facilities (including basic chemicals, specialty chemicals, agricultural chemicals, pharmaceuticals, and consumer products);
- Commercial facilities (including motion picture studios and broadcast media; casinos; hotels, motels, and conference centers; "outdoor events" such as parades; "public assembly" sites such as sports stadiums; real estate, such as apartment and office buildings; retail, such as shopping malls; and sports leagues);
- Communications (which is regarded as an "enabling" sector linked to several other sectors);
- Critical manufacturing (including primary metals, certain types of machinery, electrical equipment, and transportation equipment);
- Dams;
- The defense industrial base (including more than 100,000 companies and their subcontractors);
- Emergency services (including federal, state, local, tribal, and territorial authorities);
- Energy (including electricity, oil, and natural gas);
- Financial services (broadly defined to include institutions facilitating liquidity, investments, and risk transfer);
- Food and agriculture (including farms, restaurants, and food processing facilities);
- Government facilities (including not only federal buildings but also schools, "national monuments and icons," and election infrastructure);
- Health care and public health;
- Information technology;
- Nuclear reactors, materials, and waste;
- Transportation systems; and
- Water and wastewater systems.

For some of these sectors, federal agencies other than DHS that are already involved in regulating those industries are the "sector-specific" leads. Thus the Treasury Department is the lead agency for financial services, the Department of Health and Human Services for health and public health, the Department of Agriculture for food and agriculture, the Department of Defense (DOD) for the defense industrial base, the Department of Energy (DOE) for energy, and the Environmental Protection Agency (EPA) for water and wastewater. These other agencies had pre-existing regulatory authorities and contacts with sector stakeholders when DHS was created; they were therefore given primary responsibility to work with owners and operators of critical infrastructure in those sectors. In other cases—such as with chemical plants and facilities, communications, critical manufacturing, emergency services, nuclear reactors, materials and waste, and commercial facilities—DHS itself functions as the sector-specific agency.

Although all of these categories are designated as "critical," in reality they are not equally so. Communications, electricity, transportation, water, and financial services are "lifeline" systems that must be maintained (and restarted as swiftly as possible in the event of an adverse event) if society is to function. Other systems are "critical" in some ways but not necessarily in others. For instance, ensuring adequate security at chemical plants is critical because accidents or attacks at these facilities could kill a large number of people and because dangerous materials kept there could fall into the wrong hands; however, simple disruption in their normal production cycle is not nearly as problematic for society as a whole as it would be with the "lifeline" sectors.

One challenge with any definition of "critical infrastructure" is where the line should be drawn. For instance, local elementary schools, corner restaurants, and post offices are all considered part of "critical" sectors under the current capacious definition. In fact, such an expansive notion of critical infrastructure renders almost everything other than certain private dwellings "critical" in some way. The rationale for this encompassing and holistic approach is that if people do not feel safe going about their daily lives, society as Americans know it cannot function. But a comprehensive approach inevitably raises questions about the federal government's obligations and relationships to industry (and to state and local authorities).

The Emergence of the Voluntary System

The history of U.S. infrastructure is one of sporadically but steadily increasing federal involvement. Although Congress resisted intervening in industry for most of America's first century, by the late 1800s, the federal government had assumed an expanding role in providing and protecting infrastructure. Major increases in federal involvement came with the 1887 Interstate Commerce Act (which regulated railroads, arguably the first national infrastructure); the Depression-era creation of the Tennessee Valley Authority and other public works projects; the National Defense Highway System in the 1950s; and the establishment of a national emergency communication system during the Cold War.[3]

Growing concerns about terrorism (beginning in the mid-1990s and peaking with 9/11), combined with the increasing sophistication of the economy, led the federal government to take a greater interest in the protection of certain systems. In July 1995, a National Intelligence Estimate predicted future terrorist attacks in the United States and warned that the danger would increase over the next several years. According to the 9/11 Commission Report, this estimate "identified particular points of vulnerability, to include symbols of capitalism such as Wall Street, critical infrastructure, areas where people congregate, the power grid, and civil aviation."[4] It noted that the 1993 detonation of a truck bomb in the garage of the North Tower of the World Trade Center in New York City "had intended to kill a lot of people, and not achieve any political goal."[5] The April 19, 1995, domestic terrorist bombing of the Alfred P. Murrah Federal Building in Oklahoma City, which killed 168 people and injured hundreds of others, also revealed the potential for high-casualty attacks on civilian facilities. Meanwhile, the commercialization of the internet forced an expansive definition of critical infrastructure as "those physical and cyber-based systems essential to the minimum operations of the economy and government."[6] These included telecommunications, energy, banking and finance, transportation, water systems, and emergency services.

Building on the recommendations of the President's Commission on Critical Infrastructure Protection,[7] the Clinton administration promulgated the first comprehensive critical infrastructure policy, Presidential Decision Directive 63 (PDD-63), in 1998.[8] PDD-63 recognized that "future enemies, whether nations, groups or individuals, may seek to harm us in non-traditional ways including non-traditional attacks on infrastructure and information systems that may be capable of significantly harming both our military power and our economy."[9]

Tangibly, PDD-63 established the National Infrastructure Protection Center (NIPC) within the Federal Bureau of Investigation (FBI) to provide a national focal point for gathering information on threats to critical infrastructure. PDD-63 also encouraged the voluntary creation of private sector Information Sharing and Analysis Centers. Threat information from the NIPC was to be shared with these centers, which would gather, analyze, sanitize, and disseminate private-sector information to both industry and the NIPC. The idea was for the federal government to pull together as much information as possible, including information it had collected through classified means, and then disseminate a declassified version of it to private-sector partners.

PDD-63 also stated that market incentives should be the first choice for addressing the problem of critical infrastructure protection. Regulation was only to be used in the face of the private sector's failure to take the necessary security measures. In such cases, alternatives to direct regulation would be encouraged, including providing economic incentives to encourage the desired behavior. The overall goal was cooperative partnership between government and industry. In this partnership, the government's role would be to help the private sector identify vulnerabilities, suggest mitigation strategies, provide best practices, and offer modest resources. But the decision about when and whether to take remedial action was left up to firms.

PDD-63 was a crucial step in that the federal government officially recognized the importance of robust, resilient national infrastructure. In hindsight, however, the policy could have benefited from a more prescriptive approach. Despite its proactive language, it was designed for an earlier era. It fell victim to what the 9/11 Commission Report described as "a failure of imagination" and "a mindset that dismissed possibilities."[10]

The Post-9/11 Evolution, in Six Steps

The terrorist attack of 9/11 was the sort of nontraditional attack that PDD-63 had warned about, in that it weaponized and targeted critical infrastructure (the transportation system, government facilities, and a major commercial site that was symbolic of the financial system). The significance of critical infrastructure in this attack was not lost on Congress: post-9/11 legislation acknowledged the need for the federal government to expand its work with asset owners and operators to manage the threat of terrorist attacks on domestic soil.

The USA PATRIOT Act, which was signed on October 26, 2001, mandated that any physical or virtual disruption of the operation of the critical infrastructure of the United States be rare, brief, geographically limited in effect, manageable, and minimally detrimental to the economy, human and government services, and the national security of the United States, and that the actions necessary to achieve this be carried out in a public-private partnership involving corporate and nongovernmental organizations.[11] Broad powers were given to law enforcement agencies and the Intelligence Community (IC) to prevent and protect the country from the threat of terrorism. But how to include the private sector in this effort remained a challenge. Given the size and scope of what had come to be defined as critical infrastructure, the most viable solution was to continue to promote and enhance a voluntary framework. In general, that is the path that the United States took.

1. STRENGTHENING THE VOLUNTARY SYSTEM

In creating DHS through the Homeland Security Act of 2002, Congress established an Office of Intelligence Analysis and Infrastructure Protection (IA/IP). This office formalized the public-private framework for critical infrastructure protection while laying out more specific mechanisms to incentivize and support the private sector. Primary among its responsibilities were:

- Conducting comprehensive vulnerability assessments of critical infrastructure, including the performance of risk assessments to determine the risks posed by particular types of terrorist attacks within the United States;
- Developing a comprehensive national plan for securing the key resources and critical infrastructure of the United States; and
- Recommending protective measures necessary to protect the key resources and critical infrastructure.[12]

Information sharing between the government and the private sector had been the cornerstone of the Clinton administration's critical infrastructure policy, but insufficient protections and safeguards for sharing data had hindered its adoption. For instance, private sector firms might have faced legal liability or commercial jeopardy if they admitted certain vulnerabilities. With this deficit in mind, Congress granted DHS additional authorities, including:

- The protection of critical infrastructure information. Enacted in the Homeland Security Act of 2002, the Critical Infrastructure Information Act created an information protection regime for the private sector to voluntarily submit sensitive information about critical infrastructure, including vulnerabilities, to DHS with the assurance that the information, if it satisfies certain requirements, will be safeguarded from public release. Specifically, the information may not be used as a basis for regulatory action and is protected from Freedom of Information Act disclosure, state and local disclosure ("sunshine") laws, and use in civil litigation.

- The Critical Infrastructure Partnership Advisory Council (CIPAC). Congress instructed DHS to create an effective structure for sharing sensitive information about infrastructure with the private sector and mandated that DHS "ensure the security and confidentiality" of such information. The result was to exempt critical infrastructure advisory committees from the Federal Advisory Committee Act requirements as an incentive to critical infrastructure owners and operators to provide DHS with information and recommendations that would not otherwise be shared.[13]

The newly formed Homeland Security Council would formalize the Bush administration's critical infrastructure protection policies in December 2003 by issuing Homeland Security Presidential Directive 7 (HSPD-7), which superseded PDD-63.[14] The post-9/11 policy focused on counterterrorism. It directed DHS to develop an integrated national plan for the protection of critical infrastructure. The first draft of The National Infrastructure Protection Plan (NIPP) in 2005 laid the groundwork for an organizing structure and risk management framework. This structure reaffirmed that: asset owners and operators generally represent the first line of defense for critical infrastructure under their control; there is benefit in sector-specific planning and coordination; and government is uniquely positioned to share threat information that might inform investment decisions and operational planning.[15] Where the NIPP faltered was in its lack of connection to other plans and requirements that hindered adoption of security standards, and in the absence of a comprehensive, shared understanding of what it was trying to achieve.

Private-sector and government coordinating councils—known as Sector Coordinating Councils and Government Coordinating Councils (GCCs), respectively—formed the structure through which representative groups from the private sector and all levels of government could collaborate or share existing consensus approaches to critical infrastructure protection.[16] The councils were to work closely with their Sector-Specific Agency (SSA)—that is, the federal Department or agency that serves as the lead coordinator for each sector. Thus, DHS acted as the "lead coordinator," while the DOE was the sector-specific lead for energy-related infrastructure, the Department of the Treasury for financial services, etc.

One essential element of the regime was the definition of "critical."[17] The National Critical Infrastructure Prioritization Program (NCIPP) developed a methodology for identifying systems and assets whose loss, interruption, incapacity, or destruction would have a negative or debilitating effect on the economic security, public health, or safety of the United States, any state government, or any local government, and if destroyed or disrupted, would cause national or regional catastrophic effects.[18] The NCIPP list would be a consideration in allocating funds among states and high-risk urban areas applying for homeland security grants. Grant funds could be used for protecting a system or asset included on the prioritized critical infrastructure list, including what was known as the Buffer Zone Protection Program, an early grant program intended to increase preparedness capabilities.[19]

This program was phased out after fiscal year 2010, much to the dismay of owners and operators, who viewed it as the only funding stream available to them. Although the NCIPP remains one of thirteen allowable uses for state and local homeland security programs, owners and operators complain that the money never filters down to them. That in turn removes their incentive to make security upgrades.

2. CFATS AS AN ALTERNATIVE MODEL

Congress also set its sights on preventing terrorists and other malicious actors from gaining access to dangerous materials and technologies. Recognizing that some chemical facilities possessed weaponizable materials, and that a successful attack on certain high-risk facilities could cause a significant number of deaths and injuries, Congress gave DHS the authority to regulate security at high-risk chemical facilities in the United States through the DHS Appropriations Act of 2007.[20] The result was the Chemical Facility Anti-Terrorism Standards (CFATS) program, which represented a new regulatory model.

The CFATS regime did not mandate specific security measures, but rather permitted high-risk facilities to select layered measures that collectively met certain standards. The program's early years were marred by unforeseen (albeit preventable) problems in implementing the rules, chief among which were establishing a national inspector cadre from scratch and deploying a subjective inspection protocol. The program was also dependent on annual authorization through DHS's appropriations bill, raising questions in the minds of the owners of the covered facilities about the stability of the program and the value and rationality of making investments in security measures. Ultimately, however, the CFATS program drove more than three thousand facilities to eliminate, reduce, or modify their holdings of certain chemicals.

Despite its flexibility in allowing facilities to develop tailored security regimes, the CFATS program represented a marked departure from the purely voluntary approach. The government could fine firms and even shut down noncompliant facilities. In retrospect, the danger that hazardous chemicals would be stolen and weaponized was lower than Congress had initially feared, while the threat of natural disasters and cyber attacks to other critical sectors proved to be far greater. The result has been a mismatch between the federal authorities in regulating industry and the objective threat environment.

3. NATIONAL PROTECTION AND PROGRAMS DIRECTORATE

The bungled federal response to Hurricane Katrina in 2005 was the galvanizing force for Congress's next major piece of legislation—the Post-Katrina Emergency Management Act of 2007 (PKEMRA). The PKEMRA led to the establishment of the National Protection and Programs Directorate (NPPD) within DHS.[21] This oddly named DHS Headquarters entity included many elements of the legacy Preparedness Directorate that were not transferred to the Federal Emergency Management Agency (FEMA), including the Office of Infrastructure Protection.

The Office of Infrastructure Protection evolved from a Headquarters policy organization to a national organization with nearly three hundred field-based employees and offices in every state. Nearly two thirds of those employees were Chemical Security Inspectors responsible for enforcing the CFATS regime. The remainder were Protective Security Advisors (PSAs) that served as physical security experts in the field, working closely with private sector companies and with state homeland security advisors. Their primary roles are to conduct risk assessments; foster sharing of threat and hazard information; provide support to National Special Security Events and Special Event Activity Rating Events and incident responses; and coordinate and conduct risk-mitigation training around evolving threats.

NPPD, however, was problematic from the beginning. In 2009, the troubled and shrinking Federal Protective Service was moved into NPPD. (The rationale for this was twofold. First, "Government Facilities" was a designated critical infrastructure sector, and the Federal Protective Service is responsible for the security of more than nine thousand buildings owned or leased by the General Services Administration. Second, the Assistant Secretary of Infrastructure Protection within NPPD also chaired the Interagency Security Committee, which was established by Executive Order 12977 after the 1995 bombing of the Alfred P. Murrah Federal Building to develop best practices and set standards for nonmilitary federal facilities.[22]) NPPD also had responsibilities for cybersecurity. Finally, in the Obama administration, NPPD was tapped to address climate change risk management for critical infrastructure.[23] Unsurprisingly, it was privately characterized as the "directorate of misfit agencies."

4. RESILIENCE

By 2009, there had been two further shifts in the federal government's critical infrastructure mission. First, DHS's embrace of an all-hazards (rather than purely counterterrorism) focus filtered into critical infrastructure protection. As Hurricane Katrina had demonstrated, there were natural threats to critical infrastructure, which were worsened by the superannuated state of many systems. Second, and related, a greater emphasis was placed on the capacity of systems to rebound after a disaster. The result was a shift from "protection"— guns, guards, and gates—toward "resilience." In other words, federal efforts would focus on helping assets, systems, and communities withstand and bounce back from adverse events.

In 2009, DHS launched the Regional Resilience Assessment Program (RRAP). Regional assessments are conducted on a key industry or cluster of infrastructure assets and examine the dependencies and interdependencies, analyze the cascading effects and characteristics that make the assets and the region resilient, and report on any gaps that may impede rapid recovery from a disaster. DHS required that state and local governments nominate RRAP submissions, and any enhancements or "options for consideration" were first directed to the subnational government sponsor, not the owner or operator. The first submissions examined the cluster of chemical facilities near Exit 14 of the New Jersey Turnpike and Chicago's Financial District. By 2016, DHS had conducted more than fifty regional assessments covering almost every state and sector: the resiliency of cross-border infrastructure; the impact of climate change on coastal communities; the growing vulnerabilities of industrial control systems, etc. The RRAP was arguably one of the most valuable tools that DHS offered the critical infrastructure community. Unfortunately, like other programs targeted at owners and operators, it did not alter incentives for private-sector actors. As a result, the adoption of recommendations was inconsistent.

Another challenge to resilience policy was the lack of a clear distinction between "emergency management" (dealing with a particular incident in a particular location) and "consequence management" (understanding the consequences of a disruption, so as to mitigate its total effect). The plans and procedures that help minimize disruptions and support rapid recovery in an incident were still not well understood. FEMA not only managed the Emergency Support Function, but also had a nationally recognized brand, an authorized and well-funded regional presence, experience in engaging stakeholders, and grant money for state and local governments. In the end, its "emergency management" approach generally prevailed over the broader notion of consequence management.

5. SUPERSTORM SANDY

The whole-of-community approach to preparedness would be tested in October 2012, as Superstorm Sandy made landfall on the East Coast. The storm highlighted how an aging and failing infrastructure was more susceptible to disruptions, thus slowing response and recovery. It also showed that, while progress had been made since Hurricane Katrina, the government was still not prepared to handle a regional or national incident that disrupted infrastructure and overwhelmed the state and local response capabilities. At the same time, the storm revealed the value of partnerships between the federal government and the private sector in the context of a disaster.

In 2010, the National Infrastructure Advisory Council had published "A Framework for Establishing Critical Infrastructure Resilience Goals."[24] The writers of the report had formed a study group that included fourteen senior executives with comprehensive knowledge of power system operations and business priorities. The study group conducted a tabletop "stress test" of the electrical grid to uncover potential gaps in resilience, the results of which were subsequently shared with sector executives and used to formulate a set of recommendations to enhance resilience for the electricity and nuclear sectors. The group recommended that the White House initiate an executive-level dialogue with chief executive officers in the electricity and nuclear sector on the respective roles and responsibilities of the private and public sectors in addressing high-impact infrastructure risks and potential threats, using the CIPAC structure.

Of course, presidential advisory councils lack the authority to force government action.[25] It took the meltdown of Japan's Fukushima Daiichi nuclear power plant following a tsunami in 2011 to get the administration to act. In July 2012, chief executive officers from the nation's power companies and representative trade associations lined up on one side of the table; on the other side sat the Secretaries of Energy and Homeland Security and other top-ranking executives from their respective Departments and the National Security Council. The objective was to build trusting relationships and define clear roles and responsibilities for managing a high-impact event at the national level. The group would regularly reconvene under the CIPAC's Electric Subsector Coordinating Council. Cybersecurity and information sharing quickly dominated the agenda; grid operators were increasingly under attack and were looking for federal assistance. They pressed for better information from the government on threats to help inform security decisions and sought access to government threat-assessment tools.

The policy community was starstruck. As memories of 9/11 and Katrina had faded, getting senior executives to pay attention to security and resilience had been a Sisyphean task. The government sought to seize the opportunity in hopes of using the electricity industry as a case study for greater investment in security. In September 2012, nearly one hundred CEOs were given one-day clearance and provided with a classified briefing on threats to the power industry. This information covered low-tech, kinetic threats that the government saw in combat situations as well as a comprehensive cyber threat assessment, from espionage to control system threats. The CEOs left the room ready to engage, with cybersecurity at the top of the priority list.

On October 29, 2012, days before the next government meeting with the CEOs, Hurricane Sandy made landfall in New Jersey. It had already left a path of destruction as far south as North Carolina and would become the second costliest storm in U.S. history as it barreled up the I-95 corridor,[26] leaving nearly 8.5 million people without power.[27] The storm surge and high winds made power restoration difficult; as outages stretched and long gas lines dominated the news cycles, the CEOs began convening via conference call with their various government counterparts. Utility crews were facing issues including fuel shortages, credentialing issues, a pure shortage of qualified repair staff ("linemen"), and a region unaccustomed to housing thousands of these linemen. The nightly meeting of top executives from industry and government helped clear roadblocks, remove bureaucratic red tape, and speed recovery.

One incident highlighted the value of the collaboration. President Barack Obama joined a call in which the CEOs were lamenting the need for more linemen, and utilities on the West Coast had offered up linemen and trucks. But every available resource east of the Mississippi was spoken for, and it would take five days for the linemen to make their way east. Obama reminded the CEOs that the federal government had some expertise in logistics; if the trucks could get to a California airbase, he could shave the travel time from five days to five hours. Similar episodes played out several times during the crisis, most notably including resolution of fuel supply chain challenges that plagued New York and New Jersey. In this sense,

Sandy highlighted the importance of regular contact and collaboration between the public and private sectors.

Nevertheless, Sandy did not lead to a permanent change in the model of voluntary partnership. Private-sector participation in security upgrades came fitfully, usually in response to crises that threatened industry, and focused on securing federal resources.

6. CYBERSECURITY

On February 12, 2013, after three years in the making, Presidential Policy Directive 21 (PPD-21)—Critical Infrastructure Security and Resilience—was released.[28] PPD-21 superseded HSPD-7, aligning critical infrastructure protection with the national preparedness system and expanding the focus to consider "all hazards that could have a debilitating impact on national security, economic stability, public health and safety, or any combination thereof." It was also the aim of the policy that critical infrastructure should be secure and resilient,[29] and that the endeavor be a shared responsibility among the federal, state, local, tribal, and territorial entities, as well as public and private owners and operators of critical infrastructure.[30]

On the same day, the Obama administration also issued Executive Order 13636—Improving Critical Infrastructure Cyber Security. That order reaffirmed the policy to enhance the security and resilience of the nation's critical infrastructure and "to maintain a cyber environment that encourages efficiency, innovation, and economic prosperity while promoting safety, security, business confidentiality, privacy, and civil liberties." First, it called on the Commerce Department and the National Institute of Standards and Technology (NIST) to lead the development of a Cybersecurity Framework—a set of industry standards and best practices to help organizations manage cybersecurity risks. The Cybersecurity Framework was intended to provide a prioritized, flexible, repeatable, performance-based, and cost-effective approach to help owners and operators of critical infrastructure identify, assess, and manage cyber risk. Second, the Order called for a risk-based approach to identify critical infrastructure where a cybersecurity incident could have a catastrophic effect. The result would be the "Section 9 List," a catalogue of several dozen companies spanning the financial services, electricity, and communications sectors that would receive priority in assistance from federal government.

In some respects, these policies represented a synthesis of post-9/11 changes to critical infrastructure policy. One drawback to Executive Order

13636, however, was the bureaucratic separation of cyber-based threats to critical infrastructure from other threats. This bifurcation made it more difficult to trade off different risks to critical infrastructure. It also implied that cyber and physical threats were distinct, when in fact the convergence of the two has become increasingly clear.

Conclusion: What Should We Do Now?

Although the federal government's role in critical infrastructure protection has expanded significantly in the last twenty years, Washington still largely plays a supporting role. In most sectors, the federal government makes recommendations and furnishes information, but the private sector chooses whether to invest in security or not. This creates a conundrum: the federal government shares in the responsibility to protect its citizens and has a moral imperative to ensure the security and resilience of the nation's infrastructure, but it relies primarily on voluntary partnerships.

How far does the government's responsibility extend? Currently, it is likely that the private sector's participation in enhanced security regimes will be inadequate to protect critical infrastructure without further economic incentives or direct regulation. With this reality in mind, I focus on three levels of recommendations: steps to be taken within the existing regime, changes to the regime itself, and the larger implications of adopting an encompassing approach to critical infrastructure.

ENHANCEMENTS IN THE EXISTING VOLUNTARY PARTNERSHIP
No asset owner or operator has the resources to manage the risk environment efficiently and effectively on his own. Even state and local governments have access to only a tiny fraction of the information collected by the federal government. For this reason, the federal government must continue to lead when it comes to information collection and fusion. CIPAC-style forums also offer an opportunity for the government to assist whenever practical in the case of specific crises. Since 9/11, new legislation and policy have allowed the private sector to share information with the federal government.

One improvement that could be made to the existing system concerns information sharing from the government side. Asset owners and operators seek access to classified information, rather than reports they consider to be incomplete and watered down, in order to better understand the strategic threat environment. It is not feasible to share classified information with a range of private actors, particularly real-time intelligence around cyber threats, and the current program that provides security clearances to private-sector executives is too costly to scale. At the same time, private-sector actors do need more information on tactics and techniques than they receive, in order to assess the intent and severity of a threat. For instance, the government should be willing to share the fact that a cyberattack is state-sponsored rather than the work of a lone hacker. Such information is particularly essential in the financial and electricity sectors. It should be possible to convey this sort of information without compromising intelligence sources and methods.

A second issue concerns collaboration between the government and the private sector on planning, which has proven extremely valuable in identifying vulnerabilities and building resilience into the system. Hurricanes Katrina, Sandy, and Maria all demonstrate that infrastructure resilience is central to a region's ability to recover from a disaster and to its long-term economic viability. Additional planning and resources should be committed to better understanding the vulnerabilities of the intersection of communications, electricity, financial services, transportation, and water, and how a threat might cascade across them, thereby causing second- and third-order effects. There is an opportunity to improve strategic collaboration across sectors and to align these efforts with the most senior levels of government through a Strategic Infrastructure Coordinating Council, with a tiered approach for senior executives, operational leaders, and dedicated full-time operational staff. Responsibility for this effort should be located at DHS, within the successor to NPPD—the Cybersecurity and Infrastructure Security Agency, or CISA.

Third, attention is needed to risk management throughout the supply chain of manufactured products in critical sectors. Asset owners and operators currently do not have a trusted method to verify the provenance of components from design and manufacture to integration and use. They also lack a way to verify the security posture of suppliers, vendors, or contractors. But without these mechanisms, it is easy to infiltrate a system. Developing an adequate verification system in partnership with the private sector should again fall to CISA.

A fourth step concerns CISA itself. As discussed above, NPPD (CISA's predecessor) was formed from the leftovers of a PKEMRA-mandated reorganization and charged with protecting and strengthening the cybersecurity of the nation's critical infrastructure. Today CISA has a $3 billion budget and a workforce of eighteen thousand; its authorities include sharing and protecting sensitive information, conducting vulnerability assessments, chemical regulation, protecting federal assets, and the resilience of communications systems.[31] The reorganization of NPPD as CISA, with a mission to protect America's critical infrastructure against "all threats," including cyber, is a major step forward. As a further step, CISA security specialists in the field should be recognized as an integral part of the National Response Framework and its focus on reconstituting critical infrastructure, in particular "lifeline" sectors, in the event of a catastrophic incident.

A fifth improvement within the existing framework concerns the "education" (for want of a better word) of DHS Secretaries and their top staff. DHS leaders generally do not take office with a full appreciation of the role of the private sector in critical infrastructure. But in order to function effectively in their jobs, they must understand both the importance and the limits of partnerships with the private sector. Ways to manage the relationship between industry and government in critical infrastructure sectors is a conversation that every Secretary should have on his first day on the job, not on the first day of his first crisis.

CHANGES IN THE PRESENT REGIME

The preceding improvements can all be made within the larger framework of voluntary partnerships with the private sector. Unfortunately, even an improved voluntary structure will fall short of protecting America's critical infrastructure or guaranteeing resilience—to say nothing of protecting "public spaces" and softer targets. Continued cyberattacks against critical infrastructure raise questions about the limits of the voluntary partnership.

The principal dividends of the current voluntary approach come from enterprises that no longer view security and resilience as a cost center, but rather as something integral to corporate risk management and as a way to differentiate themselves from other firms. Such companies remain the minority. Furthermore, their decisions to invest in security may ultimately place them at a commercial disadvantage relative to firms that do nothing. Something must be done to incentivize the weak links, especially in the sectors where failures are most likely to cascade and affect other systems.

One option would be to deploy a CFATS-style regulatory regime to certain "lifeline" sectors. The water and energy (including both electricity and natural gas) sectors, in particular, are vulnerable to natural disasters and remain enticing targets for cyberattack. A preliminary step would be to undertake a full assessment of where those industries stand following Hurricane Maria, which destroyed Puerto Rico's communications system and electrical grid, and a series of Russian-organized cyberattacks. The prospect of stricter regulation could be the stick that brings about needed improvements, even if a new regulatory regime is not actually imposed.

There must also be carrots for good behavior. The 2002 Support Anti-Terrorism by Fostering Effective Technologies (SAFETY) Act provides liability limitations to companies that develop and deploy counterterrorism technologies. Owners of critical infrastructure assets are increasingly seeking certification, which allows them to display DHS-approved Safety Act grades akin to a "*Good Housekeeping* Seal of Approval." Extending this approach beyond counterterrorism to include other threats to critical infrastructure would reward firms that address security vulnerabilities. For instance, publicizing the fact that a company had received a certification (or that it had *not* received one) could affect valuations. Still other incentives might include preferential consideration for government contracts and prioritized federal assistance with business resumption in the context of a disaster.

If this combination of incentives fails, however, regulation will be needed. In the long run, there is no doubt that poorly protected critical infrastructure will be compromised. If the impact is catastrophic enough—for instance, an event leading to major loss of life or a cyberattack comparable to what Ukraine faced in 2015—then far stricter and possibly less well-conceived regulation might win out.[32] Imposing a lighter-touch, flexible regulatory regime now is a better approach.

Another much-needed change to the existing system concerns emerging sectors where technological development and commercialization are proceeding extremely rapidly, without adequate thought to security. These areas include smart grids, smart cities, autonomous vehicles, some electronic voting technologies, and the commercialization of outer space. In these cases, some measure of "security by design" is essential. The United States must avoid a repeat of the Internet of Things (IoT), where large-scale vulnerabilities were inadvertently introduced from the beginning as commercial development proceeded apace, and retrofitting security has proven almost impossible.[33] (See Chapter 12 for further discussion of the IoT and potential regulatory responses.) This means regulation, rather than voluntary standards alone.

A HOLISTIC APPROACH

Unfortunately, none of the measures discussed above will be sufficient to fully protect critical infrastructure. Simply hardening some infrastructure would be counterproductive because adversaries and human error tend to gravitate toward the weakest link. One week in April 2013—known inside

DHS as "The Week That Was"—illustrates the continued vulnerability of U.S. infrastructure, whether "hardened" or not. On April 15, two improvised explosive devices exploded within twelve seconds of each other near the finish line of the Boston Marathon, killing three and injuring hundreds of runners and spectators. The massacre was carried out by two self-radicalized brothers, Dzhokhar Tsarnaev and Tamerlan Tsarnaev, who had built the explosive devices in their kitchen from a "how-to" tutorial in Al-Qaeda's online magazine *Inspire*. A day later, still-unidentified attackers slipped into an underground vault and severed fiber optic telecommunication lines near a Pacific Gas and Electric (PG&E) substation in Metcalf, California, that sent electricity to Silicon Valley; the severed lines controlled both 911 emergency communications and downstream communications with other substations in the PG&E system. The assailants, armed with AK-47 assault rifles, also fired more than one hundred rounds from a field outside the perimeter substation in Metcalf, destroying sixteen 500-kilovolt transformers and six circuit breakers and leaving Metcalf substation down for a nearly a month. The next evening, an explosion caused by improperly stored ammonium nitrate occurred at the West Fertilizer Company's storage and distribution facility in West, Texas, killing fifteen people, including twelve firefighters, and damaging or destroying 150 buildings. It would take three years for the Bureau of Alcohol, Tobacco, Firearms and Explosives (ATF) to determine that the fire that caused the explosion had been set on purpose.

All three of these cases constitute attacks on "critical infrastructure." (The first falls under the Outdoor Events subsector of the Commercial Facilities Sector; the second under the Energy Sector; and the third under the Chemical Sector). Needless to say, the federal government was forced to be involved in all of these incidents in one way or another. But the changes proposed above would probably be insufficient to prevent such incidents.

What is to be done? One option is to accept that it is impossible to prevent all attacks, especially against softer targets, which in the grand scheme of risk pose a very small threat to most Americans, and focus resources on the higher consequence, existential threats. Another option is to keep the federal role to a minimum and let local authorities make the necessary improvements (as has occurred following the Boston Marathon bombings). Still a third option is to further incentivize investment in resiliency. In the case of Metcalf, for instance, there was enough resilience built into the system that substation operators leveraging backup communications capabilities were able to reroute power and prevent Silicon Valley from going dark.

The fourth option is greater federal involvement, including more aggressive regulation designed to create a true "culture of security." That path would require a far greater federal role. But if the United States is going to define "critical infrastructure" so expansively, it assumes an obligation that goes well beyond providing information on potential risks and hoping that others will take the necessary steps.

CHAPTER 12

Cybersecurity

John Carlin and Sophia Brill

In 2012, then–Secretary of Defense Leon Panetta described the nation's cybersecurity vulnerabilities as a "pre-9/11 moment."[1] In more recent years, nation-states, terrorist groups, and criminal organizations have probed America's critical infrastructure, planning destructive attacks, stealing personal information and intellectual property, and even attempting to influence U.S. elections. Online threats of all types are increasing in frequency, sophistication, and scope. And these threats are occurring against a background of increasing worry about the nation's overall network security. Indeed, for the past six years, cyber threats have ranked first among the U.S. Intelligence Community's annual Worldwide Threat Assessment.[2]

One unique aspect of this threat is that it applies in almost equal measure to the U.S. government itself as a target and to the private sector. In the past several years, there have been serious and alarming breaches of government networks—as occurred, for example, in the massive breach of the Office of Personnel Management's files—as well breaches of private-sector networks that have the potential to cause broad public harms. And, of course, Russia's actions during the 2016 election show how hacks against private and semi-private actors, such as the Democratic National Committee and other political campaigns, can threaten to undermine core institutions.

Just as the federal government needed a new, all-tools approach to terrorism after 9/11 and a better regime for international cooperation and working collaboratively with state and local governments, it needs the same now for cybersecurity. If anything, the challenges and stakes are even greater. The post-9/11 counterterrorism policy reforms focused on tearing down walls that impeded information sharing *within* the government. By contrast, the cyber threat also requires the government to find new ways to share information regarding threats *with the private sector*—and to do so at the speed of the internet. Information sharing must be done in a way that builds and maintains trust, protects relevant privacy interests, and does not jeopardize some of the nation's most closely guarded tools and secrets.

This chapter first describes the current threat landscape as it exists across a range of sectors, institutions, and malicious actors. This landscape can be broken down into three main categories: threats against the government itself; threats against "government-adjacent" private actors that have the potential to pose immediate threats to public safety and stability; and other types of threats implicated through emerging technologies. The chapter then describes the government's responses to these various cyber threats and discusses areas in which further improvements are needed.

Evolving Cyber Threats

The United States faces several different types of cyber threats, which require different responses from the government.

THREATS AGAINST GOVERNMENT NETWORKS

Nearly every government operation—at the federal, state, and local levels—is being carried out today with the assistance of computer networks and processes. And the government must acquire and maintain massive amounts of sensitive and valuable data in order to function effectively. Government information systems and networks are regularly targeted by a broad array of malicious cyber actors with a diverse set of motives. These motives range from foreign nation-states' desires to acquire intelligence and to identify potential security vulnerabilities to domestic and international cyber criminals seeking access to information that they can sell on the black market to ideologically motivated groups seeking to expose government secrets or even cause physical harm.[3] In recent years, these attacks have only increased in number and sophistication.

Written testimony from the Government Accountability Office (GAO) in February 2017 underscored the vast challenges to securing U.S. government information systems and networks despite the obvious importance of doing so:

> Federal information systems and networks are inherently at risk. They are highly complex and dynamic, technologically diverse, and often geographi-cally dispersed. This complexity increases the difficulty in identifying, managing, and protecting the myriad of operating systems, applications, and devices comprising the systems and networks. Compounding the risk, systems used by federal agencies are often riddled with security vulnerabil-ities—both known and unknown.[4]

The GAO report also highlighted the trend toward an increased number of attacks and other security incidents between 2006 and 2015, which can be seen in data relating to "information security incidents" reported by federal agencies to the U.S. Computer Emergency Readiness Team (US-CERT) in the Department of Homeland Security (DHS).[5] (See Figure 12.1 on the following page.)

Most people are likely familiar with at least one or two widely reported instances of government networks getting hacked. The best known is the intrusion into the databases of the federal Office of Personnel Management, which was reported in 2015 and exposed sensitive information about more than 22 million federal employees, contractors, and others.[6] This information included detailed files of individuals who had applied for security clearances—leading former Federal Bureau of Investigation (FBI) Director James Comey to describe the attack as exposing "a treasure trove of information about everybody who has worked for, tried to work for, or works for the United States government."[7]

It is not hard to imagine why foreign adversaries might want to get access to this kind of information; it can be used for blackmail against government employees or potentially even to recruit government employees as intelligence assets. Other examples of malicious actors stealing personal information from the federal government have included a breach of Internal Revenue Service (IRS) systems that allowed the attackers to gain access to information on approximately 100,000 tax accounts and an intrusion into the U.S. Postal Service's networks that compromised personal information about 800,000 employees.[8]

Adversaries are not only seeking to steal information when they conduct cyberattacks against the federal government. They might also seek to cause actual physical harm—or at least enhance their means to do so. For example, a 2015 GAO report highlighted the range of cyber threats faced by the Federal Aviation Administration (FAA).[9] Of course, a breach of air traffic control systems by someone with hostile intent could result in untold losses of life. Networks used by the Department of Defense (DOD) to control weapons systems are also natural targets for any malicious actor seeking to weaken the U.S. government's defenses or to steal designs for weapons systems.

In many ways, the federal government has long been aware of cyber threats and has taken measures to address them. In fact, as far back as 1991, the GAO reported that Dutch hackers had breached the DOD's computer systems,

Figure 12.1. Information Security Incidents Reported by Federal Agencies.

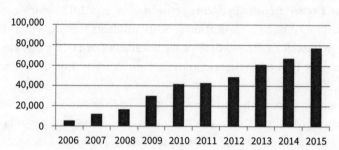

gaining access to sensitive (though unclassified) information about personnel, logistics, and weapons systems development data.[10] Although much remains to be done to secure public-sector systems, the private sector is a much more rapidly expanding attack surface and presents even more difficult challenges to secure.

"GOVERNMENT-ADJACENT" TARGETS AND CRITICAL INFRASTRUCTURE

Some of the most worrying potential risks relate to critical infrastructure entities, which are frequent targets of cyberattacks. As then–Director of National Intelligence (DNI) James Clapper testified before the Senate in 2015, "foreign actors are reconnoitering and developing access to U.S. critical infrastructure systems, which might be quickly exploited for disruption if an adversary's intent became hostile."[11] Likewise, his successor as DNI, Daniel Coats, testified in 2017 that cyber threats "pose an increasing risk to public health, safety, and prosperity as cyber technologies are integrated with critical infrastructure in key sectors."[12] Coats further noted that "if adversaries gain the ability to create significant physical effects in the United States via cyber means, they will have gained new avenues for coercion and deterrence."[13] In other words, as former Homeland Security Adviser Lisa Monaco has similarly explained: "Private companies are on the front lines. Individual defenses, as well as broader efforts to reform . . . will require our joint efforts."[14]

It is easy to imagine why an adversary would want to gain access to systems controlling dams, electrical grids, nuclear reactors, transportation systems, and financial institutions. A hostile nation-state could use that access as a means of coercive power—either as a deterrent against the

United States or offensively, to inflict harm. Terrorist groups such as ISIS could conduct an outright attack, seeking to kill or injure as many people as possible. A criminal organization (foreign or domestic) could seek to sell access to a vulnerability in our critical infrastructure systems to the highest bidder.

The defense of critical infrastructure from cyberattack poses unique challenges. Many attempts by nation-states and other sophisticated actors to penetrate critical infrastructure systems undoubtedly go undetected, while others are not reported or are revealed publicly with only a high-level description that does not convey the magnitude of the risk. Because of this, the steps taken to secure this infrastructure do not take into account the full scale of the threats. An August 2017 report from the president's National Infrastructure Advisory Council (NIAC) concluded that there is "a narrow and fleeting window of opportunity before a watershed, 9/11-level cyberattack."[15]

Consider one particularly disconcerting example: In March 2016, the Department of Justice (DOJ) unsealed an indictment charging seven experienced Iranian computer hackers for their roles in an extensive campaign of distributed denial of service (DDoS) attacks against the U.S. financial sector. One defendant was also charged with obtaining unauthorized access into the Supervisory Control and Data Acquisition (SCADA) systems of the Bowman Dam in Rye, New York.[16] The intrusion could have given the hacker control of the dam's water levels and flow rates if it had not been disconnected from the system for maintenance.

This example illustrates a few crucial points. First, there is a significant range of targets that, while not government-owned or controlled, serve important public safety and stability functions. A breach against a financial institution or against a system that controls a dam does not just threaten the entity that was hacked. It could cause broader public harm—including financial chaos or real physical damage and even death. In other words, a hack against one of these private-sector entities is different from, say, the robbery of a jewelry store; the breach is not simply a crime that harms only the immediate victim.

Second, this public harm problem poses unique policy challenges because it may not be sufficient to rely on private actors to assess the threat landscape and to provide their own security. These private entities might also be up against adversaries—like nation-state actors—who are far more sophisticated and better resourced. To continue the jewelry store analogy, imagine that the people trying to break into the store are not just ordinary criminals but entire armies. And imagine that the store holds things that, if taken, would cause widespread damage to public safety and stability.

In some ways, the U.S. regulatory system tries to bridge this gap between private resources and potentially public harms by recognizing and having special rules governing critical infrastructure. These rules were first codified in the 2001 USA PATRIOT Act, which contains a section governing "critical infrastructures protection." In enacting the law, Congress recognized that "a continuous national effort is required to ensure the reliable provision of cyber and physical infrastructure services critical to maintaining the national defense, continuity of government, economic prosperity, and quality of life in the United States." It defined "critical infrastructure" to include "the assets, systems, and networks, whether physical or virtual, so vital to the United States that their incapacitation or destruction would have a debilitating effect on security, national economic security, national public health or safety, or any combination thereof."[17]

DHS generally coordinates government programs related to critical infrastructure, but other agencies take lead roles depending upon the particular industry. There are currently sixteen sectors designated as critical infrastructure; these sectors include critical manufacturing, the defense industrial base, energy and the electrical grid, financial services, nuclear reactors and other nuclear materials, and mass transit systems.[18] Logic suggests that as more attacks proliferate, that ecosystem will expand: After Russia's interference in the 2016 election, for example, America's elections systems—which are administered by state and local governments—were added to the list.[19] As the NIAC report highlights, despite some advances to support cyber defense and resilience, there remain persistent gaps in preparedness that could lead to potentially catastrophic outcomes in these different sectors. (See Chapter 11 for a more detailed discussion of critical infrastructure.)

OTHER EMERGING THREATS

Cyber threats against the U.S. government itself and against critical infrastructure entities pose some of the most significant risks to public safety and stability. There are, however, many other potential targets for attack that exist in far less regulated spaces. And the "attack surface"—the list of potential targets and the opportunities for hackers to exploit them—is increasing daily as more and more aspects of our daily lives—right down to the cars we drive and our household appliances—are connected to the internet. As former White House Cybersecurity Coordinator Rob Joyce has explained, "During the past 25 years, we have moved much of what we value to a digital format and stored it in Internet-connected devices that are vulnerable to exploitation."[20]

THE INTERNET OF THINGS: FROM BABY MONITORS TO MOVING VEHICLES. The "internet of things" (IoT) has emerged in recent years as a key area of focus for cybersecurity efforts. This term generally refers to the growing realm of non-computer devices (things) that possess internet capabilities.[21] The IoT is growing rapidly—some estimates predict as many as thirty billion connected devices by 2020—and the range of devices includes everything from fitness trackers to pacemakers to cars.[22]

A rash of recent high-profile attacks on connected devices has called attention to the cybersecurity vulnerabilities created by the growth of the IoT. One batch of these attacks used poorly-secured connected devices as springboards for launching DDoS attacks against websites. For example, in October 2016, hackers employed a botnet (a network of computers infected by malware) to launch a massive DDoS attack against Dyn, a key player in the internet's domain name system infrastructure. The botnet achieved the scale that it did by hacking into as many as 100,000 IoT devices, including DVRs and cameras. The attack drew mainstream media attention in part because it disabled popular sites such as Twitter, the *Guardian*, Netflix, Reddit, and CNN.[23]

This was not the only such attack. Just a few weeks earlier, a French hosting site suffered two concurrent DDoS attacks orchestrated by a botnet that used IoT devices.[24] A week before that, another similar attack on cybersecurity journalist Brian Krebs's website reached such proportions that the site's hosting company had to suspend his service, forcing the site offline for multiple days.[25]

These attacks—clustered within a few weeks of each other—represent the latest in a trend that has been developing for some time. From December 23, 2013, through January 6, 2014, hackers infiltrated more than 100,000 gadgets—including televisions, multimedia centers, routers, and at least one refrigerator—and sent 750,000 malicious emails using their internet capabilities.[26] More recently, a couple in Washington walked into their baby's bedroom to learn that a hacker had taken control of their baby monitor and begun talking to their child.[27]

Additionally, the IoT era has created cyber vulnerabilities in classes of devices that for obvious reasons pose a heightened degree of risk of physical harm. Most notably, automakers are touting "smart" features that connect vehicle navigation systems and other vehicle components to the internet. According to one estimate, by 2020, 75 percent of new cars built globally will have some form of internet connectivity. There could be 220 million "connected" cars on the road, each with more than two hundred sensors. These cars will allow drivers to stream music, get real-time updates about traffic and weather conditions, and even receive help with parking.[28]

And those are just the accessories. Automakers are ramping up their investments in self-driving cars. One estimate forecasts that ten million such cars will be on the road by 2020, and that up to one in four cars may be self-driving by 2030.[29] These cars will obviously be connected to the internet, requiring navigation data and other information to be updated in real time. And that, of course, creates another critical attack surface. In September 2015, security researchers demonstrated that threat, hacking into a moving Jeep Cherokee being driven by a *Wired* reporter.[30] Later that month, Chrysler announced a recall of 1.4 million vehicles, citing concerns over cybersecurity within the network to which those cars were connected.[31]

From Barcelona to Charlottesville, we have already seen the tragic consequences that can result when a vehicle is turned into a weapon against crowds of people. If terrorists or other malicious actors are able to weaponize vehicles *remotely* by gaining access to their command and control systems, they will be all the more empowered to inflict widespread harm through technologies that most people rely on every day.

Against that backdrop, it is crucial for the government to be able to share cyber threat information with the private sector—ranging from automakers to manufacturers of more mundane devices—in as transparent and timely a manner as possible. The Trump administration took an important step in this direction in 2017 when it publicly released a charter governing the principles and processes for sharing sensitive information about the cyber vulnerabilities found in technology systems.[32] The charter prioritizes the protection of core internet and critical infrastructure systems and rightly recognizes that "unpatched vulnerabilities leave not only [U.S. government] systems, but also the systems of commercial industry and private citizens, vulnerable to intrusion."[33]

WEAPONIZED INFORMATION. Hacking can also be used to retaliate, intimidate, or coerce others—and even to undermine democratic institutions. Nation-states are able to undermine the core democratic institutions of their rivals and meaningfully punish companies that anger them in ways that were impossible in the recent past. A clear example of the former is Russia's attempt to interfere in the 2016 U.S. election. As we now know, Russian actors—operating on orders from the highest levels of their government—hacked into the servers of the Democratic National Committee and of various campaigns during the 2016 election cycle. Information stolen from those hacks, including emails, was then distributed to WikiLeaks (among other outlets), where it was used to undermine the presidential campaign of Hillary Clinton.

This is obviously a story with no shortage of dramatic plot lines to it. But many have also emphasized that it was unfortunately not a one-time occurrence. Former FBI Director Comey, for example, predicted that Russia would attack us again. As he put it, "They'll be back. . . . They introduced chaos and division and discord and sowed doubt about the nature of this amazing country of ours and our democratic process."[34] National Security Agency (NSA) Director Admiral Michael Rogers similarly testified to Congress that this type of behavior "will continue as long as autocratic regimes believe they have more to gain by challenging their opponents in cyberspace."[35] Although no major network intrusions by Russia have been reported in relation to the 2018 midterm elections, recent charges pursued by the DOJ allege that a Russian operative conducted an elaborate online influence operation targeting U.S. audiences through 2018.[36]

In addition to Russia's activities, the Intelligence Community (IC) has determined that both North Korea and Iran view their cyber programs as vital to advancing political objectives. Perhaps the most notorious example to date was North Korea's 2014 attack on Sony Pictures Entertainment. The apparent motive for the attack was retaliation against Sony for the planned Christmas Day release of *The Interview*, a comedy satirizing North Korean leader Kim Jong-un. The attackers destroyed Sony's computer systems, compromised private information, released valuable corporate data and intellectual property, and threatened employees, customers, and film distributors with violence. They stole over thirty-eight million files, totaling more than one hundred terabytes of data—including private correspondence, unreleased films, salary records, and over 47,000 Social Security numbers— and released much of it to the public in an attempt to tarnish the company's reputation.[37] The attack forced Sony to take its company-wide computer network offline and left thousands of its computers inoperable.

ECONOMIC ESPIONAGE. Individual acts of economic espionage may seem less frightening by comparison, but the aggregate threat that such activities pose is immense. As companies increasingly move to digital storage, economic espionage occurs not just through insider threats but also through cyber activity emanating from overseas. Intelligence officials have estimated that thefts of intellectual property conducted through hacking cost the U.S. economy $400 billion per year.[38]

Theft on this scale not only reduces the incentive to engage in research and development, but also undermines the trust between countries and companies that is necessary to do business in a globalized economy. As a result of the proliferation of technology—and the myriad ways to exploit it—every sector of the economy is a target: energy, financial institutions, infrastructure, entertainment, and more.

RANSOMWARE. Across multiple sectors and industries, we have witnessed the crippling effects that ransomware attacks have caused. As more and more valuable private-sector assets are placed online—including vast troves of trade secrets, intellectual property, and data needed to manage everyday operations—hackers have essentially been able to hold companies ransom by encrypting these files and threatening to destroy them unless they receive payment.

One of the most recent and notorious of these incidents was the WannaCry ransomware attack in May 2017—an attack for which U.S. officials have blamed North Korea.[39] Within days, it was reported to have infected over 300,000 computers in 150 countries. Notably, WannaCry impacted Britain's National Health Service, dramatically curtailing its ability to serve patients. The virus spread through the Windows operating system, exploiting a vulnerability that had already been patched but that continued to exist on systems that had not updated their software.

Another recent attack involved ransomware known as Petya—or, more specifically, an imitation of it. The Petya ransomware was first seen in 2016 in a form that spread mainly through email attachments. In June 2018, a new form of Petya, known as NotPetya, was used for a cyberattack that primarily targeted Ukraine. This malware relied on the same Windows vulnerability as WannaCry. NotPetya differed from Petya in that, once encrypted, a computer infected by NotPetya could not be returned to its original state and the information was lost, regardless of whether any ransom was paid. This change led many observers to suggest that NotPetya's goal was disruption, not revenue.

ANONYMIZATION OF ILLICIT ACTIVITY. As the means to launch cyber attacks continue to proliferate, malicious actors are also taking advantage of technologies that allow people to conceal their identities and their actions. For example, one often-touted feature of cryptocurrencies such as Bitcoin is the ability to facilitate anonymous transactions. Regulators around the globe are only beginning to tackle how (or if) these currencies can be regulated in order to prevent such activities as money-laundering and terrorist financing.

Social media and other types of communications providers have also built and marketed encryption technologies to consumers, including the provision of end-to-end encryption of communications. Law enforcement officials have argued that although these encryption technologies provide important security benefits, they can also protect criminals and other dangerous actors; accordingly, the officials have advocated for reforms that would facilitate access (upon obtaining a warrant) to encrypted communications. Privacy advocates and technology companies have pushed back strongly, arguing that such measures would threaten privacy rights and compromise the security of the underlying encryption.

Additionally, the "dark net" or "dark web" can provide an anonymized or quasi-anonymized forum for criminals to transact with one another and to share illicit content. The dark net generally refers to websites that are not available through conventional search engines and are often accessible only through specialized software, such as the Tor browser, which anonymizes web traffic. Some of these websites provide marketplaces for illegal drugs, child pornography, and stolen personal information that can be used to access accounts or commit identify theft; indeed, there are websites that sell cyber exploits (i.e., hacking tools) to would-be hackers.[40] (For further discussion of transnational crime, see Chapter 14.)

These and other tools that criminals can exploit pose obvious issues for policymakers in the cybersecurity realm. But they also have implications in many other spheres, ranging from child exploitation to drug policy. Consider, for example, an opioid dealer who sells his goods on the dark net and who receives payment via a cryptocurrency. His offenses could be considered "cyber-enabled," if not outright cybercrimes. Technology in that context facilitates and expands the potential markets for real-world crimes by enabling a criminal to communicate and to conduct transactions anonymously. Of course, these anonymization technologies can also facilitate cyberattacks themselves—as in the example of a hacker who purchases malicious code online using a cryptocurrency, or where a hacker profits from attacks by selling personal information online.

BLENDED THREATS. Finally, emerging cyber threats may involve many different types of actors and come in several forms. A nation-state can team up with a group of criminals, for example; or a criminal can hack for profit and turn the stolen material over to a terrorist group.

To give one example, consider the case of Ardit Ferizi. Ferizi, a citizen of Kosovo, was located in Malaysia. He stole the personally identifiable information of approximately 1,300 U.S. military service members and federal employees from a private company. He then provided that information to a notorious terrorist, Junaid Hussain, who was operating from Syria as an ISIS recruiter and attack facilitator. Hussain posted the information on Twitter and encouraged ISIS supporters to conduct terrorist attacks in the United States and elsewhere against those U.S. service members and government employees.[41]

To the organization being breached, the intrusion into its network and the theft of personally identifiable information may have appeared to be simple identity theft of the sort perpetrated every day. But the U.S. government was in the position to discover that the cyber activity was part of a transnational terrorist threat involving a Kosovar citizen in Malaysia providing personally identifiable information on American service members to ISIS. That kind of threat does not respect international borders or fall neatly within existing categories, and neither, increasingly, can U.S. preparation and response.

Developments in Government Responses

Against this landscape, it could be tempting for people to consider disconnecting all of their devices and for businesses to revert to typewriters and filing cabinets. But just as 9/11 forced the government to reshape how it shares information internally and responds to emerging terrorist threats, current cyber threats must spur Americans to rethink how government organizes itself to respond—and, most important, to reshape how government works with the private sector. Cyber threats do not recognize neat boundaries between governments and private institutions as targets. American responses have to be equally nimble.

WHO IS IN CHARGE?

A natural question might be to ask: Who in the U.S. government is in charge of cybersecurity in the United States? And who is a private company supposed to inform if it gets hacked? For the uninitiated, the answer would be a confusing alphabet soup of government agencies—DHS, the FBI, the DOJ, the ODNI, and more. And depending on the sector, even more agencies can come into play: a consumer-facing company might have to contact the Federal Trade Commission (FTC) in the event of a breach; an energy company might have to contact the Federal Energy Regulatory Commission (FERC); any publicly traded company might have to think about what it needs to incorporate into its Securities and Exchange Commission (SEC) filings; and so forth. And that is only at the federal level.

Unfortunately, asking who is in charge of cybersecurity in the United States is a bit like asking who is in charge of physical security. Just as we depend on different types of guards to protect different things in physical space, we have different agencies with responsibilities to protect cybersecurity in different sectors. Different parts of the federal government are also designed to drive different types of responses: the FBI can investigate a breach to determine who was behind it and can work with the DOJ to build a potential criminal case. U.S. intelligence agencies, including the NSA, can work to detect overseas threats, including the capabilities and motivations of hostile nation-states and terrorists. In the United States, DHS has a broad mandate over policies affecting critical infrastructure and a responsibility to ensure that those entities receive appropriate threat information and guidance. But even in that landscape, different agencies have the lead as the Sector-Specific Agency (SSA) for different sectors. For example, the DOE is the SSA for the energy sector, while the Department of the Treasury is the SSA for the financial sector.

Within DHS, as well, there are multiple offices and centers with cybersecurity responsibilities. The Office of Cybersecurity and Communications (housed within what was NPPD, now called CISA) is generally responsible for protecting the security of the nation's civilian cyber and communications infrastructure.[42] Within *that* office, the National Cybersecurity and Communications Integration Center (NCCIC) serves as "a 24/7 cyber monitoring, incident response, and management center and as a national point of cyber and communications incident integration."[43] The NCCIC, for example, coordinated with election authorities on behalf of DHS in response to concerns over cyberattacks on American election infrastructure during the 2016 election cycle.[44]

So the short answer is that, even limiting oneself to the federal government, there is no one central office in charge of cybersecurity. Nor is there any one part of government in charge of coordinating cybersecurity efforts between the government and the private sector. As new challenges emerge, there has been some progress toward finding creative solutions and improving information sharing. But the solutions to date have been slow to come together, and there is broad agreement that much more needs to be done. In particular, the diffuse nature of the cyber response at the federal level is mirrored by how responsibilities are carried out at the state and local levels—and has led to significant and vexing difficulties for public-private cooperation in the area of cybersecurity.

Against that backdrop, there are often suggestions by policymakers and commentators that the United States needs greater consolidation— some kind of unified, integrated office in charge of cybersecurity. But any such discussion must be based on practical considerations about which functions need to be served and how this can best be accomplished. The 9/11 attacks triggered a difficult process of reorganization that diagnosed core problems—mainly, a need to get better at sharing information between intelligence agencies and law enforcement, and among federal, state, and local law enforcement—and established structures that brought to bear all the tools and capabilities of government to fix those problems. While outlining how this approach would translate to the cyber threat context is beyond the scope of this chapter, it will be important to ensure that the same comprehensive, all-tools approach guides consideration of reforms.

RECENT LEGISLATION AND POLICY

In recent years, Congress and both Presidents Barack Obama and Donald Trump have taken steps toward improving structures for sharing information and protecting the government's own networks. Generally speaking, these policies have been limited in the sense that they typically have not *compelled* (and the executive branch alone often cannot compel) the private sector to take any particular security measures. Nonetheless, some of these actions provide at least early outlines for more progress that must be made. As we saw after 9/11, the government cannot effectively protect against threats if intelligence and other types of valuable data are not shared among agencies and—where possible—with the private sector and the public.

CYBERSECURITY INFORMATION SHARING ACT. In December 2015, Obama signed into law the Cybersecurity Information Sharing Act (CISA).[45] The CISA's main purpose is to bolster voluntary information sharing between the federal government and the private sector. One of the ways it does this is by clearing obstacles: businesses have often expressed concerns that they might actually *violate* a federal law called the Stored Communications Act by sharing certain types of information with the government, because that law bars companies from doing so except in cases of emergency or through the issuance of a subpoena or judicial warrant.

The CISA addresses that concern by expressly authorizing private entities to monitor their networks for cybersecurity threats and to share threat information both with the federal government and with other private entities. In addition, it gives companies liability protections for sharing that information. Among other things, the CISA also establishes a process led by DHS for receiving threat information from and sharing that information with the private sector. To accommodate privacy concerns that this type of information sharing may raise, the statute also requires companies to remove personal identifying information (if it is unrelated to a cybersecurity threat) prior to sharing that information with the government or other private sector entities.

Clearing obstacles so that companies trying to share threat information do not risk breaking the law is the least that the government can do. The CISA importantly recognized and addressed this obstacle—but companies may need more clarity on a case-by-case basis about the boundaries of what they can share. Going forward, DHS and other agencies should be accessible and responsive to businesses that may be dealing with breaches and are doing their best to comply with the law.

PRESIDENTIAL POLICY DIRECTIVE 41. On July 26, 2016, Obama issued Presidential Policy Directive 41 (PPD-41), which was designed to both codify and clarify lines of responsibility within the federal government with respect to significant cyber incidents.[46] PPD-41's framework applies regardless of whether the entity targeted by the cyber incident is in the public or the private sector. The directive assigns different types of responsibilities to different agencies: the DOJ is responsible for investigation, DHS is tasked with asset protection, and the ODNI is responsible for leading intelligence support activities. In addition to these three agencies, the National Security Council's Cyber Response Group is tasked with coordinating national policy with respect to cyber threats and attacks. By assigning responsibilities to different agencies, the intention of the directive is to describe exactly which agency is to lead in each of these different areas.

Clarifying which government agency should take the lead in certain existing tasks was an important step. From the perspective of the private sector, however, it may still be unclear who in government should be contacted in the event of a breach. There is no "cyber 911" to dial, nor is there any centralized website or email address to which reports can be directed.

EXECUTIVE ORDER 13800. Executive Order 13800, "Strengthening the Cybersecurity of Federal Networks and Critical Infrastructure," was signed by Trump on May 11, 2017.[47] As the title suggests, this order, too, was largely inward-facing: its purpose was to improve the government's own network security, as well as the security of critical infrastructure sectors. In support of those goals, it tasked numerous federal agencies with conducting various risk assessments and producing reports within certain time frames. It also directed the heads of various federal agencies to enhance cooperative measures with critical infrastructure entities where feasible.

In keeping with the voluntary regime for critical infrastructure described in Chapter 11, this order did not impose specific affirmative obligations on any private-sector entities. Significantly, however, it directed DHS and the Department of Commerce to examine efforts to promote market transparency regarding cybersecurity risk management practices in critical infrastructure entities, with a focus on publicly traded companies. This may mean that federal regulators could seek to expose whether critical infrastructure entities are lagging in their cybersecurity efforts, with potential market costs for shortcomings. Conversely, regulators could seek to reward companies that have enhanced their security efforts by ensuring that those improvements gain recognition.

Creative Approaches and New Paths Forward

As the analysis above shows, the federal government has taken incremental measures to organize itself better internally and to enhance voluntary information-sharing measures. But often these types of incremental and voluntary measures will not be sufficient. There are still too many challenges that impede the ability of government to share and exchange threat information with the private sector, as well as with state and local governments. Businesses are constantly balancing costs and benefits with respect to all types of risks; often, the only way to ensure that private entities take better measures to protect themselves is to make a business case for doing so through the use of various carrots and sticks. For other sectors that encompass core interests such as the integrity of U.S. elections and the protection of national security, the government will need to get more creative and proactive both in sharing threat information and in responding to malicious actors using whatever tools are available.

The cases below illustrate ways in which the government and the private sector are making innovations—and ways in which more improvements are still needed.

EFFORTS IN THE IOT SECTOR

The IoT is a useful example of the ways in which regulators and policy-makers are beginning to innovate. The agencies and Departments involved are as varied as the devices associated with the IoT. They include the Food and Drug Administration (FDA), which is concerned with vulnerabilities within medical devices; the National Highway Traffic Safety Administration (NHTSA), which involves internet-connected vehicles; and the Federal Trade Commission (FTC), which addresses broader issues with insufficient security and misrepresentations to clients regarding products' cybersecurity features.[48]

At present, few agencies have issued legally binding rules regarding cybersecurity requirements or procedures related to the IoT. One agency—the FTC—has relied on existing regulatory frameworks to hold manufacturers accountable for securing their devices. Most concerned agencies, however, have worked to develop nonbinding guidance. The NHTSA, for example, issued a voluntary Federal Automated Vehicles Policy in 2016—though in doing so, it asserted regulatory authority over the cybersecurity of vehicles.[49] The FDA began releasing communications on the cybersecurity of medical devices in 2013, and has issued guidance for managing the cybersecurity risks of such devices.[50] Similar to the NHTSA's guidelines, these documents are not legally binding, but instead provide recommendations for how manufacturers can address cybersecurity risks.[51]

These nonbinding advisory guidelines—while perhaps not the best long-term solution—can have effects on how businesses weigh risks. A company that meets these standards can potentially advertise that fact to consumers, gaining credit in the market for its cybersecurity efforts in a way that can be readily understood. It is not difficult to imagine, for example, that a person buying a car with internet-connected devices is more likely to buy the model that meets the NHTSA's safety standards. Moreover, a set of guidelines can become the ordinary industry "standard of care," such that a company falling short of those standards can more easily be sued for negligence.

Agencies have also emphasized that cybersecurity should be a priority at the outset in the design of connected devices, and that cybersecurity should remain a priority throughout the life cycle of the devices. Particularly concerning are devices that include default usernames and passwords that never get updated. DHS's "Strategic Principles for Securing the Internet of Things," issued in November 2017, noted the importance of creating safer passwords and enabling other security measures by default—concerns that grew following the botnet attack against Dyn.[52]

The FTC has also been proactive, using its authority under the Federal Trade Commission Act to regulate manufacturers with inadequate security in their connected devices. For example, in 2017, the agency settled charges with ASUSTek Computer, Inc., a Taiwan-based computer hardware maker, after it filed a complaint alleging that vulnerabilities in ASUSTek's routers jeopardized the home networks of hundreds of thousands of consumers.[53] The terms of the settlement required the company to establish and maintain a comprehensive security program subject to independent audits for the next twenty years.

There will undoubtedly be new challenges ahead—particularly to mitigate the risks posed by millions of old devices whose security infrastructures will inevitably become obsolete. Moreover, businesses and regulators alike should be actively considering ways to encourage consumers and manufacturers to take steps to patch known vulnerabilities in a multitude of household devices. It is one thing, after all, to ask consumers and manufacturers to update computer or smartphone software regularly when significant new vulnerabilities are detected; it is another to expect the same degree of vigilance when it comes to items like a "smart toaster" or a low-cost baby toy that requires a WiFi connection.

PREVENTING ELECTION INTERFERENCE

The ability of the United States to respond to an emerging cyber threat in real time is being tested: Americans saw Russia attempt to interfere in U.S. elections in 2016, and the clear consensus among intelligence experts is that these efforts will continue in 2020. Russia's attempts to interfere have come in many forms. Its intelligence entities hacked the Democratic National Committee and also got into the private email account of the Democratic candidate's campaign chairman, then disseminated those materials through WikiLeaks. Russian hackers also conducted cyber intrusions into state and local election boards—though DHS did not assess that these intrusions interfered in any vote-tallying.[54] Furthermore, Russia engaged in broader influence campaigns in both the 2016 and 2018 election cycles that operated through social media, including the use of paid "trolls" and bots to disseminate propaganda.

Preventing this interference in the next American election will require work on several fronts. First and foremost, the United States must ensure the security of its electronic voting systems and voter rolls. DHS took an important step in that direction by designating the nation's voting and election infrastructure as "critical infrastructure," thus enabling the federal government to offer prioritized cybersecurity assistance.[55] DHS was careful, however, to note that this designation does not constitute a federal takeover of elections (nor could it, given that the Constitution vests authority to administer elections with the states). Likewise, Congress last year allocated $380 million in funding for states to upgrade their elections systems, but states maintained the discretion to apply for funds and to determine (within certain boundaries) how to spend them.[56] So while there is a lot that the federal government *can* do—such as providing funding and sophisticated threat information and helping to harden systems against attack—it will be up to state regulators to accept that assistance.

There is also work to do on other fronts: Campaign officials, obviously, will be on heightened alert that their communications are targets for attack. So there will almost certainly be a demand for better security and increased threat awareness; it will be up to DHS and the FBI to meet that demand by proactively sharing all relevant information. As for social media platforms, Facebook (among other companies) has made clear that it does not wish to be an unwitting facilitator of foreign influence campaigns or a purveyor of "fake news." Fulfilling this commitment will require significantly increased screening of content and of advertisers. Just as social media companies stepped up their fight against ISIS and other terrorist groups in recent years—by proactively removing content and seeking to collaborate on best practices—they must engage in the same kinds of efforts in this new context.

For better or for worse, these critical steps require buy-in from entities outside the federal government, including state and local election boards, social media companies, and private citizens engaged in campaigns. Given the stakes of this issue—and the level of heightened attention it continues to receive—there are at least some limited grounds for optimism that all involved can rise to the challenge. The collaboration that results may in turn be a blueprint for addressing other threats.

USE OF CRIMINAL PROSECUTIONS AND SANCTIONS TO RAISE THE COSTS OF MALICIOUS CYBER ACTIVITY

Finally, as the government asks for more from the private sector, it must remain assertive in using all of the tools in its arsenal to identify, disrupt, and deter hackers and other malicious cyber actors. One important way in which the United States has become more assertive in responding to these threats is through pursing criminal charges. No matter where a hacker is located or with whom he or she is affiliated—China, North Korea, Iran, or ISIS—when the United States can figure out who committed the crime, by name and face, it can seek to impose real consequences.

Criminal charges reflect an increasing awareness that Americans cannot rely on defense alone; the government must also raise the costs for malicious cyber activity. The willingness of the United States to pursue a criminal prosecution sends a powerful message to the world. It demonstrates that the United States believes at the highest levels that certain activities must be considered out of bounds—and imposes a significant real-world deterrent on hackers who suddenly find themselves at risk of apprehension in much of the world. A criminal prosecution also makes clear not only that the U.S. government has established attribution but also that it stands prepared to make the case publicly in a courtroom.

A good example of how the United States has used this strategy of deterrence is the changing nature of the response to economic espionage in the cyber realm. In May 2014, the DOJ obtained the first indictment of state-sponsored computer hacking and economic espionage, charging five named members of the Chinese People's Liberation Army based on their theft of trade secrets and other sensitive business information from American companies.

These actions helped to alter the diplomatic dialogue between the United States and China on this critical issue. And a little more than a year later, Chinese President Xi Jinping publicly declared for the first time that "China strongly opposes and combats the theft of commercial secrets and other kinds of hacking attacks."[57] The United States and China agreed that neither country's government will conduct or knowingly support cyber-enabled theft of intellectual property, including trade secrets or other confidential business information, with the intent of providing competitive advantages to their companies or commercial sectors. There is clearly more work to be done to test and deepen these commitments, but there is now an important foundation on which those efforts can be built.

Of course, there are limits to the ability of the government to pursue prosecutions against every malicious actor—particularly if those actors are located overseas and are not likely to travel. An indictment may send a strong signal, but real economic consequences can also be imposed by another tool in the U.S. arsenal: the imposition of sanctions. Following the Sony attack, for example, Obama signed an executive order imposing new sanctions against the North Korean officials who were deemed responsible for the attack.[58] Several months later—recognizing the need to impose sanctions against other types of malicious cyber actors—Obama signed an executive order titled "Blocking the Property of Certain Persons Engaging in Significant Malicious Cyber-Enabled Activities."[59] That order delegates authority to the Secretary of the Treasury, in consultation with the Attorney General, to impose sanctions against people or entities who have engaged in malicious cyber activities that threaten U.S. national security, foreign policy, or economic health and financial stability.

This order was amended in late 2016 to permit sanctions against those who tamper with America's election process, and sanctions were imposed against various Russian individuals and entities responsible for election interference earlier that year.[60] Congress effectively ratified those sanctions by enacting legislation in 2017 that expressed their sense that the president should "vigorously enforce" the sanctions imposed by the previous administration.[61]

Conclusion

The threats described in this chapter are daunting. Many of the vulnerabilities in America's cyber infrastructure are receiving attention like never before. Very often, a glance at the headlines of any major newspaper will reveal some new data breach or some new vulnerability in an everyday device. But in many ways the heightened attention is long overdue. Americans can no longer claim ignorance of the fact that some of the very technological innovations that have improved countless lives have also created new risks.

The United States undoubtedly has the tools to address these risks. America's intelligence agencies and cyber capabilities are second to none. The challenge is harnessing these tools correctly—by avoiding silos within government and between government and the private sector, and by applying the same spirit of innovation that helped break down barriers after 9/11. The country has already started to recognize that the cybersecurity of private entities—be they electrical companies, movie studios, or retail stores—can affect every citizen. Now the only question is whether the United States can harness those insights to address these challenges before the country faces another 9/11 moment.

CHAPTER 13

Increasing Security while Protecting Privacy

Stevan Bunnell

THE CHALLENGE OF PROTECTING THE PRIVACY OF U.S. CITIZENS FROM a potentially overweening and intrusive state is central to the homeland security enterprise.[1] This chapter explores the interplay between security and privacy in contexts where conventional views of those concepts provide an inadequate and potentially misleading framework for thinking about policy choices. I focus on the ways in which privacy considerations affect the cornerstone missions of the Department of Homeland Security (DHS), especially counterterrorism, in three operational contexts: screening at borders and airports, information sharing and data analysis within the government, and fear management.

First, I begin with a brief overview of DHS's efforts in each of these contexts. Second, I describe different dimensions of privacy and highlight the critical importance of context in any assessment of how much privacy should matter. Third, I explore ways in which DHS's principal activities impact different aspects of privacy and discuss examples in which efforts to enhance security have also led, directly or indirectly, to enhanced privacy, especially the types of privacy about which most people seem to care the most.

In each of the three main missions that I discuss, there are opportunities for win-wins—government policies and practices that simultaneously enhance security and promote privacy, at least in the aggregate. Some of these win-wins for the public as a whole, however, do create privacy winners and losers. For individual privacy losers, I argue, the issue is frequently less about privacy itself and more about fairness, accuracy, and due process.

DHS in the Homeland Security Enterprise

DHS is a sprawling conglomerate of legacy agencies and new operational Components that loosely share a "homeland security" mission. Its range of functions outside core security operations is broad and diverse, and includes important governmental responsibilities such as naturalizing new citizens, administering the national flood insurance program, conducting search and rescue missions on the open seas, investigating financial crime, and training federal and state law enforcement officers. Many of these DHS functions raise interesting privacy issues, but they are, for the most part, different issues than the ones that arise in the context of the Department's founding mission, which was to prevent another 9/11-style attack on the homeland. Privacy issues that arise from other DHS activities are outside the scope of this chapter. Also outside my scope are all the critical national security, military, intelligence collection, and law enforcement activities that are central to national counterterrorism policy but are not responsibilities of DHS (such as the collection of metadata on cellphone users or warrantless wiretapping). It should be noted, however, that privacy concerns in all these other policy domains pale by comparison to those raised by the issues that I address here.

As other chapters in this volume discuss, DHS does both a lot more and a lot less in the fight against terrorism than many people realize. Part of the disconnect can be blamed on television shows like *Homeland*, which portray a government agency doing all sorts of things in which DHS has no role (and often things that no agency could lawfully do). But part of the confusion is also the result of bureaucratic turf battles within the federal government that occurred in the Department's early years as it tried to find a place at the table alongside more established counterterrorism players: the Department of Defense (DOD), the Central Intelligence Agency (CIA), the National Security Agency (NSA), and the Federal Bureau of Investigation (FBI). There is much greater clarity and consensus today than when DHS was first established in 2003, though the Department is still defending and refining its counterterrorism roles within the federal interagency process.

At the risk of oversimplifying, it is helpful to think in broad strokes about what DHS does not do. Operationally, DHS is not, as one of my deputies used to say, "in the business of shooting stuff down" or engaging in other types of "kinetic" counterterrorism activities overseas. (The DOD and the CIA handle that.) Nor, with very limited exceptions (e.g., counterterrorism-related intelligence collected by the U.S. Coast Guard [USCG] in the maritime environment), does DHS covertly collect intelligence related to terrorist threats. (The CIA, the NSA, and other Intelligence Community [IC] agencies handle that.) Domestically, the FBI, not DHS, has the lead—or at least first dibs—on terrorism-related national security or law enforcement investigations. (For further discussion of this issue, see Chapter 4.)

So what is left? DHS often takes the lead in filling gaps between traditional national security and law enforcement activities. In this role, DHS thinks primarily about prevention and much less about after-the-fact accountability through the criminal justice system. In particular, there are three important aspects of counterterrorism strategy where DHS plays a critical role: border and aviation security, information sharing, and what I, as DHS General Counsel, used to refer to as "fear management."

BORDER AND AVIATION SECURITY

DHS's largest Component, Customs and Border Protection (CBP), has responsibility for regulating cross-border flows. All people and goods that enter the country are subject to inspection by CBP and can be deemed inadmissible for many possible reasons. As discussed in Chapter 6, CBP has the daunting task of figuring out how to screen the hundreds of millions of people and the billions of tons of goods that come through U.S. ports of entry (POEs) every year, in ways that do not unduly impede legitimate travel and commerce. CBP's operational activity may seem simple to a typical traveler who experiences a brief routine interview with a CBP officer after an international flight, but the data analysis that informs that interview, as well as the broader screening strategies and processes that CBP uses behind the scenes, are complex and rely on far more than just the intuition of the front-line officer conducting the interview. The same can be said of the screening that the Transportation Security Administration (TSA) conducts before passengers board commercial flights in the United States: it may seem simple, even when it takes a while to get through the line, but there is much more going on than meets the eye. (For further detail on TSA, see Chapter 8.)

One of the important behind-the-scenes tools used by DHS Components (and other government agencies) to reduce the risk of terrorism is watchlisting. TSA's Secure Flight program, for example, relies heavily on the Terrorist Screening Database (TSDB), which among other things produces No Fly and Selectee lists.[2] A passenger on the No Fly list is typically a known or suspected terrorist who is believed to present a sufficient threat to aviation security that he or she should be denied boarding on a commercial flight. One could debate how much weight to give these judgments about risk, but I will assume that they have at least some predictive value. The Selectee list includes individuals about whom there may be derogatory information that creates potential security concerns, but not to the same extent as individuals on the No Fly list. An individual on the Selectee list is not denied boarding, but is subject to more intensive questioning and physical screening prior to boarding.

TSA also uses lists of trusted travelers to inform its screening operations. The popular TSA Pre✓ program allows individuals who have gone through a prior application and vetting process to go through expedited screening lines at airports. The expedited TSA Pre✓ lines require slightly less disrobing and unpacking than the regular screening lines; as a result, they are not only slightly less intrusive but also substantially quicker. (The through-put rates in the expedited lines are typically about three times the rate of regular screening lines.) CBP's trusted traveler programs, described in greater detail in Chapter 6, operate in a similar way, although with a more in-depth up-front vetting process. But once a person is accepted into the program, she can typically enter the United States without a face-to-face CBP screening interview, provided she has her passport and can establish her identity (using her fingerprints at an electronic kiosk).

Nevertheless, DHS's screening methods go beyond watchlisting and trusted traveler programs. Increasingly sophisticated data analytics are used to generate screening protocols that are tailored to statistically determined risk factors. For example, data analysis may show that known or suspected terrorists are using stolen passports most frequently from a particular country, along a particular travel route, during a particular time of the year. As a result, CBP or TSA may adjust their screening rules to increase the frequency or intensity of screening of individuals who correlate with that travel pattern. Depending on the number of travelers who fit the pattern, it may not mean that all of them will be patted down by TSA, but it may mean that a higher percentage of travelers with that pattern will receive additional screening. These data-driven adjustments to screening rules improve aviation security more efficiently than a protocol based on increasing secondary inspection rates for all travelers.

With the rapid evolution of technology and techniques for collecting, storing, and analyzing large amounts of data, DHS's counterterrorism screening efforts are likely to rely increasingly on automated detection of patterns and anomalies that correlate with terrorist risks. The better the data analytics—and the data on which they are based—the more surgical and efficient the screening procedures will be. But not all risk factors are legally or morally equivalent. Although few people object to having screening rules that take into account whether an individual is a military-aged male (because males in their twenties are more likely to be terrorists than, say, females in their seventies), if data analytics revealed that certain more sensitive or suspect classifications (e.g., religion or race) correlated with increased terrorism risks, the development of new targeting algorithms based on these criteria could raise serious legal, political, and moral issues.

The emergence of lone-wolf terrorists has further elevated the importance of data analytics in DHS's counterterrorism toolbox. Traditional intelligence collection methods, both human intelligence and signals intelligence, have proven less effective than data analysis at identifying members of amorphous terrorist groups such as ISIS, which has engaged in a crowdsourcing approach to terror rather than the more traditional command-and-control methods of other older terrorist organizations. The lone wolf (or perhaps more accurately, the "lonely wolf," because the individual is usually looking for a sense of connection and belonging) can be radicalized without any personal relationship with other members of the group. Security and law enforcement officials are concerned about individuals who "self-radicalize," not just because of the plans that they can execute on their own (and a lone actor without any sophisticated weapons or expertise can easily cause mass mayhem just by driving a car through a crowd, as a number of recent horrific incidents around the world have demonstrated), but also because they are so hard to detect, and because the time from "flash to bang" can be so short. In this context, the use of automated pattern and anomaly recognition in counterterrorism is certain to continue, if not accelerate.

For algorithms to be predictively useful, DHS needs lots of different data. The more data, and the more types of data, the more patterns and anomalies (including non-obvious connections) can be identified, and the more likely it is that a threat will be identified. Building a bigger and more searchable database combining many different types of data is thus a central part of DHS's counterterrorism strategy.

INFORMATION SHARING

The 9/11 attacks happened in part because within the U.S. government, agencies that knew critical information about the hijackers and Al-Qaeda did not share that information with other parts of the government that might have been able to disrupt the attacks. Eliminating (or at least reducing) the stove-piping of critical security information was a crucial post-9/11 goal. The hope was that putting all of the twenty-two legacy agencies and pieces of agencies under one roof (DHS) would not only improve information sharing among those agencies, but also that having a Cabinet member with statutory authority to access all information relating to homeland security would allow DHS to drive better information sharing across the homeland security enterprise (including state and local law enforcement and other public officials). The reality of information sharing often fails to live up to the ideal authorized by the 2002 Homeland Security Act, but it is much better than it used to be before 9/11, especially at the line level, and it makes the homeland security enterprise as a whole smarter and nimbler.

DHS's Office of Intelligence and Analysis (I&A) is a Headquarters element created to provide timely intelligence, information, and analysis to DHS's policymakers and operational Components. I&A works to allow for more efficient, but also tailored, access to a larger "haystack" of data in a way that enhances the probability of extracting valuable insights to inform screening and other security measures. The data analytics that I&A and other parts of DHS deploy lead to "nominations" for the No Fly and Selectee lists. These analyses can also aid in assessments of whether a particular individual is suitable for a trusted traveler program, for employment in sensitive positions, or for security clearance. And, of course, sophisticated data analytics also help to develop better screening rules for travelers.

Big data analytics only work if the government can get the right data and lots of it, which is why information sharing is critical to DHS and to security agencies more generally. I&A does not itself engage in covert collection of intelligence, but it is an avid consumer of covert intelligence collection and, in conjunction with other parts of DHS, also collects and facilitates access to data from a wide variety of nonclassified sources, including information that is reported to state and local law enforcement, information about passengers that is provided by airlines, and information obtained in the course of administering the immigration system.

FEAR MANAGEMENT

Managing risk is a crucial part of the homeland security mission. But smart risk management needs to be coupled with "fear management," a strategy to address the power of the irrational and the emotional. Fear management goes to the heart of the challenge of terrorism, which is, after all, a method of advancing political, religious, or other causes by terrorizing adversaries, i.e., making them fearful. Deaths from terrorism have an outsized societal resonance, because our concern about terrorism is not driven by the magnitude of the direct physical and economic costs of an attack. It is driven by fear, a collective fear that can snowball and become disconnected from the reality of the underlying threat. As other authors in this volume also discuss, widespread and deeply-felt fear can have more profound social consequences for a target of terrorism than the immediate loss of life, injuries, and property damage caused by a terrorist attack. Managing fear is thus an important task in its own right.

Security fears also lead to frustration and anger directed at institutions of government that may not seem to be doing enough to address perceived threats. Society then becomes vulnerable to politicians who seek to advance their political fortunes by stoking fear, rather than promoting calm and actual security. Citizens can get into a lather about security risks posed by undocumented immigrants (who in fact are statistically much less likely to commit crimes than U.S. citizens) or provoke religious bigotry by painting too broad a brush. Consequences may include disregard for individual privacy and tolerance for violations of due process, torture, and new prisons (e.g., Guantanamo Bay)—which, ironically, have been more effective as a terrorist recruiting tool than as a deterrent against future attacks.

Managing the immediate and lingering effects of fear is not a technocratic task. It requires empathetic, visible, competent government leadership. Fear management is ultimately an exercise in responsible trust-building between the government and the people. Communication during and immediately after a terror attack is essential. It should be factual, measured, and practical. The goal is to promote a return to normalcy without complacency (e.g., the British mantra of "Keep Calm and Carry On"). Careful, reassuring public communication about evolving facts is necessary, not only in statements coming from senior DHS leadership, but also across the homeland security enterprise. Sound fear management also requires the pre-crisis establishment of information-sharing and communications protocols and personal relationships across the stakeholder community, ideally reinforced through tabletop exercises and other preparatory investments.

Fear management during and after a terror attack is not just about response and recovery. Done well, it also reduces the incentive for future attacks. A terrorist attack is by definition an attempt to create terror; mitigating the general public's feelings of fear and terror denies part of the attacker's objective.

Protecting Privacy at DHS

During my confirmation process, I remember talking to senators and their staff about the importance of striking the right balance between security and privacy. As a former prosecutor, I brought a law enforcement perspective to the issue. We might have less crime, I argued, if a police officer investigating a crime could quickly search a house without having to establish probable cause for the search to a magistrate, but as a society we would all have less privacy in our homes. The constitutional choice was to let some guilty people escape justice in order to preserve privacy within all homes.

I soon learned, however, that the interplay between security and privacy is considerably more complicated in the homeland security context. One important difference is that homeland security missions, including counter-terrorism, involve a greater focus on prevention than on achieving justice after the fact (as in the classic law enforcement model). Second, rightly or wrongly, preventing deaths from terrorism is assigned a greater value than preventing deaths from common crime, because of the public reaction to terrorist attacks. A third crucial difference is the frequency with which the government already conducts intrusive inspections on a regular basis, both at the borders and for aviation security. These differences have critical implications for the weight that can be given to the importance of personal privacy; they make the standards of privacy protection found in conventional law enforcement and civilian life much more problematic.

THE LEGAL CONTEXT: THEORY AND PRACTICE

Privacy law in the United States is a fragmented patchwork, much of it developed long before the advent of the current technology that causes the most concern among privacy advocates.[3] Federal privacy protections are mandated for certain regulated industries (such as healthcare or financial services), but there is no single overarching federal law that embodies a national right to privacy akin to what exists in the European Union (EU). Some general privacy principles have become incorporated into American constitutional jurisprudence (largely through the Fourth Amendment) and provide some outer limits on state action, but constitutional law is not proscriptive. General privacy protections for executive branch records systems are required by the Privacy Act, which was enacted back in 1974, but many of its provisions do not apply to criminal law enforcement, national security, and intelligence agencies.

DHS's Privacy Office was the first statutorily created privacy office in any federal agency. The Chief Privacy Officer, with a staff of approximately thirty-five, is a senior official of the Department and reports directly to the Secretary. This office has substantial authorities and a broad mission "to protect all individuals by embedding and enforcing privacy protections and transparency in all DHS activities."[4] The eight Fair Information Privacy Principles that were set out in the Privacy Act form the basis of DHS's privacy compliance policies and procedures governing the use of personally identifiable information (PII).[5]

During my tenure as General Counsel of DHS, I worked closely with the Chief Privacy Officer on a wide variety of issues relating to screening, international agreements, and interagency information sharing. Formal Privacy Impact Assessments (PIAs) were conducted before any significant programs or systems containing PII became operational. PIAs were an important decision-making tool to ensure that privacy risks were given due consideration in the policymaking process and not regarded as merely a box-checking exercise. In my experience, whenever there was a significant policy issue being debated within DHS, the Privacy Office was part of the discussion (although there were sometimes disagreements about whether it had been consulted early enough).

DHS is legally required to conduct PIAs, but what the Department ultimately decides to do to protect privacy in the counterterrorism arena is not usually legally mandated; it is generally a function of executive branch or Departmental policy. In making those policy decisions, the Fair Information Practice Principles in the Privacy Act provide a high-level framework but limited specific guidance. In my experience, DHS policymakers, especially those who are not privacy experts, struggle to define and discuss privacy with precision or consistency. In practice, privacy turns out to be a weighty concern that is hard to weigh. Part of the problem stems from the many different interests that are often mixed together in privacy policy discussions.

THE NATURE OF PRIVACY CONCERNS

Despite its prominence within DHS and more broadly in our popular discourse, privacy is an elusive concept. Privacy can be seen either as a personal concern (e.g., how it makes you feel to know that someone else can access or use sensitive personal information about you) or as a policy question (e.g., how a government agency should manage bulk data holdings of PII).

Regarding the former, the critical question is privacy *from whom*. The most intense desires for personal privacy often arise in the context of close personal relationships: the teenage girl who wants to keep her use of birth control from her parents; the husband who does not want his wife to see his internet browsing history; the young person who is struggling with his sexual identity but not ready to share that with family or friends; and so forth. Privacy is a way for people to compartmentalize their interactions with others. People like being able to control who knows what about them, especially when it comes to potentially embarrassing facts. And beyond simple embarrassment, private information in the wrong hands—e.g., an angry ex-boyfriend, a disgruntled former employee, a vindictive boss, or a nosy neighbor—can be used to cause emotional and economic injury. These concerns about privacy rarely involve the government in general or DHS in particular. When they do, the main issue is whether DHS can be a proper custodian of the information it collects, so that such information does not fall into anyone else's hands.

Concerns about privacy from the government, on the other hand, are usually driven by fear of state power. Governments in possession of too much detailed personal data on their citizens might be better positioned to stifle dissent and impose totalitarian control. This is the "Big Brother" fear, and it motivates many of the constitutional concerns about privacy (such as the Fourth Amendment protection from unreasonable searches and seizures).[6]

This fear is really about what actions the government could take against its citizens as a result of having certain information, rather than the mere fact that such information is somehow in the government's possession. The central question, therefore, is whether this information will be used in ways that adversely and inappropriately affect citizens. The situation is least worrisome when there is less chance of adverse government action; when the effects of any adverse action would not be particularly harmful; when adverse action is not more likely to effect particular groups, especially those that enjoy special protections; and when citizens have a reliable means of redress if they are affected in inappropriate ways. As a result, "privacy debates" about what sort of information the government can collect and how it can use that information are typically blended with issues of due process.

From either an individual or a policy perspective, privacy is a matter of degree, not an absolute objective. The reality of modern life is that it would be nearly impossible for people to go about daily life without regularly sharing large amounts of information. Americans share sensitive private information in the context of their personal lives, work, purchases, internet browsing, and interactions with all levels of government (from local public schools to state registries of deeds to Medicare to the Internal Revenue Service).[7] In theory, the sharing of that information can be deemed a matter of consent, but in fact it is not generally a real choice. The collection, sharing, and analysis of personal information is thus inevitable; what actions the government takes based on the information it collects is a different matter.

In the homeland security environment, failure to appreciate this distinction can result in peculiar policy choices. Consider screening. DHS is expected to keep terrorists out of the United States, to prevent people from smuggling contraband, and to prevent people who constitute threats to civil aviation from boarding planes. To do so, both CBP and TSA have erected something approaching a universal inspection regime at borders and airports. By any reasonable definition of "privacy," these regimes can be highly intrusive. The need for physical inspection can be reduced if the government ingests and analyzes large amounts of data that help it segment travelers by potential risk, thus reducing the likelihood and intrusiveness of inspections for most people. Such an approach may sound like a threat to "privacy" (understood as what data the government might have about someone), but it would be a mistake to assume that it is inherently less protective of privacy more broadly construed (inclusive of what the government actually does to someone).

Looking for Privacy Win-Wins

In this context, DHS should be focused on finding win-wins—that is, measures that truly enhance security while also truly enhancing privacy. Because privacy from the government is so connected to the risk of inappropriate, unfair, and harmful government action, win-wins may take the form of steps that reduce the potential for due-process violations or governmental abuse rather than steps that simply limit holdings or use of data.

AIRPORT SCREENING

One of the things that TSA seeks to do to promote aviation security is to prevent weapons and other dangerous items from being carried into the passenger compartments of commercial airplanes. Many of the things that TSA worries about are small items that can be easily concealed in a passenger's clothing. Assuming that inspections do indeed prevent certain threats (and fear of threats), inspections at airports will not—and should not—disappear.

TSA can conduct its inspections by having its officers manually pat down every passenger. Full TSA pat-downs are substantial infringements on individual privacy, and can be viewed as official "searches" or potentially obnoxious government action. A passenger can ask that the pat-down take place in a private room, but because that typically involves additional delay, most passengers prefer to be patted down in public areas.

In a typical pat-down, the passenger is asked to stand with his arms extended to the sides and his legs spread apart. A TSA officer of the same gender as the passenger, wearing latex gloves, runs his or her hands over nearly every part of the passenger's body, including the passenger's hair, chest, armpits, buttocks, legs, and groin. (The officer uses the backs of his hands for sensitive and private areas.[8]) The officer also inspects the insides of the passenger's shirt collar, waistband, and pants cuffs for any prohibited objects. Although some passengers are relatively unfazed by the experience, others find it highly objectionable and complain that it feels like being groped. And, of course, TSA officers are not perfect; they have bad days, as do passengers. Add language and cultural differences that can lead to mis-communications, scared or noncompliant passengers, and the occasional mistakes by officers, and inevitably there will be instances of inadvertent, unexpected, misinterpreted, or overly robust touching of a sensitive area. The human factor creates a virtual certainty that such invasive procedures, even when performed by the book, will occasionally become offensive in practice. If the individual privacy impact of a single physical pat-down is multiplied by the seven hundred million encounters at TSA checkpoints every year, the combination of good pat-downs and the few that go bad constitutes a very large collective societal impact on privacy.

There is an alternative to patting down every passenger that is better from both security and privacy perspectives: advanced imaging technology (AIT), which is the term that TSA uses to describe body scanners that use automated target recognition software to detect potentially prohibited metallic and nonmetallic items concealed in passengers' clothing. Although the AIT machine in some sense "sees" private areas of the human body, it does not display those areas to human screeners in a detailed way that might create embarrassment. If the AIT scanner detects a concealed item on a traveler, it displays a yellow box on a generic outline of a human body. The box tells a TSA officer where to conduct follow-up screening if any is required.[9]

Properly used, the AIT scanners do not completely eliminate the need for physical pat-downs, but they dramatically reduce it. The AIT scanner is a powerful addition to the layered security measures that TSA employs at airports, but it also results in a dramatic enhancement in aggregate passenger privacy. The AIT scanners are an example of a security and privacy win-win.

An additional bonus is that the currently deployed AIT machines do not display or retain any images or personally identifiable data about the travelers.[10] Therefore, AIT machines also address the question of whether the government is a good custodian of data: there is no way that the images could be linked to individuals in such a way as to provoke embarrassment.

TSA PRE✓

Another example of a win-win is TSA's Pre✓ program. Travelers apply for the program by filling out a brief online application. Then they schedule an appointment at one of several hundred enrollment centers, where they go for a ten-minute in-person meeting that includes fingerprinting and a quick background check. If the traveler is deemed to be low risk, he is accepted into the program for five years and can become a member for a fee of $85. He would then receive expedited and less intrusive checkpoint screening.

The fingerprint-verified background check on an applicant provides significantly more information about potential security risks than the simple ID checks and ticket checks that ordinary domestic passengers encounter. The concern with Pre✓ members is less about intentional acts (e.g., secreting explosives in their shoes or clothing) and more about the traveler accidentally or unknowingly bringing dangerous items onto the plane. Accordingly, the body and carry-on bag scanning protocols for Pre✓ members are less stringent. They do not have to take off their shoes, belts, or light jackets, or remove their laptops or liquids from their bags. By expediting the checkpoint screening process for Pre✓ members, TSA is able to devote significantly more human and other resources to more intensive screening of higher-risk passengers. The net effect is more security at less expense, and less travel delay for Pre✓ members.

The privacy impact of Pre✓ is also positive. The Pre✓ experience at TSA checkpoints is expedited and slightly less intrusive, although Pre✓ members can still be randomly or otherwise selected for additional screening, including physical pat-downs.[11] The Pre✓ program, however, requires the applicant to provide fingerprints and other PII to TSA; TSA retains the applicant's PII and may share it with other agencies under certain circumstances, which creates additional, albeit usually remote, privacy risks (e.g., hacking or pilfering). Actual individual privacy injuries resulting from intentional disclosures of Pre✓ program PII by rogue government employees are extremely rare.

The Pre✓ program is a form of "whitelisting," which is a way of managing security by generating a list of pre-cleared individuals or items (or in the cybersecurity context, internet addresses) that are safe or low risk, and relying on that list to guide access decisions. It is nice to be on the list, but how does it feel not to be on the list? It is safe to assume that it feels worse for some people if they know (and can see at the time) that other travelers have been deemed to be more trustworthy and are receiving preferential treatment at the checkpoint. The resentment is worse if the ordinary traveler suspects that trusted membership correlates with illegal or inappropriate discrimination—e.g., based on race, religion, politics, ethnicity, or sexual orientation, or if the costs of the program effectively discriminate against the poor. If Pre✓ were expanded to the point where most travelers were members (and TSA adjusted its staffing and other resources to ensure that the wait in Pre✓ lines is still significantly shorter), then being a "non-trusted traveler" might take on an element of stigma, especially for a traveler who had applied for the program and been rejected. In that circumstance, the overall privacy benefits to the traveling public would clearly have increased (more people would be getting less invasive screening), but the standard screening experience would feel more negative for those not on the "whitelist."

TSA's Pre✓ program offers applicants an opportunity to correct inaccurate information that might result in the denial of membership, which mitigates some but not all of the risk of a mistaken or unfair denial. Ultimately, any trusted traveler program will be both over- and underinclusive: a few individuals who are actually high risk will slip in, and some who are low risk will be unnecessarily excluded. These are issues related to the discriminatory effects of policy and practice, and the propriety of such effects is more usefully analyzed through traditional equal protection and due process standards. In other words, the government should look for security-enhancing policies that promote overall privacy, but those policies also need to be consistent with the laws and values of the United States with regard to discriminatory impacts.

WATCHLISTING

If Pre✓ is form of whitelisting, the No Fly and Selectee lists are examples of "blacklisting": reliance on a list of previously identified individuals who present higher levels of risk to aviation security. Like the Pre✓ program, the watchlist approach is a way to target scarce screening resources where they are statistically more likely to be security-enhancing. Also like the Pre✓ program, the privacy impact is very different depending on whether a person is on the list or not on the list. The number of U.S. persons on the No Fly list is a minuscule percentage of the U.S. persons who fly on airplanes every year. If someone is on the No Fly list, he may not be able to print out his boarding pass or he may be turned away or questioned at the first stage of the screening checkpoint. Any of those experiences could be stigmatizing and embarrassing and implicitly involve the disclosure of a sensitive piece of personal information—specifically, the fact that the government thinks he might be a terrorist.

Once an individual has been denied boarding a few times, he or she is likely to stop trying to fly. This personal impact goes beyond privacy; it also impedes the right to travel.[12] Because the percentage of travelers on the list is so small, the adverse impact is outweighed by the fact that TSA does not need to conduct probing inquiries and searches of every traveler.

The Selectee list has a similar positive net effect on collective privacy, although the offsetting considerations are a bit different. The number of U.S citizens and permanent residents on the Selectee list is much larger than the number on the No Fly list, although it is still a very small percentage of U.S. travelers. On the other hand, the adverse consequences of being on the Selectee list—however real—are also much less severe. At TSA checkpoints, travelers on the Selectee list receive screening and potentially more questioning than ordinary travelers, but the traveler on the Selectee list is not prohibited from boarding the flight.[13] On balance, the use of the Selectee list provides a net privacy benefit for U.S. travelers as a whole, because providing the same level of security benefits without the list would presumably involve more intensive screening, questioning, and scrutiny of all passengers, instead of just for those who have been pre-determined to be higher risk.

Ultimately, as with whitelisting, there is a tipping point. If the Selectee list gets too long or too inaccurate—or if the consequences of being on the Selectee list become increasingly severe—then the overall privacy impact could become negative.

BIG DATA ANALYTICS

Non-intrusive scanning, whitelisting, and blacklisting, then, are strategies to enhance both security and privacy. In this sense, they are uncontroversial. A far more controversial issue concerns the collection, storage, and use of large amounts of bulk data by the government. How does this trend affect privacy?

Watchlisting is simply not nimble enough to uncover every terrorist threat, especially those that are being crowdsourced around the world by groups such as ISIS. The "going dark" phenomenon (made possible by the broad availability of inexpensive end-to-end communications encryption), the challenge of getting good human intelligence on small and insular terrorist cells, the shorter timeline for radicalization, and the almost limitless number of soft targets vulnerable to low-tech attacks (e.g., by cars or semi-automatic weapons), make it even more important for DHS to move beyond simple list-based screening.

The solution for both CBP and TSA is rules-based screening. With enough data and better analytics, it would be possible to identify patterns of travel or other objective factors in real time (or nearly so) that correlate with terrorism and other security threats, including threats that may arise suddenly or rapidly evolve. Individuals who match higher-risk patterns are selected for additional screening procedures, or tagged so that they are randomly selected for additional screening at a higher rate than other travelers. When done correctly, screening resources can be directed at a population of travelers that is statistically more likely to present threats, albeit not at the same elevated risk level as a traveler on the No Fly or Selectee lists.

On one level, the privacy implications of rule-based screening are similar to those associated with watchlisting. If done properly, rule-based screening can achieve the same overall level of risk minimization without subjecting all passengers to the same level of screening. If overall screening resources stay the same, the passengers who are not flagged by a rule are net privacy winners. The passengers who are flagged by the rule are net privacy losers. If there are more privacy winners than privacy losers, then the overall privacy impact is positive.

The policy choices on data analytics get more complicated when it comes to collecting bulk data on all travelers in order to generate higher-quality rules. A simple rule might flag military-aged male travelers who have made multiple round-trips to Turkey or Iraq in the last year. But a more sophisticated rule might combine data from a variety of public and non-public sources to generate nuanced profiles of individuals at risk for radicalization, collect similar data for individual travelers, and then flag travelers for additional screening based on how closely they match one of these profiles.

Lifestyle, biographical, financial, travel, social media, and associational data, and much more, are already commercially or publicly available for most U.S. persons. How concerning would it be if TSA or CBP started using aggregations of that data to decide who should get extra screening at airports? This privacy concern is not about individual indignity (e.g., a stranger's hand passing up and down your leg), but rather about the fear of what could happen if a government agency knows too much about you, including the discomfort of knowing that some officer at a screening checkpoint is looking at a computer that is displaying detailed personal, and potentially derogatory or embarrassing, information about you.[14]

There appear to be a wide range of reactions to the notion of CBP and TSA enhancing security by maintaining large amounts of bulk data (including "patterns of life" data) about Americans. Some people, especially those who are familiar with the practices of J. Edgar Hoover's FBI, Nixon's White House, or totalitarian governments in Eastern Europe, are deeply concerned about potential misuse, especially as the volume and diversity of digital exhaust from people's lives continues to grow at unprecedented rates. Others, however, may see the data maintained by DHS as much less extensive and concerning. In reality, actual abuse of PII for personal or vindictive purposes by DHS or other federal employees is exceedingly rare. Yet, the concern about government abuse is real and persistent.

How much of the concern about government is based on the politics or the personalities of government leaders? How much of it is about perceived competence? Would more internal oversight at DHS—from the Office of the General Counsel, the Privacy Office, the Office of Civil Rights and Civil Liberties, and the Office of the Inspector General—help build more trust in the Department's ability to responsibly collect, use, and safeguard more bulk data? Are there ways to store data so that it is only fused at a particular moment, thus preventing the permanent assignment of a risk "score"? These are among the difficult questions that DHS and other agencies will have to consider in searching for a big data win-win.

One particularly vexing issue concerns the data that people now share voluntarily with private companies such as Google, Facebook, and Amazon. As someone who has spent more than twenty years of my professional life working for the federal government, I find it puzzling, and frankly a bit sad, that so many people appear to more readily entrust their PII to private firms than they do to their own government. It is far more likely that this data will be misused by such companies in ways that create harm or embarrassment for its original "owner" than that it will be misused by the government. On the contrary, if proper control of such information were assured, government exploitation of this data could create win-wins for both security and privacy.

PARTNERSHIPS AND PRIVACY ENHANCEMENT

DHS's ability to collect data, especially in bulk from other government agencies or foreign government partners, requires DHS to be able to provide assurances about how the data will be used, protected, and retained. This can be challenging for U.S. authorities when dealing with foreign jurisdictions such as the European Union, where privacy protections are viewed as fundamental human rights and not something that can be readily waived by implied consent. Indeed, in the European Union, companies may not legally share even voluntarily-provided customer PII with DHS or other parts of the U.S. government unless special assurances are given.

Airlines that fly passengers into the United States are required to provide CBP passenger name record (PNR) data in advance of departure. Because PNR includes personal and sometimes sensitive information, and because U.S. law does not provide a general set of data-protection requirements equivalent to EU standards, DHS had to negotiate a formal international agreement requiring DHS to provide extensive privacy protections for EU PNR, including restrictions on how it could be used within DHS and further conditions on how and when it could be shared with other government agencies or third countries. This agreement also provided for periodic review to reassure the European Union that the United States was adhering to the commitments in the agreement.

The PNR agreement resulted in enhanced privacy protection for a large category of DHS's data. Some of the agreement's requirements imposed costs and burdens on DHS and diverted certain resources that conceivably could otherwise have been used to bolster traditional security measures; however, without the enhanced privacy protections, the United States might not have received the EU PNR data. And without the EU PNR data, DHS's ability to identify suspicious travel patterns would have been significantly impaired. On balance, then, DHS's willingness to provide additional privacy protections led to better security screening.[15] This model of trading restrictions on the use of certain data for access to new data could be replicated in other settings.

FEAR MANAGEMENT

Fear management is a critical part of countering the terror created by terrorism. In the aftermath of terrorist attacks, DHS and its leaders, in conjunction with the FBI and other law enforcement agencies, work to be visibly competent and make sure that accurate information is shared with the leadership of state and local governments and law enforcement agencies, its private-sector partners, the media, and the general public. Maintaining a consistent public narrative requires keeping everyone consistently informed. It is certainly not calming in a crisis to have multiple government agencies saying different things about basic facts.

Because fear is an emotional response, visual images matter. DHS officials need to be seen as well as heard. Being on the scene of a crisis matters because it symbolically says that leadership cares and is engaged. Having uniformed TSA and law enforcement officers at airports not only provides some deterrence of criminal behavior, but also makes people feel safer. This is not purely "security theater." The uniformed officers should certainly be doing something productive, but if their visual presence also reduces the false sense of insecurity that terrorism creates, so much the better.

Fear management is fundamentally an exercise in trust-building. Done well, it helps provide a sense of security. But trust in DHS also reduces anxiety about privacy risks, especially those relating to abuses of state power. We do not worry as much about the Big Brother risk from a trusted agency of government. And we trust agencies more when they do a good job.

Concerns about privacy, like concerns about security, are partly based on emotional reactions. As a result, privacy is not just about formal policies and practices; it is about tone and demeanor. In the wake of a terror attack, the public is understandably hungry for details of what happened and who was involved. When DHS professionally and calmly provides public information about the event and, in the process, also explains the need to protect the privacy of individuals who were victims or witnesses, or their families, DHS is combating the fear of terrorism and also demonstrating that it takes privacy seriously, even in the heat of a crisis. A crisis and its aftermath are teachable moments. If DHS does its fear management job well, it can also use the occasion to build its reputation for respecting privacy.

Conclusion

Security and privacy are not always at odds. By thinking through the nuances and indirect implications of policies and practices, it is possible to find security and privacy win-wins—instances where policies driven by security concerns also end up better protecting privacy, or instances where demands for strong privacy protections directly or indirectly advance the goals of security, including the goal of combating the false sense of insecurity that terrorists seek to create. Technological advances, especially in the area of big data analytics, promise to offer new opportunities for security and privacy win-wins, but only if DHS and the U.S. government more broadly continue to build domestic and inter-national trust and confidence in their commitment to privacy protection.

DHS's ability to collect and access the data that it needs is dependent on reassuring people that DHS is not and will not become a Big Brother agency. One of the keys to getting the mix of security and privacy right in the future is for DHS leaders and policymakers to focus on both tech-nology and trust-building, and to seek to make these two different aspects of the homeland security mission more mutually reinforcing.

CHAPTER 14

Homeland Security and Transnational Crime

Alan Bersin and Chappell Lawson

IN THIS CHAPTER, WE PROPOSE A NEW APPROACH TO A LONGSTANDING homeland security mission: combating transnational crime. This approach—which we call the "Disruption Model"—combines conventional law enforcement tactics such as interdiction and investigation with other tools uniquely available to the Department of Homeland Security (DHS), as well as with much more effective collection, analysis, and exploitation of data on criminal networks. Its goal is to identify the "pressure points" in criminal ecosystems and then design the best homeland security responses, which typically include a wider range of sanctions than police and prosecutors normally command. The Disruption Model, we argue, is better suited to DHS's mission and capabilities than the conventional model of domestic law enforcement embodied by the three-letter agencies in the Department of Justice (DOJ) and state or local police forces.[1]

Consider three situations that officials confronting transnational crime must address, all of which illustrate the limitations of applying conventional law enforcement approaches and the need for other tactics:

1. A (hypothetical) cybersecurity officer associated with Russia's secret services—and employed by a criminal syndicate—operates on the Dark Web from an enclave territory in Eastern Europe. His activities involve financial theft across the virtual banking world, arms trafficking, periodic freelance ransomware intrusions, and a variety of "fake news" transmissions. A team at the U.S. Secret Service (USSS) that is monitoring his illicit activities has worked with federal prosecutors to prepare an indictment against him but, because he never

---

The authors thank Peter Neffenger and Stevan Bunnell for valuable comments on previous drafts of this chapter and Kate Searle for editorial assistance.

travels outside his geographic refuge, is unable to execute it. Despite considerable investment of law enforcement resources, the classic model of "investigate-indict-arrest-prosecute-incarcerate" has not served to prevent or disrupt his activities.

2. For decades, Joaquín "Shorty" Guzmán's Sinaloa Cartel smuggled untold quantities of drugs north into the United States and, reciprocally, billions of dollars in bulk cash and huge quantities of weapons south into Mexico. Guzmán is now serving a life sentence in U.S. federal custody, but his incarceration has not materially affected smuggling across the U.S.–Mexico border.

3. In late 2014, the U.S.–Mexico border was flooded with tens of thousands of unaccompanied children from Central America who were seeking entry into the United States. Combining financial data not previously exploited by DHS with information gleaned from detained migrants, the Human Smuggling Cell (HSC)—a tiny, *ad hoc* operation with staff from different operating agencies at DHS—was able to identify hundreds of individuals (often relatives of the children in question) in the United States who appeared to have arranged for "their" child's transportation by smugglers through Mexico. The HSC's response was not to try to build a criminal case against each potential defendant; instead, agents from U.S. Immigration and Customs Enforcement (ICE) conducted "knock and talks" with those who arranged the travel with the goal of preventing further wrongdoing. Few arrests were made, but the message was clear enough; in concert with other measures, the HSC's actions helped reduce the torrent of unlawful migration to its normal trickle.

We first discuss DHS's role in combating transnational crime, including the limitations of the classic criminal justice model and the promise of an alternative approach. We then sketch out the Disruption Model. Third, we articulate the tools required to implement "disruption," drawing in part on existing efforts that employ some of the tactics we advocate. Fourth, we discuss the specific building blocks that DHS will need to assemble in order to make disruption work. In our concluding section, we anticipate some of the challenges and potential pitfalls involved in shifting toward the Disruption Model and how best to address them.

To summarize, we argue that "disruption" requires significantly greater collaboration among public safety and police agencies—both domestic and international—as well as between the government and the private sector (financial sector companies, airlines, etc.). These various collaborations are necessary for many elements of the model: intelligence collection, information fusion, strategy development, tactical responses, staffing, and the development of a "watchlist" for known or suspected transnational criminals. DHS will also need to expand its existing partnerships in the federal government, including working with the White House–led interagency process to break down persistent barriers to sharing information about transnational crime within the law enforcement community.

Finally, the Disruption Model requires new measures of success. Most of DHS's law enforcement activities involve either interdiction (attempting to stop "bad" things near the physical border) or investigation (building criminal cases against malefactors). The typical metrics used to evaluate these activities include seizures, apprehensions, arrests, prosecutions, and convictions. Disruption instead focuses on the cessation of (or insulation of the United States from) illicit activities. Because this new metric of success can run counter to existing incentives in most law enforcement agencies, implementing the Disruption Model will necessitate changes in promotion incentives and career pathways, as well as cultural reengineering and doctrinal revision within DHS agencies.

Law Enforcement and Homeland Security

Homeland security inherently blends "national security" and "law enforcement" functions. In the context of transnational crime, homeland security involves preventing the underworld of globalization from adversely affecting America and Americans. This mission makes disruption of illegal activity a more intuitive goal than it would be in many law enforcement organizations (e.g., the homicide division of the Boston Police Department), which must deal with malefactors that reside inside the country. DHS's counterterrorism mission is not designed to prosecute terrorists, but rather to help prevent terrorist attacks by keeping dangerous individuals from traveling to the United States; DHS is not judged (and should not be judged) by how many terrorists its agencies apprehend. For other species of transnational crime, we argue, the goal should be similar: keeping "bad people" and "bad things" out of the homeland. The same holds for a related homeland security mission—preventing illegal immigration.

In broad brushstrokes, DHS's law enforcement efforts are divided into agencies that focus either on interdiction (e.g., the U.S. Coast Guard [USCG] and Customs and Border Protection [CBP]) or investigation (principally ICE's Homeland Security Investigations, or ICE/HSI, and, for some financial crimes, the USSS).[2] Interdiction agencies focus on apprehending bad people and bad things, usually close to the border, before they can affect public safety. Things that get intercepted—illegal drugs, "conflict diamonds," endangered species, dual-use technologies, unlicensed firearms, pirated CDs, undeclared bulk cash, and so forth—are seized. Apprehended people—undocumented migrants, criminals with outstanding arrest warrants, drug mules, human traffickers, etc.—are processed and typically either repatriated (in the case of most undocumented migrants) or turned over to ICE/HSI and the DOJ for prosecution. Investigative agencies then focus on building legal cases against criminals and, in particular, on uncovering evidence that can be used to secure convictions.

Despite some tension between these two approaches, both pieces help deter criminal activity. For instance, many potential migrants are deterred by the prospect that they will be apprehended, repatriated, and possibly prosecuted, and many would-be smugglers are deterred by the prospect of arrest and incarceration. Unfortunately, however, these approaches do not adequately address some of the most important challenges confronting DHS, for the following three reasons.

First, as with the hypothetical cybercriminal mentioned in the opening vignette, the nerve centers of many of the criminal activities that DHS is charged with suppressing are based outside the United States, and thus beyond the reach of American law enforcement. Traditional law enforcement tactics like interdiction and investigation can, at best, cut off a tentacle here or there, but not the head.

Second, the scale of illicit activity can render the traditional criminal justice approach ineffective. Assembling cases for prosecution is time-consuming and oriented to individual acts of bad behavior. It metes out justice, but it does not necessarily solve problems at scale. International narcotics trafficking, for example, is not a problem that the federal government can resolve through arresting and prosecuting every low-level courier. Likewise, wholesale prosecuting of undocumented immigration (whether through pleas or trials), regardless of the circumstances of each case, would clog the courts with tens of thousands of cases without solving the problem.

Third, some illicit activity simply cannot be deterred through the classic criminal justice model. For example, unaccompanied minors from Central America who arrived in the United States in 2014, and the families who arrived with children in 2015 and 2016, did not attempt to elude the Border Patrol.

Rather, they immediately sought out agents to whom they could present themselves and surrender into their custody. The reason is that children migrating alone were handed over to the Department of Health and Human Services, rather than being deported automatically by ICE, and many of those apprehended believed (correctly) that they would ultimately be reunited with family members already in the United States. Even when parents accompanied the children, migrants often claimed asylum; those who met the standard of "credible fear" of persecution in their home countries were paroled into the country to wait for an immigration court hearing scheduled years in the future to adjudicate their claims. When federal courts forbade extended family detention by ICE, many migrants were simply released into the United States. (When the Trump administration decided to avoid these problems by separating apprehended parents from their children, the resulting outcry forced a change in policy.) Something more than interdiction and investigation is needed when the ordinary tools of deterrence cannot be used or fail to deter.

For all of these reasons—extraterritoriality, scale, and the potentially weak deterrent effect of standard law enforcement operations—the classic criminal justice model is often ill suited to combating transnational crime.

The Disruption Model

A different approach would be to disrupt—or to insulate the United States from—international illicit activities. Adopting this approach would not mean abandoning traditional criminal investigations, but it would shift enforcement efforts from "prosecution-centered" to "disruption-directed" measures, which "make it difficult for individuals participating in a criminal network or market to continue with their illegal activities."[3] In other words, prosecution would remain an element of the strategy, but it would be neither the ultimate objective nor the main tool.

Currently, most investigations are initiated by field-level agents with the consent of their supervisors, typically following "leads" from informants or other sources. In the disruption model, traditional investigations geared to criminal justice prosecution would still take place, but would be based on a strategic rationale rather than the simple discovery that crimes might be occurring.

Antecedents for this approach exist in some government agencies. For example, disruption as a primary strategy is common in counterintelligence, and is utilized by the Counterintelligence Division of the FBI's National Security Branch. In these contexts, arresting the architects of targeted activities is not always the desired goal, even if the identities of the perpetrators are known and legal cases could be built against them; the objective instead is to neutralize ongoing efforts at espionage by foreign powers in a continuing game of spy-versus-spy.[4]

Disruption is also a logical response to some cybercrime, where problems of detection, criminal prosecution, and extraterritoriality are patently obvious to both the outlaw and the law enforcement officer. For the great mass of cyber-enabled crime, the ecosystem is too decentralized to provide an obvious "take-down" target. As one analyst noted when commenting on the web-facilitated theft of personal data:

> The current focus to disrupt online marketplaces centres on investigation and prosecution of key players. In 2004, ShadowCrew, a stolen data marketplace, was targeted by law enforcement using a police informant. Following this operation, Federal Bureau of Investigation (FBI) agents infiltrated the DarkMarket forum, culminating in the agency running the server and hosting the communication. In 2012, international efforts involving seven countries resulted in three arrests and 36 websites being shut down. Such a takedown of stolen data markets involves substantive high-profile investigative resources, which, in the long term, may have a limited disruption effect on the larger underground economy for information.[5]

Disruption has also been invoked as a reasonable approach to money-laundering[6] and even drug trafficking.[7] It may also be a viable strategic approach to countering child pornography. In each of these contexts, the scale of criminal activity is so vast, decentralized, and disproportionate to available law enforcement resources and capabilities that it is impossible to identify, let alone prosecute, most offenders.

Although no police force has organized itself around "disruption", some law enforcement agencies have experimented with this model. One example concerns local policing in the United Kingdom,[8] with increasing attention to "law enforcement intelligence" and an effort to convert the police into an "intelligence-driven organization."[9] The goal of disruption in this context was to reduce social harm and curtail criminal activity, even if it was not possible or desirable to prosecute most offenders.

Within DHS, we believe that the changes in ICE/HSI have incorporated elements of a "disruption" strategy. In addition, as mentioned above, DHS has launched specific initiatives, such as the HSC, that fit the model, however *ad hoc* they may have been.

The Disruption Model Toolkit

Disruption requires broad statutory authorities to prevent criminal activity. Fortunately, because of its border security mandate and national scope, DHS possesses a better toolkit than the typical police force.

OPERATING ABROAD

As several contributors to this volume discuss, border security involves "pushing the borders out" so that high-risk persons and goods can be identified and interdicted as far away from the actual U.S. borders as possible. DHS now has the third-largest civilian footprint in the U.S. government (after the State Department [DOS] and the Central Intelligence Agency [CIA]), and many DHS officers abroad are engaging in precisely the kind of prevention, protection, and disruption activities recommended here. These include:

- CBP pre-clearance officers and joint security/immigration advisory program officers operating in foreign airports to determine whether passengers should be permitted to board flights bound for the United States;
- CBP officers screening cargo in distant ports through the Container Security Program or in zones contiguous to the border in the pre-inspection program;
- ICE agents conducting visa-related investigations out of U.S. embassies abroad;
- Transportation Security Administration (TSA) officers conducting airport safety and security compliance inspections abroad in "last point of departure" airports, as well as securing certain air cargo shipments bound for the United States;
- thousands of USCG personnel patrolling the maritime border to intercept migrants and interdict illicit drugs; and
- CBP officers and ICE agents stationed abroad training and advising foreign immigration officials engaged in dealing with migrants who are headed to U.S. borders.

Although DHS's foreign operations do not resolve the legal issue of extraterritoriality, they do help it to neutralize or mitigate threats to the U.S. homeland. Results range from diverting counterfeit pharmaceuticals to the repatriation by Mexico to Central America of approximately two hundred thousand undocumented migrants per year in 2014–2016.

Unfortunately, DHS activities abroad are conducted without a proper strategic framework, adequate budgetary support, needed assistance from the Intelligence Community (IC), and full coordination with port-of-entry (POE) operations and domestic law enforcement.

REGULATING ENTRY AND EXIT

DHS's legal authorities provide it with considerable power to regulate and control the entry of people and shipments into the United States, power which can be asserted aggressively against the appropriate individuals and their property. Permanently revoking the right of entry of drug "mules"— and withholding the border-crossing privileges of their known or suspected associates abroad—arguably has greater deterrent value than a short jail sentence. Similarly, severely restricting the right to import and export goods, or to transfer funds into and out of the country, by entities and individuals associated with transnational criminal activities might prevent criminal activity more effectively than years of painstaking criminal investigation. Even in the case of U.S. citizens who cannot be barred from returning, DHS can always take advantage of the fact that search authorities at the border are dramatically more expansive than they are inside the country to detain and gather information from border crossers connected with transnational crime.

WATCHLISTING

Related to regulation of entry and exit is the development of a transnational organized crime (TOC) watchlist, which is analogous to the one developed for known and suspected terrorists. The proper use of such a list can impede criminal activity without any seizures or arrests by making it harder for known or suspected criminals to travel internationally. Although the development of an intergovernmental TOC watchlist began in 2015, the list itself only contains a few dozen names (compared to hundreds of thousands in the Terrorist Screening Database). In fact, it remains a small fraction of the "No Fly" list, which comprises several thousand people who constitute a demonstrable risk to civil aviation. There is no reason that the TOC list could not grow to include tens of thousands of dangerous or undesirable individuals.

Significantly, the inclusion of an individual on a watchlist does not necessarily mean that she is automatically inadmissible. The proper response when a watchlisted person attempts to travel to the United States can consist of: denying a visa; issuing a visa but subsequently refusing entry at the border; overtly indicating to the individual that she is under close scrutiny; sending the individual to secondary inspection upon arrival in the hopes of discovering contraband; identifying travel companions of the listed individual for further scrutiny; silencing the "hit" entirely and then following the individual once she arrives in order to identify potential conspirators; alerting the relevant law enforcement authorities (those building a potential criminal case against her, those managing her as a confidential informant, her parole officer, etc.) that the individual has entered the country; or simply doing nothing.

Initial candidates for the watchlist could come from information gleaned by DHS officers abroad, as well as through the DOJ's Consolidated Priority Organization Target (CPOT) process. CPOTs are criminal entities, typically headquartered abroad, that have been designated as the top focus for federal law enforcement. (Examples might include a Russian syndicate with links to senior government officials in that country or a major Mexican drug cartel.) CPOTs, however, must be coherent organizations rather than loose networks, and U.S. enforcement efforts focus on the leadership of these organizations—a few dozen people at most. Each year, U.S. agencies decline to nominate certain criminal networks (or see their nominations fail) because the "organizations" in question are too small, insufficiently menacing, or lack a clear command and control structure. In addition, lower-level members of organizations designated as CPOTs are rarely targeted. These individuals might not be good candidates for the conventional law enforcement approach, but they would be good candidates for a watchlist. In fact, from a disruption perspective, impeding the activities of middle- and lower-level individuals (couriers, money-launderers, enforcers, etc.) can sometimes be as effective in disrupting illicit activities as multi-year investigations aimed at the organization's leader.

Multilateral organizations (Interpol, Europol, and Ameripol) and trusted partner countries (Mexico, Colombia, Panama, France, Italy, Japan, Australia, New Zealand, and the United Kingdom) could also provide candidates for the watchlist. Finally, local law enforcement agencies often possess information that is rarely integrated with federal data—for example, the San Francisco Police Department on membership in Triad organizations or the Los Angeles Police Department on MS-13.

TOC watchlisting inevitably raises many practical issues, full resolution of which is beyond the scope of this chapter. Some of these—such as procedures for nomination, protections for U.S. citizens who are watchlisted, and redress protocols—can be addressed in the same way as they have in the terrorist watchlisting process. Other issues, such as the greater risk of corruption involved in maintaining lists of organized crime figures, require novel solutions. Here we merely note that many existing efforts within the government—such as internal monitoring protocols at the Organized Crime Drug Enforcement Task Force (OCDETF) Fusion Center, procedures for handling confidential informants at various law enforcement agencies, and management of the federal Witness Security Program—suggest how such problems can be surmounted.

DATA

DHS's authorities give it control over a staggering amount of information about specific individuals that would be inaccessible to a typical law enforcement agency. Data include travel histories, information in visa applications and customs declarations forms, airline passenger name records (PNR), elements culled from cargo manifests, informant reports, field notes by Border Patrol agents, nuggets of information from the "high side",[10] and more. DHS can use this information to develop algorithms that identify potentially high-risk individuals and to paint an accurate picture of the threat environment.

Full deployment of these measures would put DHS in a strong position to disrupt transnational criminal activity.

Toward Operational Coordination

DHS's success in combating transnational crime depends on learning more about transnational criminal networks and incorporating that information into the best operational response. What specific steps are needed to accomplish this goal?

INFORMATION COLLECTION AND SHARING ACROSS THE GOVERNMENT

Disruption requires "law enforcement intelligence"—that is, information on illicit activity that has been fused together to inform operations. Specifically, DHS needs to know the lay of the land with respect to the extent and nature of illicit activity in a particular domain in order to identify vulnerabilities. This is a different approach to information than in the criminal justice model, in which the "case" is dealt with as an isolated event, the process ends after sufficient legally admissible evidence is generated to "prove" a violation of law, and potentially usable information typically remains confined to the "case." By contrast, in a sophisticated intelligence cycle, the process of converting data and reports into usable information is never "closed." This approach is central to the way intelligence is increasingly being used in policing systems, where it is repeatedly recycled, refigured, and reworked to address current problems. Thus, the same piece of intelligence can be used to support the arrest of a suspected criminal and then, on a different occasion, to inform an intervention designed to disrupt the activities of a criminal network.[11]

The most important obstacle to routinizing this process is bureaucratic: federal agencies do not do a good job of sharing the information they already possess. Although the attacks of 9/11 led to much greater information sharing about terrorism across U.S. government agencies, no remotely comparable change has occurred with regard to transnational crime. On the contrary, each investigative agency jealously guards the intelligence it possesses for fear that sharing information might lead another agency to take actions that undermine its investigations. For instance, the arrest of some members of a criminal conspiracy by Agency X could interfere with an investigation being conducted by Agency Y.[12] As a result, reticence and even mistrust reign. We believe, however, that most of the barriers to information sharing among investigative agencies could be resolved through an interagency process that includes sufficient procedural reassurances (e.g., that agencies proffering information get right of first refusal on investigations that come out of subsequent analysis). Achieving this level of collaboration will likely require political will from senior officials at DHS and the DOJ, as well as engagement by members of the National Security Council staff in the White House.

For the Disruption Model to succeed, information sharing would also have to be improved between law enforcement agencies and intelligence agencies.[13] At present, logistical, procedural, legal, cultural, and budgetary barriers impede a steady flow of information from the "high side" on non-terrorist crime. Logistically, many DHS employees do not have the necessary clearances to view classified information, and there is no automatic system for converting classified information into unclassified form (e.g., "tear sheets"). Even if they have clearances, DHS employees often operate in work environments where they cannot access classified systems. The central cultural problems concern, on the one hand, resistance by intelligence agencies to investing resources on tackling transnational crime and, on the other hand, law enforcement agencies' frequent lack of interest in classified information, because the measures required to protect intelligence sources and methods frequently prevent such information from being introduced as evidence in court. As entrenched as these problems are, we believe that they can be overcome through a senior leadership decision to develop more TOC-related intelligence and feed it swiftly to DHS.

Information sharing must also be improved between DHS and the Treasury Department. One underutilized data source is the Suspicious Activities Reports (SARs) for bank transactions and wire transfers collected by the Financial Crimes Enforcement Network (FinCEN). This information has many law enforcement applications. We also believe that wider use of these data will have a valuable secondary effect. At present, bank SARs are insufficiently standardized, based on inadequate training of bank staff, and excessively subject to editing by senior management in the banks themselves. Better exploitation of this data will encourage the government to improve its collection and quality.

DHS can also make good use of data from outside the government, such as money transfer data (e.g., Western Union) and information on corporate ownership, real estate ownership, and board memberships. Even if the current laws permitting the legal concealment of beneficial ownership are retained—an approach we consider suboptimal—the government could invest in creating more extensive records of beneficial ownership for its own use. That information would in turn enable investigators to link suspicious transactions to specific individuals and take the appropriate actions.

Finally, DHS would benefit from a continuously updated list of valid addresses and company locations. Such a list would then allow DHS to perform bulk searches of customs manifests and PNR data. If an address were flagged for whatever reason, links could then be drawn to other people at (or other shipments to) that same address.

INTEGRATION AND SYNTHESIS

Acquisition of the right data is only the first step in mapping criminal ecosystems; equally important is fusing it together in an operationally useful way. DHS benefits from some data fusion done by other agencies, such as the Special Operations Division at the Drug Enforcement Administration (DEA) and the OCDETF Fusion Center. In addition, the new system used by CBP's National Targeting Center (NTC), which provides basic automated link analysis for screeners to use in the counterterrorism context, could be readily adapted to transnational crime. Units at DHS, such as the Border

Enforcement Analytics Program (BEAP) and the HSC, have also done remarkable work in fusing data to identify criminal networks from computer-assisted analysis of big data repositories. These efforts, as well as those of entities like the Bulk Cash Smuggling Center, could be brought under a central office at DHS. One option would be to reorganize DHS's Office of Intelligence and Analysis (I&A) to assist in this effort. (See Chapter 15 for further discussion of I&A.) Such an office could also represent DHS in the interagency TOC watchlisting process.

DHS can also do a better job of synthesizing the data it already uses. One example concerns the relationship of the data on passengers and on cargo at the National Targeting Center. There are important benefits to be gained from fully merging the two sorts of information. For instance, if the address to which a series of suspicious shipments are directed is also the address listed by someone on their Customs Declaration Form or visa application, that individual would warrant greater scrutiny. In addition, information collected by Border Patrol agents in interviews with appre-hended migrants and human smugglers (known as coyotes) on the south-west border can be useful in developing a better picture of smuggling practices, routes, prices, and the like. The integration of this data with other information is incomplete and not automated. Finally, DHS has been slow to develop targeting algorithms designed to identify potential trans-national criminals; almost all of its efforts in this domain have focused on counterterrorism.

Spotting and mapping criminal networks constitute another important opportunity.[14] At present, the link analyses drawn within DHS have an artisanal quality: investigators create "maps" that depict the connections they have uncovered between criminal suspects, typically in a single net-work, over the course of a single investigation. These link analyses are sometimes used to assist investigators during an inquiry, but they are often used when preparing for a trial, and the way they are crafted reflects that purpose. In the Disruption Model, the primary purpose of link analysis would be to understand the nature of criminal ecosystems in order to develop the optimal "disruptive" response. An ideal link-analysis system would be more automated, relying on computer-generated link analyses that would then be "graded" by analysts, so that the computer-assisted process was continuously refined. For instance, investigators and analysts might "train" the computer to look only for certain types of links (e.g., between two cars registered to different individuals but garaged at the same home), but not others (e.g., two people who sat next to each other on an airplane), while still allowing the computer to find non-obvious connections among other data elements (a person, a package, a building, a company, etc.).[15]

Crucially, vulnerabilities are not the same for all criminal ecosystems. For instance, the response that works best to disrupt human smuggling would not be the best approach to combating human trafficking.[16] As a result, DHS must be prepared to use the tools at its disposal in different ways depending on the type of criminal activity it seeks to disrupt. DHS may at times have to organize operational planning around types of illicit activity, rather than by geography or Component agency.

OPERATIONAL COORDINATION

For disruption to work, intelligence collection and operational planning must be fully integrated: information must be converted into a usable form for those in charge of executing the law enforcement response (whatever it may be). This actionable information in turn would have to be shared systematically with operational planning groups from different DHS Components (ICE, CBP, the USCG, and possibly even investigators from the USSS and TSA's Federal Air Marshals). There are several possible ways to organize such an operational effort; here we simply note that there are useful examples from other parts of the federal government on which to draw, including the Joint-Interagency Task Force-South (JIATF-South) in Key West.

For disruption to be maximally effective, some of DHS's responses need to be coordinated with other partners inside and outside the federal government. Once again, the main obstacles here are bureaucratic. Greater coordination among federal agencies, better working relationships with state and local law enforcement, and closer partnerships with foreign counterparts require sustained commitment from the leadership of DHS, as well as buy-in from the DOJ, the IC, and the White House National Security Council staff.

INTERNATIONAL COOPERATION

The weakness of multilateral organizations—from the United Nations to Interpol through Europol and the World Customs Organization, International Maritime Organization, and International Civil Aviation Organization—in the face of transnational criminal activity is conspicuous and reflects antiquated notions of sovereignty. As a result, transnational information and intelligence sharing, let alone operational coordination, are woefully deficient. The consequence is that the activities of transnational criminal organizations, unlike those of terrorist organizations, are barely challenged by the international community. If foreign partner agencies would align their enforcement and disruption actions against commonly identified criminal networks, the cumulative effect would far outstrip what a handful of prosecutions by one government can accomplish. The U.S. government, including DHS, must take the lead in creating or strengthening transnational arrangements that can facilitate better operational cooperation across nation-states.

Partnership with Canada and Mexico is paramount for disruption to be effective, and existing models in North America offer examples that can be expanded to other countries. For instance, attempts to disrupt the flow of Central Americans into the United States have been much more effective when American efforts are closely coordinated with those in Mexico, including law enforcement operations and capacity building on Mexico's southern border. Likewise, attempts to prevent smuggling across a stretch of rural territory along the Arizona/Sonora border have proven vastly more effective when officials from the Border Patrol and other U.S. agencies can plan and conduct operations jointly with their Mexican counterparts (such as vetted units of the Mexican Federal Police). The same is true on the U.S. northern border, where the Royal Canadian Mounted Police and the USCG have created the Shiprider program to patrol the Great Lakes jointly. Finally, counter-cartel efforts in Mexico will be most effective when take-down operations directed against a particular cartel are accompanied by street-level enforcement in the United States targeting the domestic drug distribution networks associated with that Mexican cartel and by efforts at the border to prevent the travel of suspected cartel associates.

Avoiding Pitfalls and Mitigating Risks

DHS has a unique set of missions and capabilities that distinguish it from other law enforcement agencies. This fact poses distinctive challenges, but also creates an opportunity for DHS to pioneer a novel approach to combating transnational criminal activity. In this chapter, we have described the basics of that approach.

We believe that disruption will significantly improve both public safety and DHS's reputation; however, if the shift toward disruption is implemented haphazardly or incompetently, there could be no improvement at all. By way of conclusion, therefore, we discuss several challenges that will attend the adoption of the Disruption Model as the central organizing framework for homeland security efforts against crime.

First, the Disruption Model involves changes in operations, staffing, career paths, and culture. Law enforcement agents, especially those in investigative units, are rarely promoted for things that do not happen; rather, advancement requires involvement in "take-down" operations (often based on evidence from wiretaps). If disruption is to succeed, the incentives for investigators would have to change. One option—among several possible steps—would be to make a posting at a disruption center a requirement for promotion within certain DHS Components. DHS would also need to devise new metrics of success, linked to promotions, that would capture the cessation or reduction of illicit activity.

Second, because cultural change of this kind is not easy or automatic, transition to the Disruption Model would require sustained, high-level attention from DHS's top leadership: the Secretary, the Deputy Secretary, at least one member of their senior staff, and the heads of the relevant Components, as well as key operational leads within them (e.g., the heads of ICE/HSI, the USSS's Office of Investigations, CBP's Office of Field Operations, and CBP's Border Patrol). To address interagency issues, a Senior Director from the White House National Security Council staff will need to be charged with designing and overseeing information-sharing regimes that cut across Departments. Finally, the relevant committees in Congress will need to be apprised. In sum, coalitions will have to be built, time invested, and political capital expended.

Third, it is possible that disruption may bring DHS into conflict with investigative agencies at the DOJ, which operate on the traditional model. We believe that DHS must make appropriate accommodations to these agencies, which remain the center of federal law enforcement in the United States. When it comes to transnational crime, however, we do not believe that disruption tactics should automatically cede to conventional investigative approaches whenever the two come into conflict. This recommendation represents a sharp departure from past practice and will necessitate a robust interagency dispute resolution mechanism coordinated by White House staff.

Fourth, we note the danger—illustrated by some experiences with street-level enforcement of narcotics laws—that disruption can become an excuse for avoiding the difficult work of assembling a criminal case.[17] This danger is more pronounced if disruption is presented as part of a menu to law enforcement officers, allowing unmotivated personnel to select the least taxing option. Again, we emphasize that the Disruption Model must be based on clear metrics of performance and efficacy that are linked to promotion pathways.

Fifth, there is always the danger that link analyses and corresponding enforcement actions could be abused in ways that violate privacy or compromise due process. As noted above, we recommend that DHS adopt specific ameliorative measures, such as steps to prevent inappropriate access to government data and the anonymization of personal data used to produce link analyses until a certain threshold is reached. More broadly, we believe that the shift toward disruption must be accompanied by safeguards on investigators' access to personally identified data, clear standards of conduct, appropriate redress procedures for targets of law enforcement action, and regular oversight of the entire system (including by Congress).

Finally, to mitigate all of these risks, we note that there are opportunities to move toward the Disruption Model incrementally and assess potential pitfalls empirically. For instance, the recommendations we make regarding data analysis constitute desirable steps even if DHS hews to a more traditional approach; there is really no reason not to pursue them now, and they would lay the foundation for full-fledged adoption of the Disruption Model in the future. DHS could also build out some of the initiatives that essentially constitute "pilots" of the ideas we discuss (such as BEAP and the HSC, and the better fusion of data at the NTC). Finally, there are certain categories of transnational criminal activity for which DHS is the government's lead agency (illegal immigration, migrant smuggling, and human trafficking); DHS could begin its shift toward disruption in these areas even before building the interagency partnerships that will be required to combat other categories of transnational crime.

Adopting an incremental approach would give DHS important insight into the Disruption Model's utility and the operational experience necessary to improve it. The critical step, we believe, lies in DHS's committing to a new strategic framework which eschews exclusive reliance on the criminal justice model to counter transnational crime. For the leadership of DHS, this step entails a shift in rhetoric and doctrine (e.g., DHS's mission statement and those of some of its Components). Even if the ensuing steps are modest at first, such shifts in discourse will send a crucial signal of DHS's willingness to embrace an approach to transnational crime that best reflects its mission, authorities, and capabilities.

CHAPTER 15

The Future of Homeland Security

Chappell Lawson and Alan Bersin

HOMELAND SECURITY IS ESSENTIAL, BUT WHAT CONSTITUTES "HOMELAND security" and how best to get it remain confusing and contentious. The central purpose of this volume is to clear up that confusion and suggest ways forward for America's homeland security enterprise. In this concluding chapter, therefore, we draw on the lessons of the preceding chapters to discuss how America's homeland security enterprise can best succeed. Below we outline the key choices that need to be made in planning for homeland security over the next fifteen to twenty years.

Given the richness and detail of the issues discussed in previous chapters, we can only discuss certain points they raise parenthetically. This is particularly true when it comes to the operations of particular agencies within the Department of Homeland Security (DHS). Instead of summarizing every possible recommendation, we focus here on drawing out the larger lessons for homeland security. In particular, we concentrate on the following questions:

1. How should America's homeland security enterprise be organized?
2. How should DHS and its Components, in particular, be organized and managed?
3. How should scarce federal resources be reallocated to meet different threats?
4. How far should the United States go in "federalizing" homeland security, and how much of the responsibility for critical infrastructure, cybersecurity, and emergency management can be left to state governments, local governments, or the private sector?
5. How should the United States manage its air, land, and maritime borders in an era of globalization?

We thank Nate Bruggeman and Benjamin Rohrbaugh for valuable comments on earlier drafts of this chaper and Kate Searle for editorial assistance.

6. How should the United States incorporate DHS into federal policy-making on foreign relations?

7. How can the government identify and monitor dangerous individuals while respecting privacy and civil liberties?

8. What should be asked of American citizens and civil society when it comes to homeland security?

The answers to each of these questions represent forks in the road. In some cases, we offer explicit guidance on which fork to take. For instance, we argue against further reorganization of the homeland security bureaucracy, in favor of rebalancing priorities across threats (rather than a disproportionate focus on counterterrorism), and for ever-deeper collaboration with Canada and Mexico in managing shared borders (rather than unilateralism). In other cases, where we believe the answer is less clear, we confine ourselves to highlighting key decision points and tradeoffs involved. For instance, we acknowledge the desirability of securing the global supply system from nuclear terrorism while also noting the uncertain benefits and potentially high costs involved in doing so.

We close by restating the stakes. Failure to consolidate an effective homeland security enterprise—including a more smoothly functioning DHS—leaves Americans in harm's way. In the twenty-first century, the United States needs homeland security, and it needs it done right.

Organizing the Homeland Security Enterprise

The homeland security enterprise is a "whole of government" construct designed to protect Americans from a variety of threats, both natural and man-made. As discussed in Chapter 1, most definitions of homeland security include all or part of the following functions:

- Border security, including customs, immigration, and other inspection functions, deployed at air, land, and maritime borders;
- Transportation security (especially civil aviation);
- Disaster relief and emergency management, including response, recovery, and resilience;
- Protection of critical infrastructure, sites, and individuals (i.e., dignitaries);
- Cybersecurity;

- Combating transnational criminal activity;
- Counterterrorism;
- Counterespionage; and
- Preventing and addressing public health crises, especially pandemics of deadly infectious disease.

These are all quintessentially governmental functions; although many of them necessarily involve private actors, they cannot be left entirely to private or community organizations. Not surprisingly, two of the oldest elements of the federal government are the customs houses that eventually became part of Customs and Border Protection (CBP) and the associated revenue cutters that eventually grew into the U.S. Coast Guard (USCG). Which parts of the government should "own" which specific homeland security mission, however, is not always clear. Nor is the mechanism by which these disparate parts of the government can best collaborate.

Since the terrorist attacks of September 11, 2001, responsibilities and coordinating mechanisms for many of these functions have become much clearer. DHS is the dominant federal player in the first four (and when it comes to civilian cybersecurity, probably the fifth as well). DHS plays a secondary role when it comes to combating most transnational organized crime, which has historically been the purview of the Department of Justice (DOJ), but the primary role in countering other types of transnational criminal activity (e.g., human smuggling and trafficking). Domestic counterterrorism falls mainly to the Federal Bureau of Investigation (FBI) and the Intelligence Community (IC), though DHS plays an important supporting role. With respect to counterespionage and responding to pandemics of infectious disease, DHS's role is peripheral; the FBI and the Centers for Disease Control and Prevention (CDC), respectively, are in charge. This overall division of responsibilities within the U.S. government is now neither contested nor problematic; after fifteen years, the bureaucratic lanes are mostly clear.

Clarification of roles and responsibilities in most of these homeland security areas represents a remarkable achievement. At this point, we believe that little is to be gained by rethinking the bureaucratic structure of America's homeland security enterprise. In particular, we would caution against the temptation to move around boxes on a federal organization chart in an effort to achieve greater apparent clarity of design. Although decisions about which agencies should have been incorporated into DHS in 2002–2003 were to some degree arbitrary and possibly even mistaken at the time, changing things around again now would bring significant disruption and confusion with little expectation of actual operational improvement.

Where do we believe change is needed across the federal enterprise? As Chapters 12 and 14 in this volume make clear, coordination within the federal bureaucracy for certain homeland security functions remains weaker than it should be. Deficits mainly have to do with process, not organizational structure. For instance, whether DHS ends up being the federal government's sole lead agency for civilian cybersecurity or simply becomes an important player in a well-run interagency policymaking process led by the White House is less important than whether some coordinating mechanism exists in the first place.[1] Likewise, federal law enforcement efforts against transnational crime, which were largely unaffected by 9/11, must become far more coordinated if the United States is to respond agilely and effectively to this threat. Finally, we believe that coordination between the CDC and DHS could be enhanced, with the main opportunities for improvement being identified through joint exercises and simulations (as Juliette Kayyem recommends in Chapter 2). Focusing high-level attention on these three areas would be the best investment that senior officials and Congress could make in revisiting the organization of America's homeland security enterprise.

Organizing, Managing, and Overseeing DHS

The post-9/11 creation of DHS represented one of the largest reorganizations in the history of the U.S. government, rivaled only by the integration of the uniformed services into the Department of Defense (DOD) after World War II. Since its formation, DHS has been through several internal reorganizations—some necessary and successful, others less so. Many of its operating agencies (the "Components") have become far more professionalized, competent, and internally coherent. But how to administer a set of bureaucracies which have very different missions remains a crucial managerial challenge that DHS has failed to resolve. This challenge is compounded by the fact that most Components have a number of corollary or legacy missions that do not fit naturally with their homeland security roles. These include activities as diverse as conducting search and rescue operations at sea (the USCG), efficiently processing applications for citizenship (US Citizenship and Immigration Services [USCIS]), collecting customs duties (CBP), and investigating counterfeit currency and certain aspects of cybercrime (U.S.

Secret Service [USSS]). (For an overview of DHS Components and their roles, see Chapter 1.)

There are certainly many ways in which DHS *could* be reorganized further by moving or recombining Components, at least some of which look eminently reasonable from the perspective of an organization chart. For instance, CBP could be combined with Immigrations and Customs Enforcement (ICE), as Seth Stodder notes in Chapter 5. USCIS, ICE, and CBP could all be combined into an immigration "superagency," as Doris Meissner, Amy Pope, and Andrew Selee discuss in Chapter 9. The operational independence of all of the Components from DHS's Headquarters offices could be reduced dramatically, moving away from the current "multi-divisional" model examined by Alan Cohn and Christian Marrone in Chapter 3 toward a more centralized organization.

We would resist this impulse to move around boxes on an organizational chart. So far, attempts to re-envision and reorganize DHS have been top-down, coordinated by White House staff, Congress, or DHS Headquarters staff who were often unfamiliar with the Components' operations. In some cases, reorganizations were based on perceptions—not always correct—of how the DOD operates. A better approach, we believe, would be to begin with the actual needs of DHS as a Department and the actual requirements of each of the Components. From this perspective, we believe that there are few, if any, good candidates for bureaucratic restructuring at DHS. As with design of the larger homeland security enterprise, we incline strongly toward consolidating what DHS has already done, rather than attempting further large-scale reorganization. Not only would such an endeavor prove complex and disruptive, but it would also distract senior managers at DHS Headquarters from fixing the things at DHS that truly require urgent attention, and it would draw the attention of Component heads away from improving day-to-day operations. Change in DHS should thus be a matter of reorientation rather than reorganization, of creating new processes rather than splitting and recombining agencies.

Where, then, is change needed?

First, congressional oversight of DHS and its Components needs to be streamlined. In the U.S. system, management and organization are not exclusively the province of the executive branch; Congress also plays a role in organizational design and oversight. As several chapters in this volume note, DHS is overseen by far too many disparate congressional committees. (See, in particular, the concluding section of Chapter 4.) Even individual Components of DHS, such as CBP, must deal with a plethora of oversight and appropriations bodies.[2] Streamlining congressional engagement would be operationally valuable in at least two ways: by helping to unify strategic choices about priorities with resources in the budget process; and by allowing Component heads to focus their attention on their agencies' operations rather than spending extra time on Capitol Hill.

Second, we believe that DHS requires better decision-making processes on several issues (as noted by Cohn and Marrone in Chapter 3). These improvements will require changes within DHS Headquarters, a set of offices co-located with each other but physically separated from the Headquarters of the main Components.[3] Specific opportunities include the following areas.

Planning and budgeting. Despite incremental improvements under each of the Department's six Secretaries to date, the planning and budgeting process at DHS remains poorly integrated. Without integrated planning and budgeting, there is no way that DHS can reprioritize among known threats in response to changing conditions, let alone properly anticipate and adequately respond to new threats. Again, we would recommend against restructuring reporting relationships among the Components or recombining any of these operating agencies; rather, the Department requires a unified strategic budgeting process that is linked to planning about threats. This process must be coordinated and led by DHS Headquarters, but it must also reflect appropriate input from the Components and actively engage the Component heads.

DHS's policy shop. The experiences of the Under Secretary of Policy in the Office of the Secretary of Defense and the Policy Planning Staff at the Department of State (DOS), as well as DHS's own experience, offer useful lessons for DHS (both positive and negative). We believe that DHS's Office of Policy should serve as an instrument to ensure a Department-wide strategic vision, to prioritize among various DHS missions, to transmit recommendations from DHS to the White House–led interagency policy-making process, to incubate new ideas on homeland security, and to secure expeditious action on secretarial initiatives. (One such initiative, for instance, might include the "strategic rethink" of multimodal transportation security discussed by Peter Neffenger and Richard Ades in Chapter 8.) To do this job effectively, DHS's Office of Policy will need to be located next to the Secretary's office, rather than stranded elsewhere in the Headquarters complex, and headed by an individual who has the full confidence of the

Secretary and the Deputy Secretary. The Office of Policy must also establish much closer working relationships with DHS's Components. Accomplishing that goal will require more regular communication with the front office staff of each Component and the enlistment of detailees from the Components, rather than exclusive reliance on DHS Headquarters staff with little operational knowledge.

DHS's engagement with the federal interagency policymaking process. So far, the Department has not played a genuinely central role in policymaking on homeland security across the federal government. But, as Kayyem notes in Chapter 2, the success of America's larger homeland security enterprise depends on its doing exactly that: DHS must be the Cabinet Department that brings cross-government vulnerabilities to the attention of other agencies. And to be successful in this interagency process, DHS must speak with a single voice. As anticipated above, the most logical way to ensure that it does would be for an invigorated Office of Policy to take charge of integrating the perspectives of all Components and Headquarters offices and then representing them to the White House. Again, this approach will only work if the Office of Policy has a very clear understanding of the operational issues with which the Components must wrestle on a daily basis, as well as a close working relationship with DHS's senior leadership at Headquarters.

The Science and Technology Directorate (S&T). A fourth topic for senior leadership concerns the role of DHS's Science and Technology Directorate, known as S&T. S&T has sometimes fallen victim to the classic problem of not being close enough to its customers (the Components) to understand their operational needs.[4] Greater involvement by the heads of the Components—or even by the heads of operating entities within the Components, such as the Border Patrol within CBP, when appropriate—at each step in the design and procurement process is essential. We note that the reforms proposed by then–Secretary of Defense Ashton Carter in 2016 regarding procurement processes within the military parallel these recommendations and may help instruct DHS efforts.

The Office of Intelligence and Analysis (I&A). A fifth area where change is needed concerns DHS's Office of Intelligence and Analysis, known as I&A. I&A serves as a liaison between DHS and the IC (including the FBI); it absorbs intelligence products and produces its own briefings for the Department's senior leadership. What I&A does not do enough of—and what we believe it should do more of—is produce material that is useful for the Components in conducting their operations. In other words, I&A should view the Components, rather than Headquarters leadership, as its primary customers. It should coordinate requests from the Components to the IC that help them accomplish their central missions. In Chapter 14, we also urged an increased focus by I&A on countering transnational criminal activity, which would involve interagency advocacy with the DOJ and the IC.

Expertise and partnerships. As Kayyem argues in Chapter 2, DHS must bring people into leadership positions at Headquarters who are knowledgeable about its key partners. These include, in particular, experts from the private sector and from state and local governments. The involvement of such experts is particularly crucial for emergency management and critical infrastructure protection, but we believe it extends even beyond those two missions.

Planning exercises. Also per Kayyem's recommendations in Chapter 2, we suspect that more cross-government planning exercises would be beneficial for certain missions. We note that the relatively poor operational planning capabilities of some of the Components was one of the rationales for Secretary Jeh Johnson's Joint Task Forces (as Cohn and Marrone discuss in Chapter 3); done right, further exercises would not only yield insights but also build human capital. Pandemics of deadly infectious disease and catastrophic natural disasters are particularly appropriate topics for planning and tabletop exercises coordinated by Headquarters.

The role of the Deputy Secretary. We believe that the Deputy Secretary of DHS should design and oversee the processes discussed above and, more broadly, be in charge of enhancing the effectiveness of Headquarters. This means placing all planning, policy, and budgeting functions for the Department—as well as Headquarters offices such as I&A and S&T—under her. (The Components would continue to report directly to the Secretary on operational issues in order to keep reporting relationships clear.) This change would carve out a clearer role for the Deputy Secretary and give the policy, planning, and budgeting functions and the improvement of Headquarters operations the attention that they require.

We believe that all of these changes can be made without increasing staff levels at DHS Headquarters. In fact, they should result in cost savings in both personnel and technology investments. If made with proper involvement by the Components and greater rotation of staff to and from Headquarters, these steps will also boost morale at both Headquarters and the Components.

Third, we see several opportunities for improvement within the Components themselves. All government agencies can enhance their performance, and DHS entities are no exception. Our own list of opportunities for improvement, which is by no means comprehensive, includes:

- streamlining administrative processes at USCIS (as discussed in Chapter 9);
- planning for natural disasters in a way that focuses on what could happen rather than how to allocate existing government resources (as discussed in Chapter 10);
- improving removal procedures at ICE;
- stricter screening of newly hired agents and officers at CBP and greater investment in human capital at the top of the organization;
- improved training on the use of force by the Border Patrol (which is part of CBP);
- better integration of the lessons of red-teaming exercises within the Transportation Security Administration (TSA);
- administrative reforms within the USSS; and
- more competitive hiring of talent at the Cybersecurity and Infrastructure Security Agency (CISA, formerly known as the National Protection and Programs Directorate [NPPD]), as noted in Chapter 11.

Rather than advocate in detail for any of these (or other) measures, here we merely suggest that encouraging the Component heads to focus on the performance of their own agencies rather than on further bureaucratic reorganization will help address such opportunities for operational improvement and identify new ones. In fact, we believe that the importance of focusing Component heads on improving their agencies' operations is the central lesson from the transformation of the Federal Emergency Management Agency (FEMA) after Hurricane Katrina.

This recommendation does not mean that Component heads should think exclusively about their own agencies. As noted above, they should also be involved in interagency discussions of the larger homeland security enterprise. They should, however, be liberated from the burdensome exercise of responding to further top-down efforts at reorganization (as well as duplicative congressional oversight).

Balancing Priorities

For America's homeland security enterprise to succeed, the government must be able to reprioritize its activities in response to a changing threat environment. Currently, the most important question regarding rebalancing priorities—both at DHS and across the broader homeland security enterprise—concerns domestic counterterrorism. Although there are differences in nuance among the authors in this volume, there is general consensus that at this point, a marginal dollar spent on domestic counterterrorism is likely to yield far less public benefit than a marginal dollar spent on other homeland security missions. (The principal exception concerns Neffenger's and Ades's recommendations regarding the public spaces adjacent to transportation hubs in Chapter 8.)

This situation, as Matthew Olsen and Edoardo Saravalle point out in Chapter 4, is in part the product of objective changes in the threat environment as a result of the successes of American intelligence agencies and military forces against terrorist organizations abroad. It also reflects the fact that the United States has now developed a robust regime designed to keep terrorists out of the country, including a well-developed watchlisting process and crucial international partnerships (collaboration with Canada and Mexico being among the most essential). One indicator of these successes is that, as Stodder points out in Chapter 5, the great majority of recent terrorist incidents have involved self-radicalized individuals who were native-born citizens or had lived in the United States for a very long time before embracing *jihad*. Simply put, the nature and extent of the threat have changed.

Domestic counterterrorism must remain an important element of what the federal government (including several DHS Components) does, and we do not mean to dismiss the threat. Furthermore, we recognize (as Neffenger and Ades point out in Chapter 8) that terrorism's effect on public perceptions of safety and the corresponding disruptive effect on society justifies a greater investment of government resources than a simple actuarial calculation of mortality risk would suggest. The question is one of proportionality. In particular, we believe that threats like cyber, natural disasters, and transnational crime must move up the priority list in terms of the resources and attention they receive from the homeland security enterprise in general and from DHS in particular.

We also note that, in some cases, a focus on counterterrorism has adversely affected the legacy missions of several DHS Components to an unwarranted degree. For instance, the redirection of USCG operations toward counterterrorism has limited its ability to monitor fisheries and conduct maritime safety inspections.[5] DHS's emphasis on terrorism has also colored its principal grant program for state and local governments, which might have been better used for more common forms of disaster-related planning.[6] In the same vein, we believe that CBP devotes too much of its formidable analytical capacity in cargo screening to searching for the "bomb in a box," rather than to more quotidian smuggling. Here again, the point is not to undervalue the counterterrorism mission, but rather to highlight the importance of other missions and to ensure proper balance across multiple threats.

For this reason, more attention must be paid to "fear management" (per Stevan Bunnell, Chapter 13) and addressing "the politics of counterterrorism" (per Olsen and Saravalle, Chapter 4). One of the reasons that DHS has placed so much emphasis on counterterrorism is that ordinary citizens, the media, and politicians tend to respond disproportionately to terrorism.[7] Consequently, "officials will lose less for being wrong about a terrorist threat by over-reacting . . . even if they are proven wrong."[8] In addition, at least some parts of DHS have a budgetary incentive to exaggerate the threat.[9] For instance, constantly reminding the public of the remote possibility that terrorists might cross into the country illegally at the U.S. land borders may bring more personnel and funding, but such rhetoric distorts public understanding of the threat and makes it difficult to discuss intelligently whether an appropriate level of border security has been achieved.

Some of these political dynamics are hard to counter.[10] Nevertheless, history suggests that more could be done to inject proportionality into the debate.[11] Consider, for instance, the response of Mayor Michael Bloomberg of New York City—the epicenter of the 9/11 attacks—when commenting on a terrorist plot at New York's JFK airport nine years later:

There are lots of threats to you in the world... You can't sit there and worry about everything. Get a life... You have a much greater danger of being hit by lightning than being struck by a terrorist.[12]

Comments along these lines from senior homeland security officials—albeit perhaps in a different idiom—are essential. We believe that senior officials at DHS and the rest of the homeland security enterprise should view it as part of their mission to inform the public about the actual risks that Americans face. In fact, we believe that reassuring Americans that it is safe to go about their daily lives is itself a crucial part of any effective counterterrorism strategy. Senior officials in DHS and other parts of the homeland security enterprise need to find the right language that will permit the Department to allocate resources appropriately across a range of threats, based on dispassionate strategic analysis.[13]

As Olsen and Saravalle recommend in Chapter 4, such language should be memorialized in communication at the highest levels of the executive branch. Congressional testimony, press conferences and public speeches by senior leaders, policy statements, and private communications with experts outside of government should also clarify how dangerous DHS perceives different threats to be, and what it plans to do about them. Transparency has obvious political value, because DHS's operations will reflect a public consensus on where it should devote its energies; consequently, the Department would not be unfairly held accountable (nor be in a position to dodge blame where it is accountable). But there is also operational value in articulating the nature of the threats that America faces and developing consensus about them across the political spectrum.

DHS should also be transparent about how it approaches the protection-prevention-response-recover-resilience continuum. In many cases, DHS and the U.S. government as a whole must explicitly acknowledge that adverse events—including some kinds of small-scale terrorist attacks—will inevitably occur, and that a significant part of what the bureaucracy does must be focused on recovery rather than prevention. Again, the language of senior officials at DHS and elsewhere must reflect this fact.

Presidents, Cabinet secretaries, and agency heads are understandably preoccupied with being blamed for things that happen "on their watch," especially events that command the attention of the mass media. We believe, though, that these perceived political risks are sometimes as misunderstood as the physical risks. Leaders are typically judged more by their responses to adverse events than by the adverse events themselves; terrible events that are handled well typically result in "rally effects" for incumbent office-holders.[14] Such was the case with George W. Bush's approval ratings after the 9/11 attacks, despite the fact that the Bush administration had paid far less attention to warnings about Al-Qaeda than had its predecessor. Conversely, poor responses to adverse events can badly damage perceptions of elected leaders. For instance, the uncoordinated response to Hurricane Katrina hurt Bush's approval ratings, despite the fact that he was hardly personally responsible for FEMA's day-to-day operations and that state governments, as well as the federal government, play a major role in emergency management.[15] Therefore, redefining success to focus more on effective response and recovery rather than on prevention is not as politically impractical as is commonly believed.

In short, we believe that these adjustments in management, mission, operations, and rhetoric are both politically feasible and operationally desirable. Indeed, the current disproportionality cannot endure forever. A truly catastrophic natural disaster, debilitating cyberattack, hostile act on U.S. soil orchestrated by another nation-state, assassination, or pandemic of deadly infectious disease will force a change in priorities after the fact. The question is whether improvements in America's homeland security enterprise will happen sporadically, in belated response to painful experience, or proactively, in accordance with what those most knowledgeable about the homeland security enterprise already know should be done.

Federalizing Homeland Security and Creating Partnerships

Just as the federal role has expanded in many policy domains, homeland security functions have also become increasingly nationalized. One crucial question regarding homeland security, then, is where the boundary between federal and state government responsibilities, as well as between the public and private sectors, should be drawn.

In some homeland security missions, the responsibilities of the federal government are properly and clearly demarcated. In emergency management, for example, state and local authorities bear primary responsibility for first-response operations, while the federal government provides support to first responders and financial assistance under stipulated conditions; the government has also developed a useful incident command model to handle declared emergencies (as Kayyem notes in Chapter 2). The lines are also relatively clear in the context of immigration and border enforcement, where federal agencies plainly take the lead and states or localities have only a marginal role. In many domains, however, the rules are fuzzy. Even in counter-terrorism, federal authorities, including the FBI, may well require the assistance of local police forces to "look in on" high-risk individuals—as the case of the Tsarnaev brothers revealed.

The concept of "critical infrastructure," including the internet, is the most obvious example of tension and ambiguity. Many of the systems and facilities whose continued operations the government wishes to guarantee (the electrical grid, oil pipelines, the financial sector, the global supply system, the aviation system, etc.) are owned by the private sector, and the government requires partnerships with the private sector to adequately perform its mission in this regard.

The implicit disagreement between contributors to this volume reflects the difficulty in making firm decisions about what the U.S. government should do. In Chapter 11, for instance, Caitlin Durkovich broaches the possibility of a significant expansion of the federal government's potential role—either through direct management or indirect oversight—in order to protect the basic features of Americans' daily lives. Federalization would thus extend to sites and systems that have long been under the primary jurisdiction of state and local governments, including more direct federal regulation of "lifeline" sectors such as electricity. (In Chapter 8, Neffenger and Ades likewise implicitly suggest that a greater federal role is needed in coordinating, supporting, and overseeing efforts to improve surface transportation security.) A different approach would be to delineate more precisely where the federal role ends, and to explicitly limit the U.S. government's responsibilities. This is the view that John Carlin and Sophia Brill articulate in Chapter 12, where they differentiate between the operations of the federal government itself; the operations of state and local governments and non-governmental entities that have direct and serious systemic effects; and other threats that may not have systemic implications. In this hierarchy, the U.S. government should have full control over its own house and, in keeping with the current system, provide information about threats in the second and third categories. Carlin and Brill, however, also leave open the possibility of stealth regulation by making information available to the markets that could render private-sector firms vulnerable to liability, thus incentivizing companies to invest appropriately in security. In reality, there is no easy answer.

Here we do not offer a specific formula for the degree to which cyber-security and protection of critical infrastructure should be nationalized.

We suspect that voluntary partnerships will remain an important part of protecting critical infrastructure. At the same time, new regulation in some form or another or inducements of some sort will be necessary to protect certain sectors.

It is essential, however, that responsibilities and authorities be clearly spelled out before disasters occur, and that the entities which bear ultimate responsibility take the necessary steps to create resilient systems. It is little use to say, for example, that automakers are responsible for countering cyber-security threats to autonomous vehicles if an appropriate regulatory regime and regular exercises testing their ability to respond to worst-case scenarios are not in place. One goal in the next few years should be for roles and obligations in critical infrastructure protection and cybersecurity to be as well-defined as they have become with emergency management. The clearer these matters are, the faster the responsible agencies—whoever they are—will be able to build necessary partnerships. This is particularly true for emerging industries that will become part of tomorrow's critical infrastructure, such as "smart cities," driverless vehicles, and the commercial use of outer space.

We also underscore one crucial lesson of the last two decades: the most successful partnerships in homeland security have been exactly that—true partnerships that are the product of collaboration and negotiation with the private sector, rather than government fiat alone. Effective relationships typically involve the government gaining full access to the extensive information that private-sector partners possess in order to be able to assess risks and detect potential problems early. They also involve firms' active participation in securing their own operations in order to avoid events that would force a suspension in business operations, and to permit rapid business resumption should such an incident occur. Finally, these partnerships involve extensive discussion, so that both sides can obtain what they need with minimum cost to individual firms or to the economy as a whole. DHS must continue to reach out to the private sector (and to state or local governments) actively and, where possible, co-create the new security regime with them.

Managing Borders

Since 9/11, the United States has pioneered a remarkable change in the way that borders are conceived and managed. The core of this change, as Seth Stodder discusses in Chapter 5, involves abandoning the notion of borders as territorial *lines* to be defended and instead exploiting the extensive authorities that governments have at the borders in order to secure the *flows* of goods and people moving across them.[16] The key tools of this approach are: advance data on who and what is headed toward the country; international partnerships, which effectively push the borders of the United States outward; risk segmentation; trusted shipper and trusted traveler programs, in which merchants and travelers voluntary provide information to and are vetted by the government in exchange for expedited processing; and targeting, or the use of algorithms to identify high-risk shipments and individuals. This approach has allowed American firms to operate in an era of just-in-time manufacturing and permitted easy travel into and out of the country, while simultaneously impeding smuggling and preventing the entry of terrorists. It constitutes a remarkable achievement, and there is no real disagreement among the contributors to this volume about the wisdom and value of twenty-first century border management.

The new paradigm of border management has reached its apogee in North America. Canada, Mexico, and the United States have now institutionalized collaboration at every level, from visionary presidential declarations to *ad hoc* working arrangements at specific ports of entry (and everywhere in between). North American partnerships—at the land borders, on the Great Lakes, and for air travelers flying into the region from elsewhere—are a particularly impressive accomplishment that makes an essential contribution to homeland security. Therefore, we caution strongly against taking the fork in the road that leads back toward misguided unilateralism or unwarranted antagonism toward either of the U.S. land neighbors, which would adversely affect the safety of every American.

One major unresolved issue within the larger consensus on border management concerns how much the United States should invest in attempting to secure the global supply system—or at least the part of that system that passes through the United States—and against which specific threats it should be secured. At present, only a small fraction of maritime shipments into the United States are actually inspected either manually or by electronic scanning; the overwhelming majority of adjudications are made based on a review of data about the shipments provided by shippers and others. Securing flows of cargo would involve both better screening, including more data, and more frequent inspection, as well as closer partnerships with foreign port operators and governments.

We do not have a strong recommendation on which direction the homeland security enterprise should take. On the one hand, investing in something approaching a universal inspection regime would certainly reduce smuggling and lower the risk of nuclear terrorism, as Stephen Flynn suggests in Chapter 7. On the other hand, such a regime could impose significant costs on American firms and consumers. Therefore, as discussed at the end of Chapter 6, we lean toward gradually ramping up inspections of cargo that is not part of any trusted shipper program, prioritizing among these shipments on the basis of better data and analytics. We recognize the logic of Flynn's proposal regarding the specific risk of nuclear weapons, though, given that the creation of a new international regime could trigger technological innovations that would significantly lower the cost of inspections throughout the global supply system. In the end, decisions about this strategic choice hinge on America's willingness to invest in reducing the chance of a very low-probability but exceedingly high-cost disaster.

Another major unresolved issue with regard to U.S. borders concerns how to handle undocumented immigration. American policymakers, including the current and previous three presidents, have invested heavily in security between the ports of entry (POEs) on the U.S. southwest border, including Border Patrol agents, technology, and physical barriers (e.g., fencing). Such investments have undeniably reduced undocumented immigration. Further investment might have a small additional effect. At the same time, we believe that the United States has reached the point of diminishing marginal returns to investments in physical infrastructure between the POEs.

We also note that the physical border itself is one of the worst places to address many homeland security problems, including undocumented immigration. A more effective, efficient, and humane method would be to reduce demand for undocumented labor by sanctioning employers who hire undocumented workers. With regard to asylum claims—including those of Central Americans who have migrated through Mexico—a better alternative to current policy would be to process those claims abroad where possible, rather than at the U.S. border. (As Meissner, Pope, and Selee point out in Chapter 9, such an approach requires partnerships with other countries, especially Mexico.)

All told, the United States has adopted a lopsided approach to undocumented immigration over the last thirty years—making massive increases in security at the U.S. border while leaving in place an enormous labor-market magnet and, in the context of asylum seekers, a hopelessly clogged and under-resourced immigration court system. A better approach involves policy changes away from the border in order to prevent problems at the border itself.

Planning Transnationally across the U.S. Government

In an era of globalization, homeland security is inherently transnational in nature. Most of the incidents or threats to the homeland today are at least partly generated abroad.[17] As Stodder and Flynn discuss in Chapters 5 and 7, the new paradigm of border security does not involve defending sovereign territorial lines, but rather securing flows of people, goods, ideas, images, teledata, and cyber packets toward and across them. POEs (airports, seaports, and land ports) are the last, not the first, line of defense for nation-states. Border security begins where airplanes take off and where goods are loaded into cargo holds, not at physical frontiers. This was the central lesson of the Underwear Bomber, Umar Farouk Abdulmutallab, in 2009, and the Yemen cargo plot in 2010.

The transnational dimensions of homeland security have resulted in DHS's deploying the third largest footprint abroad among U.S. government civilian agencies (after the DOS and the Central Intelligence Agency [CIA]). Whether it is CBP officers conducting pre-clearance operations in Abu Dhabi or ICE agents pursuing visa-related investigations in Kuala Lumpur or TSA representatives working with local airport authorities in Johannesburg or Berlin, the objective is the same: securing the flow of goods and people moving toward the American homeland by safeguarding global supply chains and international travel zones.

These deployments make sense. Their implications, however, have not yet been adequately incorporated into the U.S. policymaking process—from decisions about foreign assistance to the collection of information on threats to the country. One useful step would be to designate the Secretary of Homeland Security as a statutory member of the National Security Council, at least for issues pertaining to DHS's areas of responsibility. These areas include decisions about foreign aid to countries where DHS has significant equities and, as is often the case, funding to contribute to these efforts. In addition, we believe that DHS officials at the sub-Cabinet level should also be actively involved in the White House interagency process on relevant foreign policy issues, including preparation for presidential trips.

As several contributors to this volume note, the transnational character of homeland security is particularly clear for North America. The U.S.–Canada and U.S.–Mexico relationships are neither international in a traditional sense nor domestic, given the separate sovereignties involved; instead, to borrow a phrase coined by Bayless Manning in the 1970s, they are "intermestic."[18]

Therefore, one issue in which DHS must be intimately involved is U.S. policy-making toward Canada and Mexico.

Another area in which DHS should be more actively involved in the interagency policymaking process concerns efforts to combat transnational crime. Even though DHS is not and probably should not be the lead agency for most transnational *organized* crime, it is the lead for many other species of transnational crime—human trafficking, smuggling, certain types of cyber-crime, etc.—some of which may be controlled by hierarchically structured criminal organizations. DHS should thus play a key role in identifying high-priority targets for whole-of-government action, advocating for effective strategies to protect Americans against transnational crime, and leveraging its personnel abroad in the service of those strategies.

Protecting Privacy

Many federal agencies have to wrestle with issues of privacy and civil liberties, but DHS is unique. It is the only government entity that, as part of its regular operations, conducts invasive physical searches of millions of Americans and their belongings each week without any predicate. It is also one of the only government agencies that retains huge amounts of data on individuals, using only "implied consent" for justification. In addition, it draws infer-ences based on that data in ways that are totally opaque to citizens, and takes actions that may be to their individual detriment (being selected for search and interrogation, being delayed or severely inconvenienced in their travel, etc.). As Bunnell points out in Chapter 13, the privacy and due process concerns resulting from other homeland security operations, such as infor-mation collection by the National Security Agency, pale by comparison.

A crucial challenge for homeland security, then, concerns how to reconcile the government's manifest need for information that can be used to assess the threats that individuals might pose—in order to react effectively, properly segment risk, and avoid lengthy delays in the transportation system—with the goals of transparency, privacy, due process, and equal treatment under the law. As noted above, the homeland security enterprise has delivered at least one exceedingly clever innovation over the last fifteen years, in the form of programs that encourage individuals to share infor-mation with the government voluntarily in return for expedited processing at the borders and airports. At the other end of the risk spectrum, the government has also developed watchlists and data analytics that help single out a small number of individuals for greater scrutiny, a strategy that significantly enhances public safety at very little cost or inconvenience to the overwhelming majority of travelers. As Bunnell explains in Chapter 13, these programs are win-wins for security and privacy, so long as the basis for inclusion on a watchlist is sound and DHS's algorithms actually predict risk. (It is, and they do.)

We suspect, however, that America's homeland security enterprise may be approaching the frontier of such win-win scenarios. Policy is now drifting toward greater intrusiveness in ways that serve the bureaucratic incentives of the agencies involved, but do not necessarily reflect either a strategic decision about how to value privacy or a conscious search for Bunnell's win-wins. For instance, DHS has recently noted that it "may develop analytic tools that will allow statistical analysis, geospatial analysis, link or pattern analysis, and temporal analysis among other analytic tools for approved users' use in the future." So far, these efforts stop short of full data-mining— which would involve layering human- and computer-generated algorithms on top of massive amounts of personal data in order to identify non-obvious connections—but continued movement is clearly in that direction. A better approach would be to think strategically about the relationship between privacy and security in the homeland security context. The right answer may be incremental change within the existing framework, but it might also be a thorough revision of privacy policies.

The most important privacy decisions facing the homeland security enterprise concern the large-scale collection, retention, and analysis of personally identifiable data; and the widespread use of surveillance technology, such as facial recognition, that would permit the government to more easily monitor the movements of potentially dangerous individuals through the entire transportation system.

One choice—we might call this the "right fork" in the road—would be to allow much more extensive collection and use of personal data, but also to maintain strict limits on what actions the government may take based on that data. The premise here, as Bunnell articulates it, is that the simple fact that the U.S. government collects and retains information about its citizens should not be inherently problematic. It only becomes an issue to the extent that the government either takes action against people based on it or proves to be a poor custodian of the data. Thus, the focus should be on safeguarding data and ensuring due-process protections, not on "privacy" *per se*. This approach could be made congruent with what Neffenger and Ades recommend in Chapter 8: allow citizens to decide how much information they want to share with the government, possibly including whether their facial images and electronic communications would be tracked as they move through the transportation system. In essence, travelers would temporarily sacrifice a great deal of one kind of privacy—freedom from surveillance—for more of another kind—lower probability of being physically searched by agents of the state.

A more restrictive approach—we might call this the "left fork" in the road—would be similar to the one adopted by the European Union (EU), which spells out a number of fundamental privacy rights involving data collection and retention. Some elements of the EU approach could clearly be incorporated into U.S. strategy. If the adoption of additional safeguards allowed the government to acquire more data in exchange, the result would be a win-win (as Bunnell notes in his discussion of the U.S. information-sharing agreement with the European Union). Other elements of the EU approach, however, are incompatible with DHS's current risk-based strategy; they would require a potentially significant sacrifice of security in the name of privacy (understood as government collection and use of personal data).

Here we do not recommend for or against the different paths that America's homeland security enterprise might take on privacy, though we have our own personal views. Instead, we believe that the merits of these options should be explicitly debated, and that the debate should be informed by real data on risks and by a deliberate search for win-wins. The alternative, we fear, is ill-conceived drift toward greater surveillance as agencies seek to accumulate personal information about citizens and monitor their movements "just in case," without being required to demonstrate that acquisition or retention of such information is operationally necessary. Such an approach would sacrifice privacy without necessarily providing much additional security benefit.

Engaging Citizens and Civil Society

As homeland security has become increasing federalized, it has grown more detached from local governments and civil society, with correspondingly less involvement by ordinary citizens. The modern homeland security apparatus is the antithesis of how Alexis de Tocqueville described American democracy—a decentralized government of politically engaged citizens, well-regulated local militias, citizen-juries, and volunteer fire departments.[19] Today Americans' primary role in the homeland security enterprise is to submit to being searched, literally assuming a posture of surrender for electronic imaging at airports.[20] In a disaster situation—thankfully, a circumstance in which most Americans will never find themselves—citizens are asked to comply with evacuation instructions and then await assistance from a benevolent state. At most, the government asks citizens to "say something" if they see something, and this campaign is exclusively related to potential terrorist attacks—again, an occurrence in which the overwhelming majority of Americans will never be involved. Normally, the homeland security enterprise remains distant or alien to most people. This situation is particularly unsettling given that, with the possible exception of the U.S. Postal Service, DHS Components such as TSA and CBP are the part of the federal bureaucracy with which Americans have the most regular, direct interaction. DHS is, as Neffenger and Ades put it in Chapter 8, the "retail face" of the federal government.

What more might be asked of U.S. citizens in the twenty-first century? Or, to pose the question more pointedly, should citizens be asked to do something more for homeland security than take off their shoes at the airport?

Americans clearly look to their government for protection and assistance when it comes to counterterrorism, border security, and disaster relief. Yet they also seem prepared to do their share when called upon. In Hurricane Harvey, for instance, Houstonians with shallow-water boats answered their mayor's call to help their friends and neighbors when government resources were exhausted.[21] As Stephen Flynn put it with regard to counterterrorism:

> Even with the help of their state and local counterparts…federal agencies cannot detect and intercept every act of terrorism. Police, firefighters, and other emergency responders will not always be immediately at hand to protect and rescue those in harm's way. Professionals are usually not the first responders to terrorist attacks and other disasters. A sidewalk T-shirt vendor, not a police patrol officer, sounded the alarm about Faisal Shahzad's SUV in his May 2010 car-bombing attempt on New York's Times Square. Courageous passengers and flight-crew members, not a federal air marshal, helped disrupt the suicide-bombing attempt by Umar Farouk Abdulmutallab aboard Northwest Airlines Flight 253 on Christmas Day 2009. It often falls to ordinary citizens—family, friends, neighbors, and bystanders—to lend a hand in times of crisis.[22]

Imagining how to engage citizens in homeland security is more challenging in the twenty-first century than it was in de Tocqueville's day, when communities were more clearly defined geographically and culturally. Greater citizen participation can also be harmful under some circumstances. During natural disasters, for example, some people have become looters rather than rescuers, and citizen-rescuers may perform badly—possibly even requiring rescue themselves. In the counterterrorism context, as Kayyem notes in Chapter 2, vigilance can inadvertently encourage spying on other citizens or singling them out on the basis of physical markers. The role of ordinary citizens in immigration enforcement and border control is particularly fraught. Should citizens provide information to the authorities on potentially deportable aliens they might meet? The USCG's 24,000-person auxiliary provokes little anxiety, but the prospect of a civilian auxiliary for the Border Patrol in today's political environment raises concerns about ethnic profiling, and possibly even about the motivations of those who might volunteer.[23]

Nevertheless, failing to involve Americans in their own security entails risks as well. The reality is that in some disasters, as Jason McNamara points out in Chapter 10, government resources will be inadequate for the task. In the event of a Category 5 hurricane in South Florida, a major earthquake in the Bay Area or New Madrid (where a number of nuclear power plants sit in the fault-line zone), a pandemic of highly lethal infectious disease, or some equally cataclysmic incident, citizens will be required to rely on their own initiative at a time when they most need and expect assistance from the government.[24] If local organizations that could take up the task do not exist, and citizens are not prepared to help effectively, what will happen?

Another reason to actively engage civil society echoes de Tocqueville: there is a potentially corrosive influence on democratic governance when people continually rely on the federal government to solve problems that could be at least partially addressed by citizens, civic organizations, and communities. To quote Flynn again:

> U.S. federal law enforcement agencies, border agencies, and the Transportation Security Administration (TSA) are subsumed in a world of security clearances and classified documents. Prohibited from sharing information on threats and vulnerabilities with the general public, these officials have become increasingly isolated from the people that they serve. This is the wrong approach to protecting the homeland.... It is long past time for Washington to stop treating civil society as a child to be sheltered and to acknowledge the limits and counterproductive consequences of relying so heavily on protective measures.[25]

We generally agree. America remains a country of vibrant civic organizations and extensive voluntarism. Finding institutional channels for this energy and willingness to assist others would both materially benefit the homeland security enterprise and help shape it to reflect American political culture.

Conclusion

Like all countries, the United States needs homeland security. Terrorist attacks, devastating natural disasters like Hurricanes Katrina and Maria, the challenges of undocumented immigration, high profile cyberattacks, and many other incidents make this quite clear.

The central challenge for the homeland security enterprise, and for DHS in particular, is whether the government will be able to identify the most serious threats, redirect the appropriate resources, and build the necessary partnerships with other organizations in order to execute new missions. The alternative—which we fear is entirely likely—is that the government will lurch clumsily from one threat to another, in response to disasters that might have been anticipated.

Achieving the former outcome requires planning, organization, and leadership. The chapters in this volume suggest how the United States might best organize and execute its various homeland security missions. Ultimately, however, success depends on the willingness of senior policymakers—especially the Secretary of Homeland Security—to wrestle with the difficult questions of how best to address a wide range of changing threats. In some cases, we believe that the right path is quite clear. In others, there is more than one reasonable answer. In the latter case, what matters most is making a decision, based on the best available evidence, and working from there.

Equally important, American policymakers must communicate the rationales for their decisions. They must resist exaggerating or dwelling upon certain threats—even when doing so would protect the budgets of their agencies—and confront hard choices directly. If they do not, the still-new U.S. homeland security enterprise will not be able to protect the American people.

Abbreviations

ACAS	Air Cargo Advanced Screening
ACE	Automated Commercial Environment
AEC	Authorized Economic Operator
AMRIID	Army Medical Research Institute of Infectious Diseases
APIS	Advanced Passenger Information System
AQAP	Al-Qaeda in the Arabian Peninsula
ATF	Bureau of Alcohol, Tobacco, Firearms and Explosives
ATS	Automated Targeting System
BEAP	Border Enforcement Analytics Program
CBNR	Chemical, Biological, Nuclear, and Radiological
CBP	Customs and Border Protection
CDC	Centers for Disease Control and Prevention
CIA	Central Intelligence Agency
CISA	Cybersecurity and Infrastructure Security Agency (formerly National Protection and Programs Directorate [NPPD])
CPOT	Consolidated Priority Organization Target
CSI	Container Security Initiative
C-TPAT	Customs-Trade Partnership Against Terrorism
CVE	Countering Violent Extremism
DARPA	Defense Advanced Research Projects Agency
DEA	Drug Enforcement Administration
DHS	Department of Homeland Security
DNI	Director of National Intelligence
DOD	Department of Defense
DOE	Department of Energy
DOJ	Department of Justice
DOS	Department of State
EPA	Environmental Protection Agency
EPIC	El Paso Intelligence Center
ERO	Enforcement and Removal Operations (ICE)
ESTA	Electronic System for Travel Authorization
FAA	Federal Aviation Administration
FAMS	Federal Air Marshals Service

FAST	Free and Secure Trade
FBI	Federal Bureau of Investigation
FDA	Food and Drug Administration
FEMA	Federal Emergency Management Agency
FTC	Federal Trade Commission
GAO	Government Accountability Office
HHS	Health and Human Services
HSC	Homeland Security Council
HSI	Homeland Security Investigations (ICE)
I&A	DHS Office of Intelligence and Analysis
IAP	Immigration Advisory Program
IC	Intelligence Community
ICAO	International Civil Aviation Organization
ICE	Immigration and Customs Enforcement
ICS	Incident Command System
IMO	International Maritime Organization
INS	Immigration and Naturalization Service
ISIS	Islamic State in Iraq and Syria
ISPS	International Ship and Port Facility Security
JTTFs	FBI Joint Terrorism Task Forces
NAFTA	North American Free Trade Agreement
NCTC	National Counterterrorism Center
NEXUS	Trusted traveler program for the U.S. northern border
NII	Non-intrusive inspection
NNSA	National Nuclear Security Administration
NPPD	National Protection and Programs Directorate (now CISA)
NSA	National Security Agency
NTC	National Targeting Center
OBP	Office of Border Patrol
OCDETF	Organized Crime Drug Enforcement Task Force
ODNI	Office of the Director of National Intelligence
OIG	DHS Office of the Inspector General
PII	Personally Identifiable Information
PIP	Partners in Protection (Canada's trusted shipper program, analogous to C-TPAT)
PKEMRA	Post-Katrina Emergency Management and Reform Act

PNR	Passenger Name Record
POE(s)	Port(s) of entry
Pre✓	TSA's trusted traveler program
PSI	Proliferation Security Initiative
QHSR	Quadrennial Homeland Security Review
RPM	Radiation portal monitor
S&T	DHS Office of Science and Technology
SARs	Suspicious Activity Reports
SENTRI	Secure Electronic Network for Travelers Rapid Inspection (Trusted traveler program for the U.S. southern border)
SOD	Special Operations Division of the DEA
SRTP	Secure Real-Time Platform
TECS	Main law-enforcement database used by DHS (formerly Treasury Enforcement Communications System)
TEU	Twenty-foot equivalent container
TIDE	Terrorist Identities Datamart Environment
TOC	Transnational Organized Crime
TSA	Transportation Security Administration
TSC	Terrorist Screening Center
TSDB	Terrorist Screening Database
USCG	U.S. Coast Guard
USCIS	U.S. Citizenship and Immigration Services
USMCA	United States–Mexico–Canada Agreement
USSS	U.S. Secret Service
VWP	Visa Waiver Program
WCO	World Customs Organization
WMD	Weapon(s) of mass destruction

Notes

Chapter 1: Homeland Security Comes of Age

1. Michael B. Donley and Neal A. Pollard, "Homeland Security: The Difference between a Vision and a Wish," *Public Administration Review*, Vol. 62, No. S1 (September 2002), pp. 138–144, at p. 139.
2. FEMA is pronounced "FEE-muh"; it is not referred to by its initials.
3. ICE is pronounced like the word for frozen water; it is not referred to by its initials.
4. It shares this function with the Department of Justice's Federal Marshals Service, as well as various state and local police departments.
5. Note that this figure includes only federal agencies. As the chapters in this volume make clear, state, local, territorial, and tribal agencies are also involved in many of these mission sets.
6. Overlap between two circles indicates that both are doing things related to the same mission, but their activities are not necessarily redundant. For instance, the USCG and CBP (specifically, CBP's Office of Border Patrol and Office of Air and Marine) share jurisdiction over the littorals. Likewise, ICE and CBP both deal with transnational crime but, as discussed below, CBP's role consists of interdiction while ICE's role consists of investigation.
7. See Benjamin Rohrbaugh, "More or Less Afraid of Pretty Much Everything: Homeland Security, Borders, and Disasters in the Twenty-First Century," unpublished manuscript, 2018.
8. Field personnel who operate POEs are known as CBP officers and wear blue uniforms. Field personnel in the Border Patrol, who operate in the areas between the POEs, are known as Border Patrol agents and wear green uniforms.
9. TSA does house the Federal Air Marshals Service (FAMS), which is a law enforcement entity and even has some investigative functions. FAMS constitutes a tiny fraction of TSA's total staff, however, and operates semiautonomously within TSA.
10. James Q. Wilson, *Bureaucracy: What Governments Do and Why They Do It* (New York: Basic Books, 1989).
11. DHS did, however, ultimately inherit a lead role for the federal government in countering violent extremism (CVE), a piece of the counter-terrorism mission that has grown in importance relative to the threat of terrorist attacks planned abroad.
12. Personal conversation with Chappell Lawson.

13. William W. Newmann, "Reorganizing for National Security and Homeland Security," *Public Administration Review*, Vol. 62, No. S1 (September 2002), pp. 126–137. See also William L. Waugh and Richard T. Sylves, "Organizing the War on Terrorism," *Public Administration Review*, Vol. 62, No. S1 (September 2002), pp. 145–153; Charles R. Wise, "Organizing for Homeland Security," *Public Administration Review*, Vol. 62, No. 2 (March/April 2002), pp. 131–144; and Donley and Pollard, "Homeland Security," p. 139.

14. Newmann, "Reorganizing for National Security and Homeland Security," pp. 126–137; Paul C. Light, "The Homeland Security Hash," *Wilson Quarterly*, Vol. 31, No. 2 (Spring 2007), pp. 36–44; Dara Kay Cohen, Mariano-Florentino Cuéllar, and Barry R. Weingast, "Crisis Bureaucracy: Homeland Security and the Political Design of Legal Mandates," *Stanford Law Review*, Vol. 59, No. 3 (April 2006), pp. 673–759; Harold C. Relyea, "Organizing for Homeland Security," *Presidential Studies Quarterly*, Vol. 33, No. 3 (September 2003), pp. 602–624; and Harold C. Relyea, "Homeland Security: Department Organization and Management—Implementation Phase," (Washington, D.C.: Congressional Research Service, 2003), pp. 613–623.

15. Newmann, "Reorganizing for National Security and Homeland Security," p. 131.

16. Light, "The Homeland Security Hash," pp. 36–38.

17. William O. Jenkins, "Collaboration over Adaptation: The Case for Inter-operable Communications in Homeland Security," *Public Administration Review*, Vol. 66, No. 3 (May/June 2006), pp. 319–321.

18. Paul Rosenzweig, "Homeland Security and Its Discontents," *Wilson Quarterly*, Vol. 31, No. 3 (Summer 2007), pp. 8–9. See also United States Government Accountability Office (GAO), *Department of Homeland Security: Progress Made and Work Remaining in Implementing Homeland Security Missions 10 Years after 9/11*, GAO-11-881 (Washington, D.C.: September 2011).

19. The Headquarters of DHS and of many DHS Components will be co-located at St. Elizabeth's across the Anacostia River, where the U.S. Coast Guard's headquarters is already based.

20. Jerome Kahan, "'One DHS' Revisited: Can the Next Homeland Security Secretary Unite the Department?" *Journal of Homeland Security and Emergency Management*, Vol. 11, No. 1 (January 2014), pp. 1–24.

21. Jerome Kahan, "It's Never Too Late: Restructuring the Department of Homeland Security's Regional Framework," *Journal of Homeland Security and Emergency Management*, Vol. 10, No. 1 (2013), pp. 353–369.

22. Specifically, Abdulmutallab attempted to ignite plastic explosive, which he created by combining the pentaerythritol tetranitrate (PETN) he had sewn into his underwear with triacetone triperoxide (TATP) and other ingredients. The detonation would have occurred in U.S. airspace above Detroit.

23. CNN, "State of the Nation" with Candy Crowley, December 27, 2009. A link to this video is available at Jonathan Martin, "Napolitano: The System Worked," *Politico Now* blog, December 28, 2009, https://www.politico.com/blogs/politico-now/2009/12/27/napolitano-the-system-worked-319582.

24. See Jason McNamara's chapter in this volume.

25. See the chapters in this volume by Caitlin Durkovich and Juliette Kayyem.

26. See, for example, Stephen Flynn's chapter in this volume.

27. *Health, United States, 2015* (Atlanta: Centers for Disease Control and Prevention, National Center for Health Statistics, 2015), Table 20, https://www.cdc.gov/nchs/data/hus/2015/020.pdf.

28. Ibid.

29. Ibid.

30. *Fatality Analysis Reporting System Encyclopedia* (Washington, D.C.: National Highway and Traffic Safety Administration, 2017), https://www-fars.nhTSA.dot.gov/Main/.

31. "National Hazard Statistics," Office of Climate, Water, and Weather Services, National Weather Service (Silver Spring, Md.: National Weather Service, 2015), http://www.nws.noaa.gov/om/hazstats.shtml.

32. "Lightning Victims," National Weather Service (Silver Spring, Md.: National Weather Service, 2017), http://www.lightningsafety.noaa.gov/fatalities.shtml.

33. In October 2010, Al-Qaeda attempted to destroy two cargo planes using bombs disguised as printer cartridges. Intelligence from a friendly foreign government, not DHS targeting efforts, was the source of the information used to intercept the parcels.

34. Stephen Flynn, *The Edge of Disaster: Rebuilding a Resilient Nation* (New York: Random House, 2007).

35. DHS, *Quadrennial Homeland Security Review: A Strategic Framework for a Secure Homeland* (Washington, D.C.: DHS, February 2010), https://www.DHS.gov/sites/default/files/publications/2010-qhsr-report.pdf; DHS, *The 2014 Quadrennial Homeland Security Review* (Washington, D.C.: DHS, June 2014), https://www.DHS.gov/sites/default/files/publications/2014-qhsr-final-508.pdf; and DHS, *Fiscal Years 2014–2018 Strategic Plan* (Washington, D.C.: DHS, 2014), https://www.DHS.gov/sites/default/files/publications/FY14-18%20Strategic%20Plan.PDF.

36. Sharon Caudle, "Homeland Security: Approaches to Results Management," *Public Performance and Management Review*, Vol. 28, No. 3 (2005), pp. 352–375.

37. Victor M. Manjarrez, "Border Security: Defining It Is the Real Challenge," *Journal of Homeland Security and Emergency Management*, Vol. 12, No. 4 (2015), pp. 793–800.

38. CBP's Office of Border Patrol divides the U.S. southwest border into nine "sectors," each of which contains several Border Patrol "stations." Yuma Sector, which includes

long stretches of uninhabited desert, has historically been one of the most challenging to police.

39. Discussion between Border Patrol sector and station chiefs and Chappell Lawson, Yuma, Arizona, 2009.

40. Statistically, border towns have rates of violent crime that fall below the national average. El Paso, Texas (which lies just across the Rio Grande from the notoriously violent Ciudad Juárez), has long been one of America's safer mid-sized cities. See, *inter alia*, Federal Bureau of Investigation (FBI), "Crime by Standard Metropolitan Statistical Area" (Washington, D.C.: FBI, accessed July 11, 2018), Table 6, https:// ucr.fbi.gov/crime-in-the-u.s/2015/crime-in-the-u.s.-2015/tables/table-6.

41. Frank P. Harvey, *The Homeland Security Dilemma: Fear, Failure and the Future of American Insecurity* (New York: Routledge, 2008).

Chapter 2: Building a Better Enterprise

1. Richard A. Falkenrath, "Problems of Preparedness: U.S. Readiness for a Domestic Terrorist Attack," *International Security*, Vol. 25, No. 4 (Spring 2001), pp. 164–167.

2. *Fiscal Year 2005 Homeland Security Grant Program: Program Guidelines and Application Kit* (Washington, D.C.: DHS, 2004).

3. DHS, *National Response Plan* (Washington, D.C., December 4, 2004).

4. Intelligence Reform and Terrorism Prevention Act of 2004, Pub. L. No. 108–458, 118 Stat. 3638 (2004).

5. 28 U.S.C.; 28 C.F.R. 0.85(l).

6. George W. Bush initially opposed the charge led by Senator Joe Lieberman for a Department of Homeland Security, but eventually he changed course, presenting many of Lieberman's ideas as his own.

7. "Protecting the Homeland: The President's Proposal for Reorganizing Our Homeland Defense Infrastructure, Before the Judiciary Committee" (statement by I.M. Destler and Ivo H. Daalder), 107th Cong., 2d sess. (2002).

8. "Immigration Reform and the Reorganization of Homeland Defense: Hearing Before the Subcommittee on Immigration of the S. Committee on the Judiciary," 107th Cong., 2d sess. (2002), pp. 14–16, 70–98. Dana Keener ultimately got his wish; the DOJ kept the Executive Office for Immigration Review.

9. U.S. Global Climate Change Research Program, *Global Climate Change Impacts in the United States* (New York: Cambridge University Press, 2009), p. 34.

10. Homeland Security Presidential Directive 5: Management of Domestic Incidents (Washington, D.C.: White House, February 28, 2003), p. 1.

11. Ibid.

12. Centers for Disease Control and Prevention, "The 2009 H1N1 Pandemic: Summary Highlights, April 2009–April 2010," Centers for Disease Control and Prevention, Atlanta, June 2010), https://www.cdc.gov/h1n1flu/cdcresponse.htm.

13. David Michaels and John Howard, "Review of the OSHA-NIOSH Response to the Deepwater Horizon Oil Spill: Protecting the Health and Safety of Cleanup Workers," *PLoS Currents Disasters*, July 18, 2012.

14. U.S. Coast Guard, "MEXUS Plan, The Joint Contingency Plan Between Mexico and the United States Regarding Pollution of the Marine Environment," U.S. Coast Guard, Washington, D.C., 2006, https://archive.epa.gov/emergencies/docs/chem/web/pdf/mexuspac_2006.pdf.

15. Levi J. Jordan, "Oil Spill Diplomacy: The Response from the Americas," Council of the Americas, New York, June 24, 2010, http://www.as-coa.org/articles/oil-spill-diplomacy-response-americas.

16. Azadeh Dastyari, *United States Migrant Interdiction and the Detention of Refugees in Guantánamo Bay* (New York: Cambridge University Press, 2015), p. 57.

17. Nathan E. Busch and Austen D. Givens, "Public-Private Partnerships in Homeland Security: Opportunities and Challenges," *Homeland Security Affairs*, Vol. 8 (October 2012), p. 2.

18. George W. Bush, *Decision Points* (New York: Crown, 2010), p. 331.

19. Eric Lipton, Eric Schmitt, and Thom Shanker, "Storm and Crisis: Military Response, Political Issues Snarled Plans for Troop Aid," *New York Times*, September 9, 2005.

20. British Petroleum, "Deepwater Horizon Accident Investigation Report," London, September 8, 2010, p. 29.

21. Juliette Kayyem, "The Game Changer," *Boston Globe*, April 24, 2011.

22. *State of Texas et al. v. United States et al.*, No. 15-40238 (5th Cir. 2015); and *United States et al. v. Texas et al.* (U.S. 15-674, June 23, 2016).

23. *Regents of the University of California et al. v. United States Department of Homeland Security et al.*, No. 3:17-CV-05211 (N.D. Calif. 2017); and *State of New York et al. v. Donald Trump*, No. 17-CV-5228 (E.D. N.Y. 2017).

24. DHS, "DHS Announces Grant Allocations for Fiscal Year 2017 Preparedness Grants," Washington, D.C., September 1, 2017).

25. Gersh Kuntzman, "Terror Funds Are 'Trashed,'" *New York Post*, March 15, 2005.

26. *Fiscal Year 2008 Homeland Security Grant Program: Program Guidelines and Application Kit* (Washington, D.C.: DHS, 2007).

27. Eric Lipton, "Audit Faults U.S. for Its Spending on Port Defense," *New York Times*, February 20, 2005.

28. FEMA, "Fiscal Year 2017 Homeland Security Grant Program: Fiscal Year 2017 Urban Area Security Initiative," Washington, D.C.

29. Anthony Rizzo (director), *Duck and Cover*, Archer Productions, New York, 1951.

30. NBC, Saturday Night Live, "Ian McKellen/Kylie Minogue: Ridge Address Cold Open," Season 27, Episode 15, directed by Beth McCarthy Miller, written by Tina Fey and Dennis McNicholas, March 16, 2002.

31. Development partnership examples include Axon, Raytheon, and Apptis.

32. David J. Closs and Edmund F. Mcgarrell, *Enhancing Security throughout the Supply Chain* (Washington, D.C.: IBM Center for the Business of Government, 2004).

33. Michael Barbaro and Justin Gillis, "Wal-Mart at Forefront of Hurricane Relief," *Washington Post*, September 5, 2005.

34. DHS, *Critical Infrastructure Sector Partnerships* (Washington, D.C.: DHS, 2011).

35. Busch and Givens, "Public-Private Partnerships in Homeland Security."

36. Ibid.

37. Matt Zapotosky, "FBI Has Accessed San Bernardino Shooter's Phone without Apple's Help," *Washington Post*, March 28, 2016.

38. Stephanie Goldsmith and William Eggers, *Governing by Network: The New Shape of the Public Sector* (Washington, D.C.: Brookings Institution Press, 2005), p. 31.

39. Busch and Givens, "Public-Private Partnerships in Homeland Security," p. 3.

40. Office of the Inspector General, DHS, "TSA's Role in General Aviation Security," OIG-09-69, Washington, D.C., May 27, 2009).

41. Patrick Roberts, *Disasters and the American State: How Politicians, Bureaucrats, and the Public Prepare for the Unexpected* (New York: Cambridge University Press, 2013), p. 50.

42. Ibid.

43. Ibid.

44. Use of Army and Air Force as Posse Comitatus, 18 U.S.C. § 1385.

45. Roberts, *Disasters and the American State*, p. 51.

46. Bush, *Decision Points*, p. 309.

47. Ibid., p. 323.

48. Thomas Gibbons-Neff and Helene Cooper, "Deployed Inside the United States: The Military Waits for the Migrant Caravan," *New York Times*, November 10, 2018.

49. *Fiscal Year 2018 Homeland Security Grant Program: Program Guidelines and Application Kit* (Washington, D.C.: DHS, 2017).

50. Joe Fiorillo, "Mayors Ask Homeland Security Chief for Additional Support," Global Security Newswire, October 25, 2005.

51. DHS, "Critical Infrastructure Sector Partnerships," accessed on July 11, 2017, https://www.DHS.gov/critical-infrastructure-sector-partnerships.

52. Dwight D. Eisenhower, "The Chance for Peace," speech given to the American Society of Newspaper Editors, April 16, 1953.

Chapter 3: Organizing Homeland Security:
The Challenge of Integration at DHS

1. According to a Government Accountability Office assessment, "the Homeland Security Act of 2002 required DHS to submit a plan to Congress for consolidating or co-locating certain Components' regional or field offices, among other things." Stephen L. Caldwell (Director of Homeland Security and Justice), "Department of Homeland Security: Efforts to Assess Realignment of Its Field Office Structure," GAO, Washington, D.C., September 28, 2012, p. 8, https://www.gao.gov/assets/650/649000.pdf. The Secretary's Operational Integration Staff (I-Staff) conducted this review in 2004, prepared a "Draft DHS Regional Concept of Operations" (2004), and "submitted a seven page document to Congress that presented the Department's actions and its proposed high-level approach to developing a consolidation and co-location plan." Ibid., pp. 8, 13, 22–23.
2. See DHS, "Department Six-Point Agenda," accessed July 25, 2018, https://www.DHS.gov/Department-six-point-agenda.
3. Quoted in Admiral Thad Allen, "Leading through a Major Crisis," interview with Scott Berinato, "HBR Idea Cast," *Harvard Business Review*, February 5, 2018, https://hbr.org/2010/10/leading-through-a-major-crisis.
4. Alain C. Enthoven and K. Wayne Smith, *How Much Is Enough? Shaping the Defense Program, 1961–1969* (Santa Monica, Calif.: RAND Corporation, 2005), pp. 197–198.
5. Ibid., pp. ix–x.
6. Caldwell, "Department of Homeland Security: Efforts to Assess Realignment of Its Field Office Structure."
7. Ibid., p. 9.
8. Ibid., p. 14.
9. The QHSR was modeled after the DOD's Quadrennial Defense Review. It focused specifically on DHS, not on the larger homeland security enterprise.
10. This framework reflects the 1988 Stafford Act, the 2004 National Response Plan, and the 2008 National Response Framework. For further discussion of emergency management and disaster response, see Jason McNamara's chapter in this volume.

Chapter 4: DHS and the Counterterrorism Enterprise

1. "National Strategy for Counterterrorism," White House, Washington, D.C., June 2011, p. 2, https://obamawhitehouse.archives.gov/sites/default/files/counterterrorism_strategy.pdf.
2. *The 9/11 Commission Report: Final Report of the National Commission on Terrorist Attacks upon the United States* (Washington, D.C.: National Commission on Terrorist

Attacks upon the United States, 2004), pp. 339–360, https://www.9-11commission.gov/report/911Report.pdf.

3. Department of Justice, "Fact Sheet: Prosecuting and Detaining Terror Suspects in the U.S. Criminal Justice System," News Release No. 09-564, Washington, D.C., June 9, 2009, https://www.justice.gov/opa/pr/fact-sheet-prosecuting-and-detaining-terror-suspects-us-criminal-justice-system; and "Trying Terror Suspects in Federal Courts," Human Rights First, New York, February 2018, https://www.humanrightsfirst.org/sites/default/files/Trying-Terror-Suspects-In-Federal-Court.pdf.

4. Soufan Group, "Foreign Fighters: An Updated Assessment of the Flow of Foreign Fighters into Syria and Iraq," New York, December 2015), p. 5, http://soufangroup.com/wp-content/uploads/2015/12/TSG_ForeignFightersUpdate3.pdf.

5. Tim Lister, et al., "ISIS Goes Global: 143 Attacks in 29 Countries Have Killed 2,043," CNN, February 13, 2017, http://www.cnn.com/2015/12/17/world/mapping-isis-attacks-around-the-world/index.html.

6. Abdi Sheikh, "Death Toll from Somalia Truck Bomb in October Now at 512: Probe Committee," *Reuters*, November 30, 2017, https://www.reuters.com/article/us-somalia-blast-toll/death-toll-from-somalia-truck-bomb-in-october-now-at-512-probe-committee-idUSKBN1DU2IC.

7. Karen Yourish, et al., "How Many People Have Been Killed in ISIS Attacks around the World," *New York Times*, July 16, 2016, https://www.nytimes.com/interactive/2016/03/25/world/map-isis-attacks-around-the-world.html.

8. Peter Bergen, et al., "Jihadist Terrorism 16 Years after 9/11: A Threat Assessment," International Security Program, New America, Washington, D.C., September 2017, p. 6, https://na-production.s3.amazonaws.com/documents/Terrorism_9-11_2017.pdf; and DOJ, "Sayfullo Saipov Indicted on Terrorism and Murder in Aid of Racketeering Charges in Connection with Lower Manhattan Truck Attack," News Release No. 17-374, Washington, D.C., November 21, 2017, https://www.justice.gov/usao-sdny/pr/sayfullo-saipov-indicted-terrorism-and-murder-aid-racketeering-charges-connection-lower.

9. Rukmini Callimachi, "How ISIS Built the Machinery of Terror under Europe's Gaze," *New York Times*, March 29, 2016; and "IS Spokesman Rallies Fighters against U.S.-Led Coalition, Threatens Enemy, and Calls Individual Muslims to Launch Attacks," SITE Intelligence Group, Bethesda, Md., September 21, 2014), https://ent.siteintelgroup.com/Multimedia/is-spokesman-rallies-fighters-against-u-s-led-coalition-threatens-enemy-and-calls-individual-muslims-to-launch-attacks.html.

10. Benjamin Weiser, "U.S. Seeks Death Penalty in Terror Attack on Manhattan Bike Path," *New York Times*, September 28, 2018; and DOJ, "Sayfullo Saipov Indicted on Terrorism and Murder in Aid of Racketeering Charges in Connection with Lower Manhattan Truck Attack."

11. Alexander Meleagrou-Hitchens and Seamus Hughes, "The Threat to the United States from the Islamic State's Virtual Entrepreneurs," *CTC Sentinel*, Vol. 10, No. 3 (March 2017), pp. 1–8.

12. Mark Hosenball, "U.S. Has More Than 2,000 Probes Into Potential or Suspected Terrorists: FBI Director," *Reuters*, May 16, 2018, https://www.reuters.com/article/us-usa-fbi-wray/us-has-more-than-2000-probes-into-potential-or-suspected-terrorists-fbi-director-idUSKCN1IH341; and Lisa Rose, "U.S. Has 1,000 Open ISIS Investigations but a Steep Drop in Prosecutions," CNN, May 16, 2018, https://www.cnn.com/2018/05/16/politics/isis-us-arrests-investigations-terrorism/index.html.

13. Arie Perliger, "Challengers from the Sidelines: Understanding America's Violent Far-Right," Combating Terrorism Center, U.S. Military Academy, West Point, New York, November 2012, https://ctc.usma.edu/app/uploads/2013/011/ChallengersFromtheSidelines.pdf; and *A Dark and Constant Rage: 25 Years of Right-Wing Terrorism in the United States* (New York: Anti-Defamation League, 2017), https://www.adl.org/sites/default/files/documents/CR_5154_25YRS%20RightWing%20Terrorism_V5.pdf.

14. GAO, "Countering Violent Extremism: Actions Needed to Define Strategy and Assess Progress of Federal Efforts," GAO-17-300, Washington, D.C., April 2017), pp. 4–5, http://www.gao.gov/assets/690/683984.pdf.

15. FBI, "Oklahoma City Bombing," Famous Cases and Criminals, https://www.fbi.gov/history/famous-cases/oklahoma-city-bombing.

16. *A Dark and Constant Rage*, p. 3.

17. Ibid., p. 7.

18. Kevin J. Strom, John S. Hollywood, and Mark Pope, "Terrorist Plots against the United States: What We Have Really Faced, and How We Might Best Defend against It," in Gary LaFree and Joshua D. Freilich, eds., *The Handbook of the Criminology of Terrorism* (Hoboken, N.J.: Wiley-Blackwell, 2016), pp. 479–480.

19. David J. Glawe, "Questions for the Record," Responses to the Select Committee on Intelligence, U.S. Senate, June 28, 2017, https://www.intelligence.senate.gov/sites/default/files/documents/qfrglawe.pdf.

20. "Statement of David J. Glawe, Nominee for Under Secretary for Intelligence and Analysis, Department of Homeland Security, Before the Senate Select Committee on Intelligence," 115th Cong., 1st sess., 2017, https://www.intelligence.senate.gov/sites/default/files/documents/os-dglawe-062817.pdf; and Inspectors General of the Intelligence Community, DHS, and DOJ, "Review of Domestic Sharing of Counterterrorism Information," Audit Division Report No. 17-21, Washington, D.C., Office of the Inspector General, DOJ, March 2017, p. 17.

21. DHS, "2015 National Network of Fusion Centers: Final Report," Washington, D.C., April 2016, p. i, https://www.DHS.gov/sites/default/files/publications/2015%20 Final%20Report%20Section%20508%20Compliant.pdf; and Implementing Recommendations of the 9/11 Commission Act of 2007, Pub. L. No. 110-53, 121 Stat. 317 (2007), pp. 318–324.

22. National Fusion Center Association, "2014–2017 National Strategy for the National Network of Fusion Centers," Arlington, Va., July 2014, p. 8, https://nfcausa.org/ html/National%20Strategy%20for%20the%20National%20Network%20of%20 Fusion%20Centers.pdf; and DHS, "Building Law Enforcement and DHS Partnerships: Fusion Centers and Joint Terrorism Task Forces," State and Major Urban Area Fusion Centers, https://www.DHS.gov/fusion-centers-and-joint-terrorism-task-forces.

23. DHS, "Building Law Enforcement and DHS Partnerships."

24. Brian Michael Jenkins, Andrew Liepman, and Henry H. Willis, *Identifying Enemies among Us: Evolving Terrorist Threats and the Continuing Challenges of Domestic Intelligence Collection and Information Sharing* (Santa Monica, Calif.: RAND Corporation, 2014), p. 13, https://www.rand.org/content/dam/rand/pubs/conf_ proceedings/CF300/CF317/RAND_CF317.pdf.

25. "Statement for the Record: State and Local Perspectives on Federal Information Sharing, Before the House Subcommittee on Counterterrorism and Intelligence, Committee on Homeland Security" (statement of Mike Sena, President, National Fusion Center Association, Director, Northern California Regional Intelligence Center), 114th Cong., 2d sess., 2016 http://docs.house.gov/meetings/HM/ HM05/20160908/105257/HHRG-114-HM05-Wstate-SenaM-20160908.pdf.

26. "Federal Support for and Involvement in State and Local Fusion Centers," Majority and Minority Staff Report, Permanent Subcommittee on Investigations, U.S. Senate Committee on Homeland Security and Governmental Affairs, October 3, 2012, https:// www.hsgac.senate.gov/subcommittees/investigations/media/investigative-report-criti-cizes-counterterrorism-reporting-waste-at-state-and-local-intelligence-fusion-centers.

27. "Majority Staff Report on the National Network of Fusion Centers," House Committee on Homeland Security, July 2013; "Advancing The Homeland Security Information Sharing Environment: A Review of the National Network of Fusion Centers," House Homeland Security Committee, Majority Staff Report, November 2017, https://homeland.house.gov/wp-content/uploads/2017/11/Committee-on-Homeland-Security-Fusion-Center-Report.pdf; and GAO, "Information Sharing: DHS Is Assessing Fusion Center Capabilities and Results, but Needs to More Accurately Account for Federal Funding Provided to Centers," GAO 15-155, Washington, D.C., November 2014), https://www.gao.gov/assets/670/666760.pdf.

28. Intelligence Reform and Terrorism Prevention Act of 2004, Pub. L. 108–458, 118 Stat. 3688 (2004), p. 3665.

29. White House, "National Strategy for Information Sharing: Successes and Challenges in Improving Terrorism-Related Information Sharing," Washington, D.C., October 2007, p. A1–6.

30. "Testimony of Robin Taylor, Acting Deputy Under Secretary for Intelligence Operations Office of Intelligence and Analysis, U.S. Department of Homeland Security, Before the House Subcommittee on Counterterrorism and Intelligence, Committee on Homeland Security," 115th Cong., 1st sess., September 13, 2017, http://docs.house.gov/meetings/HM/HM05/20170913/106386/HMTG-115-HM05-Wstate-TaylorR-20170913.pdf.

31. Ibid.

32. Ibid.

33. DHS, "2010 Fusion Center Success Stories: Fusion Centers Provide Critical Information to Faisal Shahzad Case," July 28, 2015, https://www.DHS.gov/2010-fusion-center-success-stories.

34. CBP, "CBP Facilitates Record Level of Travelers and Modernizes Trade Systems in FY2016," news release, Washington, D.C., January 12, 2017, https://www.CBP.gov/newsroom/national-media-release/CBP-facilitates-record-level-travelers-and-modernizes-trade-systems.

35. "The Fiscal Year 2018 President's Budget Request: Hearings Before the Committee on Appropriations, Subcommittee on Homeland Security" (statement of Thomas D. Homan, Acting Director of ICE), 115th Cong., 1st sess., 2017, p. 5, https://docs.house.gov/meetings/AP/AP15/20170613/106057/HHRG-115-AP15-Wstate-HomanT-20170613.pdf.

36. CBP, "United States Border: Sector Profile—Fiscal Year 2017," Washington, D.C., p. 1, https://www.CBP.gov/sites/default/files/assets/documents/2017-Dec/USBP%20Stats%20FY2017%20sector%20profile.pdf.

37. Marc R. Rosenblum, Jerome P. Bjelopera, and Kristin M. Finklea, "Border Security: Understanding Threats at U.S. Borders," Congressional Research Service, CRS Report No. R42969, Washington, D.C., February 21, 2013), p. 3, http://digitalcommons.ilr.cornell.edu/cgi/viewcontent.cgi?article=2042&context=key_workplace.

38. Homeland Security Act of 2002, Pub. L. 107–296, 116 Stat. 2135 (2002), pp. 2177–2178.

39. National Commission on Terrorist Attacks upon the United States, *The 9/11 Commission Report*, pp. 387, 390.

40. Ibid., p. 385.

41. "Border Security: Progress and Challenges in DHS's Efforts to Address High Risk Travelers and Strengthen Visa Security, Before Task Force on Denying Terrorists Entry into the United States, House Committee on Homeland Security" (statement of Rebecca Gambler, GAO Director for Homeland Security and Justice), 115 Cong. (2017), p. 7, https://www.gao.gov/assets/690/684443.pdf.

42. DHS, "The 2014 Quadrennial Homeland Security Review," Washington, D.C., June 2014, pp. 34–35, https://www.DHS.gov/sites/default/files/publications/2014-qhsr-final-508.pdf.

43. John Kelly, "Home and Away: DHS and the Threats to America," remarks at the Center for Cyber and Homeland Security, George Washington University, Washington, D.C., April 18, 2017, https://www.DHS.gov/news/2017/04/18/home-and-away-DHS-and-threats-america.

44. Bart Elias, David Randall Peterman, and John Frittelli, "Transportation Security: Issues for the 114th Congress," Congressional Research Service, CRS Report No. RL33512, Washington, D.C., May 9, 2016, p. 1, https://fas.org/sgp/crs/homesec/RL33512.pdf.

45. DHS, "Fact Sheet: Aviation Enhanced Security Measures for All Commercial Flights to the United States," Washington, D.C., June 28, 2017), https://www.DHS.gov/news/2017/06/28/fact-sheet-aviation-enhanced-security-measures-all-commercial-flights-united-states.

46. DOJ, "Akayed Ullah Charged in Manhattan Federal Court with Terrorism and Explosives Charges in Connection with the Detonation of a Bomb in New York City," Press Release No. 17-393, Washington, D.C., December 12, 2017), https://www.justice.gov/usao-sdny/pr/akayed-ullah-charged-manhattan-federal-court-terrorism-and-explosives-charges.

47. The GAO has also highlighted risks to surface transportation. See GAO, "Passenger Rail Security: Consistent Incident Reporting and Analysis Needed to Achieve Program Objectives," GAO-13-20, Washington, D.C., December 2012, https://www.gao.gov/assets/660/650995.pdf; and Stephanie Beasley and Brianna Garciullo, "Al Qaeda Threatens U.S. Rail," *Politico*, August 14, 2017, https://www.politico.com/tipsheets/morning-transportation/2017/08/14/al-qaeda-threatens-us-rail-221861.

48. Between September 11, 2011, and December 31, 2016, "homegrown" violent extremists caused 225 deaths over the course of 85 incidents in the United States. See GAO, "Countering Violent Extremism: Actions Needed to Define Strategy and Assess Progress of Federal Efforts," GAO-17-300, Washington, D.C., April 2017), p. 1, http://www.gao.gov/assets/690/683984.pdf.

49. White House, "Fact Sheet: The White House Summit on Countering Violent Extremism," news release, Washington, D.C., February 18, 2015), https://obam

awhitehouse.archives.gov/the-press-office/2015/02/18/fact-sheet-white-house-summit-countering-violent-extremism.

50. Jerome P. Bjelopera, "Countering Violent Extremism in the United States," Congressional Research Service, CRS Report No. R42553, Washington, D.C., 2014, p. 1, https://fas.org/sgp/crs/homesec/R42553.pdf; and White House, "Empowering Local Partners to Prevent Violent Extremism in the United States," Washington, D.C., August 2011, pp. 2–3, https://www.DHS.gov/sites/default/files/publications/empowering_local_partners.pdf.

51. Task Force on Terrorism and Ideology, "Defeating Terrorists, Not Terrorism: Assessing U.S. Counterterrorism Policy from 9/11 to ISIS," Bipartisan Policy Center, Washington, D.C., September 2017, p. 27, https://cdn.bipartisanpolicy.org/wp-content/uploads/2017/09/BPC-National-Security-Defeating-Terrorist-Not-Terrorism.pdf.

52. Bjelopera, "Countering Violent Extremism in the United States," p. 20.

53. DHS, "Department of Homeland Security Strategy for Countering Violent Extremism," Washington, D.C., October 28, 2016, https://www.DHS.gov/sites/default/files/publications/16_1028_S1_CVE_strategy.pdf.

54. "'Threats to the Homeland,' Before the Senate Committee on Homeland Security and Government Affairs" (statement of Elaine C. Duke, Acting Secretary of Homeland Security), 115th Cong., 1st sess., 2017, https://www.hsgac.senate.gov/imo/media/doc/Testimony-Duke-2017-09-27.pdf.

55. Ibid.

56. Peter Neumann, "Preventing Violent Radicalization in America," National Security Preparedness Group, Bipartisan Policy Center, Washington, D.C., June 2011, p. 7, http://bipartisanpolicy.org/wp-content/uploads/sites/default/files/NSPG.pdf.

57. Farah Pandith, *How We Win: How Cutting-Edge Entrepreneurs, Political Visionaries, Enlightened Business Leaders, and Social Media Mavens Can Defeat the Extremist Threat* (New York: HarperCollins, 2019).

58. National Commission on Terrorist Attacks upon the United States, *The 9/11 Commission Report*, pp. 116–117.

59. Ibid., p. 380.

60. White House, "National Security Strategy of the United States of America," Washington, D.C., February 2017, p. 8, https://www.whitehouse.gov/wp-content/uploads/2017/12/NSS-Final-12-18-2017-0905.pdf.

61. "Examining the Department of Homeland Security's Efforts to Counter Weapons of Mass Destruction, Before the Committee on Homeland Security, Subcommittee on Emergency Preparedness, Response and Communications" (statement of Jim McDonnell, DNDO Director, Dave Fluty, OHA Acting Assistant Secretary, and Bill

Bryan, S&T Acting Under Secretary), 115th Cong., 1st sess., 2017, https://www. DHS.gov/news/2017/12/07/written-testimony-dndo-oha-and-st-house-homeland-security-subcommittee-emergency.

62. John P. Carlin, "Remarks at Press Conference Announcing Seven Iranians Charged for Conducting Cyber Attacks against U.S. Financial Sector," DOJ, Washington, D.C., March 24, 2016, https://www.justice.gov/opa/speech/assistant-attorney-general-john-p-carlin-delivers-remarks-press-conference-announcing.

63. "The 2014 Quadrennial Homeland Security Review," p. 37.

64. Erin Miller, "Terrorist Attacks Targeting Critical Infrastructure in the United States, 1970–2015: Report to the Office of Intelligence and Analysis, U.S. Department of Homeland Security," National Consortium for the Study of Terrorism and Responses to Terrorism, College Park, Md., June 2016, p. 5, https://www.start.umd.edu/pubs/DHS_I%26A_GTD_Targeting%20Critical%20Infrastructure%20in%20the%20US_June2016.pdf.

65. Ibid., p. 8.

66. White House, "Fact Sheet: Protecting America's Critical Infrastructures: PDD 63," news release, Washington, D.C., May 22, 1998, https://fas.org/irp/offdocs/pdd-63.htm.

67. White House, "Homeland Security Presidential Directive 7: Critical Infrastructure Identification, Prioritization, and Protection," Washington, D.C., December 17, 2003, https://www.DHS.gov/homeland-security-presidential-directive-7.

68. White House, "Presidential Policy Directive: Critical Infrastructure Security and Resilience," Washington, D.C., February 12, 2013, https://obamawhitehouse.archives.gov/the-press-office/2013/02/12/presidential-policy-directive-critical-infrastructure-security-and-resil.

69. Dougherty, "Denying Terrorists Entry to the United States"; and "The 2014 Quadrennial Homeland Security Review," pp. 37–38.

70. National Commission on Terrorist Attacks upon the United States, *The 9/11 Commission Report*, p. 421.

71. Ibid., p. 419.

72. Full-page advertisement signed by sixty former officials and experts urging Congress to streamline oversight of homeland security, *Wall Street Journal*, May 21, 2014.

73. Aspen Institute Justice and Society Program, "Task Force Report on Streamlining and Consolidating Congressional Oversight of the U.S. Department of Homeland Security," Aspen Institute, Washington, D.C., September 2013, p. 10, http://cdn.annenbergpublicpolicycenter.org/wp-content/uploads/Homeland-Security-Report-09-11-13.pdf.

74. Thomas H. Kean, et al., "Reflections on the Tenth Anniversary of the 9/11 Commission Report," Bipartisan Policy Center, Washington, D.C., July 2014, p. 21,

http://bipartisanpolicy.org/wp-content/uploads/sites/default/files/%20BPC%20
9-11%20Commission.pdf.

75. Aspen Institute Justice and Society Program, "Task Force Report on Streamlining
    and Consolidating Congressional Oversight of the U.S. Department of Homeland
    Security," p. 10.

76. Adam I. Klein, "The Cyclical Politics of Counterterrorism," *Washington Quarterly*,
    Vol. 40, No. 2 (Summer 2017), pp. 95–111.

77. "The 2014 Quadrennial Homeland Security Review," p. 32.

78. Ibid., p. 35.

79. Jenkins, Liepman, and Willis, *Identifying Enemies among Us*, p. 15.

Chapter 5: Rethinking Borders: Securing the Flows of Travel and Commerce in the Twenty-First Century

1. Alan D. Bersin, "Lines and Flows: The Beginning and End of Borders," *Brooklyn
   Journal of International Law*, Vol. 37, No. 2 (2012), p. 389.

2. Ibid.

3. U2, "Invisible," *Songs of Innocence*, produced by Danger Mouse, 2014.

4. *United States. v. Flores-Montano*, 541 U.S. 149, 152 (2004).

5. *United States v. Ramsey*, 431 U.S. 606, 616 (1977).

6. *United States v. Montoya de Hernandez*, 473 U.S. 531, 538 (1985).

7. See Admission of Immigrants into the United States, 8 U.S.C. § 1181(a) (with some
   exceptions, immigrants require visa for entry into the United States); and 8 U.S.C §
   1184 (provision governing visa issuance and admissibility for non-immigrants).

8. Government Property or Contracts, 8 U.S.C. § 1361.

9. See *Kleindienst v. Mandel*, 408 U.S. 753, 765-70 (1972), which determined that
   a consular officer's decision to refuse a visa is generally unreviewable, unless the
   refusal implicates the constitutional rights of a U.S. person).

10. Some, myself included, opposed the establishment of CBP and ICE as separate
    agencies—arguing instead that they should have been combined into a single
    unified agency containing all the interrelated aspects of border and immigration
    enforcement, including border inspections, border patrol, investigations, detention,
    and removal.

11. Abraham Lincoln, "Annual Message to Congress," 37th Cong., 3d sess., December
    1, 1862.

12. "Statement of Robert C. Bonner to the National Commission on Terrorist Attacks
    Upon the United States, 108th Congress, 2d sess., January 26, 2004."

13. Ibid.

Chapter 6: The Trusted and the Targeted: Segmenting Flows by Risk

1. CBP, "CBP Facilitates Record Level of Travelers and Modernizes Trade Systems in FY2016," news release, Washington, D.C., January 12, 2017), https://www.CBP.gov/newsroom/national-media-release/CBP-facilitates-record-level-travelers-and-modernizes-trade-systems. As discussed below, "one million entries" does not mean one million unique individuals; some individuals, especially residents of communities along the land borders, cross many times per year.

2. Most illegal crossings and a good deal of smuggling take place in the areas between the POEs, where all entries are by definition illegal. The goal there is simply to intercept anything and everything. This chapter focuses exclusively on the POEs, where DHS has a dual mandate of facilitating legal flows and preventing illegal ones.

3. Author's calculations, based on (1) the total weight of freight traffic on the U.S. southwest border, as reported by the Bureau of Trade Statistics; (2) the total weight of illegal drugs seized at POEs on the U.S. southwest border, as reported by the White House Office of National Drug Control Policy; and (3) my estimate that only 5 percent of illegal drugs passing through POEs on the U.S. southwest border are seized. This assumption is likely to understate seizure rates, given the sharp price differentials between the Mexican and U.S. sides of the border, the risk premiums paid to drug mules, and the fact that smugglers are willing to invest in avoiding the POEs by creating tunnels. See David Bjerk and Caleb Mason, "The Market for Mules: Risk and Compensation of Cross-Border Drug Couriers," *International Review of Law and Economics*, Vol. 39 (August 2014), pp. 58–72, https://doi.org/10.1016/j.irle.2014.05.005; Peter Reuter and Mark A.R. Kleiman, "Risks and Prices: An Economic Analysis of Drug Enforcement," *Crime and Justice*, Vol. 7 (1986), p. 293; and Jonathan P. Caulkins and Peter Reuter, "How Drug Enforcement Affects Drug Prices," *Crime and Justice*, Vol. 39 (2010), p. 230. Even if seizure rates were as low as 1 percent, however, drugs would still constitute less than one-thousandth of 1 percent of shipments by weight. Volumetric measures would reveal a similarly tiny fraction of shipments.

4. U.S. Department of Transportation, "Border Crossing/Entry Data," Bureau of Transportation Statistics, accessed June 1, 2017, https://transborder.bts.gov/programs/international/transborder/TBDR_BC/TBDR_BCQ.html.

5. Author's calculations based on internal CBP data from 2009.

6. Illegal outbound transit includes criminals attempting to flee U.S. law enforcement, billions of dollars of undeclared bulk cash (mainly into Mexico), guns (mainly into Mexico), dual-use technologies, and the like.

7. Following CBP, I define inspection to include both (1) manual search and (2) the review of electronic images obtained through high-resolution scanning (i.e., looking

inside containers without physically opening them or peering through people's clothes without physically patting them down). I assume that ambiguous results from searches would be resolved by further scrutiny. I do not include analytical techniques that rely exclusively on data to look for anomalies without actual inspection; I refer to this as "screening." Both inspection (physical or electronic) and screening systems vary considerably in their false negative rates—that is, failure to find the bad things that they are designed to identify.

8. As noted in various chapters, border enforcement is an inefficient way to address illegal immigration or drug control, compared to interior enforcement.

9. I treat radiation scans as "inspection," even if they do not produce a full picture of the container, because they do detect emitted radiation. For discussion of this regime, which has received significant attention from researchers, see *Evaluating the Testing, Costs, and Benefits of Advanced Spectroscopic Portals* (Washington, D.C.: National Academy of Sciences, 2011); *Performance Metrics for the Global Nuclear Detection Architecture* (Washington, D.C.: National Academy of Sciences, 2013); Naraphorn Haphuriwat, Vicki M. Bier, and Henry H. Willis, "Deterring the Smuggling of Nuclear Weapons in Container Freight through Detection and Retaliation," *Decision Analysis*, Vol. 8, No. 2 (2011), pp. 88–102; Nitin Bakshi, Stephen E. Flynn, and Noah Gans, "Estimating the Operational Impact of Container Inspections at International Ports," *Management Science*, Vol. 57, No. 1 (2011), pp. 1–20; Lawrence M. Wein, et al., "Preventing the Importation of Illicit Nuclear Materials in Shipping Containers," *Risk Analysis*, Vol. 26, No. 5 (October 2006), pp. 1377–1393; Lawrence M. Wein, et al., "The Optimal Spatiotemporal Deployment of Radiation Portal Monitors Can Improve Nuclear Detection at Overseas Ports," *Science and Global Security*, Vol. 15, No. 3 (2007), pp. 211–233; *Detecting Nuclear and Radiological Materials*, RS Policy Document 07/08 (London: Royal Society, March 2008); and Laura A. McLay, Jamie D. Lloyd, and Emily Niman, "Interdicting Nuclear Material on Cargo Containers Using Knapsack Problem Models," *Annals of Operations Research*, Vol. 187, No. 1 (2011), pp. 185–205.

10. In 2016, DHS recalibrated the RPMs so as to significantly reduce false alarms.

11. RPMs (including those outside the United States) have apparently detected a small amount of nuclear "junk," such as cesium and cobalt used in industrial applications. Author's correspondence with Stephen Flynn, June 21, 2017. That material could theoretically be used in the construction of a radiological device (a "dirty bomb"), although there is no evidence that it has been.

12. See Thomas B. Cochran and Matthew G. McKinzie, "Detecting Nuclear Smuggling," *Scientific American*, Vol. 298 (2008), pp. 98–104; Dennis Slaughter, et al., *Detection of Special Nuclear Material in Cargo Containers Using Neutron Interrogation*, Report UCRL-ID-155315 (Livermore, Calif.: Lawrence Livermore National Laboratory,

2003); and Gary M. Gaukler, et al., "Detecting Nuclear Materials Smuggling: Using Radiography to Improve Container Inspection Policies," *Annals of Operations Research*, Vol. 187, No. 1 (2011), pp. 65–87. See also "Detecting Nuclear Weapons and Radiological Material: How Effective Is Available Technology? Before the House Committee on Homeland Security Subcommittee on Presentation of Nuclear and Biological Attacks and Subcommittee on Emergency Preparedness" (statement of Bethann Rooney), 109th Cong., 1st sess. (2005); and "Combatting Nuclear Smuggling: DHS's Decision to Procure and Deploy Next Generation of Radiation Detection Equipment Is Not Supported by Its Cost-Benefit Analysis, Before the Subcommittee on Emerging Threats, Cybersecurity, and Science and Technology, House of Representatives" (statement of Gene Aloise),109th Cong., 1st sess. (2007).

13. See, *inter alia*, Committee on Science and Technology for Countering Terrorism, National Research Council, *Making the Nation Safer: The Role of Science and Technology in Countering Terrorism* (Washington, D.C.: National Academies Press, 2002), pp. 39–64.

14. See, *inter alia*, Kyung Sook Cho and Yang Ho Yoon, "Fever Screening and Detection of Febrile Arrivals at an International Airport in Korea: Association among Self-Reported Fever, Infrared Thermal Camera Scanning, and Tympanic Temperature," *Epidemiology and Health*, Vol. 36 (2014), doi.org/10.4178/epih/e2014004.

15. Susan E. Martonosi, David S. Ortiz, and Henry H. Willis, "Evaluating the Viability of 100 Percent Container Inspections at America's Ports," in Harry W. Richardson, Peter Gordon, and James E. Moore II, eds., *The Economic Impacts of Terrorist Attacks* (Cheltenham, UK: Edward Elgar, 2005). See also Maarten van de Voort, et al., "Applying Risk Assessment to Secure the Containerized Supply Chain," in Igor Linkov, Richard J. Wenning, and Gregory A. Kiker, eds., *Managing Critical Infrastructure Risk* (Dordrecht, Netherlands, 2007); Maarten van de Voort, et al., "Applying Risk Assessment to Secure the Containerized Supply Chain," in *Managing Risk and Security: The Safeguard of Long-Term Success for Logistics Service Providers* (Bern: Haupt Verlag, 2009), doi.org/10.1007/978-1-4020-6385-5_5; and Nitin Bakshi, Stephen E. Flynn, and Noah Gans, *Measuring the Operational Impact of Container Inspection at International Ports: Technical Report* (London: London Business School, 2008).

16. Bjerk and Mason, "The Market for Mules."

17. Susan E. Martonosi and Arnold Barnett, "How Effective Is Security Screening of Airline Passengers?" *Interfaces*, Vol. 36, No. 6 (November–December 2006), pp. 545–552.

18. Laura A. McLay, Sheldon. H. Jacobson, and John E. Kobza, "The Tradeoff between Technology and Prescreening Intelligence in Checked Baggage Screening for Aviation Security," *Journal of Transportation Security*, Vol. 1, No. 2 (June 2008), pp. 107–126.

19. Of course, this fact leaves selective inspection regimes vulnerable to the exploitation of naïve trusted shippers.

20. How agents use their own judgment in determining what merits greater scrutiny is an important topic, which mainly applies to screening travelers rather than cargo. See Nicholas Dudley Ward, et al., "Observed and Perceived Inconsistencies in U.S. Border Inspections," *Journal of Homeland Security and Emergency Management*, Vol. 5, No. 1 (January 2008), pp. 1–22. I assume that these sorts of inspections would be part of any risk-based regime.

21. See Chris Strohm, "Investigators Call Cargo Security Program Unreliable," GovExec. com, April 5, 2006, www.govexec.com/dailyfed/0406/040506cdam3.htm; and GAO, *"Preliminary Observations on the Status of Efforts to Improve the Automated Transport System,"* GAO-06-591T, Washington, D.C., March 30, 2006.

22. GAO, "Investigators Call Cargo Security Program Unreliable, Before the Sub-Committee on Oversight and Investigations, Committee on Energy and Commerce" (statement of Chris Strohm), 108th Cong., 2d sess., GAO-04-557T, Washington, D.C., 2004; and GAO, "Homeland Security: Summary of Challenges Faced in Targeting Oceangoing Cargo Containers for Inspection, Before the Sub-Committee on Oversight and Investigations, Committee on Energy and Commerce" (statement of Richard M. Stana), 108th Cong., 2d sess., GAO-04-557T, Washington, D.C., 2004.

23. Van de Voort, et al., "Applying Risk Assessment to Secure the Containerized Supply Chain," 2007; Van de Voort, et al., "Applying Risk Assessment to Secure the Containerized Supply Chain," 2009; L. Joe Moffitt, John K. Stranlund, and Barry C. Field, "Inspections to Avert Terrorism: Robustness under Severe Uncertainty," *Journal of Homeland Security and Emergency Management*, Vol. 2, No. 3 (June 2005), pp. 1–17; Endre L. Boros, et al., "Large Scale LP Model for Finding Optimal Container Inspection Strategies," *Naval Research Logistics*, Vol. 56, No. 5 (August 2009), pp. 404–420; Bakshi, Flynn, and Gans, *Measuring the Operational Impact of Container Inspection at International Ports*; Bakshi, Flynn, and Gans, "Estimating the Operational Impact of Container Inspections at International Ports"; Noam Goldberg, et al., "Optimal Sequential Inspection Policies," RUTCOR Research Report No. 14, Rutgers Center for Operations Research, Rutgers University, Piscataway, N.J., October 2008; Jose Emmanuel Ramirez-Marquez, "Port-of-Entry Safety via the Reliability Optimization of Container Inspection Strategy through an Evolutionary Approach," *Reliability Engineering and System Safety*, Vol. 93 (2008), pp. 1698–1709; William H. Robinson, Jennifer E. Lake, and Lisa M. Seghetti, *Border and Transportation Security: Possible New Directions and Policy Options* (Washington, D.C.: Congressional Research Service, 2005); and Yuri Melnikov, et al., "Detection of Dangerous Materials and Illicit Objects in Cargoes and Baggage: Current Tools, Existing Problems and Possible Solutions," *Journal of Homeland Security and Emergency Management*, Vol. 8, No. 1 (January 2011), pp. 1–17.

24. TSA's "Pre✓" program is based on the same model, but it only exempts travelers from some elements of screening and only applies to domestic travel; therefore, it is really focused on aviation security.

25. Customs and Border Protection (CBP), "C-TPAT: Customs-Trade Partnership against Terrorism," Washington, D.C, accessed May 24, 2017, https://www.CBP. gov/border-security/ports-entry/cargo-security/c-tpat-customs-trade-partnership-against-terrorism. CBP reports this metric by dollar value. It is likely that volumetric measures are equally high for land POEs and even higher for air cargo, but lower for maritime trade.

26. CBP, "Trusted Traveler Programs," Washington, D.C., October 2015, https://www. CBP.gov/sites/default/files/documents/Fact%20Sheet%20-%20TTP%20FINAL. pdf. Specifically, the approximately 425,000 SENTRI members accounted for close to 28 million entries in 2016, meaning that each SENTRI participant on average crossed the border approximately 65 times. In fiscal year (not calendar year) 2016, 26,211,200 SENTRI entries were processed. Freedom of Information Act request, File Number CBP-2017-061895.

27. In fiscal year 2016, CBP processed 9,157,567 entries using a NEXUS card. Freedom of Information Act request, File Number CBP-2017-061895. Assuming that all of these were at the land or lacustrine borders, NEXUS would account for roughly 16 percent of northern land border entries; however, some of these entries are likely to have been air travelers.

28. DHS, "DHS Unveils Trusted Traveler Comparison Tool," news release, April 21, 2017, https://www.DHS.gov/news/2017/04/21/DHS-unveils-trusted-traveler-comparison-tool.

29. In fiscal year 2016, 1,233,751 entries were processed through Global Entry; there are approximately 129 million entries by air each year. Freedom of Information Act request, File Number CBP-2017-061895.

30. Stephen Flynn makes this point in Chapter 7 of this volume.

31. Frank P. Harvey, *The Homeland Security Dilemma: Fear, Failure and the Future of American Insecurity* (New York: Routledge, 2008).

32. See Stephen Flynn's chapter in this volume, as well as "Maritime Transportation and Port Security, Before the United States Senate Committee on Appropriations at the Hearing on Homeland Security: Infrastructure Security Port Security" (statement of Stephen E. Flynn), 107th Cong., 2d sess., 2002, https://www.cfr.org/report/maritime-transportation-and-port-security; Stephen E. Flynn, "America the Vulnerable," *Foreign Affairs*, Vol. 81, No. 1 (2002), p. 60; and Stephen E. Flynn, *America the Vulnerable: How Our Government is Failing to Protect Us from Terrorism* (New York: HarperCollins, 2004).

33. Benjamin Rohrbaugh, "More or Less Afraid of Pretty Much Everything," unpublished manuscript, 2018.

34. For a review of technologies, see Melnikov, et al., "Detection of Dangerous Materials and Illicit Objects in Cargoes and Baggage."

Chapter 7: The Challenge of Securing the Global Supply System

1. The story of the evolution of the shipping container is best told by Mark Levinson, *The Box: How the Shipping Container Made the World Economy Smaller and the World Economy Bigger*, 2nd ed. (Princeton, N.J.: Princeton University Press, 2016).

2. Stephen Flynn, "Homeland Security is a Coast Guard Mission," *U.S. Naval Institute Proceedings*, Vol . 171, No. 10 (October 2001), pp. 72–75.

3. After the September 11, 2001, attacks, I proposed and participated in Operation Safe Commerce. Stephen Flynn, *America the Vulnerable: How Our Government is Failing to Protect Us from Terrorism* (New York: Harper-Collins, 2004), p. 108.

4. International Maritime Organization, "ISPS Code: 2003 Edition," United Nations, London, 2003, http://www.ubak.gov.tr/BLSM_WIYS/DISGM/tr/HTML/20130304 _142647_66968_1_67502.pdf.

5. CBP, "CTPAT: Customs Trade Partnership against Terrorism," CBP website, https:// www.CBP.gov/border-security/ports-entry/cargo-security/ctpat.

6. CBP, "CSI: Container Security Initiative," CBP website, https://www.CBP.gov/ border-security/ports-entry/cargo-security/csi/csi-brief.

7. CBP, "Importer Security Filing '10+2,'" CBP website, https://www.CBP.gov/border-security/ports-entry/cargo-security/importer-security-filing-102 .

8. National Nuclear Security Administration (NNSA), "Core Program: The Second Line of Defense (SLD)," DOE website, https://nnsa.energy.gov/aboutus/ourprograms/nonproliferation/programoffices/international-materialprotectionandcooperation/-4.

9. NNSA, "Megaports Initiative," DOE website, https://nnsa.energy.gov/aboutus/ ourprograms/nonproliferation/programoffices/internationalmaterialprotection-andcooperation/-5

10. "Proliferation Security Initiative," https://www.state.gov/t/isn/c10390.htm.

11. United Nations, "1540 Committee," UN website, http://www.un.org/en/sc/1540/.

12. "Fact Sheet: National Strategy for Global Supply Chain Security," White House website, January 25, 2012, https://obamawhitehouse.archives.gov/the-press-office/ 2012/01/25/fact-sheet-national-strategy-global-supply-chain-security.

13. See "ISPS Code: 2003 Edition," Annex 2:13.

14. "Joint Testimony of David Heyman, Assistant Secretary for the Office of Policy, Rear Admiral Zukunft, Assistant Commandant for U.S. Coast Guard Office of Marine

Safety, Security and Stewardship, and Kevin McAleenan, Acting Assistant Commissioner for U.S. Customs and Border Protection Office of Field Operations, Before the House Committee on Homeland Security, Subcommittee on Border and Maritime Security Addressing Supply Chain Security," 112th Cong., 2d sess., 2012, https://www.DHS.gov/news/2012/02/06/written-testimony-plcy-uscg-and-CBP-house-homeland-security-subcommittee-border-and.

15. "CTPAT: Customs Trade Partnership Against Terrorism."

16. CBP reported that in FY2013, CBP officers reviewed 11,228,203 bills of lading and conducted 103,999 examinations of high-risk cargo in cooperation with host country counterparts. If one divides 103,999 examinations by 365 days in the year, this equals 285 examinations worldwide per day. If one divides 285 examinations by 58 CSI ports, this equals an average of 4.9 examinations per port per day. See Vivian C Jones and Lisa Seghetti, "U.S. Customs and Border Protection: Trade Facilitation, Enforcement, and Security," Congressional Research Service, CRS Report No. 7-5700, Washington, D.C., May 18, 2015, p. 23, https://www.fas.org/sgp/crs/homesec/R43014.pdf.

17. Ibid. In 2013, CBP reported that they subjected 0.9 percent of containers at the overseas ports of loading and 4.1 percent of containers arriving at U.S. ports to NII upon arrival in the United States. This translates into only 19 percent of containers that CBP has deemed to be high-risk enough to warrant being inspected at the overseas loading port.

18. GAO, "Combating Nuclear Smuggling: Megaports Initiative Faces Funding and Sustainability Challenges," GAO-13-37, Washington, D.C., October 2012, p. 22.

19. "Proliferation Security Initiative."

20. United Nations, "UN Security Council Resolution 1540 (2004)," United Nations Office for Disarmament Affairs website, https://www.un.org/disarmament/wmd/sc1540/.

21. Ibid.

22. "1540 Committee."

23. Andrew Curry, "Why Is This Cargo Container Emitting So Much Radiation?" Wired, October 21, 2011, http://www.wired.com/2011/10/ff_radioactivecargo/.

24. Ping Huang and Jingyuan Zhang, "Facts Related to August 12, 2015 Explosion Accident in Tianjin, China," Process Safety Progress, Vol. 34, No. 4 (December 2015), pp. 313–314.

25. "Container Scanning and Seals," Sec. 1701, in Implementing Recom-mendations of the 9/11 Commiussion Act of 2007, Pub. L. 110-53, 121 Stat. 270 (2007), https://www.gpo.gov/fdsys/pkg/STATUTE-121/pdf/STATUTE-121-Pg266.pdf.

26. UN Security Council, Resolution 1540, S/RES/1540, April 28, 2004, http://www.un.org/ga/search/view_doc.asp?symbol=S/RES/1540%20(2004).

27. "UN Security Council Resolution 1540 (2004)."

28. Hariesh Manaadiar, "What Is ISPS Code and Why ISPS Is Charged," *Shipping and Freight Resource*, January 23, 2013, https://shippingandfreightresource.com/what-is-isps-code-and-why-isps-is-charged/.

29. The Generation 3 Multi-Mode Passive Detection System (MMPDS Gen3) is a product of Decision Sciences International Corporation (DSIC). I serve on the DSIC Advisory Board. http://www.decisionsciences.com/wp-content/uploads/2017/07/MMPDS_Gen3.pdf?x93853

30. Nitin Bakshi, Stephen E. Flynn, and Noah Gans, "Estimating the Operational Impact of Container Inspections at International Ports," *Management Science*, Vol. 57, No. 1 (January 2011), pp. 1–20.

Chapter 8: Rethinking Transportation Security

1. President George W. Bush, remarks at the signing of H.R. 5005, The Homeland Security Act of 2002, November 25, 2002.

2. Bureau of Transportation Statistics, *Transportation Statistics Annual Report 2016* (Washington, D.C.: U.S. Department of Transportation, 2016), pp. 105–134, https://www.bts.gov/sites/bts.dot.gov/files/docs/TSAR_2016.pdf.

3. Four aircraft were hijacked in the terrorist attacks of September 11, 2001. Two were flown into the World Trade Center in New York City—one into each of the two towers. One aircraft was flown into the Pentagon in Arlington, Virginia. The fourth aircraft, United Airlines Flight 93, likely bound for the White House or the Capitol, crashed into a field in Shanksville, Pennsylvania, after passengers fought the hijackers for control.

4. These data come from the RAND Database of Worldwide Terrorism Incidents, January 1, 1968 through September 10, 2001, RAND Corporation, Santa Monica, Calif., https://www.rand.org/nsrd/projects/terrorism-incidents.html.

5. White House, "The National Strategy for Aviation Security," NSPD-47/HSPD-16, Washington, D.C., March 26, 2006, p. 6.

6. White House, "The National Strategy for Maritime Security," Washington, D.C., September 2005, p. 1, https://www.state.gov/documents/organization/255380.pdf.

7. The Transportation Worker Identification Credential (TWIC) program, jointly managed by TSA and the USCG, has suffered from delays and controversy since its inception. For basic TWIC program details, see TSA, "TWIC," TSA website, https://www.TSA.gov/for-industry/twic. For discussion of concerns and links to critical reports, see "Transportation Worker Identification Credential," Wikimedia Foundation, https://en.wikipedia.org/wiki/Transportation_Worker_Identification_Credential.

8. USCG Maritime Security (MARSEC) levels form a three-tiered system designed to easily communicate pre-planned scalable responses for credible threats to maritime ports. See USCG, "U.S. Coast Guard Maritime Security (MARSEC) Levels," USCG website, https://www.uscg.mil/What-Is-MARSEC/.

9. International Maritime Organization, "The International Ship and Port Facility (ISPS) Code of the International Maritime Organization," International Maritime Organization website, http://www.imo.org/en/OurWork/Security/Guide_to_Maritime_Security/Pages/SOLAS-XI-2%20ISPS%20Code.aspx.

10. The NTC further compares passenger and cargo manifests against databases and other records for clues that could reveal a high-risk traveler, such as a foreign terrorist. Paul Koscak, "Working Together: Catching Smugglers, Terrorists, and Lawbreakers Works Better through Partnership," NTC, CBP, https://www.CBP.gov/frontline/CBP-national-targeting-center.

11. World Customs Organization, *SAFE Framework of Standards to Secure and Facilitate Global Trade, 2018 Edition* (Brussels: World Customs Organization, 2018), http://www.wcoomd.org/-/media/wco/public/global/pdf/topics/facilitation/instruments-and-tools/tools/safe-package/safe-framework-of-standards.pdf?la=en.

12. The Countering Weapons of Mass Destruction Office consolidated the Domestic Nuclear Detection Office and the Office of Health Affairs. See DHS, "Countering Weapons of Mass Destruction Office," DHS website, https://www.DHS.gov/countering-weapons-mass-destruction-office.

13. For a succinct overview of maritime security, see William Johnstone, "Maritime Transportation Security: A Unique Challenge," Elsevier SciTech Connect, August 31, 2015, http://scitechconnect.elsevier.com/maritime-transportation-security-challenge/.

14. See TSA's Surface Transportation Program description, "Surface Transportation," DHS website, https://www.TSA.gov/for-industry/surface-transportation.

15. For a full discussion of this issue, see Brian Michael Jenkins and Bruce R. Butterworth, "Long-Term Trends in Attacks on Public Surface Transportation in Europe and North America," Mineta Transportation Institute, January 2016, http://transweb.sjsu.edu/PDFs/research/attacks-on-public-surface-transportation-in-europe-and-north-america-trends.pdf.

16. For insights into why this might be so, see Bruce Hoffman, interview by the Cipher Brief, "The Terrorist Threat to Aviation: Back Again," Cipher Brief, April 26, 2017, https://www.thecipherbrief.com/column_article/the-terrorist-threat-to-aviation-back-again.

17. The Secure Flight program is the primary means of such vetting. It is a risk-based passenger prescreening program that enhances security by identifying low- and

high-risk passengers before they arrive at airports by matching their names (as provided by flight reservations) against trusted traveler lists and watchlists. DHS, "Security Screening," DHS website, https://www.TSA.gov/travel/security-screening.

18. For security reasons, the Federal Air Marshal Service (FAMS) does not disclose the total number or the names of air marshals, the specific flights on which they travel, or the rationale for choosing which flights receive protection. Of the publicly available information, Wikipedia is among the most complete. "Federal Air Marshal Service," Wikimedia Foundation, https://en.wikipedia.org/wiki/Federal_Air_Marshal_ Service.

19. The FAMS program is not without controversy or critics. Some members of Congress, the GAO, DHS Inspector General, other law enforcement agencies, and the public have at times questioned the effectiveness or even the necessity of the program, especially in light of the hardening of aircraft cockpit doors and the general assumption that passengers on aircraft will no longer remain passive in the event of an attempt by terrorists to commandeer an aircraft. Moreover, it has been difficult to quantify the impact of FAMS. These and other concerns and questions argue strongly for a need to critically examine and continuously adapt the strategy and operational profile of FAMS to ensure an appropriate and justifiable federal law enforcement capability within and for transportation.

20. For a more complete discussion of this approach, see White House, "Surface Transportation Security Priority Assessment," Washington, D.C., March 2010), https://obamawhitehouse.archives.gov/sites/default/files/rss_viewer/STSA.pdf.

21. White House, "The National Strategy for Aviation Security," Washington, D.C., March 26, 2007, https://www.DHS.gov/sites/default/files/publications/nspd-47.pdf.

22. Twitter went live in July 2006; Facebook was launched on February 4, 2004; and Instagram began in October 2010.

23. See the discussion of this terrorist tactic in "Vehicles as Weapons of Terror," Counter Extremism Project, https://www.counterextremism.com/vehicles-as-weapons-of-terror.

24. On the morning of March 22, 2016, three coordinated suicide bombings occurred in Belgium: two in non-secure public areas at Brussels Airport in Zaventem, and one at Maalbeek metro station in central Brussels. Thirty-two civilians and three perpetrators were killed, and 340 people were injured. Another bomb was found during a search of the airport. The Islamic State claimed responsibility for the attacks.

25. There are, of course, other examples, including the June 2016 attack on Atatürk Airport in Istanbul, Turkey, and the January 2017 active shooter incident in a baggage claim area at Fort Lauderdale-Hollywood Inter-national Airport in Florida.

26. The U.S. Intelligence Community (IC) is a federation of sixteen separate U.S. government agencies that work both separately and together to conduct intelligence

activities in support of the foreign relations and national security of the United States.

27. This pressure will increase as passenger volume grows over the coming decades. The International Air Transport Association (IATA) predicts a doubling of air passenger volume globally by 2036. IATA, "2036 Forecast Reveals Air Passengers Will Nearly Double to 7.8 Billion," International Air Transport Association, Montreal, October 24, 2017, http://www.iata.org/pressroom/pr/Pages/2017-10-24-01.aspx.

28. This concern is well-founded given numerous recent significant data breaches, two of the largest of which were the 2017 Equifax data breach, which exposed detailed personal information on 143 million American consumers, and the 2015 U.S. Office of Personnel Management breach, in which the sensitive security files of 21.5 million current and prospective U.S. government employees were stolen.

29. CBP, "Biometrics," CBP website, https://www.CBP.gov/travel/biometrics/air-exit.

30. CBP, "Biometric Exit Frequently Asked Questions," CBP website, https://www.CBP.gov/travel/biometrics/biometric-exit-faqs.

31. For an opposing view of TSA's use of facial recognition, see Jennifer Lynch, "TSA Plans to Use Face Recognition to Track Americans through Airports," Electronic Frontier Foundation, November 9, 2017, https://www.eff.org/deeplinks/2017/11/TSA-plans-use-face-recognition-track-americans-through-airports.

32. The Senate Commerce Committee approved TSA Modernization Act in October 2017; if enacted, this bill would allow TSA to deploy biometric technology in its operations. TSA Modernization Act, https://www.commerce.senate.gov/public/_cache/files/e308d392-65e8-4f3a-828b-4c43a348b114/4C4E6267970C35B86B2BF21A5DA5529A.s.1872-TSA-modernization-act.pdf.

33. TSA, "TSA Biometrics Roadmap for Aviation Security and the Passenger Experience," Washington, D.C., DHS, September 2018, https://www.TSA.gov/sites/default/files/TSA_biometrics_roadmap.pdf.

34. FAA Reauthorization Act of 2018, Pub. L. No. 115-254 (2018), https://www.congress.gov/115/bills/hr302/BILLS-115hr302enr.pdf.

35. Harrison Rudolph, Laura M. Moy, and Alvaro M. Bedoya, "Not Ready for Takeoff, Face Scans at Airport Departure Gates," Center on Privacy and Technology, Georgetown Law School, Washington, D.C., December 2017, https://www.airport-facescans.com/#summary.

36. Marco Iansiti and Karim R. Lakhani, "The Truth about Blockchain," *Harvard Business Review*, January–February 2017, https://hbr.org/2017/01/the-truth-about-blockchain.

37. DHS, "Our Mission," DHS website, https://www.DHS.gov/our-mission.

38. For information about TSA Innovation Task Force, see Steve Karoly, "Working to Protect You: Innovation Task Force," DHS website, https://www.TSA.gov/blog/2017/06/12/working-protect-you-innovation-task-force.

39. Steven Brill, "Is America Any Safer?" *Atlantic*, September 2016, https://www.theatlantic.com/magazine/archive/2016/09/are-we-any-safer/492761/.

40. According to the National Highway Traffic Safety Administration (NHTSA), 37,461 people lost their lives in traffic accidents on U.S. roads during calendar year 2016. NHTSA, "USDOT Releases 2016 Fatal Traffic Crash Data," press release, Washington, D.C., October 6, 2017, https://www.nhTSA.gov/press-releases/usdot-releases-2016-fatal-traffic-crash-data.

41. For an interesting discussion of relative risks of terror versus other dangers, see Phil Torres, "Existential Risks Are More Likely to Kill You Than Terrorism," Future of Life Institute, June 29, 2016, https://futureoflife.org/2016/06/29/existential-risks-likely-kill-terrorism/.

42. Lawrence M. Krauss, "Thinking Rationally about Terror," *New Yorker*, January 2, 2016, https://www.newyorker.com/news/news-desk/thinking-rationally-about-terror.

Chapter 9: Fragmentation in Unity: Immigration and Border Policy within DHS

1. Doris Meissner, et al., "Immigration Enforcement in the United States: The Rise of a Formidable Machinery," Migration Policy Institute, Washington, D.C., May 2013.

2. USCIS History Office and Library, "Overview of INS History," USCIS, Washington, D.C., 2012, pp. 3–4, https://www.uscis.gov/sites/default/files/USCIS/History%20and%20Genealogy/Our History/INS History/INSHistory.pdf.

3. Ibid., p. 3.

4. The Immigration Act of 1882, 22 Stat. 214 (August 3, 1882).

5. John Moore, "The Evolution of Islamic Terrorism: An Overview," *Frontline*, PBS, http://www.pbs.org/wgbh/pages/frontline/shows/target/etc/modern.html

6. USCIS History Office and Library, "Overview of INS History," pp. 5–6.

7. Alien Anarchists Exclusion Act of 1918, Pub. L. 65-221, 40 Stat. 1012, 1013 (1918).

8. USCIS History Office and Library, "Overview of INS History," p. 7.

9. Franklin D. Roosevelt,"White House Statement Summarizing Executive Order 6166," White House, Washington, D.C., June 10, 1933, https://www.presidency.ucsb.edu/documents/white-house-statement-summarizing-executive-order-6166.

10. Franklin D. Roosevelt, Reorganization Plan No. V of 1940, White House, Washington D.C., June 4, 1940, http://uscode.house.gov/view.xhtml?req=granuleid:USC-prelim-title5a-node84-leaf90&num=0&edition=prelim.

11. USCIS History Office and Library, "Overview of INS History," p. 8.

12. Displaced Persons Act of 1948, Pub. L. 80-774, § 10. (1948)

13. "Displaced Persons in Europe, Before the Committee on the Judiciary" (statement of U.S. Senator Alexander Wiley), 80th Cong., 2d sess. (1948), p. 2.

14. Ibid., p. 26; Christopher Rudolph, *National Security and Immigration: Policy Development in the United States and Europe since 1945* (Palo Alto, Calif.: Stanford University Press, 2006), p. 50; and "Seeking a National Strategy: A Concert for Preserving Security and Promoting Freedom" (Washington, D.C.: United States Commission on National Security/21st Century, 2000), p. 5, http://www.au.af.mil/au/awc/awcgate/nssg/phaseII.pdf.

15. Moore, "The Evolution of Islamic Terrorism."

16. Anti-Terrorism and Effective Death Penalty Act of 1996, Pub. L. 104-132, 110 Stat. 1250 (1996).

17. National Commission on Terrorist Attacks upon the United States, *The 9/11 Commission Report: Final Report of the National Commission on Terrorist Attacks upon the United States* (Washington, D.C.: National Commission on Terrorist Attacks upon the United States, 2004), p. 80, https://www.9-11commission.gov/report/911Report.pdf.

18. Ibid., p. 81.

19. Ibid., p. 187.

20. Jennifer E. Lake, "Department of Homeland Security: Consolidation of Border and Transportation Security Agencies," Congressional Research Service, CRS Report No. RL31549, Washington, D.C.: May 22, 2003, p. 4.

21. Ibid.

22. Homeland Security Act of 2002, Pub. L. 107–296, 116 Stat. 2132 (2002), https://www.DHS.gov/xlibrary/assets/hr_5005_enr.pdf.

23. Lake, *Department of Homeland Security*, p. 1.

24. DHS, *Privacy Impact Assessment for the Immigration Benefits Background Check Systems* (Washington, D.C.: DHS, 2010) pp. 1–3, https://www.DHS.gov/xlibrary/assets/privacy/privacy_pia_uscis_ibbcs.pdf.

25. Ibid., p. 4.

26. Office of the Citizenship and Immigration Services Ombudsman, *Annual Report, 2016* (Washington, D.C.: DHS, 2016), p. 36, https://www.DHS.gov/sites/default/files/publications/CISOMB%20Annual%20Report%202016_2.pdf .

27. Robert D. Schroeder, "Holding the Line in the 21st Century," U.S. Border Patrol, CBP, Washington, D.C., https://www.CBP.gov/sites/default/files/documents/Holding%20the%20Line_TRILOGY.pdf.

28. Jeh Johnson, "Border Security in the 21st Century," remarks at the Center for Strategic and International Studies, Washington, D.C., October 9, 2014, https://www.DHS.gov/news/2014/10/09/remarks-Secretary-homeland-security-jeh-johnson-border-security-21st-century.

29. "Immigration Benefits Vetting: Examining Critical Weaknesses in USCIS Systems, Before the House Committee on Homeland Security, Subcommittee on Oversight and Management Efficiency" (written statement of Lori Scialabba, Acting Director of U.S. Citizenship and Immigration Services), 114th Cong., 2d sess., 2017, https://www.DHS.gov/news/2017/03/16/written-testimony-uscis-acting-director-house-homeland-security-subcommittee.

30. John Roth, "USCIS Automation of Immigration Benefits Processing Remains Ineffective," Office of Inspector General, DHS, Washington, D.C., March 2016, pp. 6–12.

31. Office of Inspector General, "DHS OIG Urgently Recommends USCIS Halt Plans to Use the Electronic Immigration System (ELIS) for Naturalization Application Processing," news release, DHS, Washington, D.C., January 23, 2017, https://www.oig.DHS.gov/assets/pr/2017/oigpr-012317.pdf.

32. "Immigration Benefits Vetting: Examining Critical Weaknesses in USCIS Systems, Before the House Committee on Homeland Security, Subcommittee on Oversight and Management Efficiency" (statement of John Roth, Inspector General), 114th Cong., 2d sess., 2017, https://www.oig.DHS.gov/sites/default/files/assets/TM/2017/oigtm-jr-031617.pdf.

33. Office of Inspector General, "DHS OIG Urgently Recommends USCIS Halt Plans to Use the Electronic Immigration System (ELIS) for Naturalization Application Processing."

34. Ibid.

35. "Visa Waiver Program: Actions Are Needed to Improve Management of the Expansion Process, and to Assess and Mitigate Program, Before the Senate Committee on the Judiciary, Subcommittee on Terrorism, Technology, and Homeland Security" (statement of Jess. T. Ford, Director, International Affairs and Trade), 110th Cong., 2d sess., 2008, https://www.judiciary.senate.gov/imo/media/doc/08-09-24FordTestimony.pdf.

36. Alison Siskin, *Visa Waiver Program*, Congressional Research Service, CRS Report No. RL32221, Washington, D.C., December 11, 2014, p. 27, https://fas.org/sgp/crs/homesec/RL32221.pdf.

37. Committee on Homeland Security, Visa Waiver Program Improvement Act of 2015, H.R. Report No. 114-369, Pt. 1 (2015), pp. 7–8, https://permanent.access.gpo.gov/gpo63633/pt.1/CRPT-114hrpt369-pt1.pdf.

38. Jeh C. Johnson, "Statement by Secretary Jeh C. Johnson on Intention to Implement Security Enhancements to the Visa Waiver Program," press release, DHS, Washington, D.C., August 6, 2015, https://www.DHS.gov/news/2015/08/06/statement-Secretary-jeh-c-johnson-intention-implement-security-enhancements-visa.

39. Donald J. Trump, "Protecting the Nation from Foreign Terrorist Entry into the United States," Exec. Order No. 13769, 82 Fed. Reg. 8977 (January 27, 2017), https://

www.whitehouse.gov/the-press-office/2017/01/27/executive-order-protecting-nation-foreign-terrorist-entry-united-states.

40. United Nations High Commissioner for Refugees (UNHCR), "Global Trends: Forced Displacement in 2015," United Nations, Geneva, Switzerland, June 20, 2016, http://www.unhcr.org/576408cd7.pdf.

41. USCIS, "Refugee Processing and Security Screening," USCIS website, December 3, 2015, https://www.uscis.gov/refugeescreening.

42. Ibid.

43. Ibid.

44. Curt Prendergast, "Most Hard Drugs Smuggled through Legal Border Crossings," *Arizona Daily Star*, May 6, 2017, http://tucson.com/news/local/border/most-hard-drugs-smuggled-through-legal-border-crossings/article_46653d40-7f63-5102-bb38-38da58c06a76.html.

45. U.S. Border Patrol, "U.S. Border Patrol Total Apprehensions (FY 1925–FY 2016)," CBP, https://www.CBP.gov/sites/default/files/assets/documents/2016-OctBP%20Total%20Apps%20FY1925-FY2016.pdf.

46. "Potential Terrorist Threats: Border Security Challenges in Latin America and the Caribbean, Before the House Committee On Foreign Affairs, Subcommittee on the Western Hemisphere" (statement of Alan Bersin, PLCY Office of International Affairs Assistant Secretary and Chief Diplomatic Officer), 114th Cong., 2d sess., 2016, https://www.DHS.gov/news/2016/03/22/written-testimony-plcy-house-foreign-affairs-subcommittee-western-hemisphere-hearing

47. "Shutting Down Terrorist Pathways into America, Before the House Committee on Homeland Security" (statement of Francis Taylor, Under Secretary, Office of Intelligence and Analysis, DHS; León Rodriguez, Director, USCIS, DHS; Dr. Huban Gowadia, Deputy Director, TSA, DHS; Kevin McAleenan, Deputy Commissioner, CBP, DHS; and Daniel D. Ragsdale, Deputy Director, USCIS, DHS), 114th Cong., 2d sess., 2016, p. 5, https://homeland.house.gov/hearings-and-markups/hearings/shutting-down-terrorist-pathways-america.

48. Blas Nuñez-Neto, *Border Security: Apprehensions of "Other Than Mexican" Aliens*, Congressional Research Service, CRS Report No. RL33097, Washington, D.C., September 22, 2005. See also Todd Bensman, "The Ultra-Marathoners of Human Smuggling: How to Combat the Dark Networks that Can Move Terrorists over American Land Borders," *Homeland Security Affairs*, Vol. 12, No. 2 (May 2016), https://www.hsaj.org/articles/10568.

49. Schroeder, "Holding the Line in the 21st Century," p. 8.

50. Ibid.

51. U.S. Border Patrol, CBP, "BP Total Monthly Apps by Sector and Area, FY200-FY2017," accessed July 15, 2018, p. 15, https://www.CBP.gov/sites/default/files/assets/

documents/2017-Dec/BP%20Total%20Monthly%20Apps%20by%20Sector%20 and%20Area%2C%20FY2000-FY2017.pdf; and Amanda Sakuma, "Mexico's Other Border," MSNBC, http://www.msnbc.com/specials/migrant-crisis/mexico.

52. William J. Krouse, "*Immigration: Visa Entry/Exit Control System*," Congressional Research Service, CRS Report No. 98-89 EPW, Washington, D.C., November 9, 1998, pp. 1–2.

53. "Alternative Technologies for Implementation of Section 110 of the Illegal Immigration Reform and Immigrant Responsibility Act of 1996 at Land Borders, Before the House Committee on the Judiciary, Subcommittee on Immigration and Claims" (statement of Michael Hrinyak, Deputy Assistant Commissioner for Inspections, INS), 105th Cong., 2d sess., 1998, http://commdocs.house.gov/committees/judiciary/hju59934.000/hju59934_0f.htm.

54. Lisa M. Seghetti, "Border Security: Immigration Issues in the 108th Congress," Congressional Research Service, CRS Report No. RL31727, Washington, D.C., May 18, 2004, pp. 5–6, https://fas.org/sgp/crs/RL31727.pdf.

55. Lisa M. Seghetti and Stephen R. Viña, "U.S. Visitor and Immigrant Status Indicator Technology (US-VISIT) Program," Congressional Research Service, CRS Report No. RL32234, Washington, D.C., February 23, 2005, pp. 8, 10, https://fas.org/sgp/crs/homesec/RL32234.pdf; and DHS, "Privacy Impact Assessment for the Advance Passenger Information System," Washington, D.C. March 21, 2005, pp. 3–4, https://www.DHS.gov/xlibrary/assets/privacy/privacy_pia_CBPapis.pdf.

56. "Homeland Security: Prospects For Biometric US-VISIT Exit Capability Remain Unclear, Before the House Committee on Homeland Security, Subcommittee on Border, Maritime and Global Terrorism" (statement of Randolph Chite, Director, Information Technology Architecture and Systems Issues; and Richard M. Stana, Director, Homeland Security and Justice Issues), 110th Cong., 1st sess., 2007, p. 4, http://www.gao.gov/assets/120/117187.pdf.

57. Ibid., p. 35.

58. Randolph C. Hite, "Homeland Security: US-VISIT Pilot Evaluations Offer Limited Understanding of Air Exit Options," GAO-10-860, GAO, Washington, D.C., August 10, 2010, p. 23, http://www.gao.gov/assets/310/308630.pdf.

59. "Biometric Exit, Before the Senate Committee on the Judiciary, Subcommittee on Immigration and the National Interest" (statement of Anh Duong, Director for Borders and Maritime Security Division, Homeland Security Advanced Research Projects Agency, Science and Technology Directorate; Craig C. Healy, Assistant Director for National Security Investigations Division, Homeland Security Investigations, ICE; and John Wagner, Deputy Assistant Commissioner, Office of Field Operations, CBP), https://www.judiciary.senate.gov/imo/media/doc/01-20-16%20 Duong-Healy-Wagner-Testimony.pdf; and Jeh C. Johnson, "Comprehensive

Biometric Entry/Exit Plan: Fiscal Year 2016 Report to Congress," DHS, Washington, D.C., 2016, p. 4, https://www.DHS.gov/sites/default/files/publications/Customs%20 and%20Border%20Protection%20-%20Comprehensive%20Biometric%20 Entry%20and%20Exit%20Plan.pdf.

60. Ibid., p. 7.

61. "Examining the Problem of Visa Overstays: A Need for Better Tracking and Account-ability, Before the Senate Committee on the Judiciary, Subcommittee on Border Security and Immigration" (statement of Michael Dougherty, Assistant Secretary, Border, Immigration and Trade, Office of Strategy, Policy, and Plans; John Wagner, Deputy Executive Assistant Commissioner, Office of Field Operations, CBP; and Louis A. Rodi, III, Deputy Assistant Director, National Security Investigations Division, Homeland Security Investigations, ICE), pp. 2–3, https://www.judiciary.senate.gov/ imo/media/doc/07-12-17%20Dougherty-Wagner-Rodi%20Joint%20Testimony2.pdf.

62. Ibid., p. 8.

63. Frank Bajak and David Koenig, "Face Scans for U.S. Citizens Flying Abroad Stir Privacy Issues," *Associated Press*, July 12, 2017, https://apnews.com/acf6bab-1f5ab4bc59284985a3babdca4.

64. "Examining the Problem of Visa Overstays," pp. 9–11.

65. Johnson, "Comprehensive Biometric Entry/Exit Plan," p. 1.

Chapter 10: Emergency Management and DHS

1. David J. Kaufman, "Bending the Cost Curve through Better Design," Domestic Preparedness, April 27, 2016, https://www.domesticpreparedness.com/preparedness/ bending-the-cost-curve-through-better-design/. For a list of billion-dollar disasters since 1980, see Adam Smith, et al., "U.S. Billion-Dollar Weather and Climate Disasters, 1980–2018," National Centers for Environmental Information, National Oceanic and Atmospheric Administration, Asheville, N.C., accessed July 25, 2018), https://www.ncdc.noaa.gov/billions/events.pdf.

2. Homeland Securitiy Act of 2002, 6 U.S.C. § 111.

3. FEMA, "About the Agency," FEMA website, https://www.fema.gov/about-agency.

4. During former Administrator W. Craig Fugate's Senate confirmation hearing before the Senate Homeland Security and Government Affairs Committee on April 22, 2009, Fugate responded to Chairman Lieberman's question about FEMA's inclusion in DHS with the following: "I believe that the next confirmed Administrator of FEMA needs to be focused on the next disaster, and being focused on that means that the debate, as far as I am concerned, is over." "Nomination of W. Craig Fugate to be Administrator, Federal Emergency Management Agency, U.S. Department of Homeland Security, Before the Committee on Homeland Security and Governmental Affairs, U.S. Senate,"

111th Cong., 1st sess., 2009, https://www.congress.gov/111/chrg/shrg50388/CHRG-111shrg50388.htm.

5. Post-Katrina Emergency Management Reform Act (PKEMRA), 6 U.S.C. § 313.

6. For "certain emergencies involving federal primary responsibility," the president is authorized to take action without the consent of the governors of the impacted states. The Disaster Relief and Emergency Assistance Amendments of 1988, 42 U.S.C. § 5191.

7. White House, "Homeland Security Presidential Directive 5: Management of Domestic Incidents," Washington, D.C., February 28, 2003, https://www.DHS.gov/sites/default/files/publications/Homeland%20Security%20Presidential%20Directive%205.pdf.

8. Reorganization Plan No. 3 of 1978, 92 Stat. 3788-3789 (1978).

9. FEMA, "Federal Response Plan," Publication No. 9230.1-PL, Washington, D.C., April 1999, http://bparati.com/Portals/0/PDF_Files/FederalDocs/DHS_FEMA/1999_04_FEMA_federal_response_plan_revision.pdf?ver=2014-09-06-105557-233.

10. FEMA, "The Federal Emergency Management Agency," Publication No. 1, Washington, D.C., November 2010, pp. 8–9, https://www.fema.gov/media-library-data/20130726-1823-25045-8164/pub_1_final.pdf.

11. Ibid., p. 9.

12. Disaster Mitigation Act of 2000, Pub. L. 106-390, 114 Stat. 1552 (2000).

13. International Association of Emergency Managers (IAEM), "History of the AEM and CEM," IAEM.com, June 2011, http://www.iaem.com/page.cfm?p=certification/history-of-cem.

14. FEMA, "Disaster Planning and Policies, Session 2: U.S. Disaster Policies: History and Institutions," Washington, D.C., accessed October 3, 2017), https://training.fema.gov/hiedu/docs/dpp/disaster%20plan-policies%20-%20session%20no%202%20-%20history%20and%20institutions_fema%20course.pdf.

15. Select Bipartisan Committee to Investigate the Preparation for and Response to Hurricane Katrina, A Failure of Initiative, H.R. Rep. No. 109-377, U.S. Government Publishing Office, Washington, D.C., 2006, p. 7, https://www.gpo.gov/fdsys/pkg/CRPT-109hrpt377/pdf/CRPT-109hrpt377.pdf.

16. Post-Katrina Emergency Management Reform Act of 2006, Pub. L. 109-295, 120 Stat. 1394 (2006).

17. Kathryn Schulz, "The Really Big One," *New Yorker*, July 20, 2015.

18. Chris P. Currie, "Federal Departments and Agencies Obligated at Least $277.6 Billion during Fiscal Years 2005 through 2014," GAO, GAO-16-797, Washington, D.C., 2016, p. 12.

19. Brian K. Sullivan, "The Most Expensive U.S. Hurricane Season Ever: By the Numbers," *Bloomberg*, November 26, 2017, https://www.bloomberg.com/news/articles/2017-11-26/the-most-expensive-u-s-hurricane-season-ever-by-the-numbers.

20. Ibid.

21. Ibid.

22. FEMA Disaster Assistance Reform Act of 2015, H.R. 1471, 114th Cong. 2nd sess. (2015), https://www.congress.gov/bill/114th-congress/house-bill/1471.

23. FEMA, "Preparedness in America: Research Insights to Increase Individual, Organizational, and Community Action," Washington, D.C., August 2014), p. 1, https://www.fema.gov/media-library-data/1409000888026-1e8abc820153a6c8cde24ce4 2c16e857/20140825_Preparedness_in_America_August_2014_Update_508.pdf.

Chapter 11: Protecting Critical Infrastructure

1. National Association of Water Companies, "Private Water Service Providers Quick Facts," National Association of Water Companies website, accessed July 24, 2018, http://www.nawc.org/uploads/documents-and-publications/documents/document_ecf5b3ac-c222-4b6c-b99f-a0128ae1e9aa.pdf.

2. Critical Infrastructures Protection Act of 2001, 42 U.S.C. § 5195c.

3. President John F. Kennedy established the National Communications System (NCS) by a Presidential Memorandum on August 21, 1963, after communications problems exacerbated the Cuban Missile Crisis. The NCS was a single unified communications system to ensure that the federal government had the necessary communications under all conditions, from normal situations to national emergencies and international crises. Its successor, the Office of Emergency Communications, ensures that the national security and emergency preparedness (NS/EP) communications community has access to priority telecommunications and restoration services to communicate under all circumstances, including when the wireless cellular network is congested.

4. *The 9/11 Commission Report: Final Report of the National Commission on Terrorist Attacks upon the United States* (Washington, D.C.: Government Publishing Office, 2004), p. 341.

5. Ibid.

6. Presidential Decision Directive/NSC-63, "Critical Infrastructure Protection," May 22, 1998, https://fas.org/irp/offdocs/pdd/pdd-63.htm.

7. In July 1996, Clinton issued Executive Order 13010, mandating a comprehensive national policy and implementation strategy for protecting critical infrastructure from physical and cyber threats.

8. Presidential Decision Directive/NSC-63, "Critical Infrastructure Protection."

9. Ibid.

10. *The 9/11 Commission Report*, p. 336.

11. USA PATRIOT Act, 42 U.S.C. § 5195c, https://epic.org/privacy/terrorism/hr3162.html.

12. Homeland Security Act of 2002, Pub. L. 107-296, 116 Stat. 2135 (2002), title II, section 203.

13. In March 2006, DHS posted notice in the Federal Register of its intent to establish the Critical Infrastructure Partnership Advisory Council, thereby exercising its authority under Section 871 of the Homeland Security Act of 2002, 6 U.S.C. 451., 71 Fed. Reg. 14930 (March 24, 2006).

14. Homeland Security Presidential Directive 7, "Critical Infrastructure Identification, Prioritization, and Protection," December 17, 2003.

15. *National Infrastructure Protection Plan, 2006* (Washington, D.C.: DHS, 2006).

16. Ibid.

17. See the Implementing Recommendations of the 9/11 Commission Act of 2007, Pub. L. 110-53, 121 Stat. 266 (2007), https://www.gpo.gov/fdsys/pkg/PLAW-110publ53/html/PLAW-110publ53.htm.

18. Implementing Recommendations of the 9/11 Commission Act of 2007, Title X, Section 2001.

19. Implementing Recommendations of the 9/11 Commission Act of 2007, Title X, Sections 2007 and 2008.

20. Pub. L. 109-295, 120 Stat. 1355 (2006), Section 55.

21. As discussed below, in November 2018, NPPD was renamed the Cybersecurity and Infrastructure Security Agency (CISA) and elevated to the status of a full DHS Component, rather than a Headquarters office.

22. Executive Order 12977 was subsequently modified by Executive Order 13286. The Federal Protective Service was later moved out of CISA.

23. DHS, "Climate Change Adaptation Roadmap," Washington, D.C., June 2012, p. 34.

24. National Infrastructure Advisory Council (NIAC), "A Framework for Establishing Critical Infrastructure Goals," Washington, D.C., October 19, 2010), https://www.DHS.gov/xlibrary/assets/niac/niac-a-framework-for-establishing-critical-infra-structure-resilience-goals-2010-10-19.pdf.

25. In 2017, NIAC released a future focus study, "Strengthening the NIAC Study Process," and identified ways in which it can improve its study process and develop more actionable recommendations, working closely through an iterative process with the National Security Council staff to achieve desired outcomes.

26. National Oceanic and Atmospheric Administration (NOAA), "Service Assessment: Hurricane/Post-Tropical Cyclone Sandy: October 22–29, 2012," U.S. Department of Commerce, Silver Spring, Md., May 2013.

27. Ibid.

28. Interagency Security Committee, "Presidential Policy Directive 21 Implementation: An Interagency Security Committee White Paper," DHS, Washington, D.C., February

2015, https://www.DHS.gov/sites/default/files/publications/ISC-PPD-21-Implementation-White-Paper-2015-508.pdf.

29. Resilience is defined as being able to withstand and rapidly recover from all hazards.

30. DHS, "Presidential Policy Directive 21: Critical Infrastructure Security and Resilience," Washington, D.C., February 12, 2013.

31. DHS, "Budget in Brief: Fiscal Year 2017," Washington, D.C., 2017; this budget covered 18,000 federal employees and contractors.

32. On December 23, 2015, the Ukrainian Kyivoblenergo, a regional electricity distribution company, reported service outages to customers. The outages were due to an attack against the utility's Supervisory Control and Data Acquisition (SCADA) systems.

33. For further discussion of this aspect of cybersecurity, see John Carlin and Sophia Brill's chapter in this volume.

Chapter 12: Cybersecurity

1. Leon E. Panetta, remarks to the Business Executives for National Security (BENS), New York City, October 11, 2012, http://archive.defense.gov/transcripts/transcript.aspx?transcriptid=5136.

2. For the most recent report, see Daniel R. Coats, Director of National Intelligence (DNI), "Worldwide Threat Assessment of the U.S. Intelligence Community," February 13, 2018, https://www.dni.gov/files/documents/Newsroom/Testimonies/SSCI%20Unclassified%20SFR%20-%20Final.pdf. Reports for 2013–17 are available at https://www.dni.gov/files/documents/Intelligence%20Reports/UNCLASS_2013%20ATA%20SFR%20FINAL%20for%20SASC%2018%20Apr%202013.pdf; https://www.dni.gov/files/documents/Intelligence%20Reports/2014%20WWTA%20%20SFR_SSCI_29_Jan.pdf; https://www.dni.gov/files/documents/Unclassified_2015_ATA_SFR_-_SASC_FINAL.pdf; https://www.dni.gov/files/documents/SASC_Unclassified_2016_ATA_SFR_FINAL.pdf; and https://www.dni.gov/files/documents/Newsroom/Testimonies/SSCI%20Unclassified%20SFR%20-%20Final.pdf.

3. Of course, with respect to nation-state actors, nearly every nation engages in espionage of one form or another—often including through cyber-related means. See Brian Egan, "Remarks on International Law and Stability in Cyberspace," Berkeley Law School, Berkeley, California, November 10, 2016, https://www.law.berkeley.edu/wp-content/uploads/2016/12/egan-talk-transcript-111016.pdf. Egan notes that "remote cyber operations involving computers or other networked devices located on another State's territory do not constitute a per se violation of international law." Indeed, the current process by which the U.S. government determines whether to disclose cyber vulnerabilities takes into account the government's potential interest

in using those vulnerabilities to conduct intelligence collection. See White House, "Vulnerabilities Equities Policy and Process for the United States Government," Washington, D.C., November 15, 2017, https://www.whitehouse.gov/sites/whitehouse.gov/files/images/External%20-%20Unclassified%20VEP%20Charter%20 FINAL.PDF.

4. "Cybersecurity: Actions Needed to Strengthen U.S. Capabilities, Before the Subcommittee on Research and Technology, Committee on Science, Space, and Technology" (statement of Gregory C. Wilshusen, Director, Information Security Issues), 115th Cong., 1st sess. (2017) https://www.gao.gov/assets/690/682756.pdf.

5. These statistics are derived from a GAO analysis of US-CERT and Office of Management and Budget data. It should be noted, however, that not all "information security incidents" necessarily represent breaches as a result of cyberattacks. They may also include incidents in which information was exposed inadvertently.

6. See Ellen Nakashima, "Hacks of OPM Databases Compromised 22.1 Million People, Federal Authorities Say," *Washington Post*, June 9, 2015, https://www.washingtonpost.com/news/federal-eye/wp/2015/07/09/hack-of-security-clearance-system-affected-21-5-million-people-federal-authorities-say/.

7. Ibid.

8. GAO, "Information Security: Cyber Threats and Data Breaches Illustrate Need for Stronger Controls across Federal Agencies," Washington, D.C., July 2015, pp. 8–9, http://www.gao.gov/assets/680/671253.pdf.

9. GAO, "Air Traffic Control: FAA Needs a More Comprehensive Approach to Address Cybersecurity as Agency Transitions to NexGen," Washington, D.C., April 2015, http://www.gao.gov/assets/670/669627.pdf.

10. GAO, "Computer Security: Hackers Penetrate DOD Computer Systems," Washington, D.C., November 20, 1991, p. 3, http://www.gao.gov/assets/110/104234.pdf.

11. James R. Clapper, DNI, "Worldwide Threat Assessment of the U.S. Intelligence Community," Senate Armed Services Committee, Washington, D.C., February 26, 2015, p. 2, https://www.dni.gov/files/documents/Unclassified_2015_ATA_SFR_-_SASC_FINAL.pdf.

12. Daniel R. Coats, DNI, "Worldwide Threat Assessment of the U.S. Intelligence Community," Senate Committee on Intelligence, Washington, D.C., May 11, 2017, p. 1, https://www.dni.gov/files/documents/Newsroom/Testimonies/SSCI%20Unclassified%20SFR%20-%20Final.pdf.

13. Ibid.

14. Lisa Monaco, speech at the 2012 Cybercrime Conference, Seattle, Washington, October 25, 2012, http://www.justice.gov/nsd/justice-news-2.

15. "Securing Cyber Assets: Addressing Urgent Cyber Threats to Critical Infrastructure," President's National Infrastructure Advisory Council, Washington, D.C., August

2017, p. 3, http://www.DHS.gov/sites/default/files/publications/niac-cyber-study-draft-report-08-15-17-508.pdf.

16. DOJ, "Seven Iranians Working for Islamic Revolutionary Guard Corps-Affiliated Entities Charged for Conducting Coordinated Campaign of Cyber Attacks against U.S. Financial Sector," news release, Washington, D.C., March 24, 2016, https://www.justice.gov/opa/pr/seven-iranians-working-islamic-revolutionary-guard-corps-affiliated-entities-charged.

17. USA PATRIOT Act, 42 U.S.C. § 5195c(e), October 26, 2001.

18. For a complete list, see DHS, "Critical Infrastructure Sectors," DHS website, https://www.DHS.gov/critical-infrastructure-sectors.

19. See U.S. Election Assistance Commission, "Starting Point: U.S. Election Systems As Critical Infrastructure," Silver Spring, Md., https://www.eac.gov/assets/1/6/starting_point_us_election_systems_as_Critical_Infrastructure.pdf.

20. Rob Joyce, "Improving and Making the Vulnerability Equities Process Transparent Is the Right Thing to Do," White House, Washington, D.C., November 15, 2017, https://www.whitehouse.gov/articles/improving-making-vulnerability-equities-process-transparent-right-thing/.

21. One helpful definition describes the IoT as "the growing body of Internet-connected devices, gadgets, and other items that do not fit the traditional concept of a 'computer.'" Lyndsay A. Wasser and Mitch Koczerginski, "Cybersecurity and the Internet of Things," McMillan, March 2016, http://www.mondaq.com/canada/x/470358/Data+Protection+Privacy/Cybersecurity+and+the+Internet+of+Things. Another describes the term as referring to "devices that collect and transmit data via the Internet." Christie Terrill, "What You Need to Know About Cybersecurity and the Internet of Things," Forbes, May 16, 2017, https://www.forbes.com/sites/christieterrill/2017/05/16/what-you-need-to-know-about-cybersecurity-and-the-internet-of-things/2/#409e43525932.

22. Stuart Madnick, "Security Surprises Arising from the Internet of Things (IoT)," Forbes, May 8, 2017, https://www.forbes.com/sites/ciocentral/2017/05/08/security-surprises-arising-from-the-internet-of-things-iot/#4f69ba582495; and Harald Bauer, Mark Patel, and Jan Veira, "The Internet of Things: Sizing Up the Opportunity," McKinsey, December 2014, http://www.mckinsey.com/industries/semiconductors/our-insights/the-internet-of-things-sizing-up-the-opportunity.

23. Nicky Woolf, "DDoS Attack That Disrupted Internet Was Largest of its Kind in History, Experts Say," Guardian, October 26, 2016, https://www.theguardian.com/technology/2016/oct/26/ddos-attack-dyn-mirai-botnet.

24. Lucian Constantin, "Armies of Hacked IoT Devices Launch Unprecedented DDoS Attacks," ComputerWorld, September 26, 2016, http://www.computerworld.com/

article/3124345/security/armies-of-hacked-iot-devices-launch-unprecedented-ddos-attacks.html.

25. Paul Szoldra, "Akamai Kicked Journalist Brian Krebs' Site Off Its Servers after He Was Hit by a 'Record' Cyberattack," *Business Insider*, September 22, 2016, http://www.businessinsider.com/akamai-brian-krebs-ddos-attack-2016-9.

26. "Smart Refrigerators Hacked to Send Out Spam: Report," NBC, January 18, 2014, http://www.nbcnews.com/tech/internet/smart-refrigerators-hacked-send-out-spam-report-n11946.

27. Chante Owens, "Stranger Hacks Family's Baby Monitor and Talks to Child at Night," *San Francisco Globe*, July 19, 2017, http://sfglobe.com/2016/01/06/stranger-hacks-familys-baby-monitor-and-talks-to-child-at-night/.

28. John Greenough, "The 'Connected Car' Is Creating a Massive New Business Opportunity for Auto, Tech, and Telecom Companies," *Business Insider*, March 11, 2015, http://www.businessinsider.com/connected-car-forecasts-top-manufac-turers-2015-2.

29. David Galland, "10 Million Self-Driving Cars Will Hit the Road by 2020—Here's How to Profit," *Forbes*, March 3, 2017, https://www.forbes.com/sites/oliviergarret/2017/03/03/10-million-self-driving-cars-will-hit-the-road-by-2020-heres-how-to-profit/#5f839cec7e50.

30. Andy Greenberg, "Hackers Remotely Kill a Jeep on the Highway—with Me in It," *Wired*, September 21, 2015, https://www.wired.com/2015/07/hackers-remotely-kill-jeep-highway/.

31. Andy Greenberg, "After Jeep Hack, Chrysler Recalls 1.4 M Vehicles for Bug Fix," *Wired*, September 24, 2015, https://www.wired.com/2015/07/jeep-hack-chrysler-recalls-1-4m-vehicles-bug-fix/.

32. See "Vulnerabilities Equities Policy and Process for the United States Government."

33. Ibid. pp. 1–2.

34. The full transcript of the hearing is available at https://www.washingtonpost.com/news/post-politics/wp/2017/03/20/full-transcript-fbi-director-james-comey-testifies-on-russian-interference-in-2016-election/.

35. "Before the Senate Committee on Armed Services" (statement of Admiral Michael S. Rogers, Commander, United States Cyber Command), 115th Cong., 1st sess., 2017, p. 2, https://www.armed-services.senate.gov/imo/media/doc/Rogers_05-09-17.pdf.

36. See DOJ, "Russian National Charged with Interfering in U.S. Political System," news release, Washington, D.C., October 19, 2018, https://www.justice.gov/usao-edva/pr/russian-national-charged-interfering-us-political-system.

37. See Keith Wagstaff, "Sony Hack Exposed 47,000 Social Security Numbers, Security Firm Says," NBC, December 5, 2014, http://www.nbcnews.com/storyline/sony-hack/sony-hack-exposed-47-000-social-security-numbers-security-firm-n262711.

38. Commission on the Theft of American Intellectual Property, "Update to the IP Commission Report: The Theft of American Intellectual Property: Reassessments of the Challenge and United States Policy," Washington, D.C.: February 2017), p. 1, http://www.ipcommission.org/report/IP_Commission_Report_Update_2017.pdf.

39. See Tom Bossert, "It's Official: North Korea Is Behind WannaCry," *Wall Street Journal*, December 18, 2017, https://www.wsj.com/articles/its-official-north-korea-is-behind-wannacry-1513642537.

40. Andy Greenberg, "New Dark-Web Market Is Selling Zero-Day Exploits to Hackers," *Wired*, April 17, 2015, https://www.wired.com/2015/04/therealdeal-zero-day-exploits/.

41. Ferizi was extradited from Malaysia in 2015 to face charges in the United States. He eventually pleaded guilty to providing material support for ISIS and to hacking charges, and was sentenced in 2016 to twenty years in prison. DOJ, "ISIL-Linked Kosovo Hacker Sentenced to 20 Years in Prison," Washington, D.C., September 23, 2016, https://www.justice.gov/opa/pr/isil-linked-kosovo-hacker-sentenced-20-years-prison.

42. DHS, "Cybersecurity Division," DHS website, July 19, 2017, https://www.DHS.gov/office-cybersecurity-and-communications.

43. Ibid. See also DHS, "National Cybersecurity and Communications Integration Center," DHS website, https://www.DHS.gov/national-cyber-security-and-communications-integration-center. The NCCIC describes its own role as "a national nexus of cyber and communications integration for the Federal Government, intelligence community, and law enforcement."

44. "Addressing Threats to Election Infrastructure Before the Senate Select Committee on Intelligence" (statement of Jeanette Manfra, Acting Deputy Under Secretary for Cybersecurity and Communications), 115 Cong., 1st sess., 2017.

45. The CISA was passed as part of a larger appropriations statute, Pub. L. No. 113-114 (2015). Its provisions are spelled out in Division N of the statute.

46. For PPD-41, see White House, "Presidential Policy Directive—United States Cyber Incident Coordination," Washington, D.C., July 26, 2016, https://obamawhitehouse.archives.gov/the-press-office/2016/07/26/presidential-policy-directive-united-states-cyber-incident.

47. For the text of the order, see White House, "Presidential Executive Order on Strengthening the Cybersecurity of Federal Networks and Critical Infrastructure," Washington, D.C., May 11, 2017, https://www.whitehouse.gov/the-press-office/2017/05/11/presidential-executive-order-strengthening-cybersecurity-federal.

48. This list is not exhaustive. The National Institute of Standards and Technology (NIST), a non-regulatory agency of the Department of Commerce, addressed cybersecurity concerns raised by the IoT in Ron Ross, Michael McEvilly, and Janet

Carrier Oren, "Systems Security Engineering: Considerations for a Multidisciplinary Approach in the Engineering of Trustworthy Secure Systems," NIST, NIST Special Publication No. 800-160, Gaithersburg, Md., November 2016, https://doi.org/10.6028/NIST.SP.800-160. Furthermore, the agencies involved have begun to collaborate to engineer solutions.

49. U.S. Department of Transportation, "Federal Automated Vehicles Policy: Accelerating the Next Revolution in Roadway Safety," Washington, D.C., September 2016, https://www.transportation.gov/AV/federal-automated-vehicles-policy-september-2016.

50. U.S. Food and Drug Administration (FDA), "FDA Outlines Cybersecurity Recommendations for Medical Device Manufacturers," news release, Silver Springs, Md., January 15, 2016, https://www.fda.gov/newsevents/newsroom/pressannouncements/ucm481968.htm.

51. FDA, "Fact Sheet: The FDA's Role in Medical Device Cybersecurity," Silver Springs, Md., https://www.fda.gov/downloads/MedicalDevices/DigitalHealth/UCM544684.pdf.

52. See DHS, "DHS Releases Strategic Principles for Securing the Internet of Things," Washington, D.C., November 15, 2016, https://www.DHS.gov/news/2016/11/15/DHS-releases-strategic-principles-securing-internet-things. See also "An Interview with Robert Silvers," interview by Stewart A. Baker, *Cyberlaw Podcast*, produced by the Lawfare Institute and the Brookings Institution, October 25, 2016, https://lawfareblog.com/steptoe-cyberlaw-podcast-interview-robert-silvers. The interview begins at roughly 20:30.

53. Federal Trade Commission (FTC), "ASUS Settles FTC Charges That Insecure Home Routers and 'Cloud' Services Put Consumers' Privacy At Risk," Washington, D.C., February 23, 2016, https://www.ftc.gov/news-events/press-releases/2016/02/asus-settles-ftc-charges-insecure-home-routers-cloud-services-put. See also FTC, "In the Matter of ASUSTek, Computer Inc.," Cases and Proceedings, Washington, D.C., last updated July 28, 2016, https://www.ftc.gov/enforcement/cases-proceedings/142-3156/asustek-computer-inc-matter.

54. The facts described here are generally taken from a joint Intelligence Community assessment, Office of the Director of National Intelligence (ODNI), "Assessing Russian Activities and Intentions in Recent U.S. Elections," Washington, D.C., January 2017), https://www.dni.gov/files/documents/ICA_2017_01.pdf.

55. See DHS, "Statement by Secretary Jeh Johnson on the Designation of Election Infrastructure as a Critical Infrastructure Subsector," Washington, D.C., January 6, 2017, https://www.DHS.gov/news/2017/01/06/statement-Secretary-johnson-designation-election-infrastructure-critical.

56. See, for example, Derek Hawkins, "The Cybersecurity 202: Here's an Early Look at How States Are Spending Federal Election Security Cash," *Washington Post*, July 10, 2018, https://www.washingtonpost.com/news/powerpost/paloma/the-cybersecurity-202/2018/07/10/the-cybersecurity-202-here-s-an-early-look-at-how-states-are-spending-federal-election-security-cash/5b43878d1b326b3348adddbe/.

57. See Shane Harris, "Obama Stares Down China on Cyberspying," *Daily Beast*, September 25, 2015, http://www.thedailybeast.com/obama-stares-down-china-on-cyberspying.

58. Carol Morello and Greg Miller, "U.S. Imposes Sanctions on N. Korea Following Attack on Sony," *Washington Post*, January 2, 2015, https://www.washingtonpost.com/world/national-security/us-imposes-sanctions-on-n-korea-following-attack-on-sony/2015/01/02/3e5423ae-92af-11e4-a900-9960214d4cd7_story.html.

59. Exec. Order No. 13694, "Blocking the Property of Certain Persons Engaging in Significant Malicious Cyber-Enabled Activities," April 1, 2015, https://obamawhitehouse.archives.gov/the-press-office/2015/04/01/executive-order-blocking-property-certain-persons-engaging-significant-m.

60. See White House, "Fact Sheet: Actions in Response to Russian Malicious Cyber Activity and Harassment," Washington, D.C., December 29, 2016, https://obamawhitehouse.archives.gov/the-press-office/2016/12/29/fact-sheet-actions-response-russian-malicious-cyber-activity-and.

61. Countering America's Adversaries Through Sanctions Act, Pub. L. No. 115-44 § 211-12, 256 (2017).

Chapter 13: Increasing Security while Protecting Privacy

1. In assessing privacy impacts, I will largely limit myself to a consideration of the privacy interests of U.S. citizens and permanent residents ("U.S. persons").

2. The TSDB is maintained by the Terrorist Screening Center, which is housed by the FBI but is effectively an interagency project within the executive branch. The information in the TSDB is based on the classified Terrorist Identities Datamart Environment (TIDE), a database maintained by the National Counterterrorism Center (NCTC) under the Director of National Intelligence (DNI).

3. The notion of a legal right to privacy in the United States is commonly traced back to a famous article published in 1890 by Warren and future Supreme Court Justice Louis D. Brandeis. Samuel D. Warren and Louis D. Brandeis, "The Right to Privacy," *Harvard Law Review*, Vol. 4, No. 5 (December 1890), pp. 193–220. Warren and Brandeis were concerned in part about what they considered to be a dangerous new technological threat to privacy—inexpensive photography—which in today's world seems quaint.

4. DHS, "2016 Privacy Office Annual Report to Congress," Washington, D.C., December 2016, p. 1.

5. These principles are: transparency, individual participation, purpose specification, data minimization, use limitation, data quality and integrity, security, and accountability and auditing. See Hugo Teufel III, "Privacy Policy Guidance Memorandum," DHS, Washington, D.C., December 29, 2008, https://www.DHS.gov/xlibrary/assets/privacy/privacy_policyguide_2008-01.pdf.

6. George Orwell, *Nineteen Eighty-Four* (London: Secker and Warburg, 1949).

7. Instinctive reactions to this fact vary. I am often struck by the differences between the privacy expectations of my twenty-one-year-old son and those of my eighty-four-year-old father. Both carry the same iPhone, but my father was surprised and concerned to learn that his was keeping a record of every location he visited, while my son just shrugs off GPS tracking as a fact of life—and something that he, unlike my father, knows how to turn off easily if he wants to.

8. TSA's website also puts passengers on notice that "additional screening involving a sensitive area pat-down with the front of the hand may be needed to determine that a threat does not exist." TSA, "Pat-Down Screening," TSA website, https://www.TSA.gov/travel/security-screening. For an example of what a properly conducted TSA pat-down looks like in practice, see "A Glimpse at the New TSA Pat-Down Procedure," RTV 6, The Indy Channel, YouTube, March 6, 2017, https://www.youtube.com/watch?v=f-W522lJtBQ.

9. For a TSA video explaining advanced imaging technology, see TSA, "Travel Tips: Advanced Imaging Technology," May 11, 2016, https://www.TSA.gov/videos/travel-tips-advanced-imaging-technology.

10. Unfortunately, the same could not be said about the Rapiscan backscatter machines that TSA used until 2013.

11. The unpredictability of random searches is considered security-enhancing because it keeps adversaries guessing.

12. A federal court has held that U.S. persons have constitutionally-protected liberty interests in traveling internationally by air, which are significantly affected by being placed on the No Fly List. *Latif v. Holder*, 28 F.Supp.3d 1134 (D. Ore. 2014). The court further held that individuals on the No Fly list are entitled to notice of the reasons (in an unclassified form) for their placement on the No Fly List and a meaningful opportunity to contest this placement. As a result of the Latif case, TSA has revised its redress procedures to provide those on the No Fly List with more notice and more information.

13. Courts have held that, as a constitutional matter, the additional delay and imposition on a Selectee is not sufficient to implicate a U.S. person's liberty interest in travel. See *Beydoun v. Sessions*, 871 F.3d 459 (6th Cir. 2017).

14. This last concern is mitigated if government officials interacting with the traveler only see a "red light" or "yellow light" indicator, rather than the information on which the "hit" is based.

15. In the wake of recent court decisions by the European Court of Justice, there is a significant possibility that the privacy protections in the current PNR Agreement will be deemed inadequate by EU courts. If that were to happen, the United States may have another opportunity to pursue greater security by providing stronger data protection.

Chapter 14: Homeland Security and Transnational Crime

1. These are the Federal Bureau of Investigation (FBI); the Drug Enforcement Administration (DEA); and the Bureau of Alcohol, Tobacco, Firearms and Explosives (ATF).

2. The distinction is not perfectly clean. CBP's Internal Affairs office is an investigative entity, as is the Criminal Investigative Service of the USCG; the National Protection and Programs Directorate (NPPD) likewise included both "patrol" and "detective" functions. Likewise, by the definition provided here, the Transportation Security Administration (TSA) would have an interdiction function; however, TSA is not primarily a law enforcement agency. On the other hand, it houses the Federal Air Marshals, who are credentialed law enforcement officers and have both preventive and investigative functions.

3. Martin Innes and James W. E. Sheptycki, "From Detection to Disruption: Intelligence and the Changing Logic of Police Crime Control in the United Kingdom," *International Criminal Justice Review*, Vol. 14, Nos. 1–24 (May 2004), p. 13.

4. We thank Stevan Bunnell for this example.

5. Alice Hutchings and Thomas J. Holt, "The Online Stolen Data Market: Disruption and Intervention Approaches," *Global Crime*, Vol. 18, No. 1 (2017), p. 12.

6. Mariano-Florentino Cuéllar, "The Tenuous Relationship between the Fight against Money Laundering and the Disruption of Criminal Finance," *Journal of Criminal Law and Criminology*, Vol. 93, Nos. 2–3 (2003), pp. 311–466.

7. Carla Morselli and Katya Petit, "Law-Enforcement Disruption of a Drug Importation Network," *Global Crime*, Vol. 8, No. 2 (2007), pp. 109–130; Nicholas Dorn, "Performance Management, Indicators and Drug Enforcement: In the Crossfire or at the Crossroads," in Mangai Natarajan and Mike Hough, eds., *Illegal Drug Markets: From Research to Prevention Policy*, Vol. 11, Crime Prevention Studies (Monsey, N.Y.: Criminal Justice Press, 2000); and Nicholas Dorn, Tom Bucke, and Chris Goulden, "Traffick, Transit, and Transaction: A Conceptual Framework for Action Against Drug Supply," *Howard Journal of Criminal Justice*, Vol. 42 (2003), pp. 348–365.

8. Innes and Sheptycki, "From Detection to Disruption"; Les Johnson, *Policing Britain: Risk, Security, and Governance* (Harlow, UK: Longman, 2000); Her Majesty's Inspectorate of Constabulary (HMIC), *Policing with Intelligence: Criminal Intelligence— A Thematic Inspection on Good Practice* (London: HMIC, 1997); National Crime Squad, *The National Crime Squad Service Plan, 1999/2000* (London: National Crime Squad Service Authority, n.d.); and National Criminal Intelligence Service (NCIS), *The National Intelligence Model* (London: NCIS, 2000).

9. Innes and Sheptycki, "From Detection to Disruption"; and Audit Commission, *Helping with Enquiries: Tackling Crime Effectively* (London: HMS, 1993). See also Justin J. Dintino and Frederick Martens, *Police Intelligence Systems in Crime Control* (Springfield, Ill.: Charles C. Thomas, 1983). For a skeptical view, see Peter Gill, *Rounding Up the Usual Suspects: Developments in Contemporary Law Enforcement Intelligence* (Aldershot, UK: Ashgate, 2000).

10. "The "high side" refers to classified information from the Intelligence Community, including, among other things, information related to telephony.

11. Innes and Sheptycki, "From Detection to Disruption," p. 9.

12. A different kind on information sharing, known as "deconfliction," refers to how different agencies can avoid interfering with each other's ongoing investigations (for instance, ensuring that a given agency knows that a particular individual relevant for their investigation is actually an undercover agent for another law enforcement agency). The prevention of "blue-on-blue" incidents between investigative agencies is handled effectively by OCDETF and, on the southwest border, the El Paso Intelligence Center (EPIC).

13. National Defense Intelligence College, "Can't We All Just Get Along? Improving the Law Enforcement-Intelligence Community Relationship," NDIC Press, Washington, D.C., June 2007.

14. Malcolm Sparrow, "Network Vulnerabilities and Strategic Intelligence in Law Enforcement," *International Journal of Intelligence and Counter Intelligence*, Vol. 5, No. 3 (1991), pp. 255–274; Malcolm Sparrow, "The Application of Network Analysis to Criminal Intelligence: An Assessment of the Prospects," *Social Networks*, Vol. 13, No. 3 (1991), pp. 251–274; P.A. Lupsha, "Steps toward a Strategic Analysis of Organized Crime," *Police Chief*, Vol. 47 (1980), pp. 36–38; and Jennifer Xu, et al., "Analyzing and Visualizing Criminal Network Dynamics: A Case Study," in Hsinchun Chen, et al., eds., *Intelligence and Security Informatics, ISI 2004: Lecture Notes in Computer Science*, Vol. 3073 (Berlin: Springer, 2004), pp. 359–377.

15. Where such computer-assisted link analyses include people, we believe the analysis should be anonymized up until the point that linkages meet a certain prespecified threshold for suspicious activity; at that point, identities could be revealed as a prelude to official criminal investigation of the individuals in question.

16. Human smuggling involves helping people to enter the United States illegally. Human trafficking is a form of enslavement (either for labor or for sex).

17. Innes and Sheptycki, "From Detection to Disruption."

Chapter 15: The Future of Homeland Security

1. Given the choice, we lean toward the former, because the partnerships with subnational governments and the private sector are similar to those that DHS has developed in other domains, as described by Juliette Kayyem in Chapter 2 of this volume. In this regard, the elevation of what was the National Protection and Programs Directorate (NPPD) to the status of a Component and its renaming as the Cybersecurity and Infrastructure Security Agency (CISA) is an important step in the right direction.

2. Jason Miller, "With 108 Congressional Bosses, DHS at Oversight 'Tipping Point,'" *Federal News Radio*, September 9, 2011. See also Paul Rosenzweig, Jena Baker McNeill, and James Jay Calafano, "Stopping the Chaos: A Proposal for Reorganization of Congressional Oversight of the Department of Homeland Security," WebMemo No. 3046, Washington, D.C., Heritage Foundation, November 4, 2010, www.heritage. org/research/reports/2010/11/stopping-the-chaos-a-proposal-for-reorganization-of-congressional-oversight-of-DHS.

3. DHS space planning envisions co-locating DHS Headquarters with Component headquarters offices in the early 2020s.

4. See Tara O'Toole and Yudhijit Bhattacharjee, "Homeland Security Science Chief Aims to Put House in Order," *Science*, Vol. 332, No. 6031 (May 2011), p. 783.

5. David M. Walker, "9/11: The Implications for Public-Sector Management," *Public Administration Review*, Vol. 62, No. 1 (September 2002), pp. 94–97; and H.D.S. Greenway, "The Unwatched Ships at Sea: The Coast Guard and Homeland Security," *World Policy Journal*, Vol. 20, No. 2 (2003), p. 77.

6. Benjamin Friedman, "Homeland Security," *Foreign Policy*, Vol. 149, pp. 22–29; and William O. Jenkins, "Collaboration over Adaptation: The Case for Interoperable Communications in Homeland Security," *Public Administration Review*, Vol. 66, No. 3 (2006), pp. 319–321. See also Richard Sylves and William R. Cumming, "FEMA's Path to Homeland Security: 1979–2003," *Journal of Homeland Security and Emergency Management*, Vol. 1, No. 2 (2004), pp. 1–21; and Jerome Kahan, "Future of FEMA—Preparedness or Politics?" *Journal of Homeland Security and Emergency Management*, Vol. 12, No. 1 (2014), pp. 1–21.

7. John Mueller, *Overblown: How Politicians and the Terrorism Industry Inflate National Security Threats, and Why We Believe Them* (New York: Simon and Schuster, 2006); Frank P. Harvey, *The Homeland Security Dilemma: Fear, Failure and the Future*

of American Insecurity (New York: Routledge, 2008); John Mueller and Mark G. Stewart, *Terror, Security, and Money: Balancing the Risks, Benefits, and Costs of Homeland Security* (New York: Oxford University Press, 2001); Edward Alden, *The Closing of the American Border: Terrorism, Immigration, and Security* (New York: Harper, 2008); Friedman, "Homeland Security"; and Benjamin Friedman, "Managing Fear: The Politics of Homeland Security," *Political Science Quarterly*, Vol. 126, No. 1 (2011), pp. 77–106.

8. Harvey, *The Homeland Security Dilemma*, p. 30.

9. Friedman, "Managing Fear," pp. 93–94.

10. Per Harvey, *The Homeland Security Dilemma*.

11. See Friedman, "Managing Fear."

12. Marcia Kramer, "Bloomberg on JFK Plot: 'Stop Worrying, Get a Life,'" Prison Planet, June 5, 2007, https://www.prisonplanet.com/articles/june2007/050607bloomberg.htm. Cited in Friedman, "Managing Fear," p. 98.

13. Within terrorism, moreover, DHS should distinguish between foreign terrorists attempting to enter the United States and the radicalization of those already resident in the country (Countering Violent Extremism [CVE]). DHS's role in the latter became more prominent during the Obama administration, but the function remains undeveloped and largely unfunded. For further discussion, see Matthew Olsen and Edoardo Saravalle's chapter in this volume.

14. John Mueller, *War, Presidents, and Public Opinion* (New York: John Wiley, 1973); Richard Brody, *Assessing the President: The Media, Elite Opinion, and Public Support* (Stanford, Calif.: Stanford University Press, 1991); Brian J. Gaines, "Where's the Rally? Approval and Trust of the President, Cabinet, Congress, and Government since September 11," *PS: Political Science and Politics*, Vol. 35, No. 3 (September 2002), pp. 531–536; Jon A. Krosnick and Laura A. Brannon, "The Impact of the Gulf War on the Ingredients of Presidential Evaluations: Multidimensional Effects of Political Involvement," *American Political Science Review*, Vol. 87, No. 4 (December 1993), pp. 963–975; and Chappell H. Lawson and Sarah Sled, "A Psychological Explanation of Rally Effects," paper presented at the annual meeting of the Midwest Political Science Association, Chicago, Illinois, April 15–17, 2004; Richard C. Eichenberg, Richard J. Stoll, and Matthew Lebo, "War President: The Approval Ratings of George W. Bush", *Journal of Conflict Resolution*, Vol. 50, No. 6 (2006), pp. 783–808; and Cindy D. Kam and Jennifer M. Ramos, "Joining and Leaving the Rally: Understanding the Surge and Decline in Presidential Approval following 9/11," *Public Opinion Quarterly*, Vol. 72, No. 4 (2008), pp. 619–650.

15. Michael A. Fletcher and Richard Morin, "Bush's Approval Rating Drops to New Low in Wake of Storm," *Washington Post*, September 13, 2005, http://www.washingtonpost.com/wp-dyn/content/article/2005/09/12/AR2005091200668.html.

16. See Alan Bersin, "Lines and Flows: The Beginning and End of Borders," *Brooklyn Journal of International Law*, Vol. 37, No. 2 (2012), pp. 389–406; and Stephen Flynn, "Beyond Border Control," *Foreign Affairs*, Vol. 79, No. 6 (2000), p. 57.

17. Austen D. Givens, Nathan E. Busch, and Alan D. Bersin, "Going Global: The International Dimensions of U.S. Homeland Security Policy," *Journal of Strategic Security*, Vol. 11, No. 3 (2018), pp. 1–34, doi.org/10.5038/1944-0472.11.3.1689.

18. Bayless Manning, "The Congress, the Executive, and Intermestic Affairs: Three Proposals," *Foreign Affairs*, Vol. 55, No. 2 (January 1977), pp. 306, 309.

19. Alexis de Tocqueville, *Democracy in America* (1835).

20. Stephen Flynn, "Recalibrating Homeland Security: Mobilizing American Society to Prepare for Disaster," *Foreign Affairs*, Vol. 90, No. 3 (2011), pp. 130–140, at p. 140.

21. John Burnett, "Riding with a Rescue Mission in the Surreal, Perilous Texas Floods," National Public Radio (NPR), August 30, 2017, https://www.npr.org/2017/08/30/547347581/riding-with-a-rescue-mission-in-the-surreal-perilous-texas-floods. See also John Burnett, "Flood Of 'Texas Navy' Private Citizens Help in Houston Rescue Efforts," NPR, August 29, 2017, https://www.npr.org/2017/08/29/546834292/flood-of-texas-navy-private-citizens-help-in-houston-rescue-efforts.

22. Flynn, "Recalibrating Homeland Security," pp. 131, 140.

23. Karl L. Schultz, "Auxiliary Policy Statement," Commandant of the United States Coast Guard, Washington, D.C., June 1, 2018, https://media.defense.gov/2018/Jun/01/2001925985/-1/-1/0/AUXILIARY-30MAY18_SIGNED.PDF.

24. Pierre Thomas, et al., "Little-Known U.S. Fault Lines Cause for Seismic Concern about Potential Earthquakes," ABC News, March 15, 2011, https://abcnews.go.com/Politics/us-fault-lines-siesmic-concern/story?id=13140354.

25. Flynn, "Recalibrating Homeland Security," p. 131.

Index

Contributors

Richard Ades was Chief of Communications and Public Affairs for TSA, where he led a team of more than fifty public affairs professionals and worked closely with senior leaders on key policy matters, communications, legislative engagements, and emergency response.

Today, as founder and senior partner of The Issues and Crisis Group, he focuses on high-stakes communications in challenging environments for companies, organizations, and individuals. He specializes in crisis preparedness and response, message development, media relations, media preparedness, writing, spokesperson training, reputation and positioning, executive communications, and risk mitigation.

Alan Bersin serves as Senior Advisor to Covington & Burling; as Inaugural Fellow in the Homeland Security Project at the Belfer Center for Science and International Affairs, Harvard Kennedy School; and as Global Fellow and the Inaugural North America Fellow at the Canada Institute and the Mexico Institute at the Woodrow Wilson Center for International Scholars in Washington, D.C.

Bersin was appointed as Obama's U.S. Commissioner of Customs and Border Protection and served as Assistant Secretary for Policy and International Affairs and Chief Diplomatic Officer for DHS. He was Clinton's U.S. Attorney for the Southern District of California, during which time he was also the U.S. Attorney General's Southwest Border Representative. He has served as Vice President of Interpol for the Americas Region and as a member of the Interpol Executive Committee, and currently serves as a Member of the Board of Trustees of the Interpol Foundation in Geneva. Bersin has also held numerous distinguished state and local government positions, including Secretary of Education of California, Superintendent of Public Education in San Diego, and Chairman of the San Diego Airport Authority.

Sophia Brill is counsel on the Committee on the Judiciary in the U.S. House of Representatives. Previously, she was an associate in Morrison & Foerster's Global Risk + Crisis Management practice, where she counseled clients on complex cybersecurity and data breach matters. She also handled a range of appellate and Supreme Court litigation in the firm's Supreme Court and Appellate Practice.

Brill previously served as an attorney advisor in the National Security Division (NSD) at the DOJ, where she advised senior NSD and Department leadership on legal matters affecting counterterrorism and other national security policies. Prior to that, she served as a law clerk to Justice Elena Kagan and to Chief Judge Merrick Garland of the U.S. Court of Appeals for the D.C. Circuit.

Stevan Bunnell is a Partner in the Washington, D.C. offices of O'Melveny & Myers, LLP, where he is Chair of the firm's Data Security and Privacy Practice. His practice focuses on blockchain regulation, cybersecurity, and government investigations. He served as General Counsel of DHS from 2013 to 2017. For seventeen years, he was a federal prosecutor at the DOJ and at the U.S. Attorney's Office for the District of Columbia, where he served as Chief of the Criminal Division and as Chief of the Fraud and Public Corruption Section. Bunnell is currently the Co-Chair of the American Bar Association's Homeland Security Law Institute and a member of the Advisory Committee of the ABA's Standing Committee on National Security.

John Carlin chairs Morrison & Foerster's Global Risk + Crisis Management practice and co-chairs the National Security practice, where he advises industry-leading organizations on sensitive cyber and other national security matters. He also chairs the Aspen Institute's Cybersecurity and Technology policy program, which provides a cross-disciplinary forum for industry, government, and media to address the rapidly developing landscape of digital threats and craft appropriate policy solutions.

Previously, he was Assistant Attorney General for the DOJ's National Security Division (NSD); under his leadership, the NSD launched nationwide outreach across industries to raise awareness of national security, cyber, and espionage threats against U.S. companies and encourage greater C-suite involvement in corporate cybersecurity matters. Prior to serving as the DOJ's highest-ranking national security lawyer, he served as Chief of Staff and Senior Counsel to FBI Director Robert S. Mueller, III. He is the author of *Dawn of the Code War: America's Battle Against Russia, China, and the Rising Global Cyber Threat* (New York: PublicAffairs, 2018), which provides an inside look into how to combat daily attacks on U.S. companies, citizens, and government.

Alan Cohn is a partner at Steptoe & Johnson LLP. He helped found Steptoe's Blockchain and Cryptocurrency practice and serves as its co-chair. He is also counsel to the Blockchain Alliance, a public-private forum established by a broad coalition of companies and organizations to help combat criminal activity on the blockchain.

Previously, Cohn served as a career member of the Senior Executive Service in senior positions at DHS for almost a decade, most recently as the Assistant Secretary for Strategy, Planning, Analysis, and Risk and second-in-charge overall of the DHS Office of Policy. In this capacity, he established the cyber policy office within the DHS Office of Policy, represented DHS on the Committee on Foreign Investments in the United States (CFIUS) and in related national security review processes for foreign investments, and created and helped implement DHS Secretary Jeh Johnson's Unity of Effort initiative, a major corporate-level DHS management reform effort. Cohn is an adjunct professor at Georgetown University Law Center and was a senior advisor to the Public Sector Practice at McKinsey from 2015 to 2018.

Caitlin Durkovich is a Director at Toffler Associates, a strategic consulting and advisory firm that provides better futures for public- and private-sector clients around the globe with an unwavering commitment to be the catalyst for change. Previously, Durkovich served nearly eight years in the Obama administration, including four years as Assistant Secretary for Infrastructure Protection at DHS, leading the mission to protect critical infrastructure and redefining public-private risk management for emerging issues such as complex mass attacks, electrical grid security, cybersecurity, GPS resilience, and climate adaptation planning. As Assistant Secretary, she served as the Chair of the Interagency Security Committee and co-chaired the Joint United States–Canada Electric Grid Security and Resilience Strategy, the Space Weather Task Force, and the Interagency Working Group to Enhance the Security and Safety of Chemical Facilities.

Durkovich has also led homeland security projects with several government agencies while at Booz Allen Hamilton and pioneered early warning cyber intelligence at iDefense (acquired by Verisign). She is a passionate advocate for the need to create a cross-sector dialogue on a modern and resilient infrastructure.

Stephen E. Flynn is Professor of Political Science and Founding Director of the Global Resilience Institute at Northeastern University. He is a member of the Homeland Security Science and Technology Advisory Council and chair of the Security Advisory Committee for the Massachusetts Port Authority. He has served as President of the Center for National Policy and as senior fellow for National Security Studies at the Council on Foreign Relations. He was a commissioned officer in the U.S. Coast Guard for twenty years, including two tours as commanding officer at sea. As a Coast Guard officer, he served in the White House Military Office during the George H.W. Bush administration and as a Director for Global Issues on the National Security Council staff during the Clinton administration.

Juliette Kayyem is the Robert and Renée Belfer Lecturer in International Security at Harvard Kennedy School, where she is also Faculty Director of the Homeland Security Project at the Belfer Center for Science and International Affairs. She teaches courses on crisis management, homeland security, and global health and security. She is also an on-air national security analyst for CNN. Previously, she was Obama's Assistant Secretary for Intergovernmental Affairs at DHS and Massachusetts Governor Deval Patrick's homeland security advisor, guiding regional planning and the Common-wealth's first interoperability plan and overseeing the Massachusetts National Guard.

She has served as a member of the National Commission on Terrorism, a legal advisor to U.S. Attorney General Janet Reno, and a trial attorney and counselor in the Civil Rights Division at the DOJ.

Kayyem is the recipient of many government honors, including the Distinguished Public Service Award, the Coast Guard's highest civilian medal. In 2013, she was named a Pulitzer Prize finalist for editorial columns in the *Boston Globe* that focused on ending the Pentagon's combat exclusion rule against women, a policy that was changed that year. She is a board member of MassINC and the Red Cross of Massachusetts, and a member of the Council on Foreign Relations, the Global Cyber Alliance, the Trilateral Commission, and, until recently, DHS's Homeland Security Advisory Committee. Her most recent book, *Security Mom: An Unclassified Guide to Protecting Our Homeland and Your Home*, was published by Simon & Schuster in 2016.

Chappell Lawson is Associate Professor of Political Science at MIT. He directs the MIT International Science and Technology Initiatives (MISTI) program and the Policy Lab at the Center for International Studies (PL@CIS). His recent academic work has focused on Mexican politics, political leadership, and homeland security policy.

From September 2009 through February 2011, Lawson was on leave from MIT as a political appointee in the Obama administration, serving as Executive Director and Senior Advisor to the Commissioner of U.S. Customs and Border Protection. Before joining the MIT faculty, he served briefly as a Director of Inter-American Affairs on the National Security Council staff during the Clinton administration.

Christian Marrone is Vice President, Civil and Regulatory Affairs for Lockheed Martin Corporation. In this capacity, he is responsible for leading the corporation's U.S. government civil customer relationships with customers outside of the DOD, NASA, and NOAA. In addition, he leads the corporation's interface with the U.S. government and Congress on regulatory matters impacting Lockheed Martin programs, products, and services. Prior to joining Lockheed Martin, Marrone served as CSRA's Senior Vice President, External Relations and Chief of Staff. In that role, he served as Chief of Staff to the President and CEO and led CSRA's Government Relations, Marketing and Communications, Security, Change Management Office, and Program Excellence functions. He was also responsible for executing the company's strategy for strengthening relationships across the U.S. government and spearheaded efforts to provide thought-leading solutions to address the critical policy issues challenging government.

Previously, Marrone served as Chief of Staff of DHS under Secretary Jeh Johnson. He has also held a number of senior positions within the DOD, including Special Assistant to then–Secretary Robert Gates and Acting Assistant Secretary of Defense for Legislative Affairs. He has received several awards throughout his career, including the Secretary of Homeland Security Distinguished Public Service Award; the Office of the Secretary of Defense Medal for Exceptional Public Service Award; and two Secretary of Defense Medals for Distinguished Public Service. Marrone is a Senior Fellow at the George Washington University Cyber and Homeland Security Center and the Aspen Homeland Security Forum.

Jason McNamara is Senior Director for Emergency Management Programs at CNA Corporation and an established emergency management and homeland security expert with over twenty-five years of senior management experience in both the federal government and the private sector. In the private sector, he has served as a Vice President at Obsidian Analysis, Inc., directed the Emergency Management and Homeland Security practice of Dewberry & Davis, LLC, and been an Assistant Vice President at SAIC.

From 2009 to 2013, he served as the Chief of Staff for FEMA, where he helped the Administrator implement organizational reforms that contributed to effective responses to some of the busiest, and most costly, disaster seasons on record. From 2003 to 2005, McNamara was a professional staff member for the House Select Committee on Homeland Security. With an early career spent responding to disasters, such as the Northridge Earthquake, the Oklahoma City bombing, and the terrorist attacks of 9/11, his knowledge and expertise cover all facets of emergency management operations, policy, federal statutes, and federal regulations.

Doris Meissner, former Commissioner of the U.S. Immigration and Naturalization Service (INS), is a Senior Fellow at the Migration Policy Institute (MPI), where she directs its U.S. immigration policy work. Her responsibilities focus in particular on the role of immigration in America's future and on administering the nation's immigration laws, systems, and government agencies. Her work and expertise also include immigration and politics, immigration enforcement, border control, cooperation with other countries, and immigration and national security. She served as Director of MPI's Independent Task Force on Immigration and America's Future, a bipartisan group of distinguished leaders. The group's report and recommendations address how to harness the advantages of immigration for a twenty-first-century economy and society.

From 1993 to 2000, Meissner served in the Clinton administration as Commissioner of the INS, then a bureau in the DOJ. Her accomplishments included reforming the nation's asylum system; creating new strategies for managing U.S. borders; improving naturalization and other services for immigrants; shaping new responses to migration and humanitarian emergencies; strengthening cooperation and joint initiatives with Mexico, Canada, and other countries; and managing growth that doubled the agency's personnel and tripled its budget. Meissner first joined the Justice Department in 1973 as a White House Fellow and Special Assistant to the Attorney General. She served in various senior policy posts until 1981, when she became Acting Commissioner of the INS and then Executive Associate Commissioner, the third-ranking post in the agency. In 1986, she joined the Carnegie Endowment for International Peace as a Senior Associate. Meissner created the Endowment's Immigration Policy Project, which evolved into MPI in 2001.

Peter Neffenger, Vice Admiral, U.S. Coast Guard (ret) was appointed in 2015 to lead Obama's TSA, a position he held until January 2017. Previously, he enjoyed a distinguished thirty-four-year career in the Coast Guard, where he served as the 29th Vice Commandant, the head of Coast Guard global operations, and, most notably, as the Deputy National Incident Commander for the 2010 BP Gulf oil spill, the largest and most complex in U.S. history. When he took the helm at TSA, the agency's challenges were substantial and numerous. His subsequent transformation of the organization led to his being named one of the twenty-five most influential business travel executives of 2016 by *Business Travel News*.

Neffenger is Chairman of the Board of Directors for Smartmatic, USA; serves on the Homeland Security Advisory Board for MITRE Corporation; and is a member of the Baldwin Wallace University Board of Trustees. He is a two-time recipient of DHS's Distinguished Service Medal, and is a Distinguished Fellow at the Atlantic Council, a Distinguished Senior Fellow at Northeastern University's Global Resilience Institute, and an Instructor in Harvard University's National Preparedness Leadership Initiative, a joint venture of the Harvard T.H. Chan School of Public Health's Division of Policy Translation and Leadership Development and the Harvard Kennedy School's Center for Public Leadership.

Matthew Olsen is an Adjunct Senior Fellow at the Center for a New American Security. After two decades of service as a leading government official in national security, intelligence, and law enforcement, Olsen now serves as the Chief Trust and Security Officer at Uber.

Olsen was appointed by Barack Obama to serve as the Director of the National Counterterrorism Center (NCTC), where he led the government's efforts to analyze terrorism information and coordinate counterterrorism operations. Prior to joining NCTC, Olsen was General Counsel for the National Security Agency. He served at the DOJ and the FBI in a number of leadership positions and worked for over a decade as a federal prosecutor. Olsen was a co-founder and president of IronNet Cybersecurity, a software technology firm. He serves on the board of Human Rights First and teaches at Harvard Law School and the University of Virginia.

Amy Pope is a Partner at Schillings, a law and consulting firm in London, where she advises corporate and individual clients on responding to and mitigating crises. She served on the National Security Council staff from 2012 to 2017, most recently as U.S. Deputy Homeland Security Advisor to Barack Obama, where she managed a range of high-profile, diverse challenges from countering violent extremism to managing Central American migration to leading the U.S. government's comprehensive efforts to combat Zika, Ebola, and other public health threats.

Prior to joining the National Security Council, Pope worked in several positions at the DOJ, including Deputy Chief of Staff in the Criminal Division, and as a trial attorney. She served as counsel in the U.S. Senate—both to the Senate Judiciary Committee's subcommittee on Terrorism, Technology, and Homeland Security and to the Senate Majority Leader. She is an Associate Fellow in the U.S. and Americas Program at Chatham House and a Senior Non-resident Fellow of the Atlantic Council.

Edoardo Saravalle is a JD/MPA candidate at Columbia University. He has been a Researcher for the Energy, Economics, and Security Program at the Center for a New American Security, focusing on sanctions, countering terrorist financing, and economic statecraft, as well as the implications of energy market shifts, and worked at investment bank Moelis & Company.

Andrew Selee has been President of the Migration Policy Institute (MPI), a nonpartisan institution that seeks to improve immigration and integration policies through fact-based research, opportunities for learning and dialogue, and the development of new ideas to address complex policy questions, since August 2017. Selee was a Co-Director of the Regional Migration Study Group, convened by MPI with the Wilson Center to look at regional migration flows among the Central American countries, Mexico, and the United States, and was part of the steering committee for MPI's Independent Task Force on Immigration and America's Future, which helped lay an important conceptual foundation for immigration reform efforts in recent years. He was selected as an Andrew Carnegie Fellow for the 2017–2018 period.

Previously, Selee spent seventeen years at the Woodrow Wilson Center, where he founded the Center's Mexico Institute and later served as Vice President for Programs and Executive Vice President. He was also a member of the Council on Foreign Relations Task Force on Immigration. In addition, Selee has worked as a staff member in the U.S. Congress and on develop-ment and migration programs in Tijuana, Mexico. Selee's research focuses on migration globally, with a special emphasis on immigration policies in Latin America and in the United States. He is the author of several books, including *Vanishing Frontiers: The Forces Driving Mexico and the United*

States Together (New York: PublicAffairs, 2018) and *What Should Think Tanks Do? A Strategic Guide to Policy Impact* (Stanford, Calif.: Stanford University Press, 2013).

Seth M. M. Stodder served in the Obama administration as Assistant Secretary of Homeland Security for Border, Immigration, and Trade Policy and as Assistant Secretary of Homeland Security for Threat Prevention and Security Policy. He previously served in the George W. Bush administration as Director of Policy for U.S. Customs and Border Protection during the three years immediately after the 9/11 attacks. He is currently a Partner at Holland & Knight LLP, and he teaches national security law at the University of Southern California Law School.

Belfer Center Studies in International Security

Published by The MIT Press
Steven E. Miller and Morgan L. Kaplan, series editors
Karen Motley, executive editor
Belfer Center for Science and International Affairs
Harvard Kennedy School, Harvard University

Acharya, Amitav, and Evelyn Goh, eds., *Reassessing Security Cooperation in the Asia-Pacific* (2007)

Agha, Hussein, Shai Feldman, Ahmad Khalidi, and Zeev Schiff, *Track-II Diplomacy: Lessons from the Middle East* (2003)

Allison, Graham, and Robert D. Blackwill, with Ali Wyne, *Lee Kuan Yew: The Grand Master's Insights on China, the United States, and the World* (2012)

Allison, Graham T., Owen R. Coté, Jr., Richard A. Falkenrath, and Steven E. Miller, *Avoiding Nuclear Anarchy: Containing the Threat of Loose Russian Nuclear Weapons and Fissile Material* (1996)

Allison, Graham T., and Kalypso Nicolaïdis, eds., *The Greek Paradox: Promise vs. Performance* (1996)

Arbatov, Alexei, Abram Chayes, Antonia Handler Chayes, and Lara Olson, eds., *Managing Conflict in the Former Soviet Union: Russian and American Perspectives* (1997)

Bennett, Andrew, *Condemned to Repetition? The Rise, Fall, and Reprise of Soviet-Russian Military Interventionism, 1973–1996* (1999)

Blackwill, Robert D., and Michael Stürmer, eds., *Allies Divided: Transatlantic Policies for the Greater Middle East* (1997)

Blackwill, Robert D., and Paul Dibb, eds., *America's Asian Alliances* (2000)

Blum, Gabriella, and Philip B. Heymann, *Laws, Outlaws, and Terrorists: Lessons from the War on Terrorism* (2010)

Brom, Shlomo, and Yiftah Shapir, eds., *The Middle East Military Balance 1999–2000* (1999)

Brom, Shlomo, and Yiftah Shapir, eds., *The Middle East Military Balance 2001–2002* (2002)

Brown, Michael E., ed., *The International Dimensions of Internal Conflict* (1996)

Brown, Michael E., and Šumit Ganguly, eds., *Fighting Words: Language Policy and Ethnic Relations in Asia* (2003)

Brown, Michael E., and Šumit Ganguly, eds., *Government Policies and Ethnic Relations in Asia and the Pacific* (1997)

Carter, Ashton B., and John P. White, eds., *Keeping the Edge: Managing Defense for the Future* (2001)

Chenoweth, Erica, and Adria Lawrence, eds., *Rethinking Violence: State and Non-state Actors in Conflict* (2010)

de Nevers, Renée, *Comrades No More: The Seeds of Political Change in Eastern Europe* (2003)

Elman, Colin, and Miriam Fendius Elman, eds., *Bridges and Boundaries: Historians, Political Scientists, and the Study of International Relations* (2001)

Elman, Colin, and Miriam Fendius Elman, eds., *Progress in International Relations Theory: Appraising the Field* (2003)

Elman, Miriam Fendius, ed., *Paths to Peace: Is Democracy the Answer?* (1997)

Falkenrath, Richard A., *Shaping Europe's Military Order: The Origins and Consequences of the CFE Treaty* (1994)

Falkenrath, Richard A., Robert D. Newman, and Bradley A. Thayer, *America's Achilles' Heel: Nuclear, Biological, and Chemical Terrorism and Covert Attack* (1998)

Feaver, Peter D., and Richard H. Kohn, eds., *Soldiers and Civilians: The Civil-Military Gap and American National Security* (2001)

Feldman, Shai, *Nuclear Weapons and Arms Control in the Middle East* (1996)

Feldman, Shai, and Yiftah Shapir, eds., *The Middle East Military Balance 2000–2001* (2001)

Forsberg, Randall, ed., *The Arms Production Dilemma: Contraction and Restraint in the World Combat Aircraft Industry* (1994)

George, Alexander L., and Andrew Bennett, *Case Studies and Theory Development in the Social Sciences* (2005)

Gilroy, Curtis, and Cindy Williams, eds., *Service to Country: Personnel Policy and the Transformation of Western Militaries* (2007)

Hagerty, Devin T., *The Consequences of Nuclear Proliferation: Lessons from South Asia* (1998)

Heymann, Philip B., *Terrorism and America: A Commonsense Strategy for a Democratic Society* (1998)

Heymann, Philip B., *Terrorism, Freedom, and Security: Winning without War* (2003)

Heymann, Philip B., and Juliette N. Kayyem, *Protecting Liberty in an Age of Terror* (2005)

Howitt, Arnold M., and Robyn L. Pangi, eds., *Countering Terrorism: Dimensions of Preparedness* (2003)

Hudson, Valerie M., and Andrea M. den Boer, *Bare Branches: The Security Implications of Asia's Surplus Male Population* (2004)

Kayyem, Juliette N., and Robyn L. Pangi, eds., *First to Arrive: State and Local Responses to Terrorism* (2003)

Kokoshin, Andrei A., *Soviet Strategic Thought, 1917–91* (1998)

Lawson, Chappell, Alan Bersin, and Juliette Kayyem, eds., *Beyond 9/11: Homeland Security for the Twenty-First Century* (2020)

Lederberg, Joshua, ed., *Biological Weapons: Limiting the Threat* (1999)

Mansfield, Edward D., and Jack Snyder, *Electing to Fight: Why Emerging Democracies Go to War* (2005)

Martin, Lenore G., and Dimitris Keridis, eds., *The Future of Turkish Foreign Policy* (2004)

May, Ernest R., and Philip D. Zelikow, eds., *Dealing with Dictators: Dilemmas of U.S. Diplomacy and Intelligence Analysis, 1945–1990* (2007)

Phillips, David L., *Liberating Kosovo: Coercive Diplomacy and U.S. Intervention* (2012)

Poneman, Daniel B., *Double Jeopardy: Combating Nuclear Terror and Climate Change* (2019)

Rosecrance, Richard N., and Steven E. Miller, eds., *The Next Great War? The Roots of World War I and the Risk of U.S.–China Conflict* (2015)

Shaffer, Brenda, *Borders and Brethren: Iran and the Challenge of Azerbaijani Identity* (2002)

Shaffer, Brenda, ed., *The Limits of Culture: Islam and Foreign Policy* (2006)

Shields, John M., and William C. Potter, eds., *Dismantling the Cold War: U.S. and NIS Perspectives on the Nunn-Lugar Cooperative Threat Reduction Program* (1997)

Tucker, Jonathan B., ed., *Toxic Terror: Assessing Terrorist Use of Chemical and Biological Weapons* (2000)

Utgoff, Victor A., ed., *The Coming Crisis: Nuclear Proliferation, U.S. Interests, and World Order* (2000)

Weiner, Sharon K., *Our Own Worst Enemy? Institutional Interests and the Proliferation of Nuclear Weapons Expertise* (2011)

Williams, Cindy, ed., *Filling the Ranks: Transforming the U.S. Military Personnel System* (2004)

Williams, Cindy, ed., *Holding the Line: U.S. Defense Alternatives for the Early 21st Century* (2001)

Xu Qiyu, *Fragile Rise: Grand Strategy and the Fate of Imperial Germany, 1871–1914*, trans. Joshua Hill (2017)

Zoughbie, Daniel E., *Indecision Points: George W. Bush and the Israeli-Palestinian Conflict* (2014)

The Belfer Center for Science and International Affairs

Ashton B. Carter, Director
Eric Rosenbach, Co-Director
Harvard Kennedy School
79 JFK Street, Cambridge, MA 02138
Tel: (617) 495-1400 | Fax: (617) 495-8963
http://www.belfercenter.org | belfer_center@hks.harvard.edu

The Belfer Center is the hub of Harvard Kennedy School's research, teaching, and training in international security affairs, environmental and resource issues, and science and technology policy.

The Center has a dual mission: (1) to provide leadership in advancing policy-relevant knowledge about the most important challenges of international security and other critical issues where science, technology, environmental policy, and international affairs intersect; and (2) to prepare future generations of leaders for these arenas. Center researchers not only conduct scholarly research, but also develop prescriptions for policy reform. Faculty and fellows analyze global challenges from nuclear proliferation and terrorism to climate change and energy policy.

The Belfer Center's leadership begins with the recognition of science and technology as driving forces constantly transforming both the challenges we face and the opportunities for problem-solving. Building on the vision of founder Paul Doty, the Center addresses serious global concerns by integrating insights and research of social scientists, natural scientists, technologists, and practitioners in government, diplomacy, the military, and business. The heart of the Belfer Center is its resident research community of more than 150 scholars, including Harvard faculty, researchers, practitioners, and each year a new, international, interdisciplinary group of research fellows. Through publications and policy discussions, workshops, seminars, and conferences, the Center promotes innovative solutions to significant national and international challenges.

The Center's International Security Program, directed by Steven E. Miller, sponsors and edits the Belfer Center Studies in International Security and the quarterly journal *International Security*.